Join the Recommended Country Inns® Travelers' Club and save!

The Recommended Country Inns® guides are the preeminent regional guidebooks to the finest country inns in the United States. Authors personally visit and recommend each establishment listed in the guides, and no fees are solicited or accepted for inclusion in the books.

Now the Recommended Country Inns® guides offer a special new way for purchasers to enjoy extra savings through the new Recommended Country Inns® Travelers' Club. For example, members can enjoy savings such as:

10% discount each night; or
25% discount each night; or
Stay 2 nights, get the third night free.

All establishments in the guide have been invited to participate **on a voluntary basis.** No fees are charged to the establishments for offering Recommended Country Inns® Travelers' Club discounts, nor are Recommended Country Inns® series authors influenced to list inns because innkeepers have participated in the Recommended Country Inns® Travelers' Club program.

How to Save: Read the listing for each inn in this guide to see if it offers special savings to Recommended Country Inns® Travelers' Club members. For participating establishments, the information appears at the end of the inn's listing.

How to Join: If you wish to become a Recommended Country Inns® Travelers' Club member, simply fill out the form on the next page, and send it, **along with your receipt for purchase of the guide,** to:

Recommended Country Inns® Travelers' Club
c/o The Globe Pequot Press
P.O. Box 833
Old Saybrook, CT 06475

Upon receipt, we will send you a membership card. Simply mention this card when you make your reservation, and show the card when you check in to participating establishments. All offers from participating establishments are subject to availability.

Sign up today and you can start enjoying savings right away as a Recommended Country Inns® Travelers' Club member!

(Offers from inns expire December 31, 1996)

Recommended Country Inns® Travelers' Club
Membership Form

Name________________________________Phone No. (   )____________

Address____________________City______________State______Zip_______

Age: under 18_______; 18–35_______; 36–50_______; over 50_______

Nights stayed at an inn per year: 0–3_____; 4–6_____; 7–10_____; more than 10_____

I usually visit inns: alone_______; with spouse or friend_______; with family_______

Annual Household Income: under $20,000______; $20,000–$35,000______;
$35,000–$50,000______; $50,000–$75,000______; $75,000–$100,000______;
over $100,000______

Credit cards you own: Mastercard___; Amex___; Visa___; Discover___; Other________

Sex: Male______; Female______ Marital Status: Married______; Single______

Book purchased at: Store name______________; City______________; State______

Send completed form, along with receipt for purchase of the guide, to:

RECOMMENDED COUNTRY INNS® TRAVELERS' CLUB
The Globe Pequot Press
P.O. Box 833
Old Saybrook, CT 06475

SW

Recommended Country Inns

THE SOUTHWEST

"For those regular or intermittent travelers with a taste for homey layovers, this guide is a must."
—*Books of the Southwest*

"Eleanor Morris has captured the flavor and scope of . . . favorite inns. Her brief, accurate descriptions provide all the information a traveler needs in selecting a relaxing spot for a week or a night. . . ."
—Frank Lively, former editor, *Texas Highways*

"Unique, highly selective Southwest travel guide."
—*Home & Away*

"This carefully researched and written guide describes . . . unique inns . . . in the three states. . . . Morris vividly notes the inn's specialty, whether architecture, menu, view, history, or atmosphere."
—*Review of Texas Books*

"Home baked muffins, gourmet meals, flowers in the room, a rocking chair on the front porch so visitors can watch the wildlife or chat with the amiable innkeeper—all these amenities are available when travelers are in-the-know. To locate non-clone travel lodging, this carefully written guide introduces and describes . . . unique inns . . . in vivid and colorful language."
—*Beaumont* (TX) *Enterprise*

"An absolute necessity for even the most infrequent Southwest traveler."
—*Northside People* (San Antonio, TX)

"Recommended Country Inns" Series

"These guides are a marvelous start to planning the leisurely trek, romantic getaway, or time-off for reflection."
—*Internet Book Review*

The "Recommended Country Inns" series is designed for the discriminating traveler who seeks the best in unique accommodations away from home.

From hundreds of inns personally visited and evaluated by the author, only the finest are described here. The inclusion of an inn is purely a personal decision on the part of the author; no one can pay or be paid to be in a Globe Pequot inn guide.

Organized for easy reference, these guides point you to just the kind of accommodations you are looking for: Comprehensive indexes by category provide listings of inns for romantic getaways, inns for the sports-minded, inns that serve gourmet meals, inns for the business traveler . . . and more. State maps help you pinpoint the location of each inn, and detailed driving directions tell you how to get there.

Use these guidebooks with confidence. Allow each author to share his or her selections with you and then discover for yourself the country inn experience.

Editions available:

Recommended Country Inns
New England • Mid-Atlantic and Chesapeake Region
The South • The Midwest • West Coast
The Southwest • Rocky Mountain Region
also
Recommended Romantic Inns
Recommended Island Inns

Recommended Country Inns®

THE SOUTHWEST

Arizona ❧ New Mexico ❧ Texas

Fifth Edition

by Eleanor S. Morris
illustrated by Bill Taylor, Jr.

A *Voyager Book*

Old Saybrook, Connecticut

About the Author

Eleanor S. Morris is a freelance travel writer living in Austin, Texas—a "refugee," she says, from the big cities of Houston and Dallas. A member of the Society of American Travel Writers and the American Society of Journalists and Authors, she has published widely in national newspapers and magazines, and she has stayed at country inns in such diverse places as Australia, Portugal, England, Canada, Mexico, and Japan.

Eleanor says a country inn is a place where you are never a stranger, no matter how far you are from home. When not traveling, she is at home in Austin with her husband and working on a novel.

ISBN 1-56440-513-3
ISSN 1078-5515

Text design: Saralyn D'Amato

Manufactured in the United States of America
Fifth Edition/Second Printing

Contents

Indexes

A Few Words about Visiting Southwestern Inns

Webster's Dictionary says that an inn is a hotel, usually a small one. *Thorndike Barnhart* says that an inn is a public house for lodging and caring for travelers. In my travels in the Southwest, I have found that an inn, or at least what we understand down here as a country inn, is much more. It is a place where, away from home, you feel at home, not necessarily because of the physical attributes of a place (although that's important, too), but more likely because of the people you find there, both the innkeepers and the guests.

Many of my innkeepers say, "Our guests are a special breed." I maintain the reason for that is because country innkeepers themselves are a special breed. As in a family, sharing your home with others makes for companionship along with sensitivity to another's moods, a concern with well-being, comfort, and need. Almost without exception my innkeepers really like other people, they are *interested* in them, and they want to *interact* with them. (Those that find they do not soon drop out of this fast-growing industry.) And since like attracts like, innkeepers attract as guests people who are open, adventurous, and who are interested in other people, too.

I think this people-interest, this interaction, is why the inn movement is growing so rapidly, at least in my section of the country where just a short time ago such a thing as a country inn was almost impossible to find. Even when people travel on business, they're learning what it means to come "home" at the end of the day to someone's home, to someone who greets them with genuine interest on a personal basis. The world is becoming so hectic, so rushed, that we often feel it's passing us by; we'd better hurry just to catch up. Along the way how nice to stop for a breather, stay with people who are interested in us and whom we can be interested in, too. It's as simple as that.

Inns of the Southwest range from romantic Victorian cottages to sprawling haciendas secluded behind high adobe walls, from grand old-time mansions to rustic country cottages, and their number is growing. Although some lodgings may disappoint you, innkeepers seldom will. Their guests become their extended family, many returning again and again. The inn movement in the Southwest is definitely "in."

About This Inn Guide

Without exception, every innkeeper in this book to whom I posed the question "Why are you doing this?" answered, "The people. We love the people."

"The people" is you, the traveler, and here are some pointers that will smooth your path to better and more beautiful inn experiences:

Inns are arranged by states in the following sections: Arizona, New Mexico, and Texas. Because it is so large, Texas is divided into five geographical areas: North Texas, East Texas, Central Texas, Gulf Coast/Border Texas, and West Texas.

At the beginning of each section is a map and an index to the inns in that section, listed alphabetically by town. At the back of the guide is a complete index to all the inns in the book, listed alphabetically by name. Additional indexes list inns by special categories.

There is no charge of any kind to an inn to be mentioned in this guide. The inclusion is a personal decision on the part of the author, who visited each inn as well as many others that were not included. Address any questions or comments to Eleanor S. Morris, The Globe Pequot Press, P.O. Box 833, Old Saybrook, CT 06475.

Menu Abbreviations:

EP: European Plan. Room without meals.

EPB: European Plan with Breakfast. Room with full breakfast. Where room rate includes continental breakfast only, this is mentioned in text.

MAP: Modified American Plan. Room with breakfast and dinner.

AP: American Plan. Room with meals.

Rates: I have listed the range from low to high, double occupancy (single where applicable), at the time I visited, realizing that it's up to you to decide how many in your party and what level of accommodation you wish. Rates change without notice, however, sometimes overnight, so I cannot promise that there will be no surprises. Always check beforehand. The rates given do not include taxes.

Reservations/Deposits: These are uniformly required, and if you do not show up and the room is not rented otherwise, you will most likely be charged. Expect to pay a deposit or use a credit card.

Minimum Stay: I have noted this wherever necessary, but most inns in this guide have no such restrictions. Check when you make your reservation, though, because policies change. Often during slow times minimum stay can be negotiable. And special rates are often available for an extended stay.

Personal Checks: All the inns in this book accept personal checks.

Credit Cards: Most inns accept the major credit cards. The few that do not are so noted in the text and listed in an index at the back.

Children: Inns that especially welcome children are listed in an index at the end of the guide. With others, it's always a good idea to ask, since many simply do not have the facilities to offer children a comfortable and happy visit.

Pets: A number of inns are prepared to deal with pets, with some restrictions, and I have listed them in an index at the back of the guide as well as in the text.

Food: I have noted which inns serve food, whether food is included in the rates as in a bed and breakfast inn, or whether there is restaurant service on the premises. Where there is food service for meals other than breakfast, the "Facilities and activities" item for the inn explains this. Where there is not, most of your innkeepers will have an assortment of menus on hand for your perusal and are happy to make recommendations.

BYOB: It is usually all right to bring your own bottle, especially to an inn that has no bar or lounge facilities. Often the innkeeper will provide setups (ice and mixes), and many serve wine where licensing laws permit.

Smoking: Many inns, particularly in Texas, have restrictions as to where, when, and if their guests may smoke. This information appears in the text. An index at the back of the guide lists inns that do permit some smoking.

King, Queen, Double, or Twin Bed: If you have a preference, always ask when you make your reservation.

Television and Telephones: I have listed where these are available, although I imagine that, like me, you may want to get away from it all when you go inning. Many inns have both television and phone located in the common rooms.

Air Conditioning/Heating: I have not listed these amenities, because almost without exception they are taken for granted in the Southwest if the climate warrants. I have noted if the climate does not.

Wheelchair Access: Most of the inns in this book unfortunately do not have total handicapped facilities, since so many of them are located in older (and often two-story) buildings. But many of them do have at least one guest room, usually a downstairs one, that can accommodate a wheelchair; in this case there will also be a ramp. It's best to ask ahead of time exactly what facilities are available.

Recommended Country Inns® Travel Club: I state the discount, free night's stay, or other value offered by inns welcoming club members. Note that all discounts listed refer to room rates only, not to meals, and that a number of offers are subject to availability.

Recommended Country Inns

THE SOUTHWEST

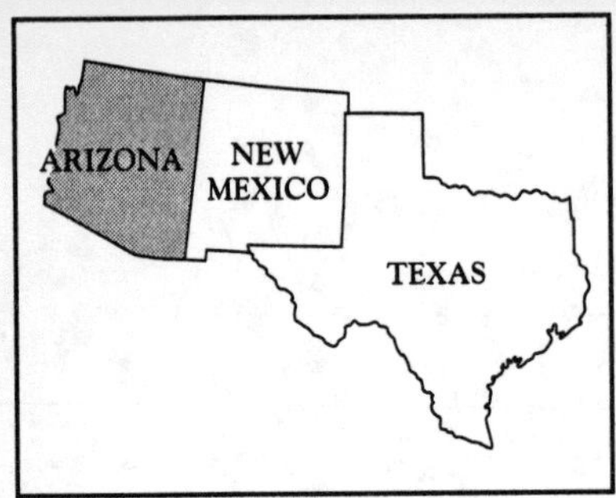
ARIZONA
NEW MEXICO
TEXAS

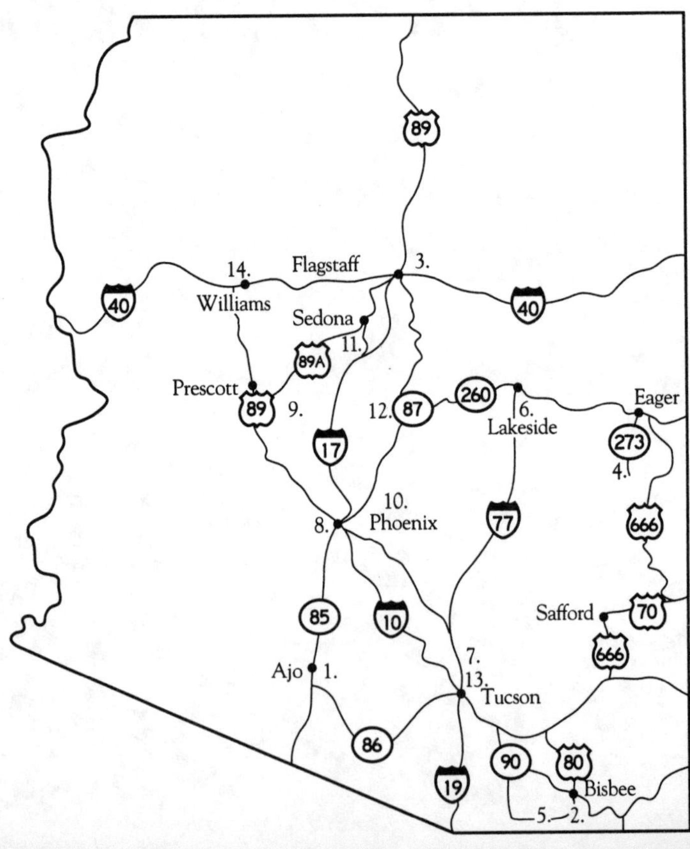
89
14.
Flagstaff
3.
40
Williams
Sedona
40
11.
89A
Prescott
89
9.
17
12.
87
260
6.
Lakeside
Eager
273
4.
10.
8.
Phoenix
77
666
85
10
Safford
70
666
Ajo
1.
7.
13.
Tucson
86
19
90
80
Bisbee
5.
2.

Arizona

Numbers on map refer to towns numbered below.

The Guest House Inn

AJO, ARIZONA 85321

This is an unusual house, with the four guest rooms square in the middle. Each room has French doors opening onto the light, bright glassed-in porch that makes a U-shape around the center rooms. The inn was designed in 1925 as a guest house for visiting officials of the Phelps Dodge Corporation, whose copper mines were the town's main industry. Now the mining is over, and Norma Walker has sort of "inherited" the lovely house.

"I was the housekeeper; I was in charge of this place until the mine closed down in 1985," she says. "The Dodges were so nice, they needed someone and my boys were in school. I was my own boss here, and I wanted the house when the mine closed down. When we found out it was for sale, my boys said, 'Mom, do you still want it?'"

Norma is a born hostess, coming from a home where, she says, hospitality was the rule. She can't get over how guests write letters of thanks for her hospitality. "I don't know why they thank me; they are paying, after all," she says in wonder. I could tell immediately why. Norma is one of nature's nurturing people, warm and giving, and she enjoys it one hundred percent. On ironing bed linens, for instance: "They are supposed to be wrinkle free, but I won't have guests sleep on them. I figure if we are going to have a nice place, we are going to do it right!"

On afternoon tea: "I give people a choice;

you never know what people want. Everything is homemade; I always want to have something to offer when people arrive unexpectedly." That's how I arrived, and I was plied with warm-from-the-oven chocolate chip cookies, vegetable soup, and didn't I want some fresh vegetables as well? "If people reserve ahead, I bake them a cake or grasshopper pie. If they are repeat guests, I bake them a different cake." Norma's repertoire includes chocolate cake, tequila cake, piña colada, "many kinds."

Breakfast on the long table in the bright dining room at the back of the house varies from pecan waffles to *huevos rancheros* with *chorizo* (sausage). Always fresh muffins with homemade jams and, for late risers, perhaps quiche. "Too heavy for early risers," says Norma.

Both sons helped decorate, and guest rooms are large and uncluttered, with lamps on nightstands for bedtime reading and dressers and chairs to put things on. Each room is furnished individually, from Victorian marble-topped antiques to handcrafted Southwestern pieces.

Bird-watchers are in for a real treat here in the Sonoran Desert, where Gambel's quail and the cactus wren are plentiful. And there's always a chance you might spot a wild javelina trotting along—just don't get in the way!

How to get there: From Phoenix take I–10 west to Highway 85 and 85 south to Ajo. From Tucson take Highway 86 west to Highway 85 and 85 north to Ajo. In Ajo turn south at La Mina Avenue (the only traffic light in town) to Guest Hill Road. Turn right, and the inn is at the end of the road. There is a sign.

Innkeepers: Norma Walker, Michael and Chris Walker
Address/Telephone: 3 Guest House Road; (602) 387–6133
Rooms: 4; all with private bath. No smoking inn.
Rates: $49 to $59, double, EPB.
Open: All year.
Facilities and activities: Patio with picnic table. Nearby: restaurants and shops in Ajo, museum, open pit copper mine, golf, scenic drives, Organ Pipe Cactus National Monument, Cabeza Prieta Game Refuge, bird watching.

The Mine Manager's House Inn

AJO, ARIZONA 85321

Ajo was the birthplace of Arizona's mining industry, and the small town was a railroad and airline stop back then. Now you pretty much have to drive, either from Tucson or Phoenix.

The Mine Manager's House was exactly that, the home of the manager of the New Cornelia Company copper mine in 1919. Eventually part of the Phelps Dodge Corporation, the mine closed in 1985. The inn is situated on the top of a hill with a view of the southwestern Arizona desert and the huge open pit mine, giving a lesson in how miners dug copper ore from the earth.

"Snow and rain brought us here," Jean says, referring to life in his hometown of Montreal. "I was sick and tired of that. After twenty years it became rough and tough. We saw an ad in the paper for the inn, and Micheline said, 'I'd like to do that!' We visited here; she said, 'I like it.'" He laughs. "I said to myself, we've just bought a place."

The inn's enclosed front porch is a small shop full of local crafts. "Indian crafts, and those made by local ladies," Jean explains. The back porch, also enclosed, is the reading room. In between, the New Cornelia Suite, the Greenway Suite, the Early American Suite, and the Nautical Room offer different motifs, with a harmonious mix of antiques and contemporary furniture, old photographs, and comfortable space. The Early American Suite overlooks the town and a lovely jacaranda tree; from the Honeymoon Suite there's a view of the mountains toward Organ Pipe Cactus National Monument. The Nautical Room is accessible for wheelchairs, and the Catalina Suite is detached, off the patio, and available to smokers.

For breakfast it's Jean who does the cooking, says Micheline: eggs Benedict, low-cholesterol Belgian waffles served with strawberries and yogurt, or tortillas stuffed with scrambled eggs and vegetables (in deference to the Southwest); orange juice, fruit cup, and blueberry muffins.

On major holidays, when Ajo restaurants are closed, guests can reserve a place at the family table. "They become part of the family; they're included," the Forniers say.

One hundred miles south of Ajo takes you to the Gulf of California, famous for fabulous deep-sea fishing in its brilliant blue waters.

How to get there: From Phoenix take I–10 west to Highway 85 and 85 south to Ajo. From Tucson take Highway 86 west to Highway 85 and 85 north to Ajo. In Ajo turn south at La Mina Avenue (the only traffic light in town) to Greenway Drive and follow the road up to the top of the hill. There is parking in front of the inn.

Innkeepers: Jean and Micheline Fournier
Address/Telephone: One Greenway Drive; (602) 387–6508
Rooms: 5, including 2 suites; all with private bath; wheelchair accessible. Smoking in Catalina Suite only.
Rates: $65 to $99, double, EPB.
Open: All year.
Facilities and activities: Jacuzzi and covered patio with refrigerator, coin laundry facilities, VCR, gift shop. Nearby: restaurants and shops in Ajo; pet care, museum, open pit copper mine, golf, scenic drives, Organ Pipe Cactus National Monument, Cabeza Prieta Game Refuge.

Bisbee Grand Hotel

BISBEE, ARIZONA 85603

Opulence, extraordinary almost-out-of-the-world opulence, is what you'll find at the well-named Bisbee Grand. Grand is a perfect adjective for this inn—so is elegant. From the red-velvet Victorian Suite to the other-worldly Oriental Suite, exotic luxury abounds in this posh, treasure-filled inn.

The modest, small black marquee over the double doors, squeezed in between two storefronts, hardly prepared me for what awaited as I climbed the red-carpeted stairs leading from the narrow entrance to the second floor and the inn rooms. Once there, faced with an iridescent stuffed peacock at the head of the stairs, I found myself in a world I certainly had never expected in the quaint and charming Old West mining town of Bisbee.

Each of the seven guest rooms is a world in itself, full of beautiful furniture and decorative details. "These antiques were collected for thirty years," innkeeper Bill says with justifiable pride. As for the three suites, they are extravaganzas, excitingly imaginative, full of unexpected appointments, such as a working fountain next to a lovely, large flower arrangement in the Garden Suite.

The Oriental Suite is unashamedly opulent, with walls covered in black, pink, and gold fabric depicting Chinese scenes. The brass bed is adorned with onyx and alabaster. "It's a unique, one-of-a-kind honeymoon bed," Bill explains. It's wide and high, with an oval mirror and paintings, while bronze dragon vases and black lacquer vie with other choice collectibles in the room.

The Victorian Suite is dripping with deep-red-velvet hangings, not only on the windows but also making a cozy nest of the canopied bed. The Garden Suite is a bower of flowers; as for the rest of the rooms, like the Coral and the Gray rooms, Deer Springs and Crow Canyon, well, I'm going to let you see for yourself. Just take my word for it: It's all outstanding.

On the main floor, adjacent to the Grand Western Saloon, the inn's old-fashioned Victorian parlor has an antique piano that you may play if you're careful. The saloon's 35-foot bar came from Wyatt Earp's Oriental Bar by way of the Wells Fargo Museum.

Breakfast will satisfy both the most eager gourmet and the health food aficionado. "All our food is from Tucson Cooperative Warehouses," Bill notes, "and we recycle and compost everything." The fruit course consisted of watermelon, cantaloupe, pineapple, and green grapes; the delicious quiche was full of cheese and mushrooms, with ham on the side; the homemade bread was delicious; and for sweets, there were cheese Danish and cinnamon rolls.

"We treat our guests very special, with all the grace and elegance of the best of a Victorian mining town," Bill says. Morning coffee, hot tea, ice tea, and a plateful of ginger snaps, lemon bars, and peanut butter and chocolate chip cookies are available in the saloon practically 'round the clock. And not the least of the pleasures of this small, elegant inn is watching the sunset, or the rainbow after it rains, over the mountains facing the front balcony.

How to get there: From Highway 80 east take Tombstone Canyon Road for approximately 2½ miles until it becomes Main Street. You can't miss the Bisbee Grand on the left.

Innkeeper: Bill Thomas
Address/Telephone: 61 Main Street (mailing address: P.O. Box 825); (602) 432–5900 or (800) 421–1909
Rooms: 11; 7 with private bath. No smoking inn.
Rates: $50 to $75, double; $95, suites; EPB.
Open: All year.
Facilities and activities: Grand Western Saloon with complimentary snacks, pool table, large TV screen, and Ladies' Parlor; Murder Mystery weekends. Nearby: Old Bisbee Tour, City Mine Tour, Bisbee Mining and Historical Museum, antiques shops, art galleries.

The Bisbee Inn

BISBEE, ARIZONA 85603

This historic inn first opened its doors in 1917 as the LaMore Hotel, overlooking Brewery Gulch, then a wild boomtown street. Owners Joy and John Timbers kept the mining hotel's spartan but comfortable Victorian atmosphere when they undertook the certified historic restoration. I like the spare but clean look that solid light oak, lace curtains, and brass bedsteads can give. It's real Victorian, all right—the brass-painted beds (innkeepers point out that they're not really brass) and oak furniture are the original hotel pieces, in excellent condition. In the closets I found flowered and plain flannel robes hanging for guests' use, a thoughtful touch.

Both lounge and dining rooms are homey. Three rooms form the dining area, the center one a small atrium. Look up and you'll see a set of stairs and a wrought-iron balcony under the skylight. Lace cloths are on the tables, with places marked by pretty ruffled mats. Furnishings are carefully restored original oak pieces.

Breakfast, made in quantity and of quality, consists of "all you can eat": two kinds of juice, fruit salad, whole wheat bread made by Joy, scrambled or fried eggs, bacon, pancakes, potatoes, waffles, and French toast made with homemade bread.

"We're in there hosting along with helpers Randy and Jill," says John, an enthusiastic innkeeper. "I like the type of person that inns attract—adventuresome people who like to try something and who enjoy it, too."

The entire crew gets into the innkeeping act. When there's a full house, Joy (who teaches) comes up after school. She and John take part, help Jill cook breakfast—everybody works together. It's the kind of place where guests often help serve evening refreshments to other guests.

The social hour can take place wherever you like—in the dining room, in the television room, out on the porch, or even in your room if by chance you want to be alone.

The inn is cooled in summer by evaporative coolers and is centrally heated during the winter. To add to guests' comfort, there are custom-made quilts on the beds. "A local lady hand-quilts them for us," says Joy.

All the crew will recommend good Bisbee eateries, and the Timbers also own the Plaza, a restaurant in the Warren area of Bisbee. (The town is really three small towns strung out along the copper mountains. Get a map, brochures, and a walking-tour map from the Chamber of Commerce on Commerce Street.) At the Plaza be sure to try the homemade cream of mushroom and broccoli soup and the pineapple pecan cake with almond cream cheese frosting. I promise you won't regret it!

How to get there: From Highway 80 take the business exit into the heart of Old Bisbee and go straight up the hill, which is OK Street. The inn is 200 yards up the steep and narrow street, and there's parking to the right, just beyond the inn building.

Innkeepers: Joy and John Timbers; Randy Pantera and Jill Thomas
Address/Telephone: 45 OK Street (mailing address: P.O. Box 1855); (602) 432–5131
Rooms: 18 share 5 shower rooms and 7 rest rooms; all with washbasin. Pets permitted. No smoking inn.
Rates: $29 to $51, double, EPB.
Open: All year.
Facilities and activities: TV room, laundry facilities. Nearby: Brewery Gulch, Copper Queen Mine Tour, Lavender Pit Mine Tour, Bisbee Mining Museum.

Clawson House

BISBEE, ARIZONA 85603

Built in 1895, Clawson House is another of those lovely mansions built for lucky mine executives of bygone times. Sitting atop famed Castle Rock, the hill that is one of Bisbee's most outstanding features, the inn offers views far and wide. On a clear day you can even see Mexico from the porches that surround the house.

Clawson House is the oldest house on the hill, which, according to Jim, used to be called Nob Hill after Judge Bisbee moved here from San Antonio. "This, and all the early homes, were built out of redwood, so I guess he had a lumber interest as well as mining," Wally says with a laugh.

Bisbee, in the heart of the Mule Mountains, was quite a mining town in its heyday. Founded in 1889, it once was the most highly populated town in Arizona, thanks to copper.

The Watertower, the inn's breakfast room, is a reminder of the 30-foot copper water tank that was filled every day for the mine superintendent and his men. The home has been completely restored, and its spacious rooms are furnished elaborately: This is one of those wonderful places where you hardly know where to look and what to admire next. There are Oriental rugs, northern California brass and copperware, and an extensive collection of original Currier and Ives prints, which "I've collected all the way from Buffalo to Boston," Wally says. He's also pretty proud of his complete collection of forty Richard Timm wildlife prints.

Retired from careers as giftshop proprietors in northern California, Jim and Wally spent two years restoring the house for themselves, using their thirty-year collection of beautiful objects. "But when we got involved with the Chamber [of Commerce] as volunteers, they encouraged us to open the house as an inn," Jim says. "We really encourage people to use the whole house; nothing is off-limits."

The entry has Italian etched crystal windows leading into the grand parlor, which has a fireplace. The formal dining room is huge, and guest rooms also are large as well as elegant. I loved the unexpected collection of kachina dolls lining the stairs, the brass bedsteads, the antique quilts, the rawhide furniture on the screened veranda, and the reversed painted glass lampshades inherited from Jim's mother and grandmother.

The two innkeepers work well together as a team. "I do the outside, he does the inside," says Wally. "Jim is the baker, I'm the banker."

The baker makes morning glory muffins with apples, carrots, and raisins, and a sour cream coffee cake with a cream cheese filling topped with raspberries and sliced almonds—just remembering makes my mouth water. The zucchini nut bread is delicious, too.

You can have poached eggs if you like, but "I also do a healthy buffet," Jim says, "A Southwest quiche, modified for guests—young people are conscious of health."

"So are the old folks—because of their age," Wally adds with a laugh. It's all served on china, crystal, and silver; and if guests are there for more than one morning, the settings as well as the menu are changed.

How to get there: Take Main Street to the intersection of Clawson and Main; the intersection is marked by the copper-colored Iron Man statue. Turn right on Clawson, and the inn is the first house up the hill on the right. Turn into the driveway, which circles around the house. There's parking in the rear.

Innkeepers: Jim Grosskopt and Wally Kuehl
Address/Telephone: 116 Clawson Avenue (mailing address: P.O. Box 454); (602) 432–5237 or (800) 467–5237
Rooms: 3; 1 with private bath. No smoking inn.
Rates: $55 to $70, double, EPB.
Open: All year.
Facilities and activities: Verandas and views, walking distance to Historic Center. Nearby: Old Bisbee Tour, City Mine Tour, Bisbee Mining and Historical Museum, antiques shops, art galleries.
Recommended Country Inns® Travel Club Benefit: 10% discount.

Park Place
BISBEE, ARIZONA 85603

I didn't have to ask the reason for Park Place's name once I turned the corner and saw it facing the park. "We didn't inherit a horror story; the house has always been well taken care of," Janet says of the large, 1910 Mediterranean-style home that they've turned into a wonderful inn. "The only thing I couldn't stand was what had been added to the fireplace. I said to Bob, `I'll have that off the minute we sign the papers!'" What she couldn't stand was a blue wormwood facade covering the fireplace from floor to ceiling.

"Luckily, we had a picture of the original fireplace, so we were able to reproduce it," Janet says with satisfaction, although she mourns what was done to the wood in the house. "It's all golden oak—can you imagine painting it white? But I've been in the antique business, and I'm not about to strip it!"

Bisbee natives into the fourth generation, Janet and Bob were in the real estate business when they got the inn by trade. My first impression was of windows, windows everywhere, which I love, and every room is exceptionally large in the 5,000-square-foot house. The glassed-in solarium, known in these parts as an Arizona room, is a favorite gathering place.

The dining room is spacious, too, with antique walnut furniture. "Everybody else wanted oak," Janet says, explaining how she got her hands on that hard-to-find wood.

The library has a fireplace to make you cozy while you read, and more bright windows. Each guest room is a corner room, with large windows letting in the view of the broad park across the street or the rose garden on the grounds. The Green Room, in pastels and with twin beds that can be made into a king, opens onto a large side porch. "The man next door has a fabulous garden, especially in the spring," Janet says, "and guests love to sit out here and enjoy it. Peace, quiet, and rest!"

Both the Yellow Room and the Blue Room also open onto the porch. The Blue Room is made special by a huge mirrored headboard over its waterbed, while the Yellow Room is graced by a plate rack lined with quite a collection of plates. The Pink Room is a spacious suite with a queen bed.

Janet and Bob are relaxed, comfortable, and caring innkeepers. A departing guest inquired where she could buy French bread in town. "Oh!" responded Janet. "I wish you'd asked me yesterday! I would have baked you one!"

She and Bob are becoming absolutely famous for their breakfasts. One guest was so carried away that she exclaimed, "I have *never* eaten that well for breakfast!"

The meal is an hour- to an hour-and-a-half-long, four-course feast of fresh fruit compote, German pancakes, ham, bacon, breakfast steaks or pork chops, and homemade muffins. From food to table, the presentation is worthy of a gourmet magazine. "I'm very concerned with correct presentation," Janet says. "It's Bob who puts out the gourmet food."

"Janet does detail work on serving, on the table," Bob elaborates. "I do it on the food." They make quite a team, serving the feast in the formal dining room, sun porch, or on the garden patio, weather permitting.

How to get there: From the circle where Highways 80 and 92 meet, take the fourth road (Bisbee Road) to Congdon. Turn left to East Vista. Turn right, and the inn is on the left, on the corner of East Vista and Tener.

Innkeepers: Janet and Bob Watkins
Address/Telephone: 200 East Vista; (602) 432–3054 or (800) 388–4388
Rooms: 4; 2 with private bath. Pets at discretion of innkeepers. No smoking inn.
Rates: $40 to $60, double, EPB.
Open: All year.
Facilities and activities: Lunch and dinner by reservation; workshops in weaving, spinning, fibers. Nearby: Historic Old Bisbee, shops and restaurants, Lavender Mine tours, Bisbee Mining and Historical Museum, birdwatching, golf, bike rental, horseback riding, rock hounding.

Schoolhouse Inn

BISBEE, ARIZONA 85603

A guest wrote that the Schoolhouse Inn is so homey, she felt she was visiting a dear friend's home. Innkeepers Marc and Shirl Negus believe that they *are* home. "We dropped out of the corporate world," Marc says. "What it boils down to is you only have one life to live. I like working around the house and I thought this would keep me busy." He laughs. "We're working just as hard as we did in the corporate world, but—we're home."

Their home now is a fascinating place, a big, old-fashioned schoolhouse—really! Built in 1918 at the height of Bisbee's prosperous mining days, Garfield School accommodated grades one through four in four huge classrooms. When things died down in Bisbee in the 1930s, the school was converted into apartments.

Shirl's son lives in nearby Douglas, and when he got married a few years back, the Neguses, then living in California, came to the wedding. "We saw Bisbee . . ." and that was the end of their hour-long commute to Apple Computer.

They had a great time creating a schoolhouse theme for each room. "We do have a good time with it," Marc says. You can pick your favorite subject: Music? History? Geography, Art, Reading, Writing, maybe Arithmetic? You can "cut class" in the Library or play chief in the Principal's Office.

Check out the original school blueprints

hanging along the walls of the main stairway. Even more fascinating is the old class picture hanging in the upstairs hallway. "A gentleman we met here went to this school in the 1920s," Shirl says. "He gave us that class picture."

Rooms are decorated in pastel colors; there are pretty quilts on the beds; the 12-foot ceilings make everything seem extremely spacious. In the suites, cozy sitting areas are separated from the bedrooms by arched openings, and the writing desks are perfect for your "homework": writing postcards home, describing quaint Bisbee.

The dining room/lounge contains a soft sectional sofa facing three large lace-covered tables. The French doors lead to a patio shaded by a huge black oak tree, "probably a hundred years old," Shirl says. It's very relaxing out there, swinging on the covered swing, listening to the wind chimes, and looking at the darting hummingbirds.

Breakfast is fulsome. Shirl brags: "We have never-throw-away recipes," by which she means that everything always gets all eaten up! Sometimes it's walnut French toast, other times Shirl's special Schoolhouse Quiche—a crustless egg delicacy with two cheeses and green chilies—not to mention the deliciously healthy walnut oat bran muffins. And there are always at least two fruits.

Good lounging places, besides the lounge and the patio, are in the upstairs hall or the small porch upstairs over the front door. There's an old Dr Pepper cooler with soft drinks. Also of interest: the napkin ring collection on the sideboard in the inn office.

How to get there: On Highway 80 pass through the Mule Pass Tunnel and take the Tombstone Canyon exit. Go 1 block on Tombstone Canyon and turn right onto Pace Avenue. The inn is up the hill, past the fenced-in school playing courts on the left.

Innkeepers: Marc and Shirl Negus
Address/Telephone: 818 Tombstone Canyon (mailing address: P.O. Box 32); (602) 432–2996 or (800) 537–4333
Rooms: 6, plus 3 suites; all with private bath; wheelchair accessible. No smoking inn.
Rates: $45 to $65, double; $10 extra person; EPB.
Open: All year.
Facilities and activities: Lunch by reservation, groups only; cable TV; board games and chess; basketball, volleyball, horseshoes. Nearby: Historic Old Bisbee, shops and restaurants, Lavender Mine tours, Bisbee Mining and Historical Museum, bird watching, golf, bike rental, horseback riding, rock hounding.

Birch Tree Inn

FLAGSTAFF, ARIZONA 86001

How do two women decorate one house? Good friends for years, Sandy and Donna hit on a perfect plan when they decided to go into the inn business together. "I have an idea," one of them said. "You take two rooms and I do the same, and no questions asked!"

The result is a lovely inn that everyone is happy with. The house was built in 1917 by a Chicago contractor who moved to Flagstaff with a large family. "It was never considered a mansion, so we decided to decorate in comfortable country," Sandy says. All four innkeepers are from Southern California, and the ties go back since Donna and Ed knew each other in the fifth grade!

They work together well, with Sandy doing the cooking and Donna taking care of the artistic touches. "She does the flowers, folds the napkins, decorates real pretty," Sandy says. Sandy's specialty is a Farmer's Breakfast, with skillet potatoes and a healthy frittata of eggs, cheese, broccoli, carrots, and green beans, served with fresh fruit and muffins. "Depends upon the mood I'm in, maybe they'll be banana-apple with nuts and orange." Sometimes there will be German pancakes with apples and syrup or strawberries and whipped cream.

"We like to serve afternoon refreshments in the parlor," both Donna and Sandy say. "It gives us a chance to know our guests."

Pella's Room has Dutch lace curtains and a handmade quilt. In Carol's Room they let a daughter pick out the wallpaper. The antique armoire was hauled all the way from California. The pale-lemon-painted Wagner/Znetko Room, named after Ed's grandparents, has a basin in the room and a private bath attached.

The Wicker Room speaks for itself, in blue and white and a queen-sized bed. The aqua Southwest Suite has a king-sized bed, corner windows, and a huge bath with the house's original fixtures on a black-and-white tile floor. Downstairs, the soft rose and blue color scheme is restful—and so is the swing, out on the veranda. A wheelbarrow in the front yard is filled with bright flowers.

The innkeepers keep a book of restaurant menus handy for guest information; but in desperate situations, "like being snowbound," Sandy says with a laugh, they've served guests soup and fresh bread. "Donna is a good tour guide," she adds, which is a handy thing to know if you want to see some of the many attractions of the area.

How to get there: At the intersection of I–17 and I–40, take exit 195B (which becomes Milton Road). Follow it around to Highway 180 (which becomes Humphry's Street) and go left 2 blocks to Birch Avenue. Turn left to the inn at 824. But if there's still construction going on, take Aspen left across the construction to Beaver, left on Beaver to Birch, and right on Birch.

Innkeepers: Sandy and Ed Znetko, Donna and Rodger Pettinger
Address/Telephone: 824 Birch Avenue; (602) 774–1042
Rooms: 5; 3 with private bath; no air conditioning (elevation 7,000 feet). No smoking inn.
Rates: \$55 to \$90, double, EPB.
Open: All year.
Facilities and activities: Bicycles, tennis rackets (tennis courts nearby), pool table, game room, piano. Nearby: restaurants and Downtown Historical District, cross-country skiing, Grand Canyon, Museum of Northern Arizona, Coconino Center for the Arts, Lowell Observatory, Pioneer's Historical Museum, Northern Arizona University.

Dierker House

FLAGSTAFF, ARIZONA 86001

"All my boys were boatmen on the Colorado River," Dottie Dierker says as she points out the joys of the nearby white-water rafting. "Of course," she says, "you have to plan way ahead."

She plans way ahead for her guests, too, providing baskets in her guest rooms for toothbrushes and other commodities that people use regularly. Her rule is that nobody leaves anything in the bathroom. Even towels used once go in the hamper, so "Nobody need touch a towel or a washcloth twice."

Dottie was a nurse before she retired. She also raised six children. "I kind of like taking care of people," she says. "And my house really helps. It gives everybody privacy. I can go to market and leave it open, leave a note.

"I've been in bed and breakfasts in other parts of the world. All over, in Budapest, all over Greece . . . mostly Europe and the Mediterranean. Of course," says this well-traveled innkeeper, "everyone does it in England and Germany." Wherever her guests may have been, they certainly enjoy Dierker House and keep coming back.

Dottie lives downstairs in her house, and guests have the run of the upstairs, which is really a three-bedroom suite. It's so cozy that guests sit around in the kitchen and raid the cookie jar or the refrigerator for refreshments. "They get together and exchange addresses," Dottie says with satisfaction. The single bath is large, with a skylight, plants, a scale, and a stocked medicine chest. "It's the nurse in me, I guess," Dottie confesses.

The three guest rooms, cozy under the eaves with down comforters and antiques and filled with green plants, are a travelogue in themselves. Would you rather sleep in France, Germany, or Greece? Posters and other mementos will take you there in your dreams.

For breakfast in the dining room, Dottie will serve one of four menus ("If you stay longer, you get a repeat," she warns): bran muffins, blueberry muffins, a meat dish, or an egg dish, all served at 8:00 A.M. "That's the only time I cook." But not to worry if you're early or late: "There's the option of a big continental breakfast in the guest kitchen."

Dottie is pretty much settled into her house. "I've only lived here more than forty years!" she told me. She raises orchids and she quilts, comfortable with her three Shih Tzu dogs and her many canaries, who live in cages in the long garden room behind the dining room. "They sing every morning—such a happy sound."

Skylights light the pool table standing on the Mexican tile floor. A wall of windows opens onto a small bright garden. There's an old Wurlitzer jukebox that lights up like a Christmas tree and plays all those old tunes. Guests occasionally indulge in a game of pool after breakfast. "Fun!" says Dottie.

How to get there: At the intersection of I–17 and I–40, take exit 195B (which becomes Milton Road). Follow it around to Highway 180 (which becomes Humphry's Street), turn left, and go 3 blocks to Cherry Avenue.

Innkeeper: Dorothea (Dottie) Dierker
Address/Telephone: 423 West Cherry Avenue; (602) 774–3249
Rooms: 3 share 1 bath; no air conditioning (elevation 7,000 feet). No smoking inn.
Rates: $45 to $65, double, EPB. No credit cards.
Open: All year.
Facilities and activities: Lightly equipped kitchen, microwave. Nearby: tennis courts, Downtown Historic District, museums, Indian ruins, skiing, white-water rafting on Colorado River, Grand Canyon.

The Inn at Four Ten

FLAGSTAFF, ARIZONA 86001

The Inn at Four Ten is a pretty gray-and-white house enclosed by a rock fence. The porch railings are painted white; so is the pretty gazebo in the yard to the right. Welcoming—and tempting—are the cookies waiting in the jar by the front door.

"This is certainly a lot friendlier than manufacturing!" Howard says happily, delighted to be finished with his past as a maker of purchase displays to advertise products in stores.

"Indeed it is a friendlier industry. We've already made friends," Sally adds. "It took me ten years to do that in a Chicago suburb!"

The Krueger motto is "there's no such thing as too much service," which may be part of the reason Sally and Howard find everyone so friendly. "We've liked to go on vacation ourselves, so we thought we'd like to help others enjoy their vacations." Howard says that he had a fortunate childhood, with help in the house, so he knows what service is. "We don't call for Jeeves; Jeeves is already here," he says with a laughing reference to the famous P. G. Wodehouse butler. "We can see the comings and goings in the parking lot, and I stop what I'm doing so I can welcome guests at the door. We want our guests to know they're appreciated."

Well, that explains how Howard is able to fling open the door almost before I have my hand on the doorknob!

The entrance opens onto a large living/dining area with cozy ticking-covered sofas and white wicker. Little touches make the inn cozy and friendly: Birdcages are suspended from the ceiling and doilies decorate tables, even the newel post of the staircase. An old sewing-machine cabinet is used as a sofa table, and pretty flowers in a white china pitcher bloom over an assortment of antique children's boots on the linen doily.

Sally and Howard are concerned with the health of their guests. "I won't serve quiche!" he says rather vehemently. But you won't miss it when you see the bountiful basket of fresh-baked goods like popovers and lemon pecan muffins, pumpkin chocolate chip muffins, and toasted homemade bread. French toast, too, and toasted bagels. All this is accompanied by a fresh fruit compote, and there's pineapple shrub to drink. This latter item sounds to me like something in an old-fashioned novel, and it turns out to be fruit juices blended with pineapple sherbert—delicious!

Sally and Howard coddle their guests with cookies in the afternoon, and wait until you taste the recipes that Sally brought with her from Chicago. Two favorites are cinnamon kiss cookies and Mrs. King's Cookies, concoctions of white and dark chocolate chips, oatmeal, and granola—you'd never know they were healthy. Hot chocolate, coffee and tea, and apple cider are available for "whoever's around in the afternoon," Sally says. "We love to eat, so we love to recommend restaurants."

Box lunches are a great option when you want to go sightseeing—the crowds at the Grand Canyon restaurants are daunting. Howard says, "This way you can unpack your lunch and enjoy it at the edge of the canyon away from the crowds."

How to get there: From the east on I–40 (or the south on I–17 to I–40), take exit 195B, and go about 1½ miles through town. After you go under an overpass, take the third street on the left, which is Leroux. Go up the hill, and the inn is on the right. There's a sign.

Innkeepers: Sally and Howard Krueger
Address/Telephone: 410 North Leroux; (505) 774–0088 or 774–1424
Rooms: 9; 7 with private bath. No smoking inn.
Rates: $59 to $89, double; $15 extra adult; $10 extra child; EPB and afternoon refreshments.
Open: All year.
Facilities and activities: Box lunches available. Nearby: Northern Arizona University, Museum of Northern Arizona, Lowell Observatory, Pioneer's Historical Museum, Arizona Snow Bowl with skiing and other winter sports, golf.

Greer Lodge

GREER, ARIZONA 85927

Here's another great place for communing with nature. On the inn grounds you might spot a blue heron or two, or perhaps an owl zooming down and buzzing the pond, catching his dinner. If he doesn't get a fish he'll get a duck; owls have been seen pulling full-sized ducks out of the water. Such is the view from Greer Lodge's magnificent two-story greenhouse lounge at the back of the inn, all glass with plants everywhere. The room overlooks the pond and away to the pine-covered mountains in the distance, where you can strike out for a hike or horseback ride into the National Forest.

The inn's spacious, comfortable rooms also have windows with views. The color scheme is rust and white: rust carpets, rust curtains and coverlets with little white flowers sprinkled all over, fresh comforters, linens, and towels—"the whole atmosphere is bright," say the Allens, who pride themselves on the way the inn sparkles, bright and shiny.

Chef Brandon Bell makes sure that everything served in the restaurant is homemade, from the biscuits and gravy to the cinnamon rolls. Breakfast is ordered off the menu, and you can have homemade croissants with your "eggs any way," or waffles, or pancakes. (Breakfast is not included in the rate for Little Lodge.) Lunches are available, packed for picnic, hiking, or fishing trips.

Homemade soups are wonderful here, soups like clam chowder, or my favorite cream of cauliflower or broccoli soup. Fresh homemade Kaiser rolls or whole wheat bread makes the thick roast beef, turkey, or ham sandwiches special.

Come winter, the inn's one-hundred-year-old Mennonite sled is available for romantic rides. "We had two marriage proposals right away!" Brandon says.

After lunch (or maybe early in the morning?) in the summer, sit on the back porch and just throw your line in the stream feeding the pond, which is stocked with two-pound rainbow and German brown trout, as well as Canloupes fresh from the Canadian lake of the same name. Flyfishing schools have become popular at the lodge, taught both on the pond and on the Little Colorado River nearby. Sitting out on the sun deck facing the pond, I see fish jumping out of the water, just waiting for Greer Lodge guests to catch them. Horses graze in the meadows in the distance. Elk and deer graze in the sunny alpine meadows. The hurly-burly of the city is far, far away. "This is Arizona's most beautiful setting," cheerful assistant Bob Pollack says, bragging that "even the governor thinks so!"

How to get there: Greer is at the end of Highway 373, a short road that runs south from Highway 260 between Eager and Indian Pine. The inn is at the end of the road on the left.

Innkeepers: Barb and Rich Allen
Address/Telephone: P.O. Box 244; (602) 735–7515
Rooms: 26; 9 with 9 baths in Main Lodge; 17 in 8 cabins; no air conditioning (elevation 8,500 feet); cabins wheelchair accessible. Smoking permitted except in dining room.
Rates: Main Lodge: $60 to $95, double; $15 to $20 extra person; EPB in Main Lodge only; two-night minimum stay on weekends, three nights on holidays.
Open: All year.
Facilities and activities: Restaurant serving breakfast, lunch (May to October) and dinner; picnic lunches, cocktail bar, stocked trout pond, hiking, horseback riding, skiing, bobsledding, bird watching, canoeing; corporate meeting space.

White Mountain Lodge

GREER, ARIZONA 85927

Mary is the daughter of original owners Sophie and Russ Majesky, and she and Charlie have taken over from the "old folks." I had loved Russ's answer when I asked why he liked being an innkeeper after supervising in Tucson's main post office. Not only did he say that both he and Sophie liked caring for people and that, although a lot of work, it was enjoyable; he added energetically, "and—I gotta have something to do!" Now he's finding that he's just as happy with "a little less work to do."

Mary and Charlie say they are "refugees" from busy Tucson, where Mary was a health care administrator and Charles also was in public administration. "Mom kept asking us when were we going to come up and take over, and I kept telling her to wait until our kids were grown." She laughs. "When I told her and Dad that finally we were ready, Dad said, 'I'm going to bed early!'"

White Mountain Lodge, the oldest building in Greer, began as a farmhouse, built in 1892 by one of the first Mormon families to settle in Greer. The Majeskys have preserved a wonderful landmark in a cozy and comfortable way and Mary and Charlie have done nothing to change it, except for enhancing the breakfast menu a little.

The enclosed front porch and the main lodge room are comfortably furnished, and the word *cozy* keeps returning to my mind. The feeling is of warmth and interest in guests—genuine hospitality.

"We've never charged a single cent for a cup of coffee in the years we've been in business," Charlie says. And the pot is on as early as 5:30 in the morning. This is the place for people who wake up early just dying for a cup of coffee.

The full breakfast is served in the family dining room. In addition to orange juice, coffee, and toast and jam, you'll have fresh fruit, a hot main entree, and homemade breads and rolls. "I'm the baker, Charlie's the cook," Mary explains as she serves honey-wheat bread, an apple or cherry coffeecake, melt-in-your-mouth butterhorns, maybe a German sour cream coffeecake.

"It really is a partnership. Wait until you taste Charlie's Grand Slam Breakfast!" It's a hum-dinger of a Mexican *chorizo* (sausage) casserole, served with hot tortillas and refried beans, and a fruit salad to cool things down a little.

Breakfasting together with other guests, the Basts believe, "provides spontaneity in talk and in striking up friendships while at the lodge." And they find that such friendships often are ongoing.

They say that they're seeing people from an entirely different perspective than from their former work: "As guests in your home," Charlie says.

Mary finds that innkeeping in no way compares with what she used to do. "Putting on heels and a dress and going to an office? We love the independence of the lifestyle here!"

"We have been blessed with seeing more elk, deer, and antelope grazing in the surrounding meadows," Mary says, "and of course the beaver continue to play in the ponds created by the Little Colorado River."

"The elk kept me up, bugling last night," Charlie adds. "They say two things—baby, come my way, and hey, stay outa my way!"

How to get there: Greer is at the end of Highway 373, south off Highway 260 between Eager and Indian Pine. The inn is on the left as you enter the village.

Innkeepers: Mary and Charlie Bast
Address/Telephone: P.O. Box 139; (602) 735–7568
Rooms: 9; 2 with private bath, 2 with connecting bath; wheelchair accessible; no air conditioning (elevation 8,500 feet). Pets permitted.
Rates: $40 to $70, double; $5 extra person; EPB. No credit cards.
Open: All year.
Facilities and activities: Nearby: fishing, hunting, and downhill and cross-country skiing at Sunrise Ski Area 13 miles away.
Recommended Country Inns® Travel Club Benefit: 10% discount, Monday–Thursday, subject to availability.

Ramsey Canyon Inn

HEREFORD, ARIZONA 85615

Ramsey Canyon Inn sits under tall pine trees at the very entrance to the Ramsey Canyon Preserves Nature Conservancy. Innkeeper Shirlene is a member of the conservancy and of the National Audubon Society, and she says the main reason people come to Ramsey Canyon is that more species of hummingbird have been recorded here than anywhere else in the United States. "Plus two hundred other species!" Ron adds. "This is a bird watcher's paradise, made for people who love nature and hiking."

Shirlene also loves to bake pies, and she modestly owns up to winning more than two hundred ribbons for her pastry. A native of the Ramsey Canyon area, she migrated to Alaska for a while and took pie honors at the Kenai Peninsula Fair, only to come home and take sweepstakes honors at the Cochise County Fair. What is her favorite pie? "I like them all!" is her laughing answer. The blackberry slice I had was rich and thick and tasted too much like more! Fruit for the pies comes fresh from her own orchard, and she bakes the pies daily.

Oh, it's quiet in Ramsey Canyon, birds notwithstanding. "Most of my guests tell me they haven't had a night's sleep like this in years," Shirlene says. From the windows of Room 7, you might catch a glimpse of a pair of golden eagles that nest up in the cliffs every spring and stay all summer. All the rooms are comfortable and cool, furnished with antiques, refinished by Shirlene, who is both artistic and handy. She has stenciled decorations along the walls of each room with designs she painted to match comforters, pillow shams, and bed ruffles. "I like things to match," she says. Shirlene also bakes birthday and anniversary cakes and presents flowers to birthday guests, flowers that she has cultivated in spite of the voracious forest creatures that surround her. "The javelina and the deer eat everything I plant but snapdragons!" Along with the birds, the deer, and the javelina, you may see raccoons, coatimundi, ring-tailed cats, mountain lions, foxes, and small black bears in Ramsey Canyon.

Shirlene serves a full gourmet breakfast. Individual puffed Dutch pancakes with sliced strawberries and whipped cream; cooked apples, peaches, and blueberries; sausage; and cranberry-pecan or banana muffins will fuel a lot of hours of bird watching. And you can do it lounging on the covered porch or under the tall black walnut, chokecherry, oak, maple, and sycamore trees of the picnic area if you wish, because Shirlene brings the show to her door. "We go through fifty pounds of sugar a week, feeding literally hundreds of hummingbirds," Ron says.

How to get there: From I–10 take Highway 90 south, turning onto Highway 92 south through Hereford 6 2/10 miles to Ramsey Canyon Road. Turn right and follow the trail 3½ miles to the inn, on the right just before you enter Ramsey Canyon Preserves.

Innkeepers: Shirlene and Ron DeSantis
Address/Telephone: 31 Ramsey Canyon Road; (602) 378–3010
Rooms: 6; 4 with private bath; 3 one-bedroom housekeeping cottages; no air conditioning (elevation 5,400 feet); handicapped accessible. No smoking inn.
Rates: Rooms: $85 to $95, double, EPB. Cottages: $85 to $105, double; $10 extra person; EP. No credit cards.
Open: All year.
Facilities and activities: Picnic area. Nearby: Ramsey Canyon Preserves, bird watching, hiking trails in Huachuca Mountains.
Recommended Country Inns® Travel Club Benefit: 10% discount, October–February.

Bartram's White Mountain Inn

LAKESIDE, ARIZONA 85929

"We never hear traffic noises," Petie Bartram says happily. "Instead we hear birds and see wild horses, elk, eagles, and bears. The inn overlooks the Apache Indian Reservation, and the other day a herd of wild horses was grazing in the field shared by the inn and the reservation." Petie, having decided that if she kept on the way she was going, she'd be dead, gave up a well-paid job for life here in the woods. "I'm going to be dead a long time when I die," she says, "and this is what I want to be doing now."

Ray is a long-distance truck driver, but with the inn Petie never gets a chance to be lonely. "My guests are fun," she says. "It's such fun when you have people who are willing to be fun back!"

"But Petie," her guests protest, "it's you who's fun." And indeed, Petie works hard to make the inn special; she wants it to be an affordable escape for people who can't manage an expensive getaway resort. She and Ray do things like make homemade ice cream in the summer. "We do whatever fits into someone's lifestyle," she says.

In winter guests like to curl up with an afghan on the sofa in front of the petrified-wood fireplace and take a cozy nap. The fireplace heats the entire house. On the wall above, there's a collection of Apache snowshoes that guests who want to trek in the snow can borrow.

There are notions and hand-decorated towels

in the bathrooms. Rooms were decorated with great enthusiasm by Petie, and it's a hard choice between the Blue Room, the Peach Suite, and the Satin Room.

Petie is proud of her seven-course breakfast—a whopper. We had: (1) juice, coffee, tea, and hot chocolate; (2) "cheesey eggs" with mushrooms, scallions, cream, and cheese sauce; (3) hashed brown potatoes with paprika and parmesan cheese (or sometimes she serves potato cakes with curry and sesame seeds); (4) two kinds of muffins (banana sour cream with walnuts, and bran raisin sticky buns); (5) bacon (sometimes smoked turkey, ham, smoked pork chops, or Italian sausage); (6) a fruit platter with cream sauce; and (7) (time to holler *Enough!*) stuffed French toast.

The inn has delightful pets, most unusual ones like Farnsworth, the house-trained pig, and Nugget, the parrot, who lives in a cage in the back room. "Nugget can walk right out here now; he's housebroken," Petie says. "All of our animals are strays. Ray was making a delivery in back of a store at 3:00 A.M. and there was this big green parrot sitting out there. Ray held out his hand and the bird jumped on. They fell madly in love. We advertised, but no one came to claim him." There are also four outside cats and three dogs: the poodle, Shammy, a collie named Samantha, and another collie, Yum-yum. "But we call him Yummy," say the two animal lovers.

How to get there: From Highway 260 in Lakeside, turn right at the only traffic light, onto Woodland Lake Road; go to the stop sign and turn right. The inn's on the right at the end of the road.

Innkeepers: Petie and Ray Bartram
Address/Telephone: Route 1, Box 1014; (602) 367–1408
Rooms: 3; all with private bath and patio; no air conditioning (elevation 7,000 feet); electric blankets. No smoking inn.
Rates: $70, double; $20 extra person; EPB.
Open: All year.
Facilities and activities: Infant equipment, ski storage, volleyball, badminton, horseshoes. Nearby: restaurants, Woodland Lake Park, Apache Indian Reservation, fishing, hiking, biking, tennis, horseback riding, skiing, golf, and antiques shops.
Recommended Country Inns® Travel Club Benefit: 10% discount.

Villa Cardinale

ORACLE, ARIZONA 85623

You won't need to ask why this inn is named for cardinals—they're all over, both the real thing and artistic representations of them.

You'll see lots of other wildlife in this small inn, which is so high up that the temperature is always twenty degrees cooler than in Tucson. The air is clearer, the sunsets more spectacular, and the evening sky glitters with stars. You're out in the country, and the only pets the inn has, says Donna, are the wild ones. Besides the many small birds, there are quail, turkeys, javelinas, and chipmunks. Glenn draws the line at feeding them, though: "I don't want any of those boars to come around close!"

Breakfast and dinner are wonderful in the huge atrium/dining room. With the green plants inside and the flower gardens outside, it's like dining in a greenhouse.

The inn is furnished with an eclectic mix of antiques. The Hummingbird Room is dainty, with blue-and-white lace; Road Runner has a queen bed and Mexican leather table and chairs; Cactus Wren has a four-poster bed and Ethan Allen chairs; Quail Room, with a view of the live quails out the window, has an unusual four-poster, Shaker-style pencil-post bed.

All four rooms open onto a shady entrance patio; you can come and go via your own entrance if you want, through the arched entrance to the patio. Just be careful not to bump into the old locomotive bell over the wrought-iron gate if you don't want to be heard!

The small refrigerator out on the patio is for ice and soft drinks. There is coffee as well that Donna puts out first thing in the morning. Soft music plays on the stereo, which is there for guests to use.

There's a small fountain in the patio, too, to keep things even cooler. Around the patio window boxes brighten each window, and the brick is lovely used adobe from Mexico.

Glenn is the chef, and breakfast is hearty, with tasty dishes like breakfast burritos, a colorful medley of eggs, red peppers, green onions, and spices topped with cheese. "It's a tribute to the Southwest," says Glenn, who hails from New York City. He was a paramedic on a helicopter—until it crashed. "That took care of that!" he says.

Donna is from Minnesota originally. She is a registered nurse, so guests know they're always in good hands, no matter what!

New to me, and super delicious, was Glenn's breakfast dessert of carmelized bananas. "I was dreaming the other night, and when I woke up, I thought, hey, that sounds good!" How's that for a talented chef—one who actually dreams up wonderful dishes! Add to that red-potato home fries, blueberry bran, banana nut, and pumpkin raisin bread, and you'll have more than enough energy to hike all around Aravaipa Canyon.

And if you want to go prospecting, why, "There's gold in them thar hills; we've had geologists visiting, and they tell us so . . ."

How to get there: Take Highway 89 north from Tucson to Oracle Junction, then Highway 77 to Oracle. Don't take the business route; go on to Rockcliff Boulevard. Turn left; the first right is Oracle Ranch Road. The inn is 500 yards on the right.

Innkeepers: Donna and Glenn Velardi
Address/Telephone: 1315 West Oracle Road (mailing address: P.O. Box 649); (602) 896–2516
Rooms: 4; all with private bath, 2 with TV; wheelchair accessible; no air conditioning (elevation 4,500 feet). One smoking room. Pets permitted.
Rates: $60 to $75, double, EPB. No credit cards.
Open: All year.
Facilities and activities: Dinner by reservation, spa, patio. Nearby: hiking trails in Oracle State Park, horseback riding, bird watching, biking, Biosphere II, Aravaipa Canyon; 30 miles from Tucson.

Maricopa Manor

PHOENIX, ARIZONA 85011

Life wasn't busy enough for Mary Ellen and Paul, raising twelve children; now they've opened their lovely Spanish-style home as a very luxurious inn, which they're calling an urban inn instead of a country inn. The house is a combination of surprises: Off the spacious entry hall is a very formal living room with some beautiful French antiques. In fact, two of the fragile-looking end tables are 1937 reproductions of tables that Marie Antoinette had, probably at Versailles. Two satin love seats face each other in front of the fireplace, which has a screen made of Dutch lace.

"But we move it in the winter, when we want a fire," Mary Ellen assures me. There's a harp, and guests make themselves at home both here and in the large, modern Gathering Room, with a cathedral ceiling and The Pit, a sunken corner that's the television area. Amusing and entertaining is an antique slot machine that still works. "Some guests are in high heaven with that," Paul says. "If it's your nickel, you keep your winnings; if it's our nickel, we keep."

The dining room is large, and according to Mary Ellen, "It's seen many a family celebration dinner." Three of the children they raised were their own, the others were foster boys, as well as a Salvadoran exchange student who never went home! Married now, he and his family are part of the family.

Mary Ellen serves breakfast—fresh fruit, homemade bread and jams, and gourmet coffee—in a basket and delivers it to each suite. "We've had people take it to Sedona and even the Grand Canyon!" she says. "I change the china, and every morning there's a surprise." This morning it was a delicious quiche.

The inn's five unique and luxurious suites are a delight. The Library Suite has several hundred leather-bound books to read. Well, not all at once, but "that's what they're there for," Paul says. "People should enjoy them."

The Palo Verde Suite, named for the state tree, has an original Franklin stove amid green and pink Laura Ashley fabrics; the Victorian Suite is done up in satins and lace with a mirrored armoire.

Reflections Past has antique mirrors and a canopied bed; Reflections Present, adjoining, is a study in black, gold, and white modernity reflected in a collection of mirrors. "Our son said, 'Let's get out of the antiques for a change'—and it just seemed like a wonderfully crazy idea," Mary Ellen says with a laugh. She's enjoyed the change, even adding her own artistic touch, painting a lacy black tree silhouette on two of the walls and adding the perfect touch of a red, red rose in a vase.

Both the large, beautiful home, with its luxurious space and lovely grounds, and the gracious innkeepers make this a wonderful place to stay. "It's our home," Mary Ellen says simply, "and we now share it with anyone who chooses to come. People," she adds, "are so interesting. They [inn guests] are a special breed."

How to get there: From I–17 take Camelback Road east on Third; then go north on Third to Pasadena Avenue. The inn is one house west of the intersection of Pasadena and Central.

Innkeepers: Mary Ellen and Paul Kelley
Address/Telephone: 15 West Pasadena Avenue; (602) 274–6302
Rooms: 5; all with private bath, phone, and TV; wheelchair accessible. Smoking in designated areas.
Rates: $49 to $99, double, continental-plus breakfast.
Open: All year.
Facilities and activities: Hot tub. Nearby: Camelback Road with restaurants and shops; museums, state capitol and park, botanical and Japanese gardens, golf, tennis, festivals.

The Marks House Inn

PRESCOTT, ARIZONA 86303

High on a hill overlooking Courthouse Square and Whiskey Row, the historic Marks House stands in regal splendor, a fine old dowager of a mansion built in 1894 by an early Arizonan who was reputed to be the wealthiest man in the area at the time he built the home for his bride, Josephine. Jake Marks, trader, mine owner, and general merchandizer, evidently was quite an adventurer, joining General Crook in fighting the Pitt River Indian Wars. When he wasn't off fighting Indians, he also was involved in both the liquor business and the politics of the time. "He and General Crook were great friends, and the general stayed at the house when he was in town," says Dottie as she serves hors d'oeuvres in the late afternoon on the veranda.

Gorgeous sunsets are on view from the veranda and the curved windows in the circular corner turret of both the parlor and the Queen Anne Suite above. The old house is on the National Register of Historic Places, and it took seven years to restore it. The spacious mansion certainly bears witness to wealth, with polished hardwood floors and beautiful wood moldings and doors. The dining-room floor is inlaid with a pattern of walnut, oak, and mahogany, and there is a fireplace back to back with the parlor one. The original wood floors creak even when lightly trod upon, and there seem to be several resident ghosts. One is a man "who apparently is a prankster," says Dottie. "He opens doors, turns on lights, and generally misplaces things." The other, according to old tales, is a lady who is looking for her child. "But she lives at the back of the house," Dottie says reassuringly, "and doesn't seem to bother anyone." And the creakings, thumps, and bumps that generally come with an old house add to the mystery.

What was wonderful, if not mysterious, to me was the surprise at finding such lovely features in a house built so shortly after the first settlers arrived in Prescott. Barely thirty years later here was this two-story Queen Anne Victorian with sunburst window designs, a turret, and my favorite detail, the ornately decorated front porch that wraps around the turret.

The two bedrooms of the Ivy Suite on the main floor are decorated in soft greens, which complement the Victorian antiques; the Princess Victoria Room has an 1890s copper tub from a bathhouse in Syracuse, New York. The Tea Rose Room has a queen-sized bed and is close to the hall bathroom.

Mornings, Dottie serves a main dish of some sort of breakfast casserole, along with fresh or cooked fruit, homemade muffins, coffee, tea, cocoa, and juice, and a side dish of breakfast meat if there's none in the casserole. "My Overnight French Toast Casserole is what most guests seem to like best," Dottie said, generously giving me the recipe. Hint: It's so rich because there's cream cheese in it, too.

How to get there: From Courthouse Square go east up the hill of Union Street to Marina. The inn is at the corner of Marina on the right.

Innkeepers: Dottie and Harold Viehweg
Address/Telephone: 203 East Union Street; (602) 778–4632
Rooms: 4 suites; all with private bath; no air conditioning (elevation 5,300 feet). No smoking inn.
Rates: $75 to $135, double; $5 less, single; special rates for extended stays; EPB.
Open: All year.
Facilities and activities: Nearby: Historic Prescott Courthouse Square, restaurants, shops, and museums; golf, boating, hiking, tennis, and swimming at area lakes Lynx, Walker, Goldwater, and Watson.
Recommended Country Inns® Travel Club Benefit: 10% discount, Monday–Thursday, subject to availability.

Pleasant Street Inn

PRESCOTT, ARIZONA 86303

Innkeeper Jean is another person who has had enough of the corporate world. "I decided I wanted to make my own choices and decisions," she says. Visiting another inn in town, the idea of having one of her own "started rolling around in my head." With teenage son Charles in tow, she found the pleasant house on Pleasant Street. She sort of rescued the 1906 home, which had been moved from another location.

"It was going to be demolished to make room for a new police station. A local contractor said, 'You can't destroy historic property!' and he moved it." When I ask Jean what had to be done, she laughs. "Everything!"

It's hard to imagine that it once was rather dark and gloomy; Jean has let a lot of light in. "The house evidently had a hard life, but we figured out how to open it up." There are windows everywhere, from the bay in front to the big ones opening onto the two terraces. In summertime she really enjoys the terraces, serving breakfast there. Guests also gather there for afternoon and evening sociability.

In the winter they gather around the fire in the living room, enjoying hors d'oeuvres and beverages and the good company. One of Jean's guests observed, "There must be a tremendous amount of love in this house." Jean said she was surprised, a little taken aback, not knowing what to answer him. But she certainly was pleased: "I was delighted; that's what I want people to feel!"

The Pine View Suite, complete with a fireplace in the sitting room, has a king-sized bed; the bright and sunny Coventry Room, with its view of Prescott's tree-covered mountains, has twin beds that can be made into a king. Jean hopes that the Garden Room, with flowered fabric and white wicker furniture, will make guests think of an English garden. Downstairs, the Terrace Suite has both a sitting room and a private covered deck.

The color scheme in the living room, of soft rose, blue, and gray, is restful. The old chestnut-pegged game table was inherited from Jean's parents, while many of the other pieces are antiques collected by Charles's father. "He was curator of the Arizona Historical Society," says Charles.

He is quite a help to his mother; he'd just mowed the lawn the day I was there, and the sweet smell of freshly cut grass was pleasant at the Pleasant Street Inn.

Jean's breakfasts are delicious. She'll serve you a continental one if you insist, but "nobody's asked for that yet," she says. I had warm spiced fruit with sour cream for starters. Next came stuffed French toast, chock full of cream cheese, cinnamon, and nuts. With it there was ham, but sometimes it's sausage or bacon, "whatever I'm in the mood for." The morning glory muffins were glorious, too. Like the French toast, they were stuffed with such goodies as apples, nuts, and raisins. Jean's pumpkin muffins are not to be sneezed at, either.

Prescott has some interesting historical sights, not the least of which is Whiskey Row, once a lineup of maybe hundreds of bars and brothels during the days when Prescott was a wild territorial capital. "Today the only relic is the Palace Bar," Jean reports. She has two favorite restaurants to recommend: the old-fashioned and elegant Peacock Room, at the historic Hassayampa Inn downtown, and trendy Murphy's, both serving delicious continental dishes.

How to get there: From I–17 take Highway 69 into Prescott. It becomes Gurley Street in town. Go about 4/10 mile on Gurley to Pleasant Street, turn left, and go 2 blocks.

Innkeeper: Jean Urban
Address/Telephone: 142 South Pleasant Street; (602) 445–4774
Rooms: 2, plus 2 suites; all with private bath. No smoking inn.
Rates: $80 to $120, double; $10 extra person; EPB.
Open: All year.
Facilities and activities: Nearby: Historic Prescott Courthouse Square; historic Whiskey Row; Prescott Fine Arts Association Theater & Gallery; Elks Opera House; hiking trails, boating, swimming, golf, and tennis at area lakes Lynx, Goldwater, Walker and Watson.

Victorian Inn

PRESCOTT, ARIZONA 86303

Irene, who is artistic, loves to set a beautiful table.

"When you walk into the dining room, the mood is set," Irene says. "I want guests to think, 'This is elegance.'" Which we do, and very fitting it is, too, in this elegant Victorian mansion built in the 1890s. Painted blue with white trim and a peaked-roof turret and enclosed in a formal wrought-iron fence, the house is a showplace on the corner of the street.

Inside, the inn is furnished with a twenty-year collection of antiques, seventeen chandeliers, sliding wood doors, and stained-glass windows.

Guest rooms are large and airy, with wallpapers that are exact reproductions of 1890s Victorian wallpaper. The canopy queen bed in Eve's Garden Room is draped with soft creamy chiffon, and an armoire and rockers in fresh white wicker add to the ambience. The Teddy Bear Room contains a four-poster that was a family piece, and yes, of course, a teddy bear. The Rose Room is bright and soothing; the bathroom has a footed tub and a hand shower of brass.

The settee in the Victorian Suite is a conversation piece. "It's a lovers' seat," Irene says. "For a man and a woman. One sits, the other lies down—and gets their feet rubbed!"

Breakfast at the table elegantly set by Irene is more than a feast for the eyes. Fresh fruit, Canadian bacon, and a repertoire of hot cross or cashew coconut buns, main-dish strata, Linzer Torte, vanilla yogurt soufflé, Swedish pancakes—it's all delicious (but of course you don't have it all at once).

After such a feast all I wanted to do was to sit on the front porch swing and relax. Just for a while, though. Because I could see Courthouse Square and its attractions just a block away, beckoning to me over the housetops. . . .

There is a small gift shop in the entrance of the inn, with hand-painted porcelain objects, dried flower arrangements, and mementos of the inn.

How to get there: One block south of Courthouse Square and 1 block east of Montezuma (Highway 89).

Innkeeper: Irene Cameron
Address/Telephone: 246 South Cortez Street; (602) 778–2642
Rooms: 4, including 1 suite; suite with private bath; no air conditioning (elevation 5,300 feet). No smoking inn.
Rates: $90 to $135, double, EPB.
Open: All year.
Facilities and activities: Gift shop. Nearby: restaurants, antiques shopping, Courthouse Square, historic homes, museum, horseback riding, hiking trails up Thumb Butte, fishing in Goldwater and Lynx Creek lakes, many festivals.
Recommended Country Inns® Travel Club Benefit: Stay two nights, get third night free, Monday–Thursday.

The Inn at the Citadel

SCOTTSDALE, ARIZONA 85255

"Everything has family meaning," Kelly Keyes says of this posh, family-built inn in chic Scottsdale, at the foot of outstanding Pinnacle Peak. "It's all been built in threes and fives; those three arches over there are for three daughters—me and my two sisters."

The sentiment goes beyond the immediate family. Kelly points out that the brands decorating the Marque Bar are those of everyone who had anything to do with the building of the inn. "Architects, builders, my parents—theirs is the flying double K," she explains.

The inn had a propitious beginning. Built on Hopi Indian land, the Hopis were invited to a blessing of the land. "Everyone, even the children, came. It was a black-tie-and-jeans event, jeans and boots."

This is a pretty sumptuous establishment for the casual Southwest, more like a fine European-style hotel than a country inn, but "we try to put guests at their ease," Adam Wilson says. "Sometimes they're a little taken aback, awed by the location." This is grand country, with Pinnacle Peak just overhead.

Kelly's mother, Anita Keyes, is an interior designer, and each of the eleven rooms is decorated with careful detail, down to the smallest item. Original artwork by such artists as Jonathan Sobel and Armond Laura hang on the walls, and antiques are used extensively. The armoires in six of the rooms were painted by local Arizona artists Liz Henretta, Skip Bennett, Sherry Stewart, and Carolyn Baer.

Rooms have safes, robes, hair dryers, bath amenities, and an honor bar, stocked with not only premium liquors, wine, and champagne, but also playing cards, along with the expected soft drinks, crackers, and candy bars.

Fresh hot coffee comes along with the complimentary newspaper each morning. A massage, facial, or manicure can come to your room, too, if you wish. Each room has cable TV with HBO.

The larger rooms are more like suites, with large sitting areas and desks. The king-sized beds are covered with quilted satiny spreads, and the pillow shams match the dust ruffles.

Actually, the Citadel is not only an inn. It's a restaurant and shopping complex in a shady courtyard complete with a pond and a bubbling waterfall. The continental breakfast is served either in The Market or in your room, whichever you prefer. Fresh-squeezed orange juice is followed by a large serving of seasonal fresh fruit—I had raspberries—and then moist zucchini, bran, or corn muffins, and, of course, coffee or tea.

At The Market you can get anything from blue corn waffles to hamburgers, pastas, salads, and enchiladas, and it's all deliciously fresh and nicely served. The award-winning 8700 at the Citadel really goes all out, with the finest regional American cuisine. One of chef Leonard Rubin's specialties is roast rack of black buck antelope. "It's pretty popular," Adam says. The menu also features 8700 Mixed Grill, poached salmon, and coffee toffee crunch cake.

How to get there: From I–17 take Bell Road 30 miles east to Scottsdale Road, then go north 4 miles to Pinnacle Peak Road and east 2 miles to the inn.

Innkeepers: Kelly Keyes, Jane De Beer, and Adam Wilson
Address/Telephone: 8700 East Pinnacle Peak Road; (602) 994–8700 or (800) 927–8367
Rooms: 11; all with private bath; wheelchair accessible. No smoking inn.
Rates: $195 to $265, double, continental breakfast.
Open: All year.
Facilities and activities: Two restaurants, piano bar, limo tours of the desert, health and beauty spa facilities, boutiques. Nearby: Hiking to Pinnacle Peak; golf.
Business travel: Located in Scottsdale (not downtown). Desk in room; conference space, boardroom, secretarial services, computer and fax facilities, banking, banquet, and catering facilities.

Canyon Villa

SEDONA, ARIZONA 86336

Instead of remodeling or rebuilding for their inn, Marion and Chuck began from scratch. "We built from the ground up," Marion says. Driving up to the Moorish arches of the entrance, it's hard to tell whether this is real or an illusion. The beautiful, pale-pink stucco villa with its Mediterranean look lies at the base of one of Sedona's fantastic red rock formations, and the ensemble looks like a movie set. The blue Arizona sky and the clear, rarified air of Sedona add to the thought that the picture is too perfect to be true.

But Canyon Villa is as real as it is beautiful, and staying here is a wonderfully refreshing adventure. The villa's tall windows and wide doors open onto exhilarating vistas. "Just open the French doors to your patio or balcony and enjoy the view," Marion points out invitingly. Beyond the pool, which is bordered by bright green grass and fenced in by ornate white grillwork, Bell Rock and Courthouse Butte tower over the scene, seeming almost close enough to touch.

Marion and Chuck have lived all over the country, and although they like the four seasons, "We're warm-weather people at heart." And, like many others, they were looking for a change. "We were tired of the same old things and wanted to find something new before we got too old." She adds with a laugh, "It turned out to be a little more than we expected!"

The pride that Marion took in decorating the villa shows in every room of the spacious inn. Her grandmother's cut glass collection is displayed in a large, mirrored breakfront along with Waterford and Svartski crystal. The fireplace in the huge, vaulted-ceilinged common room opens through to the dining room, a large room containing two dining sets. "My Mom's, and mine," Marion says. "We can seat twenty-two."

For those who like to plan ahead, tomorrow's breakfast menu is out for perusal and anticipation. Today's delicious mushroom and artichoke omelet and homemade cinnamon rolls just might be upstaged by tomorrow's four-cheese herb quiche and angel biscuits.

Late afternoons, from 5:00 to 6:00, there are refreshments: maybe chips and guacamole, cream cheese chutney, crab spread, or crackers and nuts, with ice tea and punch. Complimentary soft drinks and juices are available all day long and Marion's homemade Sweet Dreams cookies every night.

Her grandparents' sofa is comfy in the library off the patio, and there's a nice collection of reading matter. "We've even sent people home with books they want to finish—and they mail them back!"

Guest rooms, described by Marion and Chuck as a blend of Old World charm and Southwestern style, are wonderfully imaginative. Decorating eleven separate rooms so charmingly takes a lot of talent. "Several pieces of furniture, like the dining-room sets, and art pieces have been handed down through our family," Marion explains. The rooms are named for regional flora; what a choice—and what a chance to exercise every woman's decorating dream: Indian Paintbrush (country charm), Claret Cup (traditional elegance), Evening Primrose (Victorian), Ocotillo (Southwest Santa Fe), Spanish Bayonet (Old World Spain), Desert Daisy (Americana and quilts), Strawberry Cactus (garden wicker), Manzanita (rustic antique), and Prickly Pear (Old West and brass)!

How to get there: From Highway 89A in Sedona, go south on 179 through Oak Creek Village; turn right on Bell Rock Road, go 1 block, and then take a right on Canyon Circle Drive.

Innkeepers: Marion and Chuck Yadon
Address/Telephone: 125 Canyon Circle Drive; (602) 284–1226 or (800) 453–1166
Rooms: 11; all with private (whirlpool) bath, 1 with wheelchair access. No smoking inn.
Rates: $95 to $155, double; $25 extra person; EPB and afternoon refreshments.
Open: All year.
Facilities and activities: Heated pool. Nearby: golf, tennis, and massage at Sedona Golf Resort; Oak Creek Country Club; Sedona Racquet Club.
Recommended Country Inns® Travel Club Benefit: 10% discount, subject to availability, for reservations made by guests only.

Casa Sedona

SEDONA, ARIZONA 86336

You're apt to get a little bit of Hollywood at breakfast at beautiful Casa Sedona: Innkeeper Dick Curtis is the very same Dick Curtis who performed with Dick Van Dyke, Jonathan Winters, Andy Griffith, and many others. Singer, dancer, actor, comedian, TV host—Dick is an entertainer, whether on camera or hosting breakfast at his inn.

"He's entertained all his life," fellow innkeeper Misty says, "and now he just likes to entertain our guests." He also has discovered the joys of gardening, as the gorgeous hanging baskets around the inn, dripping with bright flowers, testify.

"Dick and I both wanted to do something different," Misty says, although they were cautioned not to indulge in the innkeeping dream. "Don't do it, cost you a million easy," was the advice from Hollywood, Misty laughs. Luckily for future guests, they ignored it and set about creating a beautiful, luxurious inn.

"We want our guests to feel like very special guests in our home," says Misty, placing fine crystal goblets on the table she's setting for breakfast, where enthusiastic discussions of the day's activities are apt to occur. If you'd rather, breakfast can be served in the Sunrise Alcove, to catch the first rays of the morning sun, or outside on the deck overlooking Dick's gorgeous garden, amidst two huge cypress trees. "This is our adult playground," Misty says as she points to a hammock-for-two among the trees.

Food can be fancy: a feta cheese and spinach puff for breakfast; an afternoon appetizer of stuffed mushrooms and pizza. Coffee, tea, and hot chocolate are available 'round the clock. There's no smoking inside or out at this inn.

Guest rooms are lovely, each one more restful and pleasing than the next. They all have a terrace, spa tub, and fireplace.

"I started each room with an idea," Misty explains. The Serena Room was inspired by the wallpaper; the Kachina Room, of course, was inspired by the dolls. Not surprisingly, an MGM poster with a photo of Dick in the center gave birth to That's Entertainment, while Juniper Shadows pays tribute to the beautiful old trees on the property on which the inn was built.

The Cowboy Room is accessible to wheelchairs, and a sidewalk around the building leads directly to a dining deck. As for the Hopi Room, Misty went to a Hopi dance and was enchanted by a little boy leading the dance. "I just had to call this the Hopi Room," she says.

The Sierra Room is the television and music center. The library, with its cozy fireplace, is planned for reading and relaxing—the furniture was designed with that in mind.

The inn itself was designed by architect Mani Subra, a disciple of Frank Lloyd Wright. He said, "I wanted to bring the view toward Casa Sedona, to have the surrounding natural environment and sky become part of the structure, so wherever guests sit or stand, they will be able to enjoy the view."

How to get there: From the intersection of Highways 89A and 179 in Sedona, follow Highway 89A into West Sedona. Go 3 miles west to Southwest Drive (or Tortilla Drive, which comes next), and turn right. Follow either road around to Hozoni Drive. The inn is at the end of Hozoni.

Innkeepers: Misty and Lori Zitko and Dick Curtis
Address/Telephone: 55 Hozoni Drive; (602) 282–2938 or (800) 525–3756
Rooms: 16; all with private bath, 1 with wheelchair access. No smoking inn.
Rates: $95 to $150, double, EPB and afternoon refreshments.
Open: All year.
Facilities and activities: Saturday night buffet in June, July, and August; holiday dinners. Nearby: walking trails, golf and tennis, Indian ruins, jeep tours, hiking, hot-air ballooning.
Recommended Country Inns® Travel Club Benefit: 10% discount, Monday–Thursday.

Cathedral Rock Lodge

SEDONA, ARIZONA 86336

Carol and her son Samyo had no problem deciding what to name their inn—wait until you see Cathedral Rock! From almost every window of the inn, you can see this glorious hunk of the beautiful red rock that the Sedona area is famous for. This is the scenery you oohed and aahed at during all those western movies where the bad guys chased the good guys among gigantic formations of red rock.

Carol, who is from Tempe, camped here with her children for several years before she acquired the inn. "I wanted to live in this gorgeous country," she says, and she gave up her work as volunteer coordinator between the city's museums, libraries, and senior citizens. Now she earns a living where she once only dreamed of living.

"Since so many people are on cholesterol-free diets, my biggest challenge is finding eggless dishes," she says with a laugh. One specialty is sour cream Belgian waffles with pecans along with ham, fresh fruit, and fresh-ground coffee. A Mexican breakfast is a guest favorite, too, a Mexican soufflé with green chilies, not too spicy unless you want it that way. "You make Mexican food *picante* (hot) with the sauce," Carol reminds me. "And Mexican food stays with you," she promises—in case you're worried about going hungry! Afternoons, she sets lemonade, iced tea, and homemade cookies out in the lounge.

The lounge has a wall of windows, and that huge Cathedral Rock outside, red red rock against deep blue Arizona sky, looks too good to be real. "Viewing Cathedral Rock, that's our most popular local activity," Carol announced one afternoon as she served lemonade to two contented Easterners sitting at the picnic table under the huge old shade trees. "We fell in love with these monster elms. There's nothing like them in Sedona; they must have been planted when the house was built in the forties."

Both guest rooms in the main house are furnished with family antiques, and the beds sport handmade quilts. Connected in back are the Garden Room, with its own wildflower quilt and photographs of Carol's mother and sister, and the Homestead Room, with lace curtains and room for three. The Amigo Suite overhead, with a private deck, has a king bed, a double-bed couch, and a kitchen. When I visited, a pair of grandparents were happily ensconced up there with a small grandchild.

The cabin, a guest addition in the back connects with back stairs to the kitchen of the main house. "In cold weather, guests just come down in their robes," Carol says. Informality and comfort are the rule here. The common room is packed with books and magazines, children's films for the VCR, and information on hiking, historical sites, and Indian ruins to visit—once you decide to quit loafing at this happy inn.

How to get there: Go south on Highway 89A through Sedona and West Sedona to traffic light at Y in road. Go 4⅒ miles farther to Upper Red Rock Loop Road. Turn left onto a well-graded dirt road and go 2⁷⁄₁₀ miles, passing Disney Lane on the left. Cathedral Rock is the next lane on the left.

Innkeepers: Carol and Samyo Shannon
Address/Telephone: Star Route 2, Box 856; (602) 282–7608
Rooms: 3, including 1 suite; all with private bath, suite with kitchen and TV; cabin with full kitchen, deck, bath, bedroom and upstairs loft. No smoking inn.
Rates: $65 to $90, double; $5 extra person; EPB, continental in cabin. Two-night minimum weekends; three-night minimum for cabin; special rates for longer stays.
Open: All year.
Facilities and activities: Picnic equipment, library of local history and videotapes of movies filmed in red rock country. Nearby: Sedona with restaurants and arts and crafts, shopping at Tlaquepaque; 300-acre Red Rock State Park for environmental education; hiking, horseback riding, Indian ruins.

Cozy Cactus

SEDONA, ARIZONA 86336

"No pets, please, but you are welcome to enjoy ours," innkeepers Lynne and Bob say. So you might be greeted by three little doggies at the door, but Lynne calls them off immediately if they're not wanted. Katie, the black miniature Schnauzer, Chev (short for Chevis Regal), a gray miniature poodle, and Fudge ("an old cockapoo," says Lynne) are all very well behaved.

"We had always wanted to do this [innkeeping]," Lynne and Bob say. "But we never wanted to leave East Texas." Until they saw Sedona. "We fell in love with Sedona!" which is a familiar cry here in this gorgeous red rock country. The inn backs up to Cocomino National Forest, and the scenery is grand.

Their ranch-style home is furnished both with family heirlooms and theatrical memorabilia from Bob and Lynne's past careers as professional actor (Bob) and professional singer (Lynne). "I especially like singing to the senior citizens here who can't get out," Lynne says. Both have done community theater in Sedona, and Bob is Cultural Commissioner. He has a background in science and math as well as acting, and his current interests include cooking.

"I loved to cook when we got here," Lynne says enthusiastically. "Now Bob's learned to love it, too."

"Well, almost," Bob adds with a grin.

Breakfast was a mutual effort and the results

were delicious enough to convince me that both love the culinary arts equally. Beginning with a stuffed baked pear, we went on to wholewheat buttermilk raspberry pancakes served with turkey sausage. "We're as low-sugar, low-cholesterol as possible," Lynne says, and adds that she always asks about allergies.

"I've reminded many a guest who will say, 'Oh, that's right, I can't eat nuts.'"

Guest rooms are furnished in differing styles and decorated with the hosts' interesting collections. The Music Box Room has a fascinating assortment of music boxes displayed on the solid cherry bedroom set from Michigan (this was Lynne's parents' wedding set). The music box collection began when grateful newlyweds made Lynne presents of the boxes in return for her singing at their weddings.

Bob's special collection of nutcrackers decorates the Nutcracker Room, which has an antique, high-backed queen-sized bed. The American Room has a small collection of quilts, while other collections include pretty glass objects on some of the window ledges.

And there's more.

"I love angels and cherubs," Lynne says, but the confession is unnecessary. The evidence—angel and cherub figurines—is everywhere.

The bedrooms come in pairs, and each pair shares a sitting room with a fireplace—and the convenience of a small kitchen. So you can cook your own breakfast, but much preferred is the one Lynne and Bob serve up in the great room, where we watched the sun come up and warm the south face of Bell Rock. Beverages are served on the patio later in the day, while we watch the late afternoon sun dip behind Castle Rock to the west of the inn.

How to get there: From Highway 89A in Sedona, go south on 179 through Oak Creek Village; turn right on Bell Rock Road, go 1 block, then take a right onto Canyon Circle Drive.

Innkeepers: Lynne and Bob Gillman
Address/Telephone: 80 Canyon Circle Drive; (602) 284–0082 or (800) 788–2082
Rooms: 5; all with private bath. No smoking inn.
Rates: $75 to $90, double; $15 to $20 extra person; EPB. Two-night minimum on weekends; special rates for longer stays.
Open: All year.
Facilities and activities: Dinner on holidays, bicycles, croquet, tennis racquets. Nearby: golf course, public pool, wilderness trails, Cocomino National Forest.

Graham's Bed & Breakfast Inn

SEDONA, ARIZONA 86336

Graham's Inn is located in the heart of Arizona's red rock country, surrounded by jagged strata of bright orange rock jutting dramatically against the blue, blue sky. The inn, smooth and square and white, makes a cool contrast to its surroundings.

Traveling through Sedona, Carol and Roger, like so many others, were awestruck by the beauty of the famous red rock formations. I think it's called "red rock fever"! They purchased the inn from Marni and Bill Graham, who were such wonderful innkeepers that the Redenbaughs decided to keep the inn's name.

"I wouldn't trade places with anyone in the world," Carol says of Sedona, "and we're close to my sister Linda and brother-in-law John"—Linda and John Steele, who own Sedona's Territorial House Inn.

The inn was decorated by the Grahams, with the help of a California-trained designer, and the results were outstanding. Each room has a name with a theme to match. Hoping to maintain the ambience created by the Grahams, yet wanting to put their own mark on the inn, Carol and Roger compromised by keeping the Heritage Room and the San Francisco Room as they were but redoing the Southwest Room and the Country Room anew for themselves. The Heritage Room has remained red, white, and blue, with military memorabilia in honor of Marni Graham's father.

The San Francisco Room has kept the soft grays and peach colors of the Sedona sunset. The large-scale, California king-sized bed and matching bedside tables face the balcony.

The new Country Room is a tribute to Carol's mother, who used to be a schoolteacher in Kansas. The old ledger she kept reveals what schoolteachers in Kansas were paid in 1940: $70 a month! The room is for Carol a memory of her childhood on a Kansas farm. The redecorated Southwest Room reflects the glorious Sedona colors: sand beige, canyon red, teal green. The rustic queen-sized bed is Taos, New Mexico, style, The bath has a Jacuzzi.

The Garden Room has kept its white wicker furniture, dark-green-and-crimson wallpaper, and deep-green carpet. There's a private balcony here, too.

The Sedona Suite, in teal, gray, and clay colors, also has a Taos-style king-sized bed. There are comfy robes, an oversized bath with Jacuzzi, and a patio.

When Carol is chef, it's a delicious German pancake; when Roger cooks, it's a special cheese strata. Whichever, the food is always delicious.

How to get there: Canyon Circle Drive circles off Bellrock Boulevard, which is in the south Sedona suburb of the Village of Oak Creek. From Highway 179 turn west at the intersection that has a convenience store and a service store on the right—that is Bellrock Boulevard. Canyon Circle Drive and the inn are on the right about a block down the road.

Innkeepers: Carol and Roger Redenbaugh
Address/Telephone: 150 Circle Canyon Drive (mailing address: P.O. Box 912); (602) 284–1425
Rooms: 6; all with private bath. No smoking inn.
Rates: $90 to $190, double, EPB.
Open: All year.
Facilities and activities: Pool and spa. Nearby: restaurants, tennis, golf, racquetball, shopping at Tlaquepaque, horseback riding, jeep rides, hiking, Indian ruins.
Recommended Country Inns® Travel Club Benefit: 10% discount, Monday–Thursday, December 1–January 31, except holidays.

Lantern Light Inn

SEDONA, ARIZONA 86336

Kris and Ed have named their inn for Kris's collection of lanterns, which are an interesting sight, especially if you arrive after dark and see the entrance one all lit up. Two posts at the entrance make the inn easy to find: On one post there's the inn sign, and on the opposite post is, of course, a lantern, and a huge one at that.

This small, cozy inn is also fresh with green plants and bright flowers. The curved drive of earth-colored stones leads to an open breezeway, also full of plants and hung with lanterns. "I've collected them from everywhere," Kris says. "I even have eighteen more, in the garage, waiting for a place!"

She and Ed are from Los Angeles, where Ed was involved in the Premier Market, his family's gourmet food market. "We thought we'd probably open a food store," Kris says, "but I'm really pleased with the inn." She was a department store buyer, and in furnishing the inn her merchandising experience came in handy. "I love furniture," she says, as she beams at the antiques that fill the room. "Being in merchandising for so many years, I know how to shop," she adds when she's complimented on the inn's rich red, blue, and green color scheme. Right now she's excited about the new oriental rug in the long hall, all lovely reds and blues.

The inn has a unique arrangement, in that the guests get the downstairs and the Valjeans have the upstairs. The well-furnished common area is a long room that's for both sitting and dining, with books and brochures, as well as a television/VCR corner. Up the stairs are the innkeepers' living quarters and the kitchen.

Two guest rooms are off the long hall in the main building: The Queen's Room, mauve and pink, opens onto a lovely back garden with a sun deck; the King's Room next door is done in blue with oriental rugs. The Ryan Room across the breezeway is large, with a sofabed and a kitchen as well as an entrance all its own.

Kris is the cook, although she gives Ed credit for helping. But she says he's better at charting out trips for guests. "He really sits down with them and plans outings," she says. "He's much better geographically than I am."

She comes into her own at breakfast, with fulsome meals that include fresh-squeezed orange juice, mixed fruit salads with lemon yogurt sauce, and hashed brown or home-fried potatoes with a Southwest casserole of chilies, egg, and three cheeses. Other specialties are cheese blintzes with raspberries, Belgian waffles, and thin blueberry hotcakes, all served with sausage—"No pork; all sausage, bacon, and ham are really turkey. Kris is health-conscious," says her sister, Mary Sica, who helps out now and then. "She's an angel," Kris says, and I certainly found her to be a very pleasant addition to Lantern Inn. So are Kris's pies (vanilla, yogurt, coconut, Grand Marnier) that she plies guests with in the evening.

"We've always had guests in our home, people coming and going," Kris says. "We're not thrown by having people around. We give guests the freedom of the downstairs and we have ours upstairs. We find it's perfect, if that's the way they prefer it."

How to get there: Take Highway 89A west. The inn is on the left.

Innkeepers: Kris and Ed Valjean
Address/Telephone: 3085 West Highway 89A; (602) 282–3419
Rooms: 3; all with private bath. No smoking inn.
Rates: $65 to $95, double, seasonally, EPB.
Open: All year.
Facilities and activities: Nearby: restaurants, shops, hiking, horseback riding.

The Lodge at Sedona

SEDONA, ARIZONA 86336

Barbara and Mark make welcoming and eager innkeepers, despite the fact that they really didn't expect to be doing this. "We weren't looking for an inn," Barbara says with great good humor, "although I'd stayed in one in Ireland and decided it's the best way to travel. We were out biking and came by to look this property [The Lodge] over for someone else, who was interested in it as a treatment center. We fell in love with the property, but what we went through to get it!"

The Lodge began life in 1959 as a home for a doctor and his family of twelve. It went on to become a home for the elderly, a minister's home and church, and finally an in-patient rehab treatment facility. The friend wasn't interested in The Lodge, but Barbara and Mark were, thereby beginning two years of frustration and tenacity. "Just as we submitted our proposal, someone else bought it," Mark says.

"We were devastated," Barbara adds. "So we began a two-year journey, searched all over Phoenix for another property, and I finally had to say, oh well, maybe we're not meant to do this." But eventually there was a happy ending. "This fell out of escrow, and it was wonderful the way the community welcomed us."

The Lodge is secluded, shrouded in greenery and almost hidden from the road. Friends came to help with the restoration. "They'd come to do landscaping," Mark says. Barbara laughs. "And we'd end up in a bedroom discussing decor."

Innkeeping assistant Michelle says Barbara is too modest about her decorating prowess. "When I ask her how she did such a wonderful job, she always says, 'Oh, my sister came up' or 'A friend helped out.'" She laughs. "But I've heard her family say, 'We always knew Barbara could do it.'"

Seven guest rooms are downstairs, six are up above. The Nature Suite has a king-sized bed and a comfortable sofa. French doors lead to the porch, and the pink tub in the bathroom lends itself to a luxurious soak. English Garden has an undisturbed view of the colorful Sedona sunset, while the Master Suite and Cherokee have private entrances. So does Susannah, cozy with a pretty quilt and wicker chairs.

Both the Renaissance Room and Traviso have a charming Old World European air, which is only fitting, since the latter is named for the Italian town that Mark's family came from.

Things have gotten so busy that the inn boasts an Italian chef for weekend cuisine: Antonio Fiznoglia, who studied his art in New York. Besides breakfast, afternoon refreshments are served from 5:00 to 6:00. Accompanying sodas and juices, some days you'll find homemade pizza slices or chicken taquitos, other days guacamole, salsa, and chips or crackers and cheese to nibble on.

The Lodge is situated on two and a half acres of wooded land, so there's lots of room to breathe. I awakened to the fragrance of pine and went eagerly to breakfast. We began with pears simmered in port wine with cinnamon and grated orange peel; next came The Lodge's specialty of the day, layered egg, cream cheese, and roasted red and yellow peppers. Other choices (or additions) were assorted juices and Barbara's special Lodge Granola with yogurt. The grand finale was a delicious blueberry crumb cake.

How to get there: From the intersection of Highways 89A and 179 in Sedona, follow Highway 89A into West Sedona for 2 miles west. Kallof Place is on the right, The Lodge on the left.

Innkeepers: Barbara and Mark Dinunzio and Michelle Bordelon
Address/Telephone: 125 Kallof Place; (602) 204–1942 or (800) 619–4467
Rooms: 13; all with private bath; 1 room for the handicapped. No smoking inn.
Rates: $85 to $195, double, EPB and afternoon refreshments.
Open: All year.
Facilities and activities: Boardroom, sports court, horseshoes, basketball, holiday dinners.
Nearby: uptown Sedona's shops and restaurants; walking trails, golf and tennis, Indian ruins, jeep tours, hiking.

Saddle Rock Ranch

SEDONA, ARIZONA 86336

This luxurious home is not what you would expect from a place that calls itself a ranch. Today the historic homestead, built in 1926, is on the edge of a residential area. But it sits on three acres of hillside overlooking Sedona, and it has starred in many Old West films.

"I just saw a late-night 'thirties movie, *Angel and the Bad Man*," Dan says, "and there was our whole house! It was a dude ranch back then, and the wife of the owner always played an Indian princess in the films," he adds with a laugh.

Fran and Dan, who met while both were employed at a prestigious California hotel, are experts in providing special attention to guests. What you'll get is the same VIP treatment that they gave to many of the "rich and famous." And before that Dan had a rather adventurous career: You might recognize his name, because he played football for the Pittsburgh Steelers.

"He's lived every man's fantasy," Fran says. "He also raced with Mario Andretti on the Indy circuit." They moved to Sedona for the climate, and now Dan and Fran are having an adventurous time innkeeping. "Our guests are wonderful, outstanding, and we want them to have the same total experience throughout their visit. It's a point of pride to us that our guests get the best of not only what we have to offer, but what Sedona has to offer as well," Dan says, so you can expect full concierge service with restaurant reservations at Sedona's finest—concerts, theater, tours, and anything else you, or they, can think of.

Guest rooms are elegantly comfortable, as is the living room. Large Saddle Rock Suite has a country French canopied bed and a rock fireplace; furniture in the Rose Garden Room was Dan's great-great-grandfather's, and the room has its own private, walled rose garden; The Cottage in back, with wood-paneled walls, is surrounded by panoramic vistas. Robes, nightly turndown, chocolates, bottled water, afternoon snacks, guest refrigerator and microwave oven—just make yourself at home in this just-about-perfect inn.

There are cuddly teddy bears everywhere, and it's Dan who collects them! "I was born at home, and the doctor brought a bear when he delivered me—I still have it," he says. It lives in retirement with other teddy bears on a daybed that belonged to his great-great-grandfather.

Breakfast is served in the large and sunny dining room, and specialties are heart-shaped peach waffles and individual Dutch babies (pancakes) filled with apples and vanilla ice cream or yogurt. "I like to use our local Sedona apples, peaches, and pears," Fran says. Orange juice is always fresh-squeezed, and if you prefer tea to coffee, there are sixteen different ones to choose from.

At the rear of the property, a national forest shelters wildlife; deer come to the salt lick, and quail abound. The inn has tamer specimens in Diana and Fergie, miniature schnauzers. "But guest quarters are off-limits to them," Fran says, "unless you particularly request some puppy love!"

How to get there: Take Highway 89A (Airport Drive) to Valley View; go south 1 block to Rock Ridge Drive, left to Forest Circle, and right to Rock Ridge Circle; continue beyond Rock Ridge Drive and take the gravel road on the left up the hill to Saddle Rock.

Innkeepers: Fran and Dan Bruno
Address/Telephone: 255 Rock Ridge Drive; (602) 282–7640
Rooms: 3; all with private bath. No smoking inn.
Rates: \$110 to \$130, double; \$15 extra person; minus \$5 single; EPB and afternoon snacks. Two-night minimum stay; extended stay specials.
Open: All year.
Facilities and activities: Swimming pool and spa, concierge service, Sedona airport transportation. Nearby: restaurants, shops, hiking, fishing, horseback riding, Hopi Mesa tours.

Territorial House

SEDONA, ARIZONA 86336

Little angel figures scattered around the inn illustrate Territorial House's creed: "Do not neglect to show hospitality to strangers for by this some have entertained angels unaware." Linda has been collecting the figures for more than a dozen years. "John was a seed corn distributor and we traveled Kansas, Nebraska, Colorado—all over the Midwest together. I've found angels in many places," she says.

Now she, John, and her angels have come to rest in beautiful Sedona, which they discovered on a golfing vacation. Both are appreciative of nature and take great pleasure in the beauty of the desert cacti and the birds and wildlife so accessible in this part of the world. "Come sit out amidst the juniper and cottonwood and watch our family of quail march through the landscape," they say. They mention, but don't promise, the possibility of hearing the lonesome call of the coyotes at bedtime.

They delight in showing Old West movies that were filmed in and around Sedona. Linda's late-day snack of homemade gingerbread goes quite well with this activity.

After so many years of travel, Linda and John really understand the kind of hospitality that other travelers enjoy. "We call our decorating Territorial Southwest, not Territorial Santa Fe," Linda says. All the guest rooms are named after areas or eras of Sedona history.

Red Rock Crossing, opening off the porch, has a Southwest-style canopy bed and other rugged furniture, with a lighted breakfront chock full of Precious Moment angels for contrast. Schnebly Station consists of two rooms, the Sedona Room and Carl's Cabin, and can sleep up to four persons. Carl's, up a curving stairway, has two cozy window seats under the eaves, and out on the balcony there's a telescope for long-distance mountain and moon viewing.

"You can see the lights of Jerome from here," John boasts. Jerome is an old-timey mining town sitting on the top of a high mountain peak on the road to Prescott.

The Sedona Room boasts a king-sized bed, a fireplace—and a needlepoint angel. The bright red dresser was Linda's when she was a child.

The entire first floor is paved with Saltillo tile, and several pieces of furniture were made by the Steeles' son Kent. The harvest table on which breakfast is served was one of Kent's high school projects. Kent also built the three-section wallpiece in the Great Room. The big stone fireplace there is great for chilly nights. And as for the small child's table and chair set painted as bright red as the dresser in the Sedona Room: "You've guessed it," Linda says. "That too was mine as a child."

The Steeles have been collecting Charles Russell prints from taverns all over the Southwest and you'll find them, as well as original paintings by John's mother, who lives in Parsons, Kansas, decorating the rooms.

Breakfast, beginning with bananas and grapes and strawberry yogurt, continued in true Southwest style with blue corn waffles and sizzling country links. "The syrup is 'light,'" Linda promises, and there's a delicious choice of maple and boysenberry. Homemade bran muffins, too, and an assortment of coffee; you can choose Morning Blend or Folger's regular or decaf.

How to get there: From the intersection of Highways 89A and 179 in Sedona, follow Highway 89A west into West Sedona 3$\frac{1}{10}$ miles to Dry Creek Road. Turn right, go $\frac{2}{10}$ of a mile, then take a left on Kachina Drive. Piki Drive is on the left, about $\frac{4}{10}$ of a mile.

Innkeepers: Linda and John Steele
Address/Telephone: 65 Piki Drive; (602) 204–2737
Rooms: 4; all with private bath. No smoking inn.
Rates: \$90 to \$160, double, EPB.
Open: All year.
Facilities and activities: Exercycle, hiking, biking. Nearby: uptown Sedona's shops and restaurants; walking trails, golf, tennis, Indian ruins.
Recommended Country Inns® Travel Club Benefit: 10% discount, Sunday–Thursday, January–February and July–August.

Strawberry Lodge

STRAWBERRY, ARIZONA 85544

I knew this was a happy place the minute I walked in the door. If it hadn't been the vibrations telling me so, it would have been the happy voices in the crowded restaurant, which is where everybody enters the lodge, although there's a perfectly good entrance to the inn lounge.

The restaurant is packed all the time. "This is the best meal I've had since I left home," customers constantly tell Jean. The "coffee klatch table" next to the fire is filled with regulars, and their wives join them at 3:00 P.M. They're always sold out of the Saturday night prime rib and apple pie. "We have never compromised on quality," Jean says firmly.

Many wonderful things have been added to the menu, "most of them 'healthy,'" Jean says. "Lower fat—broiled, vegetarian dishes—we are trying to cater to our health-conscious customers." But don't worry, she is still making her super homemade pies and still serving her great prime rib on Saturday nights; also specialties like Mexican food on Monday and barbecued ribs on Wednesday. If you're interested, you had better make a reservation. Otherwise, lots of other people will get there before you!

Back when Jean's children were small and her husband, Richard, was alive, the family drove through Strawberry on a holiday.

"Oh," she said then, with her wonderful enthusiasm, "Wouldn't this be a heavenly place to live!" It seemed like fate when later on they saw "a little two-line squib about a hunting lodge for sale" in that very place. Richard was a Zane Grey fan (Grey wrote about the Mongollon Rim area) and that clinched it: They became innkeepers. Now Jean runs the inn herself, and she is doing a grand job of it.

The lodge was so neglected that it was a big challenge. "My husband, who had never built a thing in his life, built all the fireplaces and did all the woodwork." Each of the newer guest rooms has a real wood-burning fireplace, and each is different. Richard used all native materials in remodeling the inn, learning how to do it himself. Rooms are rustic but warm and comfortable, with wood-paneled walls and nice touches like coordinated print wallpaper in the bathrooms.

The entire family pitched in to make the inn the great place that it is. As a Christmas present for her folks one year, daughter Cindy made a set of hand-carved tiles for each shower.

For her part, Jean learned how to cook for crowds. "I was known for my piecrusts, but not in such quantity!" she says with a laugh. "Some people go through life with talents they never develop. I'd never cooked for anyone but my family, so it was a traumatic thing for me." Now the lodge is famous for her pies as well as all the other good food.

I was dying to know how the town got its name. "The original settlers found this whole valley a mass of wild strawberries—at least that's the story," Jean says. Now the only strawberries are at happy Strawberry Lodge.

How to get there: Strawberry is on Highway 87/260, and the inn is on the left just as you drive into the town from the south.

Innkeeper: Jean Turner
Address/Telephone: HCR 1, Box 331; (602) 476–3333
Rooms: 12; all with private bath; wheelchair accessible; no air conditioning (elevation 6,000 feet). Pets permitted.
Rates: $40, double, ground floor; $48 to $50, upstairs with fireplaces; EP. No credit cards.
Open: All year.
Facilities and activities: Restaurant, barbecue patio. Nearby: gateway to the Mongollon Ridge with fishing, hunting, horseback riding, hiking, scenic attractions.

Casa Alegre

TUCSON, ARIZONA 85705

"One of the nicest things about being near the university," Phyllis says, "is the interesting people who come to stay here. Italy, Belgium, South Africa, a biologist/anthropologist from Argentina . . ." The guest books she's placed in each room make fascinating international reading.

Phyllis became an innkeeper because, she says, "people are fun." Once busily managing the service branch of a California bank, she suddenly asked herself, "What do you *really* want to do?" Sitting down then and there, she wrote a list of her requirements. "Sunshine, cultural action, history . . . and then, I had gone to high school and college here in Tucson, so it was like coming home."

Casa Alegre has a great location, right between the University of Arizona and downtown Tucson. Built in 1915, it has been home to a pharmacist, a doctor, and an artist. Phyllis has furnished her inn with pieces that reflect highlights of Tucson history, from its beginnings as an Indian nation to the mining industry that figured so largely in Arizona's development.

The inn's parlor, with its white walls and shining dark woodwork, has a period look. The golden wood floor is graced by large, colorful rugs, and an upright piano is angled in a corner by the door to the sunroom. Off the formal dining room, a door opens onto that bright and sunny room, furnished with yellow wrought iron and white wicker.

"Someone in California gave me the fabric, and a friend and her parents brought a sewing machine here and made the curtains," Phyllis says—how nice to have such friends! The same pretty fabric is used for the looped valances and the windowseat cover. "This is a favorite place for winter breakfasts," Phyllis adds, and I can see why.

Books and games are in the hall. "When people come in and sit down, it's fun to see what they choose to play," Phyllis says.

The Arizona Room has the television set. "No television or telephone in your room to interrupt your relaxing visit with us." (Three guest rooms have phone jacks if you're serious about communicating with the outside world.) This common room opens onto the patio, a courtyard bright with Mexican morning glories and mesquite around a fountain. "Gee, you don't realize you're in the middle of town!" was one guest's surprised comment.

The furnishings of the Saguaro Room, with its own fireplace, were inspired by the cactus of the same name: The handmade armoire and the queen-sized lodgepole bed sport ribs from the sturdy desert plant. Mining memorabilia sets the theme for the Rose Quartz Room—Phyllis's father was a mining engineer. "My mother says he spent most of his life in a hole in the ground," she says jokingly. The Spanish Room's queen-sized headboard was made originally for a Mexican priest, and the Amethyst Room is decorated with early 1900s antiques.

Phyllis carries her decorating philosophy to the breakfast table. "It's the mental image," she says. "If people can say, 'Oh, that looks good!' they know it's going to taste good." Raisin bread French toast stuffed with cream cheese, "very health-conscious turkey sausage," sliced plums on green lettuce—yes, it tasted as good as it looked!

How to get there: From I–10 take Speedway east 1 mile to 5th Avenue. The inn is on the right, on the southeast corner of Speedway and 5th.

Innkeeper: Phyllis Florek
Address/Telephone: 316 East Speedway; (602) 628–1800 or (800) 628–5654
Rooms: 4; all with private bath. No smoking inn.
Rates: $70 to $80, single; $75 to $85, double; EPB. Weekly, business, and seniors rates available.
Open: All year.
Facilities and activities: Swimming pool, hot tub, holiday dinners. Nearby: University of Arizona campus, University Medical Center, Tucson Community Center, Fourth Avenue businesses and restaurants.

El Presidio Inn
TUCSON, ARIZONA 85701

Patty is strongly dedicated to two things. The first is the landmark historic district that surrounds the El Presidio Inn. The second, in my opinion, is the marvelous food she serves her guests.

The Tocis have won several awards for their restoration of the old property. "My focus," Patty says, "is this landmark historical property and the entire district. This is where Tucson began, at El Presidio, when Tucson was a walled city to protect the settlers from Apache Indians."

The delightful Territorial Victorian adobe building looks deceptively small. Built on a corner, it hides a large back courtyard—the pride of Patty and Jerry's gardening talents, centered with a fountain that Jerry found in Mexico and shaded with a huge magnolia that provides greens for Christmas celebrations.

"I'm a good old Southern girl," Patty says. "We always had magnolia greens back home for Christmas, and when old friends visit us here, they can't believe our big magnolia, growing right here in Tucson, Arizona!"

"Innkeeping is a great lifestyle," Patty says. "It's your social club as well." Breakfasts on the glassed-in sun porch are leisurely feasts, so don't be in a hurry. Patty says she has so many repeat guests that she makes notes on what she fed them last. The long table is beautifully appointed. On my visit we began with fresh orange juice, then progressed to a magnificent fruit cup of kiwi, strawberry, orange, pineapple, and cantaloupe. Next came two kinds of French toast, one made of cinnamony raisin bread, the other stuffed with homemade peanut butter and bananas. Canadian bacon came with this, and yet I really could not resist having two of the lemon nut muffins topped with streusel. Like every good cook, Patty was pleased as punch to see me stuff myself!

"The recipe for the lemon muffins isn't original with me," she says. "But the streusel topping is." She puts her happy touch on everything. Guest rooms are provided with fruit, juice, coffee, teas, and snacks. There are bathrobes to wrap up in. The Victorian Suite, with a huge sitting room furnished in cool white wicker, has a photograph of Patty's grandmother, setting the period mood. The Carriage Suite combines an Eastlake lady's desk with a collection of Southwest antiques, including a trunk that held a pioneer's goods. The Gatehouse Suite has Bar Harbor–style wicker furniture. The Zaugan Room, the lovely common room, has a tile fireplace, wreaths of fragrant dried flowers, books to read, and current magazines providing information on the best of Tucson. "We've been living here long enough to know the best things to do," the Tocis say. "The Mexican and craft festivals here in our neighborhood during spring, summer, and fall have become grand affairs."

How to get there: From I–10 take the St. Mary's exit and go right 4 blocks to Granada. Cross Granada to the next street, which is Main. Turn right onto Main and Franklin, and the inn is on the southeast corner. Curbside parking is permitted if you get a permit from Patty to put on your windshield.

Innkeepers: Patty and Jerry Toci
Address/Telephone: 297 North Main Avenue; (602) 623–6151
Rooms: 4; all with private bath, phone, and TV. No smoking inn.
Rates: $55 to $90, single; $65 to $105, double; EPB. Weekly and monthly rates available. No credit cards.
Open: All year.
Facilities and activities: Courtyard garden. Nearby: restaurants, historic district, Sonora Desert Museum, Old Town Artisans handicrafts.
Recommended Country Inns® Travel Club Benefit: Stay a week, get the seventh night free; stay five nights, get 50% off on the fifth night.

La Posada del Valle

TUCSON, ARIZONA 85719

La Posada del Valle occupies a lovely villa designed in 1929 by a renowned Tucson architect, Josias T. Joesler. Built of adobe and stucco, the inn is a perfect example of early Santa Fe–style architecture moving westward.

"We love to stay in bed and breakfast places ourselves," Debbi says, "and after we took a trip to California several years ago, we just fell in love with the idea. Tucson had none, and it took us two and a half years to open the inn, but by George, we did it!"

The patio is lovely, with a fountain and ornamental orange trees. The trees were planted by nuns from a nearby church who lived in the house a while back. But I doubt the nuns would recognize it now, divided as it is into Pola's Room, Isadora's Room, Claudette's Room, Sophie's Room, and Zelda's Room. All have private entrances.

"We picked out names of women who were popular back when the house was built, carrying out the twenties and thirties theme." Each room has black-and-white still photographs of the actresses and the dancers. Fresh flowers from the gardens make each room fragrant, and Debbi and Charles provide personal touches such as turned-down beds, freshened rooms, and candy and mints. There's a menu basket in the living room; the innkeepers make a point of helping with guests' plans and reservations for dinner.

It's delightful to sit out under the orange trees and breathe in their fragrance. The oranges there are not for eating, alas, but grapefruit and lemons from inn trees are served. Breakfast might be cream cheese blintzes with raspberries, and there are always home-baked bread, muffins, and coffeecakes.

Debbi has a helper, Pattie Bell, whom she claims as her "right arm." But, she adds, "We make Charles fix breakfast on Saturday mornings." Not to worry: he fixes Eggs a la Charles, "something he made up, and it's delicious!"

Afternoon tea, with the beverage either hot or cold, is served with cookies, almond shortbread, poppyseed muffins, and butter scones in a living room appointed with fine art deco furnishings from the 1920s and '30s. "At teatime we either mingle with the guests or leave them alone," Pattie says, sensitive to the prevailing mood.

Charles is a hospital administrator and Debbi was a homemaker. "But I never knew what I *really* wanted to do until I fell into this. Then I found my calling!"

How to get there: From I–10 take Speedway Boulevard exit and go east on Speedway to Campbell Avenue. Take Campbell north to Elm Street. The inn is on the corner of Campbell and Elm; the inn entrance is on Campbell, but there is guest parking at the side of the inn on Elm.

Innkeepers: Debbi and Charles Bryant
Address/Telephone: 1640 Campbell Avenue; (602) 795–3840
Rooms: 5; all with private bath, 2 with phone. No smoking inn.
Rates: $90 to $115, double, EPB.
Open: All year.
Facilities and activities: Lunch and dinner catered by reservation, bicycles, patio. Nearby: restaurants, Sonora Desert Museum, art and photography museums, Old Town Artisans handicrafts.

Mariposa Inn

TUCSON, ARIZONA 85719

Oliver, the big black watchdog, gives a bark of welcome when you arrive at the Mariposa Inn and then, satisfied, he barks no more. "He makes people feel safe," Maria says. "More so than does KC." (KC stands for Kiss Cat.)

Easily identified by the huge black-and-blue-painted butterfly spreading its wings at the inn's pink adobe entrance, this private, small inn began its second life as a haven for travelers with a different name: The Brimstone Butterfly.

"But although that's the name of a pretty butterfly, people seemed to find something sinister in the word 'brimstone,'" Maria says. So she changed the name to Mariposa, which is Spanish for any sort of butterfly.

Maria carries the butterfly theme through the artwork she does for her brochure and notes, and they're quite attractive. Attractive, too, are the three guest rooms, each entirely different. Painted Lady has a king-sized four-poster bed, nineteenth-century Southern style, so wide and high that you need an angled stepladder to get into it. It's draped in lacy sheers, covered in an eyelet-trimmed white spread, and bounded by a white quilted bedskirt.

The soft pink walls add to the simple elegance of the room, which also has a stained-glass window and a beehive fireplace for cool Arizona nights. The bath has a deep tiled tub.

Maria kept the Brimstone name for the

Brimstone Room, which boasts an 1890s Brazilian-rosewood queen-sized bed, brought from Brazil by David and Maria Tod. A small-town attorney from Youngstown, Ohio, he became the first U.S. ambassador to Brazil. Later on he was governor of Ohio. How do we know all this? David and Maria Tod were Maria's great-grandparents.

In case you want to get up to some private deviltry, the Brimstone Room has its own separate patio and entrance as well as a refrigerator and cooking space, which are especially convenient if you want to stay awhile.

Spanish Moon is a two-room guest house with a double bed and a comfortable sitting room. It's just steps away from the swimming pool and patio, draped with pink bougainvillea.

This classic 1933 mud adobe structure has a few ups and downs. It's a few steps down to the quiet common sitting room, with its cool green glass window, white furniture, and a fireplace that opens off the pool. An interesting note is the old schoolhouse desk.

The dining room has a tiled fireplace, and the TV room off the kitchen is filled with bright wicker and colorful print fabric. Maria's collection of baskets hangs from the rafters.

Whether you elect to eat the three-course breakfast in the breakfast area, the dining room, or the patio, it is always delicious. The full gourmet meal, served complete with china, silver, and table linens, offers a choice of menus, either creamed turkey hash on freshly made waffles and eggs florentine popovers or sautéed rosemary chops and fried bananas. "Or," says Maria, "both!"

How to get there: From I–10 take Speedway east, crossing Campbell Road. Go 2 more blocks on Speedway to Olsen. Turn right onto Olsen, and the inn is in the second block.

Innkeeper: Maria Johnstone
Address/Telephone: 940 North Olsen; (602) 322–9157
Rooms: 3; all with private bath, 1 with kitchen. Limited smoking. Pets at discretion of innkeeper.
Rates: $95, double, EPB. No credit cards.
Open: All year except July.
Facilities and activities: Swimming pool; use of laundry facilities; off-street parking. Nearby: University of Arizona campus; University Medical Center.
Business travel: Located in downtown Tucson. Conference room; corporate rates, $55 to $75.

Rimrock West

TUCSON, ARIZONA 85749

This Southwest hacienda is a haven of peace and quiet; even the road leading to the spread-out, low, pink stucco building is a private one. The Catalina Mountains are spread out on the northern horizon, the Rincon Mountains to the east. Terra-cotta pots spilling over with pretty pink flowers line the portales of the entrance, and a hammock is strung under the roof in a corner.

If an artist's easel is sitting out in front, you'll know for sure you've come to the right place: The whole Robbins family is artistic. Val is a sculptor and furniture maker; Mae does enamel work, as her beautiful tiles, which enhance the blue-and-white kitchen, proclaim. Artwork by both hosts and son Christopher beautifies the inn. Mae and Christopher are self-taught.

"Christopher's all grown up now, but he's been painting since he was a little kid," Mae says.

Val studied at the famed Pratt Institute, but when he wanted some tiles for a table he was making, he said, "Mae, I need some tiles, can you do this?" And she did. "I got a book, we got a kiln . . ." Now a pro, she has just finished making tiles for the bathroom they've put in their Rimrock West Art Gallery on the property, a family gallery showing work by this talented trio.

"We built two rooms for clean work and one for dirty work," Mae laughs. It seems that painting, oil, or watercolor is clean work; Val's woodwork is the dirty work!

Like so many Southwest innkeepers, Val and Mae are transplants, from Pennsylvania. But unlike many innkeepers, they came with plenty of experience.

"We had a resort in the Poconos for years, near the Delaware Water Gap. But when our son Dain came here eighteen years ago to go to college, we found that we were constantly going back and forth to visit him." They got tired of that, and when they found this lovely hacienda, they were Easterners no more.

"Except," Mae explains, "we didn't sell our house in Pennsylvania until a few years ago. But we found we were staying in Arizona longer and longer periods of time; we just love it here."

Val's handiwork is evident, beginning with the cocktail table in the TV room and continuing on to the chests in the dining room. He's been making furniture for more than twenty years, and some fine pieces of sculpture as well.

Not everything is newly crafted; there's a lovely antique desk in the foyer and a wonderful handcarved antique headboard in the Queen Room, brought with them from Pennsylvania.

Breakfasts are works of art, too. Strawberry waffles, smothered with whipped cream, sinful! All-bran muffins, though, are healthy enough, and there are also cornbread muffins, or crunchy apple streusel ones for your sweet tooth. Mae is famous for her smoothies, too. "I just throw everything from the fruit bowl into the blender, and add orange juice. Everybody loves them!"

What Mae loves is to garden. "It's my life," she declares passionately. The only problem is the jackrabbits. They eat everything, even the cactus. "But we're planting them faster than they can eat them," she says with satisfaction.

How to get there: From I–10 take Grant east to Wilmot (which becomes Tanque Verde) for approximately 4 miles to Catalina. Turn left and go 1 mile to Prince. Turn right on Prince; in 1 mile turn right onto North Drake Place. There is a sign on Prince; the inn is at the end of short North Drake Place.

Innkeepers: Mae and Val Robbins
Address/Telephone: 3450 North Drake Place; (602) 749–8774
Rooms: 3, plus 1 cottage with kitchen; all with private bath and TV; wheelchair accessible. No smoking inn.
Rates: $85 to $120, double; $20 extra person; EPB. No credit cards.
Open: All year.
Facilities and activities: Twenty acres with swimming pool; art gallery, hiking, bird and other wildlife watching. Located 20 minutes from the University of Arizona, airport, and metropolitan Tucson.

The Suncatcher

TUCSON, ARIZONA 85748

"I've tried to take all the qualities of a first-class hotel and put in the charm of a bed and breakfast," Dave says of his luxurious inn. A sure clue is each guest-room name: There's the Connaught, the Four Seasons, the Regent, and the Oriental. With the hotels as his inspiration, Dave gave up his law practice to become an innkeeper.

"I was traveling a lot and I was ready for a change," he says. "I began thinking about other things I could do." Now Dave likes to open the door wide and call, "Welcome to The Suncatcher!" He was pleased with my delighted reaction, which was just what he has learned to expect.

"I see the guests' eyes open," he says, "and it's such a pleasure. As for the name, The Suncatcher, why do people come to Tucson?" he asks. "The sun, the dry heat, the desert," he answers himself. "And I thought, what do I want my place to be? A retreat, a getaway—so I invented the name." Dave also created the inn emblem, little terra-cotta faces that are on the walls and elsewhere.

The huge common area (70 x 70 feet), with its soaring ceiling, has several focal points. In one corner there's a large, copper-hooded fireplace; in another, a mirrored mesquite bar. A centerpiece is the grand piano that Dave's parents bought for him when he was fifteen. "I play a little," he says modestly; he'd rather encourage guests to entertain. Display cases contain many personal treasures he collected on his travels.

The room is done so well I assumed it was decorated by a professional—it would make a beautiful spread in a fashionable home-decorating magazine. "But," says Dave, "I did it all myself, and I'm pretty proud of that." The entire area—sitting, dining, kitchen—is open, and you can watch the chef prepare breakfast, beginning with grapefruit halves, juices and coffee, on to cold cereals, egg strata, bagels, and honey date muffins. "I always ask the night before what time you'd like breakfast," he tells me, which I think is pretty accommodating. Any time is fine, and late in the day there are complimentary hors d'oeuvres. "My pleasure is sitting down and speaking with my guests," Dave says.

One guest room opens off the huge airy and spacious common area, two have French doors opening off the pool, and a fourth is around the corner with its own entrance.

The Connaught (London) is furnished with Chippendale-style furniture in gleaming dark mahogany; the Four Seasons with a formal canopied bed; the Regent (Hong Kong) has lovely original oriental scrolls; and the Oriental (Bangkok), the largest room, has among other splendors its own Jacuzzi. All have at least one comfortable chair, writing desk, original artwork, and fresh flowers.

How to get there: The inn is on the edge of Saguaro National Monument. From I–10 and downtown Tucson, take Broadway east, crossing, as a last landmark, Houghton. Continue on to Avenida Javelina, bearing in mind that Avenida Javelina is beyond the DEAD-END sign on Broadway. Turn north on Javelina, and the inn is on the left in the middle of the block.

Innkeeper: David Williams
Address/Telephone: 105 North Avenida Javelina; (602) 885–0883 or (800) 835–8012
Rooms: 4; all with private bath, phone, TV, and VCR; wheelchair accessible. No smoking inn.
Rates: $125 to $145, double; $25 extra person; EPB. Two-night minimum stay.
Open: All year.
Facilities and activities: Heated pool and spa, bicycle. Nearby: restaurants, tennis and health club, hiking, horseback riding, Saguaro National Monument; 15 minutes to downtown Tucson.

Canyon Country Inn

WILLIAMS, ARIZONA 86046

If it's an inn you want, the Canyon Country Inn is the closest place to the Grand Canyon you can find. Don't be put off by the large motel sign on the end of the building; there's a reason for that.

"We wanted a country inn, not a motel," Sue says of the building they constructed to replace a defunct motel, and they built a Colonial-style frame house right in the center of Williams. "But as soon as we opened, all the motels in town tacked 'inn' onto their names, so we had to add 'motel' in self-defense." (She's pleased, however, that they've earned a prestigious "motel" rating.)

Although the entry is small, coffee and tea are waiting for the traveler, and the innkeepers greet you warmly. Up the stairs on the right is a cozy sitting room, and the guest rooms off the sitting room are almost master-suite size. The many windows under the eaves make for nice, bright space, and rooms have flowered carpet and spreads or pale rose carpets and patchwork spreads; all are different. Sue has worked hard to create what she hopes is a "romantic, charming, and elegant country inn." She and John are from California, where they remodeled houses *and* inns, so she had definite ideas about what she wanted to do.

Two things are in particular abundance; teddy bears and intriguing lamps. "I like teddy bears," she confesses, as though it weren't apparent! "I used to make them myself, before I got so busy," she adds with a laugh. "But now I get homemade ones from a lady in town." She also collects antique lamps. One in particular, in a small upstairs sitting area, caught my eye: It was a cherub half covered with a gold silk lampshade dripping with long, black fringe.

While the upstairs rooms have the most ambience, the smaller downstairs ones, with outside entrances along the long porches running the building's length both front and back, reveal careful attention, too. Beds are comfortable pine copies of antiques, and the rooms, most with a color scheme of soft rose and blue, have decorator touches, such as decorative wallpaper moldings along the ceilings. A great deal of thought has gone into the decorative wallpapers, towels and linens, comforters and spreads, satin clothes hangers, ceiling fans, and lace curtains that make Canyon Country Inn a cozy hideaway in this rural area of northern Arizona.

Breakfast, what Sue likes to call "a beary special continental," is brought to your door. Coffee, tea, fresh juice, home-baked pumpkin bread, cinnamon rolls, banana cinnamon muffins, and a fruit cup can be eaten in your room or in the small common room at the head of the stairs.

How to get there: From I–40 take Highway 64 south to Bill Williams Avenue, which is one-way running east. If you're coming from the east (Flagstaff), turn right and go west on Railroad Avenue instead, turning south at 5th Street. The inn is on the corner of West Bill Williams and 5th.

Innkeepers: Sue and John Einolander
Address/Telephone: 442 West Bill Williams Avenue; (602) 635–2349
Rooms: 9, plus 1 cottage; all with private bath, phone, and TV, cottage with wheelchair access. No smoking inn.
Rates: $45 to $125, double, continental breakfast.
Open: All year.
Facilities and activities: Nearby: small town with walking map of shops and restaurants; Grand Canyon, Grand Canyon Railway, Grand Canyon Helicopter tours, 9-hole golf course, hiking, hunting, fishing, skiing.

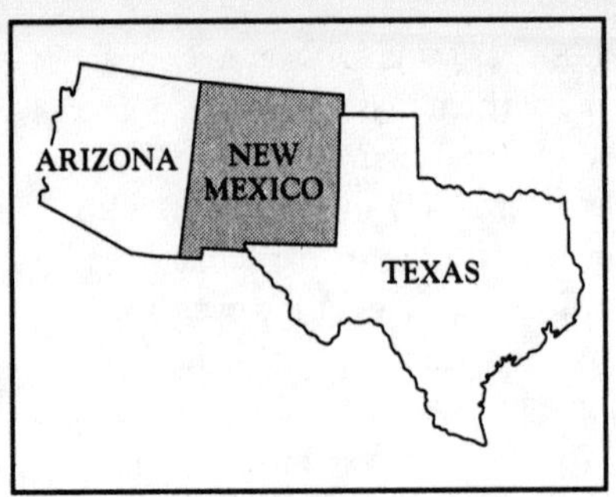
ARIZONA
NEW MEXICO
TEXAS

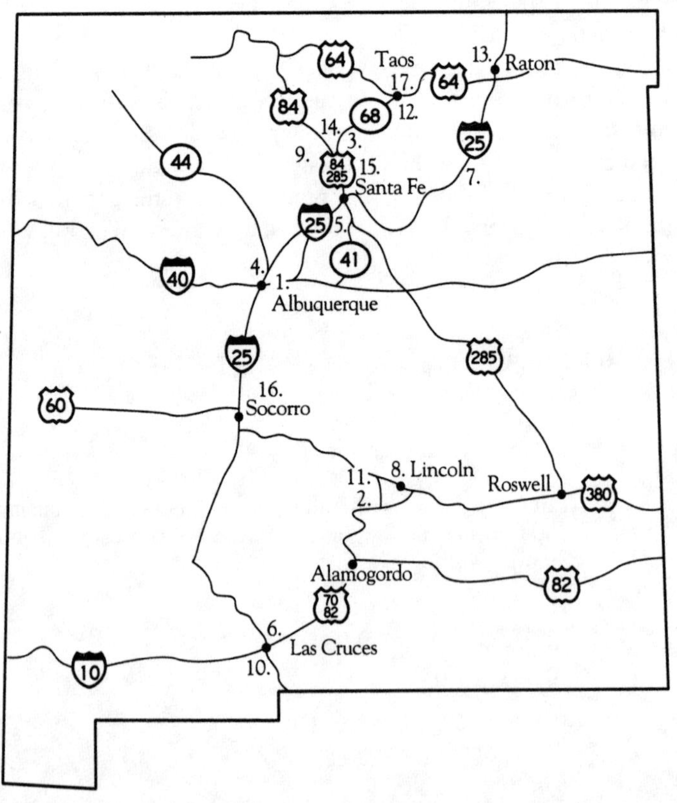
64
Taos
13.
Raton
17.
64
84
68
12.
14.
3.
25
9.
84 285
15.
44
Santa Fe
7.
25
5.
41
4.
40
1.
Albuquerque
285
25
16.
60
Socorro
11.
8. Lincoln
Roswell
380
2.
Alamogordo
82
70 82
6.
Las Cruces
10
10.

New Mexico

Numbers on map refer to towns numbered below.

Adobe and Roses

ALBUQUERQUE, NEW MEXICO 87114

Adobe and Roses is tucked away in a corner of Albuquerque that you could never find without directions. That's because Dorothy is a horse person and she wants to be out where there's a lot of room, which makes the inn peaceful and private. She boards horses, and although you can't ride them, you can enjoy watching them.

"People from an urban area, especially, really like seeing the horses out the window," she says. "I used to ride seriously; I tried out for the Olympic team in the sixties. Didn't make it," she adds. Now she's a fan of contemporary crafts as well as a booster of local cultural affairs with strong connections with the Albuquerque Symphony. She has musical evenings, which guests as a matter of course are invited to join.

Innkeeping, says Dorothy, suits her personality. "I always have liked having guests—interesting, adventurous people who are fun to talk to." Even before she went in for innkeeping, she had the suite built for house guests "so they wouldn't feel in the way." She goes all out, especially for honeymooners in the suite. "I get out my Limoges, I use table linens, crystal, when people have a really big do."

Busy, energetic Dorothy is a whirlwind at improving the property she has lived in for more than thirty years. In addition to gardening (her brother is a horticulturist, and her garden reflects his expert advice), she laid the adobes and tile for the two guest rooms that are housed in a separate building, built the small ponds with water lilies and goldfish, and created the rock garden. She planned it, she says, "so that from every room you will look at something wonderful." At sunset the Sandia Mountains in the distance turn to pink; closer in, the lily ponds reflect the sinking sun and the towering cottonwood trees.

"I want people to feel comfortable, to be at home. I don't know," Dorothy says with a laugh, "maybe I get a lot of ego satisfaction from it."

Rooms have fresh flowers; a bowl of fruit and a plate of homemade cookies wait; in the suite a dart board hangs on the wall and there's a piano. Since nights at 5,000 feet are chilly, down comforters and pillows are on the beds.

Breakfast, served in the main house family room or out on the portale (arched walkway–porch) of the guest house, might be Dutch baby, a giant popover with powdered sugar and lemon juice (my mother used to call it a German pancake), along with strawberries and bananas in whipped cream, a heavenly delight.

How to get there: Take Rio Grande exit off I–40 west; go north on Rio Grande 6 miles to Ortega Road; turn right on Ortega for approximately 4/10 mile until you see a blue mailbox on the right side of the road with 1011 on it. The inn is to the left. Dorothy likes to keep a low profile, so there is no sign.

Innkeeper: Dorothy Morse
Address/Telephone: 1011 Ortega NW; (505) 898–0654
Rooms: 3, including 1 suite; all with private bath, kitchen, fireplace, private entrance, phone, TV, and wheelchair access. Pets at discretion of innkeeper. No smoking inn.
Rates: \$55 to \$85, double; \$10 extra person; EPB. \$10 surcharge for single-night stay, discount for six or more days. Two-night minimum unless there is last-minute space. No credit cards.
Open: All year.
Facilities and activities: Laundry facilities, tennis court, handball court, barbecue grill. Nearby: tennis courts and handball, Indian Pueblo Cultural Center, Albuquerque Old Town, Rio Grande Nature Center, Natural History Museum, skiing, 8 miles from downtown Albuquerque.

Bottger Mansion

ALBUQUERQUE, NEW MEXICO 87104

The Bottger Mansion was built between 1910 and 1912, before New Mexico was granted statehood. Patsy says the builder, Charles Bottger, was from Germany. "He operated an inn and a lounge and he married a local lady, and their children married into the Garcia and Gallegos families," she says. "My husband, Vincent, is a Garcia, so Charles Bottger is one of his ancestors." Which explains one of the reasons why Vincent and Patsy call their inn the Bottger Mansion; the other reason is that it's built in a more European style of architecture than most buildings in this Southwest Spanish-heritage town.

"Through the years the house was passed down from one family to another," Patsy adds. Until—it went up for sale.

"We hate to let property out of the family!" Patsy exclaims. "So—we decided, this was it, we'd open an inn!"

I thought this was fascinating; imagine all these years of continuity in the same family for this house. No wonder the innkeepers—and their guests—feel so at home here. And for even more continuity, Vincent's family were original settlers in Albuquerque's Old Town, although of course it wasn't called "old town" back in the mid-1600s. His grandparents had a home and store on the south plaza, and the restaurant down the street is located in the house he grew up in.

Patsy has turned the glassed-in front porch of the inn into a bright café, with white wrought-iron tables and chairs, red tablecloths, wine-bottle vases with flowers, and a charming rose trellis painted on the white wall. Coffee, tea, and sodas are set around an ice machine, and in the afternoon you can dip into corn chips and salsa and nibble on nuts to recharge your batteries after a day of sightseeing in fascinating Albuquerque.

Breakfast is served in the café too, and it's a Southwestern treat: Spanish omelets and flour tortillas with red and green chilies made a spicy contrast to cool cantaloupe, honeydew, and green grapes. This was topped off with orange and cherry sweet rolls and Swiss chocolate almond coffee. Breakfast may also be enjoyed on the patio in the garden.

The Garcia–Sanchez families are very supportive of Patsy and Vincent's endeavor, proof of which is the appearance of Patsy's mother, Priscilla Sanchez, who says, "I thought you might need a hand."

I learn more about the family in the Mercedes Room, which is named for Patsy's grandmother, whose picture is on the wall. "This room was the dispensa," Patsy explains. "The grandkids ate out here in the summer." Now it's a luxurious suite with a black Jacuzzi in the huge bath. The color scheme of gray, rose, and black is pleasing, and there's a pink heart pillow on the queen bed. "We like to think of this as the honeymoon suite," Patsy says.

The Lola Suite is named for another grandmother, this time on Vincent's side. The lovely mural was painted by George Gallegos, who, Patsy says, married Julia Bottger, Charles Bottger's daughter. Vincent's other grandmother is honored in the Sophia Suite; she had to open a restaurant during some of the family's hard times. The room has a king-sized bed, and there are twin beds in the adjoining sunroom overlooking the garden. Each room is tastefully furnished.

"Ever since we opened, I've looked for different and unique pieces," Patsy says of her interesting collection. Particularly noteworthy are the red velvet sofa and the antique chess table in the Main Parlor.

How to get there: From I-25 north take Lomas West approximately 5 miles to San Felipe. The inn is on the right at the south entrance to Old Town, on the corner of Lomas and San Felipe.

Innkeepers: Patsy and Vincent Garcia
Address/Telephone: 110 San Felipe NW; (505) 243–3639
Rooms: 3, including 1 suite; all with private bath. No smoking inn.
Rates: $59 to $139, double; $20 extra person; EPB and afternoon refreshments.
Open: All year.
Facilities and activities: Mexican-style high tea. Nearby: Old Town Plaza, Historic San Felipe Church, Museum of Natural History, Albuquerque Museum, Albuquerque Little Theater, skiing; Country Club Golf Course.

Casa del Granjero

ALBUQUERQUE, NEW MEXICO 87114

The name of this inn (pronounced "gran-hair-o") means "the farmer's house." When Victoria and Butch found this wonderful old adobe hacienda nestled in the historic North Valley of Albuquerque, "we knew we were home."

More to the point for the likes of us, right from the beginning they were encouraged to open their home to guests. "Everyone told us, this is the kind of a house everyone wants to see and explore." Victoria says happily. She immediately set to work furnishing and decorating the home in a manner worthy of its size and history. The main house was 110 years old when they arrived, with beams from an 1860s bakery and bricks from famous old Route 66 (acquired when the highway was paved).

The first surprise at Casa del Granjero is opening the front door and walking into the huge common area, with Mexican tiles and a pool sunk in the middle of the room. It's surrounded by soft pink brick walls, a corner fireplace, and cushy white sofas. Cactus, clay pots of other green plants, a huge oriental rug in tones of soft reds and blues—and overhead, glass clerestory windows add even more dimension to the spacious area.

For Victoria the inn has many happy memories of Butch's grandmother, now deceased. "Granny didn't know what a bed and breakfast was. When we told her she said 'Oh. I can maybe make quilts!'

"She came across the country in a covered wagon when she was five; she died at eighty-seven," Victoria says. "She was my best buddy." Her name was Lilla Farmer and she regaled guests with stories of old Taos (north of Albuquerque and Santa Fe). She evidently is sorely missed, and I say how sorry I am not to have known her. Victoria takes me out on the patio.

"Those are Granny's wind chimes. There are days when there is no wind . . . yet we hear the chimes . . ."

In the dining room the long Spanish-mission–style table and chairs rest on another huge oriental rug, while two breakfronts display an assortment of glass and objets d'art. The overhead dark brown wood beams are older than the house.

In Quarto del Rey the old radio actually works; handcrafted Mexican tiles accent the kiva fireplace, and the view is of not only the courtyard but also the mountains and trees. Quarto de Flores (Flowers Room) boasts great-grandmother's flower needlepoint as well as Granny's colorful quilts. French doors lead to the patio and the portale that winds around to the main courtyard.

The Allegre Room presents an entirely different ambience: Butch made the four-poster that is hung with white satin and Battenburg lace.

Breakfast is a wonderful concoction of blue corn pancakes with sour cream and a caramelized apple topping, cool apricot-pear-pineapple frappé, a molded rice custard (a variation of the Mexican flan, with rice instead of eggs but still with the traditional delicious baked-on caramelized sugar sauce), and crisp bacon. "But I find that people don't always like breakfast meats, so I often serve chicken instead," Victoria says.

How to get there: From I–40 north take Alameda Boulevard west to Fourth Street. Turn left at C de Baca, then take a right to the inn, which is on the left.

Innkeepers: Victoria and Charles (Butch) Farmer
Address/Telephone: 414 C de Baca Lane NW; (505) 897–4144 or fax (505) 897–9788
Rooms: 4; all with private bath; wheelchair accessible. No smoking inn.
Rates: $85 to $105, double; $20 extra person; EPB.
Open: All year.
Facilities/activities: Hot tub, rose garden, lily pond and waterfall, gazebo; horses (to pet), pygmy goats. Nearby: hiking trails; Albuquerque with Old Town Plaza; Historic San Felipe Church; Museum of Natural History; Albuquerque Museum; skiing.
Business travel: Located in an Albuquerque suburb; fully equipped office, special meals for business meetings.
Recommended Country Inns® Travel Club Benefit: 10% discount, subject to availability.

Casas de Sueños

ALBUQUERQUE, NEW MEXICO 87104

Be prepared for a wild surprise when you drive up to this adobe inn. Above the entrance gates looms a most unusual structure, added to the inn in 1976 by Albuquerque's famous artist Bart Prince. "I tried to call it the Nautilus, but our neighbors call it 'the snail,'" Robert says. "People become different in that space." Robert, who sold his law practice to become a full-time innkeeper, adds: "When you're in it, there's no contention, no divorces. People let go of their preconceptions."

Nautilus or snail, whatever you call it, it's a fascinating structure, and I wasn't surprised to hear that people come knocking on the door to ask, "What *is* that thing?" Just as fantastic inside as it is out, it's entered by a spiral staircase, and it serves as a lounge as well as a television and meeting room. The view of nearby mountains is impressive from any of the amazing structure's three levels.

You'd think it would be hard for the rest of the inn to live up to such an introduction, but not so. These "houses of dreams" (casas de sueños) were built in the 1930s by artist J. R. Willis, growing into a cluster of small casitas around a huge old elm in the courtyard. "To support his painting, Willis kept building these casitas to rent to friends," Robert says. Today the innkeepers have turned them into a delightful collection of suites, each one unique.

Guest rooms are furnished with antiques, heirlooms, art, oriental and Indian rugs, goosedown comforters, bath amenities, and luxurious towels; some have kitchens, and most have fireplaces as well as adjoining sitting rooms and outdoor garden areas. Cascada even has its own waterfall. The Cupid Suite has a skylight; the Georgia O'Keeffe Suite features reproductions of her work; the Rose Room blends the romance of yesteryear with the comfort of today; Route 66 Suite is so named because it's just 1 block off the famous highway. (That's why the rate remains $66, too! even though other room rates may increase in time.) But I won't tell everything; I'll let you make discoveries for yourself.

The dining room was the artist's studio, and the large northern wall of windows faces the gardens. There's always coffee, tea, and cake on hand, and breakfast is a buffet of gourmet coffee and tea, fresh fruit, cereal, yogurt, and a specialty such as decadent French toast with fresh fruit sauce, or perhaps a Southwest dish. "You can stay a week and never have a repeat, and we always accommodate special dietary requests," helper Shay Tindall says, as she serves late-afternoon guests moist poppyseed cake crunchy with Brazil nuts, along with their coffee.

The inn often hosts public receptions for visitors to the local university, and since inn guests are welcome to attend, it's a real treat to stay here. "Lots of buildings need to be held up," Robert says. "This is the first that needs to be held down!"

How to get there: From I–40 west take Rio Grande exit south toward Old Town. Cross Mountain Road and Central Avenue and go 2 more blocks. The inn is on the left, facing the Albuquerque Country Club Golf Course.

Innkeepers: Robert Hanna and Mary Sacco
Address/Telephone: 310 Rio Grande SW; (505) 247–4560 or (800) 242–8987
Rooms: 14 casitas; all with private bath, phone, and TV, 1 with wheelchair access. No smoking inn.
Rates: $66 to $225, double, seasonal; $15 extra person; EPB.
Open: All year.
Facilities and activities: Dinner by reservation, hot tub. Nearby: Old Town Plaza with restaurants, shops, and galleries; health club, museums, zoo, festivals, golf, swimming, horseback riding, longest aerial tram in North America, skiing.
Business travel: Minutes from downtown Albuquerque; modem hookups and fax machines.

The W. E. Mauger Estate

ALBUQUERQUE, NEW MEXICO 87102

The Mauger (pronounced "major") Residence has been on the National Register of Historic Places since 1985. The inn, once an old boardinghouse, won a blue ribbon for elegant restoration from the local board of realtors. Now the new owners are carrying on the inn's aim of "offering comfortable Victorian accommodations for sixteen souls in a style reminiscent of an era when graciousness, thoughtfulness, and elegance were a way of life."

The Queen Anne house was built in 1897, for the whopping sum of $1,600, by the daughter of a local tavern owner named Talbot. An unhappy marriage sent her into the arms of a New Yorker, and she left the house to be sold to William and Brittania Mauger, who were in the wool business. The Wool Room, on the second floor, was the business office.

There are three other guest rooms on the second floor. The Brittania, the original master bedroom, has three windows overlooking downtown and the beautiful Sandia Mountains. The Boston Sleeper was a screened sleeping porch for summer dog days—now it's all glassed in with an additional room for use as a suite. The Tuers Room was a bedroom/sewing room, and it too has a fine mountain view, as well as morning sun.

Upstairs on the third floor, the Graystone is a spacious two-bedroom attic suite, presenting an interesting and surprising contrast to the nostalgic Victoriana below. The two rooms are furnished in an almost art deco style, with color schemes of pink and gray and pink and black and wild print linens to match.

The Talbot Room, named for the original owner of the house, has a sleigh bed, a comfortable lounge chair, and a huge old desk. The Garden Room is bright with green plants.

The inn is cozy, with lace curtains in the windows, and there are green plants in the two dining rooms. Chuck does wonderful soufflés, crab and spinach being specialties, as well as spinach and egg burritos and crab quiche. Also delicious is an omelet with cilantro, green chilies, and tomato. Add fresh home-baked scones, blueberry and bran muffins, and bagels to a fruit dish such as fruit of the season served with yogurt and granola, orange juice, and coffee, and you're more than set for the day! (If not, head on back later in the day—afternoon refreshments are also served.)

Chelsea, a blond cocker spaniel, lives primarily in the back of the inn with her owners, but if you want her, she's delighted to be friendly.

How to get there: From I–25 take the Grand Street exit west to 7th Street. Turn right on 7th, go 1 block to Roma, and the inn is on the northwest corner.

Innkeepers: Chuck Silver, Brian Miller, and Lorraine Day
Address/Telephone: 701 Roma Avenue NW; (505) 242–8755
Rooms: 8; all with private bath. Pets permitted in one room.
Rates: \$59 to \$109, double, EPB and afternoon refreshments.
Open: All year.
Facilities and activities: Nearby: historic old town, Indian Pueblo Museum, Rio Grande Zoo, museums, restaurants, shopping, Sandia Peak Tramway to Sandia Peak and the ski area.
Recommended Country Inns® Travel Club Benefit: 10% discount, subject to availability.

Hacienda Vargas
ALGODONES, NEW MEXICO 87001

Algodones was a Spanish military garrison in the 1620s and '30s, and caravans crossed the Rio Grande to travel up and down the narrow road. Often there were raids by bandits and Navajos in spite of the military presence. Later the village was a stagecoach stop and trading post and eventually the site of a U.S. Post Office.

This inn is truly a family affair. "Each of us has different skills, different talents," Paul says of himself and his brothers and sister. They couldn't resist combining their various abilities to the making of an inn when they found this historic spot. Paul contributed his professional corporation and banking experience, Jule his marketing expertise, Lawrence his gardening talents, and Frances her culinary skills.

Hacienda Vargas is on that bit of El Camino Real once called the Chihuahua Trail. Paul imparts an interesting bit of history that also explains the name. "Until 1821 this territory was part of Mexico. The Spanish would not allow Mexicans to trade with Americans. They could trade only with Chihuahua [the city and state directly south of the border]."

The adobe building, more than 200 years old, has lived through a lot. "Three or four families lived in smaller areas on the one-acre site," Paul says as he points out the old bell tower and the family chapel (complete with candles, fireplace, and benches if you want to sit and meditate a while). I was fascinated by the glassed-in openings that the innkeepers have installed in several places to reveal the original adobe walls.

The long, wide Delgado Sala, with an entire wall of French doors leading out to the courtyard, is both entry and art gallery. Care has been taken to combine the spirit of the Old West with the influence of the early Spanish settlers and the original Pueblo Indian culture. The furniture is all authentic New Mexico antique, and there are many fascinating pieces like the old ice box, now used to store table linens, and the old dentist's medical cabinet in the Peña Room.

In the Peña Room you'll also find three signed pieces by famous Southwest artist Amado Peña. "He sent us them as a gift," Paul says with pleasure. The bed and headboard are of a unique design, and here the innkeepers have framed and glassed-in one of the openings showing the original walls.

The Wagner Room, the largest of the guest rooms, was inspired by the composer, of whose music Paul is fond. "I lived in Austria, in Innsbruck, for a while when I was a student," he says. The room has a kiva fireplace, a separate sitting area, and a Jacuzzi tub with a skylight view—pretty luxurious! The Piñon Room, with its white wrought-iron bed, has a great view of the gardens (Lawrence's handiwork) and a 200-year-old elm tree. The old-timey bath has a claw-footed tub and a pullchain commode.

Frances comes into her own with pancakes and waffles served with a homemade nectarine topping, or a fluffy four-layer soufflé of eggs, ham, vegetables, and such. She's a real professional who has studied and worked under chefs in large hotels and restaurants.

How to get there: North on I–25 to Algodones exit (approximately 5 miles past the Bernalillo exit), west to El Camino Real (Highway 313). Turn left on El Camino Real, and Hacienda Vargas is behind the adobe wall, immediately on the right. The front door is at the second entrance.

Innkeeper: Paul, Jule, Frances, and Lawrence de Vargas
Address/Telephone: 1431 El Camino Real (mailing address: P.O. Box 307); (505) 867–9115
Rooms: 4; all with private bath; wheelchair accessible. No smoking inn.
Rates: $69 to $99, double; $15 extra person; EPB.
Open: All year.
Facilities and activities: Hot tub, barbecue area, Murder Mystery Weekends. Nearby: golfing, river and lake fishing, water sports, snow skiing. Albuquerque is about 25 miles south, Santa Fe about 30 miles north.
Recommended Country Inns® Travel Club Benefit: 25% discount, Monday–Thursday, subject to availability; in January, stay one night and get one night free.

Sierra Mesa Lodge

ALTO, NEW MEXICO 88312

"We'd been planning this for years," Lila says of the bright blue-and-white inn high above the Sierra Blanca range of New Mexico, just north of Ruidoso. "Larry took early retirement, and we thought of emigrating to New Zealand; we checked out the Caribbean; we went all over the world." When they saw this area, they were hooked. Larry wanted to build a small hotel, but Lila argued that "meeting people is what an inn is all about."

She enjoys her guests; she says it's like having family in the home. "We play cards, dominoes with our guests; we're good friends by the time they leave." If the guests want television, they're banished upstairs to the television room, where there's a telescope, too. "We want them to visit, we don't want the television on; that ends the conversation," she says with a laugh.

Lila has two hobbies: cooking—and making delicate porcelain dolls. Each guest room has an occupant, a china doll that she created from scratch. "I walked into a paint store for some paint and a woman was demonstrating doll making. Just like that I was lost!"

Guest rooms are individually decorated with flair. The mirrored black enamel queen-sized bed in the Oriental Room is an eye-catcher, and the other authentic oriental pieces are outstanding, too. A magnificently embroidered oriental marriage robe hangs on the wall.

Each room has a window seat, but otherwise variety reigns. There are the Victorian, French Country, Country Western, and Queen Anne rooms, each ruled over by one of Lila's dolls. Comforters, goose down pillows, kimonos, rockers, and chaise longues may spoil you rotten.

So will the food, Lila's and Larry's other area of expertise. For breakfast you are at the mercy of the cook, but not to worry—you'll manage to live through waffles, quiches, poppyseed bread, fruit parfait with honey and sour cream, perhaps Lila's blintz soufflé. Lila will even pamper you with breakfast in bed.

Afternoon tea means a special chocolate bread with cream cheese, peanut-butter cream pie, chocolate streusel. In the evenings guests gather around the cheery fire for wine and cheese and good conversation. If you don't object, Magnum, a big, friendly mix of a dog, will join you.

The lodge is now offering exciting Murder Mystery weekends if you get five friendly couples together for two evenings of fun and fine food: breakfast, afternoon tea, dinner, and late-night wine and cheese.

How to get there: Take Highway 48 north from Ruidoso approximately 6 miles to Fort Stanton Road on your right. Keep to the left at the fork in the road and you'll find the inn on your left about 2 miles down the road. There is a sign.

Innkeepers: Lila and Larry Goodman
Address/Telephone: Fort Stanton Road (mailing address: P.O. Box 463); (505) 336–4515
Rooms: 5; all with private bath; no air conditioning (elevation 7,000 feet). No smoking inn.
Rates: \$80 to \$90, double, EPB and high tea.
Open: All year.
Facilities and activities: Indoor spa, games, Murder Mystery weekends. Nearby: skiing, horseback riding, fishing in Alto Lake, Ruidoso Downs race track and golf, hiking trails in Lincoln National Forest, restaurants in Ruidoso.

Hacienda Rancho de Chimayo

CHIMAYO, NEW MEXICO 87522

Chimayo is a very small town with an interesting history bound up in Hacienda Rancho de Chimayo and in the Restaurante Rancho de Chimayo, which serves native New Mexican cuisine just across the road from the inn. Both establishments belong to a family that has lived in Chimayo since the 1700s and traces its roots to the first Spanish settlers.

In the 1880s two brothers, Hermenegildo and Epifanio Jaramillo, built family homes facing each other across the road. Their descendants restored the homes, creating in 1965 the Restaurante Rancho de Chimayo in Hermenegildo's home and in 1984 the Hacienda Rancho de Chimayo in the house that once belonged to Epifanio and his wife, Adelaida. I found the sense of history here intriguing.

The inn's rooms open off a walled courtyard with a sparkling fountain and bright flowers. The view is toward the mountains, and my room had the same view. French doors opened onto a little balcony, and that's where I had my simple continental breakfast, although I was tempted to join other guests in the courtyard. The restaurant is justly famous: Lunch was a small *sopapilla* (a puffed, slightly sweet Mexican roll) stuffed with chili and cheese, served with guacamole. For dinner I had *carne adovada* (pork marinated in chili), another specialty. The inn has a cookbook if you want to make these delicious dishes yourself.

All guest rooms have fireplaces, and my very large room had twin mahogany beds forming a king-sized bed. At the foot was a taupe velvet sofa, a coffee table, and two wing chairs; every room has a similar area.

I appreciated such details as the pink linens, rose lace shower curtain, and old prints on the walls. It seemed just like home—or like home ought to be!

"We've traveled a lot in the States, and we always like to sit for a while in our room, perhaps have some wine and cheese and relax, before we go out to dinner," says Florence Jaramillo. There's wine in the kitchen of the office/lobby for whoever wants it, and a bottle of wine is placed in your room if you notify ahead of a special occasion.

Other evidences of thoughtfulness were the small cans of fruit juice I found in my room. Each room is practically a suite, there's so much space, and the antique furniture is well selected. I particularly admired my room's mahogany dressing table and the antique blanket stand holding a white woven afghan in case I got chilly. I asked Florence how they were lucky enough to have so many lovely pieces.

"We searched all of San Antonio, Austin, and Denver for our antiques," Florence says. She and Laura have done a wonderful job, re-creating the distinctive charm of the colonial New Mexico of their ancestors.

How to get there: From Highway 285 north of Santa Fe, take Highway 503 east 8 miles to Highway 520 north; continue for 3 miles to Chimayo. The highway runs right between the inn and the restaurant.

Innkeepers: Florence and Laura Jaramillo
Address/Telephone: P.O. Box 11; (505) 351–2222
Rooms: 7; all with private bath.
Rates: $54 to $81, double, continental breakfast.
Open: All year except January.
Facilities and activities: Restaurant (closed in January). Nearby: 1850s Church of Santuario, the "Lourdes of the U.S."; weavers' shops famous for rugs, jackets, cushions.

Casa la Resolana

CORRALES, NEW MEXICO 87048

The Thomases describe their inn as "a house splashed by the sun," which is a good description, for two reasons. One is that it's located on four and a half acres of sunny Rio Grande Valley land, and the other is that it's solar heated—even the water used in the inn is heated by the sun. Twenty solar collectors gather up all the warmth and energy of the hot New Mexico sun.

Casa la Resolana may look like an old adobe hacienda, but don't let it fool you. "The house was built by us," Jerry says, bragging just a trifle. He laughs as he says, "You're looking at the plumber, carpenter, electrician . . ."

"And it's true adobe, not fake," Nancy says of the spacious, 4,500-square-foot home with brick floors, beamed ceilings, and three kiva fireplaces. "I know. We set every adobe brick!"

When they began to build this family home in Corrales (which is sort of a suburb north of Albuquerque), the Thomases were living in Albuquerque and raising a family. Jerry worked with his architectural supply company, and Nancy was teaching. It took them five years to build, which is not surprising when you learn they did it only on weekends.

"Our son was five, and he's grown now. So are our two daughters, and a foster son." But it sounds like it was quite a lark for everybody, even the youngest, to hear Nancy and Jerry tell the tale.

There's still a lot of teamwork in the innkeeping. While Nancy's applesauce muffins are made with applesauce Nancy makes herself, "I picked the apples," Jerry says.

Breakfast might be *huevos rancheros*, homemade granola, the applesauce or hot raspberry bran muffins, and spiced peaches. Fruits served with the breads are from the inn's orchards, which seasonally yield peaches, apricots, cherries, and pears, so you know they're fresh. Especially if Jerry's been out there picking. "I used to be slow, but I'm a quick person now!"

When Jerry sold his business and retired (by then the house was long finished), he thought he would take it easy. "But Nancy let me stay retired for about six months," he laughs.

After breakfast it's off to some of the pastoral acreage to pet and feed the horses, hike the trail to the Rio Grande, or just sit on the patio, portale (an arched walkway–porch), or in the rose garden, breathe the fresh air, and admire the view of the Sandia and Jemez mountains on the horizon.

The common area has a fireplace and a piano, a coffee and juice bar, a record player (remember them?), and a poker/game table. Out on the portale there's an inviting swing that just asks to be napped on. But not at breakfast time—the portale is also a dining spot.

The pink adobe brick walls of the Queen Room are curved around the corners, and the bath has a bright-yellow sunken tub, which matches the bright-yellow dust ruffle under the soft white quilt on the queen-sized bed. The King Room, of course, has a king-sized bed, and the East Room has a lot of books, so ask for that if you're a reader.

How to get there: North on I–25, take the Alameda exit to the corner of Coors and Corrales Road (Highway 448). Turn right onto Corrales Road and follow it north to number 7887 (approximately 6 miles).

Innkeepers: Nancy and Jerry Thomas
Address/Telephone: 7887 Corrales Road; (505) 898–0203
Rooms: 3; all with private bath. No smoking inn.
Rates: \$70 to \$95, double; \$15 extra person; EPB.
Open: All year.
Facilities and activities: Hot tub. Nearby: golfing, hiking, skiing, historical pueblos; 15 minutes from Albuquerque, 50 minutes from Santa Fe.

Corrales Inn

CORRALES, NEW MEXICO 87048

Laura and Mary spent many years in Europe and learned what an inn should really be like. The sophisticated continental atmosphere in this spacious, almost luxurious, inn makes for a wonderfully relaxing stay. "We are often told this inn is one of the best in the country," they say with pride. Both women are originally from Chicago and taught there before setting out in the world. Mary taught French; Laura taught drama and performed in New York and Europe. They both lived in Europe at the same time but didn't know each other then. It was a lucky day when they met up; they are a perfect combination.

"Mary is gifted—she's the chef. I'm the people person," Laura says. The gifted chef learned from a French mother-in-law; it was like having "your own Cordon Bleu." Mary specializes in country French and continental cuisine, and people practically beat down the door to the inn as well as plead with them to reopen the restaurant they used to have in front of the inn.

"We have people who return just for the breakfast," Laura says with a laugh. "We have people who will do anything, even beg. We're known for our food. We used to offer a public brunch, and people keep hoping we'll return to it." They long for the stuffed croissants, the New Mexican green chili and mushroom omelets, the blue corn pancakes, the country-fried potatoes, homemade applesauce, Denver pie, wild rice with fruit—need I go on?

But there's food for the soul, too. The stars at night are just marvelous, and a walk through the *bosque* (woods) is like being carried back to the France or Italy of two centuries ago—timeless. Laura is busy with a reclamation project, claiming the land around the inn for native grasses and wildflowers to attract birds, "for people to get an idea of what the land was like before cattle and people made it into a desert," she says.

Sherry and port evenings in the Great Room are part of the ambience. The room is surrounded with bookshelves, classical music plays softly (Laura is a violinist), and the walls are hung with interesting collections—old iron keys, masks, the yoke used on the first plow on Indiana's soil.

Rooms are spacious and bright. I especially liked the Balloon Room, decorated with balloon bedspread and posters in honor of nearby Albuquerque's hot-air balloon festival. "The prevailing winds bring the balloons up here, and we're filled up from one year to the next for the occasion," Laura says.

The American Indian Room, the Victorian Room, the Southwest Room, the Kiva Room, the Oriental Room—each one is imaginatively decorated. Two rooms have twin beds, two have queens, and two have king-sized beds.

How to get there: From I–25 north of Albuquerque, take Alameda exit 233 west approximately 4⁶⁄₁₀ miles to traffic light at Corrales Road. Turn right (north) and go approximately 2⁷⁄₁₀ miles until you see a restaurant in small Plaza San Ysidro on your left. (You'll pass a school on the right.) Turn left onto a dirt road just edging the south wall of the restaurant. The inn is immediately behind the restaurant.

Innkeepers: Laura Warren and Mary Briault
Address/Telephone: 58 Perea Road (mailing address: P.O. Box 1361); (505) 897–4422
Rooms: 6; all with private bath and wheelchair access, TV upon request. Pets welcome. Smoking in designated areas.
Rates: $65 to $85, double; $15 extra person; EPB. Weekly rates available.
Open: All year.
Facilities and activities: Hot tub. Nearby: Rio Grande irrigation ditch, a 9-mile trail along irrigation system; the bosque, with muskrat, beaver, ducks; horseback riding on Sandia Indian Reservation trails, 12 miles from Albuquerque.

The Galisteo Inn
GALISTEO, NEW MEXICO 87540

Of this more-than-250-year-old classic Spanish adobe inn, Joanna says, "It looks even better than ever." Wayne is a landscape contractor, and they have beautified the inn even further to please their artistic eyes. But they have no quarrel with the pink and blue mountains that surround them.

"We fell in love with New Mexico," Wayne says. "The clean air, the serenity . . ." So these two fugitives from California gathered up young daughter Paige and headed for these hills.

Centuries ago The Galisteo Inn was the hub of a Spanish trading post, a fourteen-room hacienda owned by the Ortiz y Piño family. All remodeling was done carefully so that the inn continued to fit in with its surroundings, which include some of the oldest colonial buildings in America. (Remember that the Spanish were here long before the Pilgrims landed in the Northeast.)

The inn is situated on eight acres of land under huge old cottonwood trees. It's a long, low adobe building hidden behind a long, low stone wall, and I almost missed it. Galisteo is not much more than a mark on the map; I don't advise looking for it in the dark!

But what a wonderful place to discover, no matter if I had a little difficulty finding it. Staying here is like going on a retreat. The simple rooms have whitewashed walls with wood vigas above. Handmade furniture and handwoven rugs are the decor; some rooms are angled, some have adobe fireplaces, all are clean, simple, and uncluttered, yet with what Joanna calls "lots of decorative upgrades."

Breakfast is a refreshing eye-opener with fruit smoothies (a kind of fruit milk shake) and a fruit platter, and may include waffles, breakfast breads, or quiche. "We use seasonal and local foods whenever possible," Joanna says.

Dinners are superb, a heavenly feast in the wilderness (the inn is 23 miles south of Santa Fe). The food is a delicious combination of Southwest and nouvelle cuisine. Spinach-and-*chorizo* (sausage)-stuffed duck and blue corn polenta are specialties. The innkeepers tend their own garden—they use fresh lettuce, peppers, squash, and herbs, as well as fruit from their orchards—and a vegetarian meal can be requested. "We have a lot of health-conscious people who come here," Joanna says.

They come for what I was delighted to find, a beautifully decorated Southwestern retreat, quiet and low-key. Two cozy cats, Rudy and Murphy, are still on the premises, legacies from the previous owners. Smart animals: They know The Galisteo Inn is too good a place to leave.

How to get there: From Albuquerque take I–40 east to Moriarty, 41 north toward Santa Fe through Galisteo. From Santa Fe take I–25 north to 285 south toward Lamy, 41 south to Galisteo.

Innkeepers: Joanna Kaufman and Wayne Aarniokoski
Address/Telephone: Box 4; (505) 982–1506
Rooms: 12; 8 with private bath; no air conditioning (elevation 6,300 feet); wheelchair accessible. No smoking inn.
Rates: $60 to $175, double, EPB.
Open: All year except last three weeks in January and first week in December.
Facilities and activities: Box lunches, dinner by reservation Wednesday through Sunday, horseboarding and horseback riding, swimming pool, hot tub, sauna, trail bicycles, hiking, skiing the Turquoise Trail and the Santa Fe Ski Basin. Nearby: old pueblo, old church, old Spanish graveyard, museum, petroglyphs (Indian rock paintings) 8 miles south of town, Old Turquoise Trail mines.

Inn of the Arts

LAS CRUCES, NEW MEXICO 88005

Walking in one front door of the Inn of the Arts, you'll find yourself in an art gallery first and foremost, with wonderful paintings by such New Mexico artists as Keb Barrick, who studied with Grant Wood. A side entrance, located off the quiet, tree-shaded patio, leads directly into the Merienda Room, two stories high with enormous arched windows. This common room, also filled with art, was designed by Gerald to connect the two historic Llewellyn Houses that make up the inn.

Gerald is an architect, Linda has the gallery, and both are wide-awake, vital, energetic people who make guests feel part of the electricity in the air. Both are actively involved with the arts in Las Cruces; they print a newsletter that keeps guests informed.

"Our guests are part of the family immediately—we treat them like that," says Linda. "We have a man from Bogotá, Colombia, a regular guest, who needs a phone, so we put a jack in his room." The inn has all sorts of international guests, and you're bound to meet very interesting people, perhaps even in the kitchen! I liked having the freedom of the modern, attractively tiled kitchen, where a guest from Portugal was poaching his own eggs, an actor fixing his health breakfast, and a vegetarian woman preparing her own special brought-along food.

The *Merienda*, an afternoon social hour

from 5:00 to 7:00 P.M., is complete with wine and Southwestern hors d'oeuvres: *chili con queso*, guacamole, perhaps shrimp soufflé. If it's an off day, there will be a basket of fruit in your room instead.

Downstairs guest rooms lead right and left off the two-story Merienda Room. A circular stairway leads up to a balcony overlooking the large room and into the upstairs guest rooms.

Each room is named for an artist famous in the Southwest—names like Georgia O'Keeffe, Fritz Scholder, Olaf Weighorst. The Weighorst Room has headboards cunningly made from antique gas-grate hoods padded with decorator fabric matching the bedspreads. I loved the bathroom's footed tub, painted bright red.

Two weeks of every month are devoted to the Elderhostel program, with the knowledgeable Lundeens holding forth on "Ancient Art and Architecture" and "Historic New Mexico Art and Architecture." Gerald has built a *horno*, an Indian oven, at the end of the garden; guests helped make the adobe bricks. Now every third morning or so, the Lundeens bake thirty-six loaves of fresh bread! While watching the oven work, you can play croquet or toss horseshoes or perhaps watch a filming. The inn was used by a film studio last year to make a movie, which gives you an idea of the vibrant atmosphere and architecture here.

"We all interact," says Linda, and it's easy to see how, at the Inn of the Arts.

How to get there: The inn is on Alameda Boulevard next to the First National Bank Tower, the only high rise on the street.

Innkeepers: Linda and Gerald Lundeen
Address/Telephone: 618 South Alameda Boulevard; (505) 526–3327
Rooms: 15; all with private bath, 2 with kitchenette, 6 with phone and TV; wheelchair accessible. Pets permitted. Limited smoking permitted.
Rates: $50 to $90, per room, continental breakfast.
Open: All year.
Facilities and activities: Kitchen open for guest use, bicycles, Elderhostel program. Nearby: Old Mesilla, Herschel Zohn Theater, Rio Grande River, hiking in Gila Mountain Wilderness and Bosque del Apache Bird Refuge.

Carriage House Inn

LAS VEGAS, NEW MEXICO 87701

Anne and John are from Suffolk, England, but they had been in California for quite a while. John imported British stereo equipment and Anne worked in the hotel industry. "But I decided that basically the hotel industry can no longer call itself the hospitality industry," Anne says, "when the bottom line is more important than the guests." She laughs. "I decided that poring over budget sheets is not my forte."

Deciding that an inn would fulfill their urge to offer more friendly hospitality, John and Anne hoped for a location that would meet their three requirements. "A small town, a university town, and one with some historical significance." They feel they were pretty lucky.

"Being here in Las Vegas is a mere fluke," Anne says. "We told a friend who was going on vacation in New Mexico to let us know if he saw any properties of interest."

When he came back to California and told them, "I think I've found it!" they were off to take a look.

"I just got about a yard inside the front door, and I knew this was it," Anne says. "We've had years of joy since."

The Carriage House is one of Las Vegas's special Victorian houses, a relic of the gracious days of long ago. The polished and well-preserved golden woodwork is lovely; there's some interesting gingerbread crowning the hall between the living room and the stairs.

Anne and John have filled the inn with an eclectic collection of period pieces and antiques.

"Thirty years of marriage and lots of china," Anne says with a laugh. Of course I wasn't surprised to see her choice collection of English tea cups, and she serves tea in them "upon request." (Cups you can see through, little crustless sandwiches, tea cakes . . .)

Guest rooms are large, ceilings are high, and baths are spacious with claw-footed tubs. The rooms are bright with flowered bedspreads and curtains, except for the Blue Room, which is rather tailored.

"That's a concession to John," Anne confesses. "It's masculine because he did get fed up with all my flowers!" The bedspread, drapes, valence, and swag over the bed are done in a lovely dark paisley pattern in navy and deep red. The bedside tables are solid squares of wood and the brass lamps are tailored, too.

Downstairs, the long entry hall leads straight to the dining room with its lace-clothed table and old hutch. The plates on the wall are another collection of Anne's. On the way the comfortable common rooms are to the left, with wing chairs and lounge chairs to relax in. There's a television set and games to play.

Breakfast might be what Anne calls her "thingamajig" (English muffin with bacon and cheese) or orange French toast, carrot and fresh ginger muffins, pumpkin bread—and, of course, fruit and juice, coffee and tea.

The town's Plaza is a treat; Las Vegas has 918 buildings listed on the National Register of Historic Places, the highest count in the state. Anne and John can guide you to copies of a self-guided walking tour if you're feeling ambitious.

How to get there: Take University exit off I–25 to 6th Street. Turn right to number 925; the inn is on the left.

Innkeepers: Anne and John Bradford
Address/Telephone: 925 6th Street; (505) 454–1784
Rooms: 4; 2 with private bath; $10 extra person. Smoking in common rooms only.
Rates: $55 to $75, double, EPB.
Open: All year.
Facilities and activities: Nearby: historic square, Plaza Bridge Street art galleries, Douglas Street shopping district, Fort Union National Monument, Rough Riders Museum, Montezuma Castle, National Wildlife Refuge, golf, Highland University.

Casa de Patron

LINCOLN, NEW MEXICO 88338

Innkeepers Cleis (pronounced Cliss) and Jeremy used to camp in nearby Lincoln National Forest, and she fell in love with the little town of Lincoln.

"I told Jerry I *had* to live here," Cleis says with a laugh. "He thought I was bananas; this house was a wreck. But it had great charm, and after it was fixed, we decided to share it with others."

The historic nineteenth-century house was the home of Juan Patron, born in 1855. The Jordans decided to name the inn after his family, who lived in the house and kept a store there during the mid-1800s. Young Juan lost his father in an 1873 raid on Lincoln, forerunner of the Lincoln County Wars. Billy the Kid, Sheriff Pat Garrett, murders, and rival mercantile establishments—these are the ingredients of the bloody Lincoln County Wars. I'll leave it to you to visit the museums and flesh out the story, but it was pretty wild in Lincoln back then.

Today there's peace and tranquillity in the beautiful forested country, the calm broken only by the many festivals and pageants in the tiny town and in nearby Capitan (home of Smokey the Bear) and Ruidoso.

Each guest room in the spanking white adobe-and-viga house is decorated with collectibles and antiques like the 1800s spinning wheel from Jerry's family back in Deerfield,

Illinois. The number 1 Southwestern Room has twin beds and a full bath; number 2 Southwestern Room has a queen bed and washbasin and private bath around the corner; the Old Store has a queen bed, private bath, and outside entry to a patio. The casitas are completely private, and the Jordans are understandably proud of the fact that they built them from scratch. Casa Bonita has a cathedral ceiling in the living area and a spiral staircase winding up to the loft bedroom.

Breakfast might be Cleis's baked egg soufflé, strawberry walnut muffins, home-fried potatoes, and fresh fruit—in the clear mountain air, appetites are hearty. The huge kitchen has a wonderful collection of washboards, those old-fashioned thingamajigs for scrubbing clothes. Hot or cold drinks in the evening are enhanced by music, with Cleis at the baby grand in the parlor or at the real live pipe organ in the dining room. You can be sure the music is professional—Cleis has a master's degree in organ music.

As for dinner, you can drive to La Lorraine in Ruidoso, Chango in Capitan, or Tinnie's Silver Dollar in Tinnie; but, says Cleis with a laugh, "that's one of the reasons why we went into the dinner business (by prior arrangement only): People said, 'What, you mean we have to get in the car and drive 12 miles?'"

A Salon Evening might be a night of ragtime and American cuisine, or German specialties accompanied by suitable music. "But it's the people, that's the fun part," says Jerry.

How to get there: Casa de Patron is located at the east end of Lincoln on the south side of Highway 380, which runs between Roswell and I–25. The highway is the main and only road through the tiny town.

Innkeepers: Cleis and Jeremy Jordan
Address/Telephone: P.O. Box 27; (505) 653–4676
Rooms: 3, plus 2 two-room casitas; 3 rooms with private bath, casitas with private bath, hide-a-bed, and kitchen; no air conditioning (elevation 5,700 feet). No smoking inn.
Rates: $73 to $93, double; $13 extra person, single deduct $10; EPB for main house, continental for casitas; afternoon drinks and snacks.
Open: All year.
Facilities and activities: Dinner by advance reservation. VCR, special entertainment such as German Evenings and musical Salon Evenings. Nearby: Billy the Kid country with state monuments and Heritage Trust museums, Lincoln National Forest, hiking, skiing, horse races at Ruidoso Downs, soap-making and quilting workshops.

Orange Street Inn
LOS ALAMOS, NEW MEXICO 87544

You have to wind your way up the mountain to reach this homey inn on a mountaintop. And there's only one way down, too. But you'll be glad you made the climb when you meet innkeepers Susanne and Michael.

"We feel we're a nice change from Santa Fe, and people use Los Alamos as a hub," Michael says. "They'll go down to Santa Fe, to Taos, and then come back. We're an excellent location for hitting the high spots." They're also an excellent location for meeting international scientists—people from Scandinavia, Austria, or Germany, for example, who come for a time to work at Los Alamos—if, says Susanne, "we can keep them from talking too much shop!"

Shop or not, and scientists or not, people linger over the table at Orange Street breakfasts. In addition to fresh fruit and juices, there will be Susanne's homemade pot cheese to spread on homemade granola breads and muffins, and perhaps chicken soufflé, or maybe delicious Southwestern specialties like breakfast *quesadillas* or *sopapillas*. "We certainly emphasize our good food," Susanne says, especially since Michael has added oven puff pancakes, Italian frittata, oatmeal soufflé, French breakfast sandwiches, and *huevos los Alamos* with corn crepes to the menu.

I could emphasize their other objectives: to provide nicely decorated rooms (not large but comfortable, in country or New Mexican motifs) as well as unusually good food—"and cleanliness is important to us." Michael adds that being sensitive hosts is important; they try to ask guests what they want and like. "If someone picks up the newspaper, we leave them alone. Otherwise, we'll talk."

Guests can make themselves at home in the kitchen, make popcorn, use the microwave or the dishwasher, check the refrigerator for beverages, frozen yogurt, and other good snacks. "People can bring food in if they want," Michael says. There's also access to a copier (some of their scientists are busy with laptop computers) as well as such homey things as sewing and ironing needs, shampoo, conditioner, or anything else you might have forgotten. "I've even fixed people's cars," Michael says with a laugh.

The Paisleys are from Los Angeles, and they were looking for a nice mountain hamlet with friendly and accommodating people. This they have found in Los Alamos, but perhaps because they are so friendly and accommodating themselves! There are books to read, a dartboard to toss at, games of checkers to play.

There's a lot to do nearby, too, from the Larry Walkup Aquatic Center a few streets away to more rugged outdoor activity. "If you're any kind of outdoors person, you can do anything," Michael promises. "Great biking, ice skating, rock climbing at Bandolier National Monument, great trout fishing . . ." What a grand place for an all-around vacation!

How to get there: From Central Street (in center of town) go west to Canyon Street. Turn left to Diamond Street (next signal), right on Diamond to Orange Street (next signal), right on Orange, and down the hill. The inn is on the left.

Innkeepers: Susanne and Michael Paisley
Address/Telephone: 3496 Orange Street; (505) 662–2651
Rooms: 7; 3 with private bath; wheelchair accessible; no air conditioning (elevation 7,500 feet). No smoking inn.
Rates: \$55 to \$75, double; \$5 extra person; EPB.
Open: All year.
Facilities and activities: Group lunch and dinner by reservation, gourmet cooking classes; bicycles, golf clubs, tennis racquets, and skis and assorted boots available. Nearby: restaurants, Aquatic Center, golf, tennis, hiking, skiing, canoeing, rafting, Indian pueblos and prehistoric ruins, shops, Bradbury Science Museum.
Business travel: Airport pickup, town and lab shuttle, fax, copier, government rates.

Mesón de Mesilla

MESILLA, NEW MEXICO 88046

Mesón de Mesilla is innovative in that it is solar heated. Innkeeper Chuck Walker did research at nearby New Mexico Solar Institute before building the inn.

Everything is new and fresh and bright. All rooms open off the wide balcony that encircles the building. The painted tile work in the entry is especially attractive.

The parlor has a fireplace (great for chilly New Mexican evenings). A pile of towels waits by the door for guests heading for the pool just outside.

Chuck left the insurance business to become an innkeeper, and he is serious enough about his hosting to be very disappointed when a guest declines the gourmet breakfast he takes pride in. He didn't have that trouble with me. My problem was deciding whether I would have the eggs Benedict or the lemon soufflé French toast! I chose the latter, and the plate was garnished with fresh fruit in a positively French manner.

"You have to love people to be in this business," said Chuck, "and I meet the most marvelous people in the world." He joked that when he was in the insurance business, people avoided him at parties, but now they don't run anymore. "I've turned eighteen years of total rejection into these years of total acceptance," he said happily.

He and his late wife Merci patterned their inn after California ones that they admired, those with "a fine restaurant, good food, small size, and an intimate atmosphere."

Chef Bobby Herrera, who has been with the inn since its opening, offers three specials for lunch each day. Lunch is either buffet or a la carte; the dinner menu features such specialties as fillet of salmon champagne, scampi *alla pescatora,* and beef Wellington, and Chef Herrera checks on diners to make sure they're happy and satisfied. No doubt about that, because reservations are a must. "We're offering more fish and seafood," Bobby says, "and it's all fresh—no frozen, which always surprises people who think that's not possible in New Mexico." The all-you-can-eat Sunday champagne brunch is crammed with good food, and the inn offers full service cocktails.

Chuck delights in sending guests to "the best theater in the Southwest," the American Southwest Theater, directed by playwright Mark Medoff. The inn will also pack lunches for hikers to Aguirre Springs, a hiking trail overlooking the New Mexican missile range.

How to get there: Take exit 140 off Highway 10 or I–25 to University Avenue to Avenida de Mesilla.

Innkeeper: Chuck Walker
Address/Telephone: 1803 Avenida de Mesilla; (505) 525–9212
Rooms: 13; all with private bath, phone and TV provided as requested. Pets permitted by prior arrangement.
Rates: $52 to $82, double, EPB.
Open: All year.
Facilities and activities: Restaurant open for lunch Wednesday, Thursday, and Friday, for dinner Tuesday through Saturday; Sunday brunch; banquet room for sixty-five people; swimming pool; bicycles. Nearby: Old Mesilla Plaza, with shops and restaurants, where Gadsden Purchase Treaty was signed and Billy the Kid was imprisoned.

Monjeau Shadows Inn
NOGAL, NEW MEXICO 88341

Monjeau Shadows is the perfect answer to just what makes a country inn different from a motel: There's a lot more ambience, even if there's probably no swimming pool. One of the supreme pleasures in this almost perfect setting is to sit on the porch and watch the hummingbirds, or hike down one of the nature trails to the treehouse.

The inn is famous for the hummingbird watch in summertime. J.R. sets up feeders, which also attract many other species, making great bird watching. "We take the feeders down every September so the birds can go to a warmer climate, but we sure miss them," Kay says. The sundeck and the porch beneath it offer a gorgeous view of the mountains all around. The house, perched high on a hill, is surrounded by 200-year-old alligator junipers as well as piñon and ponderosa pine.

"See over yonder?" J.R. gestures. "We'll have all those acres around the trees trimmed so you can walk under them." The driveway is lined with flowers; so is the house, and the patch of grass in front is smooth and green. "I love to do the work," he adds, gazing about fondly.

More famous, perhaps, than the hummingbirds, are Kay's musical evenings. "I had my own band in Lubbock [Texas]: Kay Calloway's," she says, and from her bubbling, enthusiastic personality, you know she was good. Better yet, she hasn't stopped being musical. "Now we have jam sessions on Sunday nights. Local groups come over and we have a ball. We set up outside, weather permitting, and guests can stay over and join in." One member of a local group is Kay's sister Jean Rhotan from Ruidoso.

Monjeau Shadows, a charming Victorian-era farmhouse, was built as a private home before it was opened as a country inn. The two-story living room has a stained-glass skylight; the bright colors shine with sunlight by day and are illuminated by lights at night. A lot of weddings take place here—"Do we ever have a lot of brides!" Kay says—and one of the reasons might be the long staircase, which is a picture-perfect setting for a wedding gown and train. The balcony above has bookshelves and a French door leading to a sun deck.

"It's not only for weddings, but for anniversaries, too. We decorate the room with balloons and banners and have a fruit basket waiting," Kay says.

There's also a lounge with books and a television set. In the inn's lower level, there's a large game room with bar, pool table, and a separate lounge with a sofa bed which can be put into service for extra guests.

J.R. not only keeps up the eight and a half acres of wilderness beauty, he's also the chef, serving Spanish eggs, bacon, and an artistic fruit plate of grapes, canteloupe, watermelon, and strawberries with a flourish. His biscuits are a dream, almost eclipsing the muffins.

Ruidosa, 13 miles south, has shops and good restaurants, and Kay and J.R. can recommend the best. But the horses at Ruidoso Downs? For that, you're on your own!

How to get there: Take Highway 48 13 miles north of Ruidoso to Highway 37 and go west approximately 2⁹⁄₁₀ mile markers (between markers 15 and 16). Turn left at the inn sign.

Innkeepers: Kay and J.R. Newton
Address/Telephone: Bonito Route; (505) 336–4191
Rooms: 5, plus two-bedroom suite; 4 with private bath.
Rates: $75, double; $90, suite; EPB.
Open: All year.
Facilities and activities: Dinner by reservation, game room with pool table, picnic tables, hiking paths on ten acres, musical evenings. Nearby: fishing on Bonito Lake, skiing at Ski Apache, Ruidoso Downs horseracing, shops and restaurants.

Adobe & Pines Inn

RANCHO DE TAOS, NEW MEXICO 87557

Even the innkeepers admit that if you're not watching for the orange, blue, and turquoise poles that mark the road to the inn, you'll miss the turn-off. But, like me, you can always turn around and look again. And once you find it, you'll get a friendly welcome from Rascal, the cocker-terrier, who, says Charil, "along with our horse Desi, requests no other pets at the inn."

And what an inn; it's full of beauty, beginning with the lovely mural at the end of the 80-foot-long portale, a 1950s scene of the famous Taos Pueblo. "We didn't come into this blind," Charil says. "We even hired a consultant who told us what to expect from innkeeping." She laughs. "We've had our eyes opened more ever since."

Like so many happy innkeepers, they were looking for a lifestyle different from their hectic one in San Diego. They sold everything they owned and traveled in Europe for a year. "We didn't know we were doing our homework," Chuck says. They landed in Taos because Chuck had a birthday and Charil surprised him with tickets to the balloon festival in Albuquerque. While there they chanced to look at an advertisement on business opportunities. "Taos was not a plan, but we fell in love, made an offer.

"Then we had three and a half months of intense renovation," Chuck says ruefully of the 150-year-old adobe home on four acres of fruit and pine trees. He brightens up. "But it's all

Charil's decor. She does a dynamite gourmet breakfast, too!"

This was true. It was so gorgeous that guests left the table to get cameras for photos before we destroyed the 4-inch-tall puff pastry hiding banana yogurt and the German pancakes smothered with fresh raspberries and golden raisins.

Chuck is no slouch, either, when it comes to muffins. Lemon poppyseed, apple cinnamon . . . "Guests dub them Chuck's killer muffins," Charil says. They've had so many requests for recipes that Chuck has compiled their own Southwest cookbook.

Rooms are beautiful, too. Two open off the portale: Puerta Azul, a blue room with an antique writing desk and a hand-painted kiva fireplace, and Puerta Verde, green and rust colors with a romantic canopy bed and sitting area by the fireplace. "We utilized the one hundred-year-old 'Dutch' doors," Charil says: They open at the top for a view outside without opening the entire door.

Puerta Rosa, off the courtyard, conceals a surprise under vaulted ceilings: an oversized, sunken bathroom with Mexican tiles surrounding a large cedar sauna (and a separate shower). There's a fireplace to warm the room and another in the bedroom by the sitting area. Puerta Turquesa, a separate guest cottage off the courtyard, has a jet whirlpool bath as well as two fireplaces. There's a kitchen here, too, if you want to stay a while and make yourself at home.

During afternoon hors d'oeuvres, relax and ask about the underground tunnel built for escaping from Indians.

How to get there: The inn is off Highway 68 in Rancho de Taos, a small settlement 4 miles south of Taos. The turn-off to the inn, which is on the east side of the road, is marked by orange, blue, and turquoise poles 3/10 mile south of St. Francis Plaza and 4 miles north of the Steakout Restaurant. Both landmarks are on the east side of the road.

Innkeepers: Charil and Chuck Fulkerson
Address/Telephone: P.O. Box 837; (505) 751–0947 or (800) 723–8267, fax (505) 758–8423
Rooms: 5; all with private bath, 1 with TV. No smoking inn.
Rates: $85 to $145, double; $15 extra person; EPB and afternoon snacks.
Open: All year.
Facilities and activities: Jet tub. Nearby: Historic Church St. Francis de Assisi; shopping; art galleries; seven minutes from Taos with its historic Plaza, galleries, shops, and restaurants; historic Taos Pueblo; Kit Carson House; Rio Grande Gorge; Taos Ski Valley.

Red Violet Inn

RATON, NEW MEXICO 87740

The first thing I asked John was why the inn was called the Red Violet. He laughed. "We wanted our name to be memorable. There's no such thing as a red violet—but there's a Red Violet Inn!" It's a good thing, too, since there's not another inn for miles around. "We're right between Denver and Albuquerque, and Santa Fe and Amarillo, a real good halfway stop for wherever you're going," he says.

The red-brick Victorian home was built on the Santa Fe Trail in 1902 by the Reverend Orvil Eldridge and his wife, Eileen. She played the organ at church, and in those days a lady was known by the hats she wore. "She left us a dozen hats," Ruth says, "and people actually send us more." They festoon the walls of the Hat Room.

Handsome Jacks Room is named for John's Pony Express rider great-uncle. "When I get my Dad in a silly mood," John says, "he tells stories. . . ." So far he hasn't been telling them to guests—maybe you'll be luckier than I!

"Our policy is gourmet food and pampering," Ruth says, "especially since Raton hasn't many really great places to eat." Breakfast may be Mexican soufflés, quiche, crepes, cheesecake, muffins; the lunch menu (by reservation) presents such offerings as Colorado Mountain Chili, chicken asparagus crepes, garlic chicken with wontons, or a surprise called the Go For It Banana Split Lunch.

The pampering that comes with the inn includes fresh flowers, robes, candy, fruit, cookies, and sherry waiting in your room, coffee and tea trays available always, and a 5:00 to 6:00 P.M. social hour with hors d'oeuvres such as an artichoke dip with garlic toast points or a vegetable dip with mini-tostados, wine, and iced tea. Ruth can serve from two to thirty people, and she's generous with her recipes—I left with two, for mushroom/bacon quiche and a flan garnished with orange peel.

Both Ruth and John, casual and relaxed hosts, are collectors of many things, all displayed somewhere or other in the inn. John's plate collection—old Norman Rockwell plates and a row of colorful Chinese children—surrounds the dining room. The stair landing boasts Ruth's bottle collection, and high on the walls of the Homestead Room you'll find an intriguing collection of washboards and other reminders of the hardships of pioneer life while you loll in the comfort of bright modern furnishings and linens. The entry hall is filled with many green plants. The twin sofas in the parlor, brightly Victorian, are an eyeful.

Ruth was a librarian at the University of Colorado, and John had a silkscreen manufacturing business. "We've worked together successfully as partners and friends for more than twenty years," they say, and it looks as though this team will go on together for a lot more than the next twenty.

How to get there: From I–25 coming from the north, take exit 455; from the south take exit 450. Both exits form the I–25 Business Loop, which becomes 2nd Street in town. The inn is just north of the downtown historic district and on the west side of the street at the corner of 2nd Street and Parsons Street.

Innkeepers: Ruth and John Hanrahan
Address/Telephone: 344 North 2nd Street; (505) 445–9778 or (800) 624–9778
Rooms: 4; 2 with private bath, all with telephone. No smoking inn.
Rates: $45 to $65, double; $10 extra person; EPB and afternoon snacks.
Open: March through January.
Facilities and activities: Lunch and dinner by reservation; washer/dryer, iron, guest fridge, transportation from bus or rail (Amtrak). Nearby: historic downtown area, live performances at Shuler Theater, art gallery and antiques shops, golf, racetrack, hiking, and fishing; skiing 45 miles away.
Recommended Country Inns® Travel Club Benefit: 25% discount, Sunday–Thursday; 2-for-1 dinner, with advance reservations; subject to availability.

Chinguague Compound

SAN JUAN PUEBLO, NEW MEXICO 87566

You pronounce *Chinguague* "ching-wa-yea," which isn't hard at all—my difficulty was in remembering it! The name of the arroyo you have to cross to get to this fascinating inn means "wide place" in the language of the San Juan Indians.

Before I could cross the arroyo, I had to drive through the town of San Juan Pueblo and ask for help in finding it. The obliging switchboard operator at the town police station said they often send guests on their way with a police escort! But she called Philip Blood, who came and got me. (He was coming in to town to get the mail, anyway.)

By now I imagine you've tumbled to the fact that this is an unusual place. Situated close to the banks of the Rio Grande in the midst of the San Juan Indian Reservation, Chinguague Compound is an idyllic retreat of several adobe casitas. Contented guests take long walks along the river, go fishing, or bird watching, read the hundreds of books, play the classical music records, loaf, and watch the sunrise and sunset over the Sangre de Cristo Mountains.

"When people come here the first time, they don't believe it," says JB, who claims to be on perpetual vacation. Both she and Philip are fugitives from back East, delighted to be in the inn business.

"It's fantastic—we've met people from all

over the world. We find bed and breakfast people just wonderful. We invite all our guests to breakfast, though they can cook their own; but we've even had a guest with dietary restrictions who would come—she'd just bring her own breakfast!"

It's hard to stay away. Aside from the good company, guests dine on JB's blue corn waffles or cornmeal pancakes with New Hampshire maple syrup, sausage, homemade granola and coffeecake, and fruit-and-yogurt parfait. Wheat and corn are freshly ground as needed for baking; JB and Philip grow their own corn and grow the fruit to make apricot and plum preserves or peach-flavored honey.

As if grinding your own flour is not enough, I caught JB actually ironing sheets. "I don't like polyester," she said firmly. "There's something about sleeping between freshly ironed sheets . . ." It all fits in with the salubrious atmosphere at Chinguague Compound, where the resident Dobermans, Hildi and Clio, are as friendly as their owners. And as relaxed.

Jim Petty is artist-in-residence. "That's his work on the walls," Philip points out. His work is also shown in a gallery in Santa Fe.

How to get there: Take Highway 84/285 to Route 68 and exit at San Juan Pueblo. Turn right at the white water tank and ask for help at the police station on the right by the post office! (Or call, and help will be forthcoming.)

Innkeepers: JB (Joan) and Philip Blood
Address/Telephone: P.O. Box 1118; (505) 852–2194
Rooms: 3 casitas of from 1 to 5 rooms; all with private bath, kitchen, living area with kiva (Indian "beehive" fireplace), screened porch, TV, AM/FM tape player. No smoking inn.
Rates: $78 to $159, double, EPB. Deposit for one night's lodging required. Reservations strongly recommended; two-night minimum; 10 percent discount for 7 or more days.
Open: All year.
Facilities and activities: Library, games, TV. Nearby: Indian events in the Eight Northern Pueblos; Santa Fe Opera House 17 miles south, July–August season.

Adobe Abode

SANTA FE, NEW MEXICO 87501

"I'm a collector of all types of things," Pat says, and wherever your eyes alight they rest on something beautiful, interesting, fascinating. I loved the colorful Mexican *animalitos* (little animals) and the Philippine overseer's chair.

"I go off to the flea markets and come back with treasures," she says. Could be because Pat and her daughter, Allison Harbour, have an artist's eye: Pat's background is fashion and advertising and Allison studied at New York's Parson's School of Design. It was she who created the inn's award-winning logo, a colorful, stylized bed-and-fried-egg combo.

The inn is hung with many fine paintings; a painting by Allison takes pride of place over the living-room fireplace. The room is Southwestern-style, complete with Indian artifacts, vigas, a fireplace—and cable television.

The sixty-eight-year-old small adobe house, pink with blue trim, is just 4 blocks from the Plaza. Set on a corner, it's bounded by a low stone fence, with a narrow sitting area on the side of the house and a lovely garden hidden behind high walls in the back. There's comfortable wicker furniture in which to relax and enjoy the blue skies and fresh Santa Fe air, which Pat says "has been polluted by nothing more than the Indian smoke signals of ages past."

The room called The Casita has its own private, walled patio, and the wall beside the

Southwestern–style four poster is hung with a collection of western hats, typical of the originality with which Pat has decorated her inn.

Pat's artistry hasn't stopped with decorating; every meal boasts a different menu and place setting. Two guests stayed for fourteen days and returned for a sixteen-day stay. "It was a challenge to come up with breakfast menus and place settings for their entire stay, but we did it!" Pat says.

I got to sample only one menu, but it was delicious. Fresh orange juice and pineapple were followed by carmelized French toast (which I had to agree with Pat was absolutely decadent) and crusty cinnamon muffins. I hope to return for Pat's famous Santa Fe Cheese Casserole, Apple Skillet Cake, and Fiesta Baked Tomatoes, all of which have been selected for inclusion in a regional cookbook. But of her blueberry muffins, Pat says "Unfortunately, that's a family recipe I have sworn not to divulge."

I love the questionnaire that Pat hopes each guest will fill out. It includes such questions as What I like *best* about AA's breakfast (muffins, entrees, etc.) and what I like *least* about AA's breakfast.

Pat keeps adding things "to make your visit a little nicer," she says. There are Adobe Abode terrycloth robes embroidered with the inn's crest, special Adobe Abode soap, shampoo, conditioner, and lotion in little Adobe Abode bottles; morning newspapers; and Santa Fe cookies. These last were new to me, so I had to taste each flavor; I have to recommend chocolate piñon nut.

As for seeing the sights of Santa Fe, "My guests tell me I'm the best travel guide in the area," Pat boasts.

How to get there: From I–25 north take the St. Francis exit and go 3 miles north to Cerrillos. Turn right onto Guadalupe, crossing Alameda. Go 3 more blocks on Guadalupe to McKenzie, and turn right to Chapelle. The inn is on the left-hand corner.

Innkeeper: Pat Harbour
Address/Telephone: 202 Chapelle; (505) 983–3133
Rooms: 5; all with private bath, 1 with wheelchair access. No smoking inn.
Rates: $85 to $150, double; $20 extra person; EPB.
Open: All year.
Facilities and activities: Nearby: Governor's Palace; Santa Fe Plaza with shops, galleries, and restaurants; Fine Arts Museum; St. Francis Cathedral; Mission of San Miguel; Santa Fe Opera; Indian pueblos.
Recommended Country Inns® Travel Club Benefit: Stay two nights, get third night free, Monday–Thursday, November 1–March 31.

Alexander's Inn

SANTA FE, NEW MEXICO 87501

Alexander's Inn is a surprise in New Mexico—it's not an adobe hacienda. The two-story American country–style house is located in a residential area on Santa Fe's historic east side. Built in 1903, it has retained the cozy feeling of a family dwelling. With the help of a resident gardener, the beautiful flower gardens, both front and back, are filled with a riot of roses, tulips, lilacs, poppies, and peonies most of the year.

"I'm a born hostess," Carolyn says as she sets a plate of warm-from-the-oven raisin oatmeal cookies right under my nose. "I love setting the table, arranging flowers." She used to manage a restaurant, but managing the inn is better by far, she says enthusiastically. "I love being at home, being a homemaker, nurturing people where it's quiet, intimate, where I can interact with guests."

At Alexander's Inn guests are encouraged to make themselves at home, make themselves coffee or tea, put food in the refrigerator, have friends over and visit in the cozy living room/dining area. The roomy entry, too, has a corner by a window where guests can relax.

There are plants and books and a collection of menus. Carolyn herself is a fount of information. "I've lived here for years and I can help people really get around."

The quaint inn is full of nooks and crannies, skylights and eaves. The Master Bedroom has a four-poster king bed, a skylight, a large bricked bath, and a sitting area in front of the fireplace. Rooms 3 and 4 have four-poster queen beds and private baths. Up the narrow stairs, two guest rooms share a large bath; one has twin beds and the other an iron-and-brass queen bed.

Check-in brings tea and cookies, a nice afternoon pick-me-up. Both breakfast and afternoon tea are as often as not served outside on the patio to take advantage of Santa Fe's lovely weather. Homemade granola, blueberry muffins, cereals, and fruit—such as a mélange of pineapple, strawberries, and kiwi—are served for breakfast.

And the teatime plate of cookies I almost finished single-handed weren't just everyday oatmeal cookies. "They're pear, raisin, walnut oatmeal cookies," Carolyn says, explaining the different taste I detect. "It's the pear."

Alexander's Inn guests can snack with impunity—they can work it off with swimming, indoor or outdoor tennis, exercise classes, and machines at the El Gaucho Health Club.

How to get there: Exit I–25 at Old Pecos Trail, which turns into the Old Santa Fe Trail. Turn right at Paseo de Peralta and follow around curve to Palace Avenue. Turn right and go 3 blocks. Alexander's Inn is the old brick-and-wood building on the left. There is a sign.

Innkeeper: Carolyn Lee
Address/Telephone: 529 East Palace Avenue; (505) 986–1431
Rooms: 5; 3 with private bath; no air conditioning (elevation 7,000 feet). No smoking inn.
Rates: $65 to $150, seasonal, double; $15 additional person; continental breakfast and afternoon tea.
Open: All year.
Facilities and activities: Sun deck, patio, mountain bikes; guest privileges at El Gaucho Health Club. Nearby: Santa Fe Plaza, with shops, art galleries, museums, and historic buildings, is within walking distance.
Recommended Country Inns® Travel Club Benefit: Stay two nights, get third night free, Monday–Thursday, November 15–March 1, except holidays.

Dos Casas Viejas
SANTA FE, NEW MEXICO 87501

Santa Fe seems to be a happy place for people to embark upon new careers. Back in San Francisco, Jois (pronounced "Joyce") was an interior designer and Irving had retired as a dentist.

"We wanted to be in Santa Fe, but we still wanted to work," Jois says. "This is absolutely perfect for us. We like to decorate, cook, entertain, talk with people—we've taken our favorite hobbies and turned them into a business."

It took two years of hunting to find what they were looking for, and what they found was not quite what they expected: not one, but a pair of 1860s adobe buildings! Which is how the inn called Dos Casas Viejas was born: the name means "two old houses."

Jois doesn't exactly say they were in bad shape, but "as a designer, I saw them the way they would be, not the way they were." Irving was optimistic, too, when she said, "We could fix them up." He loved it: "Goody, I get to do some work." What a husband!

But it wasn't all a bed of roses (although Irving is quite a rose gardener). There are strict regulations in Santa Fe when it comes to historic property. "You keep everything the way it is" is the edict, which presents quite a challenge.

The historic buildings lie within a half-acre compound enclosed by walls 18 inches thick. Passing through the gate into the courtyard is like driving into the narrow street of a pueblo in

Old Mexico. The walls of the courtyard blend into the thick walls of the buildings, and you're surrounded by pink adobe; the only thing missing is the cobblestones.

To the right is the main house, with its long, shaded portale. It contains the lobby/library and dining room. Straight ahead and a little to the left is the second house, which houses the guest rooms. Each one has a private entrance off the secluded courtyard.

Guest rooms are furnished with authentic Southwest antiques, and you know Jois and Irving had a great time seeking them out. All have original vigas (beams) and great lighting; the mirrors are flattering. Jois says, "A good decorator knows how to take care of these things." There are also flowers, bath sheets, and wood-burning kiva fireplaces for chilly days and nights. On warm, sunny days guests like to sit outside by the heated lap pool (and exercise in it, of course) and listen to the fountain cascading into the far end of the pool.

Breakfast can be served there, or in the dining room, or, if you like, you can carry a basket back to the privacy of your room. It's a continental meal, but more than just coffee and doughnuts—fresh-squeezed orange juice, fresh raspberries or blackberries, chocolate yogurt coffeecake, or maybe pistachio yeast bread.

Irving does the yeast breads, Jois the others, and they pride themselves on never repeating with the same guests. "We have twenty-eight different recipes," they brag.

How to get there: From I–25 north take the St. Francis exit, and go 3⁸⁄₁₀ miles into town. At Agua Fria Street, turn right. The inn is 2 blocks on the right, next to Guadalupe Inn. There is a sign.

Innkeepers: Jois and Irving Belfield
Address/Telephone: 610 Agua Fria Street; (505) 983–1636
Rooms: 5; all with private bath, phone, and TV, 1 with wheelchair access. No smoking inn.
Rates: $125 to $185, double, EPB.
Open: All year.
Facilities and activities: Lap pool. Nearby: Governor's Palace; Santa Fe Plaza, with shops, galleries, and restaurants; Fine Arts Museum; St. Francis Cathedral; Mission of San Miguel; Santa Fe Opera; Institute of American Indian Arts Museum; Santuario de Guadalupe; Loretto Chapel; Cross of the Martyrs; Indian pueblos.

El Paradero en Santa Fe

SANTA FE, NEW MEXICO 87501

El Paradero is Spanish for "the stopping place," a lovely name for this warm and cordial inn. Innkeepers Ouida and Thom are professionals in the best sense of the word, dedicated to and loving the work they have chosen for themselves.

The innkeepers have extensively remodeled this old Spanish adobe farmhouse but have kept its rambling, rabbit-warren character. Santa Fe's Historic Styles Commission approved the plans to leave the old structure a hodgepodge, and the effect is delightful.

The front part of the building is more than 200 years old. Space was doubled circa 1850 with a Territorial-style addition. To complete the charming polyglot effect, the front door is 1912 Victorian, with oval beveled glass. The walls are textured buttermilk and sand, painted, and all is concealed behind a high adobe wall.

Inside, all is light and airy, with high viga ceilings, big windows, and Mexican-tile floors. Green plants hang from the skylight in the breakfast room; the picture window opens the view to the patio; and through the serving window I could see the hand-painted tile decorating the bright, clean kitchen.

The inn has a recent addition: the small Victorian house next door. In it are two luxury suites, each with a fireplace, bedroom, bath, and kitchenette. This house, too, is on the state Historic Register.

There's a lot of common space in this inn: a main *sala* (living room), a cozy television lounge, two dining rooms, patios, and the courtyard are available to guests all day and evening. Tea and treats are served, along with convivial company, in the afternoons. "A lot of our guests are artists and writers, and it's fun for them and fun for us," says Ouida.

Ouida is active on the city council, but she still has time to be a gracious hostess. She also grows parsley and other herbs, and each breakfast is a gastronomical adventure. *Huevos avocado*, two poached eggs on an avocado half with salsa and cheese, take my vote. And there is always freshly squeezed orange juice, fresh fruit, freshly ground coffee—and for tea-sippers like me, forty-five varieties!

Santa Fe, a tourist town, has many fine restaurants. Ouida and Thom will gladly recommend their favorites, most around the Plaza, within walking distance of the inn.

How to get there: From I–25 south take the Old Pecos Trail exit into town. Take a left on Paseo de Peralta and turn right on Galisteo. The inn is on the southeast corner of Galisteo and Manhattan. From I–25 north take the St. Francis exit, follow it to Hickox, turn left before it becomes Paseo de Peralta, cross Cerrillos Road, and turn left on Galisteo.

Innkeepers: Ouida MacGregor and Thom Allen
Address/Telephone: 220 West Manhattan Avenue; (505) 988–1177
Rooms: 14, including 2 suites; suites with private bath and kitchenette, all with phone, some with air conditioning, 2 with TV. Pets permitted.
Rates: $60 to $120, double, EPB and afternoon snacks. No credit cards.
Open: All year.
Facilities and activities: Picnics by reservation; dinners for groups that fill the whole inn. Nearby: five-minute walk to historic Santa Fe Plaza, with art galleries, restaurants, and historic buildings.

Four Kachinas
SANTA FE, NEW MEXICO 87501

Kachinas are Hopi dolls—but they're not toys. They are sacred objects for Hopi children to study. Bright and elaborate, they represent a variety of gods, spirits, departed ancestors and such. They make a wonderful theme for this inn: Each room represents one of these supernatural beings, with the decor reflecting the kachina's persona.

Tawa represents the Hopi Sun God; it's the only room on the second floor. It has a window seat with a view of the Sangre de Cristo Mountains. Each of the other three rooms, downstairs, has a small, private garden patio. As for the kachinas, they're from John's collection; you might have Poko the Dog, Hon the White Bear, or Koyemsi the Mudhead Clown. All four rooms are decorated with custom-made furniture, colorful Navajo rugs, and lovely antiques.

Andrew is an architect, and in California John was a combination of caterer and social services worker. "He's used to soothing people," Andrew says.

"This is a people business, too," John answers. "We're very much in people's lives. Sometimes they show up late, are cranky, we help them get oriented, give them a soothing cup of tea. . . ."

Sounds great to me! Being pampered is a large part of the charm of staying at an inn, and John and Andrew have made a serious study of this. Having been to Japan three times, they were very impressed with Japanese hospitality. They've patterned Four Kachinas after an inn in Kyoto. "We like the Japanese style of hospitality, the personal contact, the bringing of breakfast."

Consequently, your continental breakfast can be brought to your door if you like. You're presented with a form ready to be filled out, with your selections of juice, fresh fruit, yogurt, and homemade pastries to be checked, as well as the time you'd like to have it. "I've never been keen on waking up on my travels and facing a bunch of strangers," John says. "I want to have my coffee in my room."

But if you prefer to be sociable, the old adobe garage in the courtyard has been converted into a guest lounge. You can shop there too if you like: There's a variety of travel books, maps, and guidebooks, as well as a nice collection of art, silver jewelry, and Indian crafts for sale.

John is the pastry chef, and he's good. A lot of noses were out of joint when his coconut pound cake took "Best of Show" at the 1992 Santa Fe County Fair. John laughs. "Yes, I won the prize. People are still bitter about it!" (It's usually captured by women bakers, not a man who's a newcomer to Santa Fe.)

Kachinas are not the only history connected with this interesting inn. Andrew and John built it from scratch, but the land it's on has an interesting history. It belonged originally to the Digneo family, who came from back East to build Santa Fe's St. Francis Cathedral. The family was sponsored by the very archbishop, Jean Baptiste Lamy, who is the central figure in Willa Cather's novel *Death Comes to the Archbishop*.

How to get there: From I–25 north take the Cerrillos exit north to Paseo de Peralta. Go right on Peralta to Webber, across from the New Mexico State Capitol. Turn right on Webber. The inn is at 512 Webber.

Innkeepers: Andrew Beckerman and John Daw
Address/Telephone: 512 Webber Street; (505) 982–2550 or (800) 397–2564
Rooms: 4; all with private bath, phone, and TV, 1 with wheelchair access. No smoking inn.
Rates: $85 to $110, double, continental breakfast.
Open: All year.
Facilities and activities: Nearby: Santa Fe Plaza, with shops, galleries, and restaurants; Governor's Palace; Fine Arts Museum; St. Francis Cathedral; Mission of San Miguel; Santa Fe Opera; Institute of American Indian Arts Museum; Santuario de Guadalupe; Loretto Chapel; Cross of the Martyrs; Indian pueblos.
Recommended Country Inns® Travel Club Benefit: 10% discount, Sunday–Thursday, December, February, and March, except holidays.

Grant Corner Inn

SANTA FE, NEW MEXICO 87501

On each guest room door of this handsome Santa Fe Colonial home hangs a red-velvet-and-lace heart that says WELCOME. This should give you a hint of the cordiality of this inn. But there's a sense of humor at work here, too. The reverse side of the stuffed velvet heart on your door will say BEWARE OF OCCUPANT.

"We can't really pamper our guests, but we can come pretty close," says Louise. Close—like fruit, fresh flowers, and ice water in your room, plus a terry robe if you're sharing a bath. Like a personal welcome card. Like warm, personal care not only from the family but from all the inn staff.

Begin with this truly outstanding tall blue-and-white house on the corner of Grant Avenue. It's surrounded by a spanking-white picket fence and absolutely draped in weeping willows. Inside, blue-and-white walls, white drapes, and the warm woods of antique furniture meld with the large antique oriental rugs covering polished wood floors. There's a convenient restroom on the first floor.

Guest rooms have antique pine and brass beds, and you can have twin, double, queen, or king (some of them four-poster), depending on which room you choose. Double Deluxe rooms—numbers 7 and 8—have their own porch, and four rooms have space for a rollaway.

Louise is an interior designer with a background in the hotel business, so you can see why Grant Corner Inn is pretty much of a masterpiece.

She also doubles as chef, creating eggs Florentine, banana waffles, and a special New Mexican soufflé. Louise compiled the *Grant Corner Inn Breakfast and Brunch Cookbook*. Need I say more?

In the winter breakfast is served in front of the blazing dining-room fire. In the summer you can have it on the front veranda, under the willows. Complimentary wine and hors d'oeuvres are offered to inn guests in the evening.

Louise is eager to provide guests with information on local events, such as the Indian pueblos and their dances and music and art festivals, as well as the renowned Santa Fe Opera, with a July–August season. Santa Fe Plaza, practically on the inn doorstep, is lined with shops and restaurants, art galleries, and curio shops. Don't miss the art museum, housed in one more of Santa Fe's pink adobe buildings.

How to get there: The inn is on the corner of Grant and Johnson just south of Santa Fe Plaza. Grant is the street that borders the Plaza on the west.

Innkeeper: Louise Stewart
Address/Telephone: 122 Grant Avenue; (505) 983–6678
Rooms: 13; 11 with private bath, all with phone and TV, 1 with wheelchair access. No smoking inn.
Rates: $70 to $140, double, EPB and evening refreshments.
Open: All year except January.
Facilities and activities: Picnic, lunch, and dinner for 12 or more by reservation; afternoon tea, open to public; yearly bazaar between Thanksgiving and Christmas. Nearby: historic Santa Fe Plaza 1 block away, Anthropological Museum.

The Guadalupe Inn

SANTA FE, NEW MEXICO 87501

Don't be put off by the deserted-looking, old-fashioned store to the right of the entrance into The Guadalupe Inn's Courtyard. The inn is a family business, built by two sisters and their brother on family property, and that little store was their grandfather's. Which makes this a family business in the best sense of the term.

The street in front of the inn, Agua Fria, was once the famous Camino Real, connecting northern New Mexico (only it wasn't that then) with Mexico. First Indian, then Hispanic traders traced the route. This is the historic Guadalupe District, less than a mile from Santa Fe Plaza.

"We used to work in the store," Dolores says, "since I was eight and Henrietta was seven. The front buildings were our grandparents' home and store. When they died the family said if anybody wanted it, they'd listen. So we bought it from the estate, but we couldn't decide what to do with it."

They let it sit for four or five years, until inspiration struck. Pete is in heating and air conditioning and metal roofing, and in New Mexico, Dolores says, you can construct your own building. So, Eureka! They decided to build an inn.

"We each got three rooms to decorate," Dolores says. "I never decorated anything in my life!" But wait until you see the rooms—each is more delightful than the next.

Guest rooms have no names, just numbers,

and number 3 is one of Dolores's creations. She carved the back of the wooden luggage rack in the room, and it's amazing. "Henrietta carves," she notes, "and I wanted to see if I could do it, too." The rooms, off galleries or balconies, with views of the Sangre de Cristo and Jemez mountains, are furnished with wonderful Southwestern pieces, and a surprising number were made by these artistic innkeepers.

I loved Henrietta's multicolored bed in number 11. The room also has an old-fashioned bathtub, surrounded by mirrors. Number 5 has a colorful sunburst bed and a desk in an alcove. Number 8, one of Pete's rooms, has blue-covered beds. Colors are all soft Southwest blues and pinks and grays, warmed by the golden tones of the wood and cooled by the white adobe walls.

And—I did say it was a family business, didn't I?—nephew Chris Quintana made the beautiful metal sconces covering the gallery lights, and a little niece even decorated one of the guest rooms.

Mother Quintana comes in to lend a hand. "Mom loves it," Dolores says. "She used to work at La Fonda (a local hotel) in her youth. She met a lot of artists who are real famous now. Back then they were just trying to begin. She comes in every morning and fries bacon; then she has breakfast with guests, tells them all her art stories." Which is a real treat.

Breakfast is a feast. In addition to Mother Quintana's bacon, we had our choice of *huevos rancheros*, burritos, or a western omelet, finishing off with turnovers of cherry, strawberry, apple, apricot, or peach. "Our turnovers are terrific," Dolores says as she hands me a peach one, and oh my, are they ever!

How to get there: From I–25 north take the St. Francis exit 3⁸⁄₁₀ miles into town, to Agua Fria. Turn right, and the inn is 2 blocks on the right, next to Dos Casas Viejas Inn.

Innkeepers: Henrietta Quintana, Dolores Quintana Myers, and Pete Quintana
Address/Telephone: 604 Agua Fria; (505) 989–7422
Rooms: 12, including 2-bedroom suite; all with private bath, phone, and TV, some with Jacuzzi, 1 with wheelchair access. No smoking inn.
Rates: $125 to $175, double, EPB.
Open: All year.
Facilities and activities: Hot tub. Nearby: Santa Fe Plaza with shops, galleries, and restaurants; Governor's Palace; Fine Arts Museum; St. Francis Cathedral; Mission of San Miguel; Santa Fe Opera; Institute of American Indian Arts Museum; Loretto Chapel; Indian pueblos.
Business travel: Located in downtown Santa Fe. Phones in every room; meeting room.

Preston House

SANTA FE, NEW MEXICO 87501

This charming house is the only Queen Anne in New Mexico, Signe told me. "This house has been a real pleasure. It's different from anything in Santa Fe, or in all of New Mexico, and the minute I saw it I wanted to own it!"

It was built in 1886 and has some wonderful features. The large arched window halfway up the stairs faces west, and the window seat on the large landing is a favored spot for afternoon refreshment.

The staircase itself, all gold and black lacquer, is very unusual. "It looks oriental," I said to the innkeeper. "It is," she replied. "It was built by Chinese workmen who came to build the railroad. This is the only way they knew to build."

Signe, an artist, remodeled the house and turned it into an inn because that seemed the perfect thing to do with it after it became hers. Many of Signe's paintings grace the walls and are for sale.

With her artist's vision, Signe wanted guests to see her inn as an exciting experience, not just as a place to spend the night. My favorite room is number 1, whose fireplace is of tile with a built-in wood cupboard. The flowered wallpaper, high ceilings, and lacquered oval oriental nightstands on each side of the king-sized bed were a hit with me. From the third-floor room, another favorite, there's a wonderful view and an outside spiral staircase to the garden below.

The parlor has a communal television in case you want company, as well as an antique armoire, furniture upholstered in cool white, and a tile fireplace. Recently renovated and decorated is the adobe building adjacent to the inn, with rooms furnished in traditional Southwest adobe style. "Now," Signe says, "guests have a choice of Southwestern architecture and furnishings there, or Victorian in the main house."

Breakfast is served in the large dining room, and it's generous. Pear streusel, bread pudding, sour cream coffeecake, four cold cereals, yogurt, and fruit salad are accompanied by homemade jams and jellies. New bread recipes are being added, alternating with standbys, continuously. An afternoon tea is also served between 4:30 and 6:30.

Signe's helpers bake in the evening as well as serve breakfast. "But mostly, everybody here does everything," she says. "They find that after a waitressing stint elsewhere, innkeeping is infinitely superior. This is such a different atmosphere—you get to know people instead of merely serving them." That pretty much sums up the spirit of innkeeping, I think.

How to get there: Take Palace Avenue 4 blocks east of the Plaza. Turn left on Faithway, just 1 block long, and the inn is on the right. (There's Holy Faith Episcopal Church on the corner for a landmark.)

Innkeeper: Signe Bergman
Address/Telephone: 106 Faithway; (505) 982–3465
Rooms: 15 share 14 baths; all with TV, 5 with air conditioning. No smoking inn.
Rates: $48 to $155, double, continental breakfast.
Open: All year.
Facilities and activities: Nearby: historic Santa Fe Plaza, with restaurants, shops, art galleries, and the Palace of the Governors.

Water Street Inn

SANTA FE, NEW MEXICO 87501

What caught my eye upon walking into this award-winning adobe restoration was a bouquet of yellow tulips in such full bloom that they looked like peonies. Then I noticed full pots of flowers blooming everywhere, as well as a candy dish half full of Hershey kisses. "Yes, those are very popular," Dolores explained. "We're small, and we like to take care of individual needs." Nearby were coffee, tea, and soft drinks for guests.

Dolores and Al redid the building as office space, and it gradually evolved into an inn. Al was born in his family's hotel in Louisiana and he had never lived in a house until he married Dolores. "He said he'd never have a hotel—and now we have this!" Dolores exclaims.

The whole family thinks it's a great idea, and youngest son Thomas works alongside his parents. "I made all the curtains," Dolores says, "and Thomas and I tiled all the new bathrooms." And Aurora, who is not a member of the family but fits in as though she is, helps with everything. "She retired from thirty years of nursing, but she just couldn't stay home," Dolores says. "Now she is everything here. If she ever leaves, I'm leaving too!"

The adobe inn has brick floors and oriental rugs, beamed ceilings, four-poster and other antique beds, fireplaces, decks, and patios; some rooms have a sofa, trundle, or futon for extra guests. "This is a quiet, personal place," Dolores says. "Our guests enjoy one another as well as the inn. We have hors d'oeuvres at night, and many guests then go out to dinner together." She and Al run the inn the way they like to live: reading, relaxing, hanging loose.

Dolores does the cooking, but once in a while Aurora surprises her with bread and rolls, or shepherd's pie with potatoes and chili. Another breakfast might be eggs Benedict or eggs Dijon, with muffins and breads, cold cereal, and yogurt sent to your room on order. You can eat there in privacy or in the common room upstairs with comfy furniture, fireplace, and fabulous views. Evenings, wine and cheese or other snacks are served either downstairs or in the upstairs common room.

Rooms are spacious and fresh, bright with new furnishings, and there are blackout curtains if you want to sleep late and waste that good Southwestern sun! Room 1 is a large blue-and-white creation off the downstairs hall next to an interesting hat rack festooned with straw hats and canes. It opens off a patio, as does Room 2. Room 3 is a junior suite, with nice heavy shutters on the windows and a Louisiana cypress four-poster bed. "This is called either acorn or rolling pin," Dolores says of the four posts, and I'm not sure either; I just know it's attractive.

Room 6, upstairs, has pine twin beds and a balcony for breakfast, lounging, and sunset viewing.

How to get there: From I–25 take St. Francis exit (U.S. Highway 84–285) north 2 miles to Cerrillos Road. Go east to Guadalupe until you cross Alameda. Water Street is the next street to the left.

Innkeepers: Dolores and Al Dietz
Address/Telephone: 427 West Water Street; (505) 984–1193
Rooms: 8; all with private bath, phone, and TV; wheelchair access to first floor rooms. Pets upon discretion of innkeeper. No smoking inn.
Rates: $75 to $135, double; $15 extra person; EPB and afternoon refreshments.
Open: All year.
Facilities and activities: Nearby: Santa Fe Plaza with restaurants, galleries, and shops; museums, Santa Fe Opera, Indian pueblos, skiing.

Eaton House

SOCORRO, NEW MEXICO 87801

"This is infinitely more fun than what I did before, and the people are wonderful," Anna says, but I think it works both ways: Both Anna and her inn are wonderful. The building, on the New Mexico Historical Register, was built in 1881 and is a cross between eastern Victorian and New Mexican Territorial. It was built by Colonel Ethan W. Eaton, who was an important figure in the $30-million Magdalene Kelly Mine back in the 1880s. The area is rich in silver, lead, zinc, and copper, as well as more ancient points of interest, such as the Piro Indian petroglyphs in nearby San Acacia.

Socorro in Spanish means "aid" or "help," and the town got the name back in 1598 when Spanish explorers received aid from the Piro Indians, who are believed to have been the area's first inhabitants. The climate, typical of high desert, makes for a great bird-watching area, and many Eaton House guests have come for just that.

"We have hundreds of hummingbirds from April to September, as well as dozens of other species," Anna says. "I pack what I call my early-birder special for guests who want to go out before I serve breakfast. They go out with hot coffee, chocolate, or tea and sweet rolls, and they come back later for a full breakfast." Anna, who used to travel 200,000 miles a year in her field of marketing and interpersonal skills, wanted to live a higher quality of life than what she describes as a "bubble existence. You live in a car, office, plane—you have nothing to do with reality."

Now Anna is into the reality of making sure her guests are taken care of. She feels strongly about no-nitrate meats, range eggs, organic vegetables. Breakfast is a cheese soufflé with apricot topping, brioche, turkey sausage, fresh fruit in season. The lunches she packs to order have tuna or ham and cheese on homemade bread, fruit juice and bottled water, homemade cookies, brownies, fruit cobbler, and her celery-and-carrot "trail mix." Especially good and healthy are Anna's apple-and-raisin crispy cookies!

Guest rooms, bright and comfortable, contain Southwestern furniture, much of it made by a local artisan. In spacious Colonel Eaton's Room, though, there's a four-poster from Santa Fe and an antique 1859 desk and old liquor cabinet. A closet wall in Daughter's Room is all mirrors, and the twin beds were hand carved for twin daughters of the colonel.

"We've had great-granddaughters and sons [of the original family] stay here," Anna says. The *trastero* (combined bench and armoire) in the Vigilante Room is an interesting piece. There's luxury in the down comforters and the huge bath sheets, but the iron bars in the windows of the hallway are a reminder of a 1906 earthquake—that's when the colonel put them in. The only thing changed of the original house are the portales (covered walkways) added so that each room could have its own entrance.

How to get there: From I–25 in Socorro, take Manzanares west to California. Turn south on California for 2 blocks to Church; go west on Church 4 blocks to Eaton, and then south on Eaton to 403.

Innkeepers: Anna Appleby and Tom Harper
Address/Telephone: 403 Eaton Avenue; (505) 835–1067
Rooms: 4 in Main House, plus 2 casitas; all with private bath; handicapped accessible. No smoking inn.
Rates: $75 to $120, seasonal, double, EPB, except June to August continental.
Open: All year.
Facilities and activities: Lunch to take out. Nearby: historic town walking tour, Mineral Museum, New Mexico Tech Golf Course, petroglyphs, observatory, Bosque del Apache Wildlife Refuge, Alamo Indian Reservation, Festival of the Cranes, Fat Tire Fiesta (mountain-bike tours).
Recommended Country Inns® Travel Club Benefit: Stay two nights, get 15% discount on second night, Monday–Thursday, subject to availability.

American Artists Gallery House

TAOS, NEW MEXICO 87571

American Artists Gallery House was one of the first fine inns in these parts, with bright, comfortable guest rooms decorated in pleasing Southwest style and hung with art by local artists. Judie and Elliot Framan were guests at the inn when Judie overheard two of my favorite innkeepers, Ben and Myra Carp, say that they wanted to retire to travel and to spend more time with their grandchildren.

Judie was concerned at the time because Elliot's work as a project engineer for Cal Tech was taking him abroad, and she worried about him traveling out of the country. "Actually, I was spooked," she confesses, "and I wanted to find a way I could keep him at home."

Although at first Elliot looked at her as though he thought she'd lost her mind, she says, he soon came around to her way of thinking. "Retirement?" he now says with a laugh. "What retirement?" They both are dedicated to continuing in the American Artists Gallery tradition of showcasing local, regional, and national artists, as well as developing Elliot's photography. They are dedicated to hospitality as well, continuing the entertaining "happenings" involving guests in the local Taos art scene, which the inn's former owners were known for.

"I have changed Myra's New York Experience breakfast specialty to my New York/California Experience, since we're from

California," Judie says. Now the dish is a wonderful mixture of avocados, jicama, and California red onions. Another delicious breakfast is Judie's quiche Florentine, with fresh spinach and mushrooms, whereas Elliot's specialty is blue corn pancakes with blackberries and syrup. Often served are fresh-baked pecan cinnamon rolls.

The sunroom has become a large dining room facing the inn's famous outdoor garden, thus enlarging the already good-sized common room. The Honeymoon Cottage is new, and Judie plans on having the cottage overlook what she hopes will be an English garden. "Well, an English-type garden, with lots and lots of flowers. We'll have to see what grows here," she says as a concession to the climate, "but I'm hoping for lilacs and roses." Now her interesting cactus collection graces the guest rooms, but she's looking forward to fresh garden flowers, too, as well as raising fruits and vegetables to be used in meal preparation.

"We plan to continue the tradition of making every guest a part of the family, and a friend," she says. "We're eager to learn, along with our guests, the lore and the magic that is Taos."

How to get there: Coming into Taos from the south on Old Santa Fe Road (the main highway through Taos), turn right on Frontier, alongside the Ramada Inn. The inn is on the right a short way down the road.

Innkeepers: Judie and Elliot Framan
Address/Telephone: Frontier Road (mailing address: P.O. Box 584); (505) 758–4446
Rooms: 7, including 1 suite and 1 cottage; all with private bath, 1 with kitchen; no air conditioning (elevation 7,000 feet). No smoking inn.
Rates: $65 to $95, double; $25 extra adult; $15 extra child; EPB.
Open: All year.
Facilities and activities: Hot tub, small conference room, contact with the art community, history, and culture of area. Nearby: historic Taos Plaza with restaurants, shops, and art galleries; hiking, horseback riding, skiing, tours, Taos Indian Pueblo, and museums.

Casa Benavides
TAOS, NEW MEXICO 87571

Barbara Benavides McCarthy is a native *Taoseña*, as is her husband Tom. She wanted to buy the inn property, a mélange of seven adobe buildings, because she had a very personal interest: Her father was among the carpenters who built them.

"Actually, it was a whim," she says. "One of these was my family home; the others belonged to good friends of both our families. Tom said I could buy the property, but I had to make it pay for itself. (Tom has been the businessperson in the family.)

"My cousin said, why don't you open a bed and breakfast, it's no work at all!" This is Barbara's supreme joke. She collapses in helpless laughter. "No work at all!"

Tom has three retail shops in Taos, and Barbara swears that even so, she works harder than Tom does, "although Tom helps me here," she admits. "He helps me serve. I've never worked so hard in my life," she says; but it has turned out to be work she loves. She adds that the nicest thing is how different this is from meeting people in a shop. "They've already bought what I have, and we can just enjoy each other."

The guest rooms Barbara has designed are an interior decorator's dream yet authentically New Mexican, with kiva fireplaces for chilly nights, skylights, and Mexican tile. The inn started with fifteen rooms and keeps on a-building. A true-blue *Taoseña*, Barbara is proud that all her carpenters are Native Americans. "I've dedicated my Taos Pueblo Room to them," she says. Her favorite guest room, decorated in a western gambling and bordello style, is named Doña Tules.

"She was my kind of woman," Barbara confides with a twinkle. "The townspeople dress up in local costumes on Padre Martinez Day, and once a year I get to be her. She was the mistress of a former state governor." The padre, a Taos celebrity, brought the first printing press to the town, "but he had nothing to do with Doña Tules," she hastens to add.

Each guest room contains something from either Barbara's or Tom's family. In La Victoriana you'll find Barbara's great-grandparents' wedding certificate on the wall. The San Tomas Room's walls are hung with *retablos*, tin religious paintings from churches all over New Mexico. The Rio Grande Room has log furniture and red-and-black Indian weavings. Each room is a masterpiece, and you can tell that Barbara had a ball designing them.

Barbara also has a ball cooking, which she does with equal flair. Mexican eggs with green chilies and cheese, jalapeño salsa, homemade flour tortillas, pecan pancakes, French toast, and muffins, all family style. "You eat all you want," she says.

Casa Benavides means "the house of good life." I enjoyed the joy of life that radiates here. Even young Jason wants to be included as one of the innkeepers. He checked to make sure I was spelling his name right.

How to get there: The inn is located ¾ block east of Taos Plaza and the main intersection of Highway 68 and Kit Carson Road. There is parking, perfect for exploring the town on foot.

Innkeepers: Barbara, Tom, and Jason McCarthy
Address/Telephone: 137 Kit Carson Road; (505) 758–3934
Rooms: 28; all with private bath and TV, some with kitchenette; no air conditioning (elevation 7,000 feet); wheelchair access to inn, guest rooms, and dining room. No smoking inn.
Rates: $80 to $190, double; $15 extra person; EPB.
Open: All year.
Facilities and activities: Hot tubs, patios. Nearby: historic Taos Plaza with shops and restaurants a half block away; Indian pueblos, museums, hiking, fishing, skiing area, mountain-bike and horseback rentals.

Casa de las Chimeneas

TAOS, NEW MEXICO 87571

Chimeneas is Spanish for chimneys, and the inn is named for the traditional New Mexico kiva fireplaces in each room. There are two in the Library Suite, one each in the Blue Room and the Willow Inn, and three more in the main house.

Susan and her assistant, Isabelle, are responsible for the delicious breakfasts served each morning: eggs Benedict or perhaps Ron's multigrain corn pancakes; *huevos rancheros*, breakfast burritos—always a delicious hot dish following a fresh fruit course.

Guest rooms have French doors opening onto a grassy walled courtyard where fountains play and flowers bloom. Both innkeepers are avid gardeners and have planted more than 2,000 bulbs. I have to agree with Susan when she says the results are spectacular! Near the hot tub are herb, vegetable, and rose gardens, with paths for strolling and enjoying, and there's a new garden in the rear where the innkeepers grow corn, squash, and raspberries. Pretty flowers for the house are grown in the greenhouse.

Inside, designer linens, down pillows, skylights, and hand-carved furniture make for a luxurious stay. Unexpected are the color cable television sets and the ice makers concealed behind carved wooden screens.

The large common area is light, bright, and sunny. Paintings by Ron and other local artists' work enhance the thick adobe walls. Sodas and juices are complimentary, and so is the homespun treatment of guests, typical of the warmth of Taos.

"Although we don't serve either lunch or dinner, we did have a guest who got the flu, and we made him homemade chicken soup," Susan told me. "And of course, if anyone wants a cup of tea . . ."

I noticed a rack of brightly colored quilts and learned they are all handmade, by Susan's mother, and are for sale. So is much of the art on the walls, not at all unusual for Taos, where almost every inn is also a gallery. Art with a capital A is king and queen in Taos; it seems to be something in the air!

Susan is a Taos publicist and active community volunteer. Ron, who paints in both oil and watercolor, has work hung in galleries in Santa Fe, as well as in Taos and other parts of the country. "In Taos, most everyone usually does three things in order to be able to live here," she said with a laugh.

How to get there: Going north on the South Santa Fe Road, turn right at the traffic light on Los Pandos and continue a short way, keeping a lookout for Cordoba, a small unpaved road to your right. The inn is behind an adobe wall to your left almost as soon as you turn the corner.

Innkeepers: Susan Vernon and Ron Rencher
Address/Telephone: 405 Cordoba Road (mailing address: Box 5303); (505) 758–4777
Rooms: 3, including 1 suite; all with private bath, phone, and TV; wheelchair accessible; no air conditioning (elevation 7,000 feet). No smoking inn.
Rates: $118 to $143, double, EPB.
Open: All year.
Facilities and activities: Hot tub, ski racks. Nearby: trolley to Taos Plaza with shops, galleries, and restaurants; Taos Pueblo, museums and seasonal events, skiing.

Casa Encantada

TAOS, NEW MEXICO 87571

Casa Encantada means "enchanted house," and behind the all-encompassing pink adobe wall there's an interesting combination of peace and quiet—in the garden—and activity around the portales, with children playing and guests mingling happily and busily.

The old hacienda imparts a feeling of history, of generations of family and friends who have lived and visited here. In the garden there's the scent of sage and piñon; the fresh mountain air is exhilarating and chirping songbirds greet each new day.

Sharon is from Wichita, Kansas. "I went on a job search and learned to be an innkeeper," she says. The inn's lounge is a spacious, warm, and welcoming area, tastefully decorated in Southwestern style. Comfortable sofas are grouped around the large fireplace, which divides the room from the dining room. There are books, magazines, brochures, and restaurant menus; Frances and Sharon can recommend several restaurants.

Under the skylight in the dining room, the long mission-style table is prettily set. Sunlight pours in, and puffy white clouds drift through the deep blue New Mexico sky above. The table accommodates a large group of contented guests who are helping themselves from the bountiful breakfast buffet.

"Our energy bars are nonfat," Frances

assures me, but I'm drawn to the green chili strata, the French toast, and the fresh-baked English muffins, not to mention the banana walnut coffeecake. There's yogurt, and a fresh fruit platter, and coffee and herbal teas.

In the afternoon salsa and chips and beverages are served, and during the ski season, guests can warm up with an appetizer of taco soup after skiing, before going out for dinner.

All guest rooms have private entrances—they open off the long portale along the side of the house facing the garden. Five of the ten rooms are suites, which make them perfect for families. The Rio Grande Suite originally was the family living area of the old hacienda; it has two bedrooms in addition to the cozy sitting room.

Santa Fe Suite has ticking-striped sofas in front of the fireplace in the living room. There are two rocking chairs in the spacious bedroom with a queen-sized bed. Casita ("little house") originally was the estate's chapel, and it also has two bedrooms in addition to a living room. Both the living room and the larger bedroom have kiva fireplaces for cozy winter warmth. There are a kitchen and a private walled courtyard, too.

There's another kitchen in El Pueblo, a quiet retreat with a sunny bedroom with kiva fireplace and a sofa/sleeper in the family room. The Kit Carson has a touch of Territorial Taos in its furnishings. It has a kitchenette and a private alcove all its own. Rose is named for the rose-painted kiva fireplace in the corner; there are soft-rose-and-blue printed spreads on the twin beds.

"We want our guests to have warm memories of Taos's Magic Mountain and Casa Encantada," Sharon and Frances say.

How to get there: From the traffic light on Highway 68 at the Plaza, turn right on Kit Carson Road (Highway 64) and go 5 blocks east to Liebert Street. Turn right and make a jog; the inn is behind the large adobe-walled property on the right.

Innkeepers: Sharon Nickelson and Frances Mondragon
Address/Telephone: 416 Liebert Street (mailing address: P.O. Box 6460); (505) 758–7477 or (800) 223–TAOS
Rooms: 5, plus 5 suites; all with private bath and TV, some with kitchen. Pets welcome. No smoking inn.
Rates: $65 to $145, double, EPB and afternoon refreshments.
Open: All year.
Facilities and activities: Nearby: within walking distance of historic Taos Plaza with shops, galleries, and restaurants; historic Taos Pueblo; Kit Carson House; Millicent Rogers Museum; Rio Grande Gorge; Taos Ski Valley; hiking; fishing; white-water rafting on Rio Grande.

Casa Europa

TAOS, NEW MEXICO 87571

Marcia and Rudi list young son Maximilian as one of the innkeepers; he is such a fine host when guests include children. "They're all welcome to play with his toys," Marcia told me. Maxi also gladly shares a special place where children can play. "Where Rudi comes from in Germany, everyone has a garden house. Rather than putting a garden house here, we have one on stilts—it's Maxi's private clubhouse."

Rudi and Marcia are the hospitable models their son patterns himself after. Both are used to the public and enjoy entertaining. Before coming to Taos, they were proprietors of a fine restaurant in Boulder, Colorado, for many years.

"But," Rudi says, "I needed to do something with people again."

"He needs to work about eighteen hours a day," Marcia adds with a fond laugh.

"Well, we get our guests started, we introduce them, and then they are fine," Rudi explains. I certainly was fine, my only problem being one of indecision at teatime; should I choose the chocolate mousse–filled meringue or the raspberry Bavarian? Or perhaps the Black Forest torte or one of the fresh fruit tarts? (I really wanted one of each, all made by chef Rudi, who was trained at the Grand Hotel in Nuremberg, Germany.)

Breakfast is another such feast prepared by chef Rudi. For the grownups, fresh fruit salad, a mushroom-and-asparagus quiche, lean bacon edged in black pepper, home-fried potatoes, and fresh homemade Danish that absolutely melted in my mouth. Children dive into the blue corn pancakes with bacon and eggs, "or they come into the kitchen to choose their own cereal. I've learned," Marcia says. "Once I put fruit on cereal and the child said, 'Yuk!' so I leave it alone!"

The house itself is a treasure, with fourteen skylights and a circular staircase to the gallery above the main salon, displaying the paintings, pottery, and sculpture of local artists as well as wonderful Navajo rugs. The inn appears deceptively small from the outside; inside, the large common rooms (but very uncommon!), both upstairs and down, lead to six exceptionally spacious and elegant guest rooms. It's also very comfortable. The wood floors are graced with oriental rugs; the white stucco walls are hung with original art. The front courtyard is bright with flowers around the Spanish fountain; the European garden in back offers quiet relaxation. The English Room is a departure, with fine antique English furniture. "It goes into a place where people can see it," Marcia says.

How to get there: Driving into Taos from the south on Highway 68, take Lower Ranchitos Road left at the blinking-light intersection just north of McDonald's and south of Taos Plaza. Go 1½ miles southwest to the intersection of Upper Ranchitos Road, which will be on your right. (For a landmark, there's a James Mack Studio on the right-hand corner.)

Innkeepers: Marcia, Rudi, and Maximilian Zwicker
Address/Telephone: 157 Upper Ranchitos Road; (505) 758–9798
Rooms: 6; all with private bath, several with built-in bancos that convert to twin beds; no air conditioning (elevation 7,000 feet). No smoking inn.
Rates: $80 to $110, double; $20 extra person; EPB and afternoon tea.
Open: All year.
Facilities and activities: Swedish sauna, hot tub, three private courtyards for play, a special clubhouse. Nearby: historic Taos Plaza with restaurants, shops, and art galleries; hiking, horseback riding, and winter skiing; Taos Indian Pueblo and museums.

Casa Feliz

TAOS, NEW MEXICO 87571

This warm and welcoming artistic inn has won the gratitude of local authorities for the restoration of Casa Feliz, bringing back the ambience of the days when Georgia O'Keeffe, Becky James, and John Dunn frequented the old adobe home. Now on the National Register of Historic Places, Casa Feliz is a treat, just off the Plaza right in the middle of town. And like many Taos inns, it's a gallery as well, showing works of many fine local artists. Bonnie's aim is to show in her main gallery the works of local artists who don't have a regular space, including the art of the Taos Indians who live in the Taos Pueblo.

While she runs the gallery, Bonnie also runs the inn, serving a very generous breakfast.

"One of the ideas when I started was that people should not feel they are being served; they should feel at home," Bonnie says. "I pile the tables with homemade breads, cakes and muffins, and New Mexican dishes as well." Delicious is Frittata Feliz with green chilies and Monterey Jack cheese; different are the piñon-nut waffles, and wonderful are many of Bonnie's other dishes "that I don't even have names for," she says as she serves scrambled eggs with hominy and pinto beans. Her muffin repertoire is large, with ginger and blueberry ones both favorites.

There's also the thoughtful touch of a snack for tired travelers when they check in, usually with something cold and wet—wine, beer, soda—all welcome in this dry climate. Evenings, there's wine and cheese by the fire in the cozy sitting area of the gallery.

"I've wanted to create a calm, peaceful, and relaxing atmosphere here for my guests to make it inviting and comfortable," Bonnie says. Guest rooms are spacious and uncluttered, with adobe walls of soft rose. And each has unique New Mexico–style handcrafted furniture and queen-sized beds. The Romantic Room is romantic; the Vega Room, of course, has vegas on the ceiling; and the Desert Room's colors and cactus give it a light and airy feeling. The cottage at the back of the garden has three connecting bedrooms, all sharing one bath, ideal for a family or "a family of skiers," Bonnie suggests. "People can come and go."

All the rooms have electric blankets on the beds, a nice amenity in this mountain town, where people can be more concerned with keeping warm than being air conditioned. The large enclosed garden, perfect for picnics and barbecues, has a wonderful view of magic Taos Mountain. It's just a half-hour's drive up to the Taos Ski Valley for winter fun and the same amount of time to the Rio Grande for summertime river rafting.

Lately, Bonnie has become infected with the artistic atmosphere surrounding her. "I've started to dabble in little things, like bolo ties, made from found objects," she confesses. "There's a jewelry class here in town. . . ."

How to get there: The inn is located on historic Bent Street, 1 block from the Plaza behind the northwest corner. There is parking in the rear.

Innkeeper: Bonnie McManus
Address/Telephone: 137 Bent Street; (505) 758–9790
Rooms: 3, plus a three-room cottage; all with private bath; no air conditioning (elevation 7,000 feet). No smoking inn.
Rates: $75 to $115, single; $85 to $125, double; $10 extra person; EPB and evening refreshments.
Open: All year.
Facilities and activities: Large enclosed garden with picnic table and barbecue grill; parking. Nearby: Taos Plaza with shops and restaurants around the corner; public swimming pool across the street; mountain-bike and snowmobile rentals; skiing, Indian pueblos, museums.
Recommended Country Inns® Travel Club Benefit: 10% discount, two-night-minimum stay, holidays and feast days excluded, subject to availability.

Hacienda del Sol

TAOS, NEW MEXICO 87571

"I was in education for thirty years," Marcine says, "and John was a traveling salesman. A long time ago we decided we'd retire at age fifty-five and do something together." They used to visit Taos twice a year at least, and like so many happy innkeepers, once they saw this inn, they fell in love with it.

"It's our home," Marcine says, "and that's how we treat it. We don't come in the morning; we're already here." She likes to recount how they moved in the door as previous innkeepers Carol and Randy Pelton were moving out. "The Peltons made breakfast Monday, and we made breakfast Tuesday."

The inn's story is part of Taos history. Mabel Dodge Luhan, the wealthy arts patron who brought Georgia O'Keeffe and D. H. Lawrence to Taos, bought the home as a hideaway for her Taos Indian husband Tony, so he wouldn't feel like a fenced-in bear. What's more, Georgia O'Keeffe painted her *Sunflowers* here.

The inn, like so many New Mexico homes, is an old adobe building hidden behind a wall. But it backs up to 95,000 acres of Indian land, with a beautiful view of Taos Mountain, the Magic Mountain of the Taos Indians. "Now I can't imagine living any farther from that mountain than I have to," Marcine says.

The Sala de Don was Tony's room; Escondido has two skylights; and my room was attached to another room just as large, in which the centerpiece, surrounded by windows, was a huge, dark-blue Jacuzzi. Talk about luxury!

Luxurious, too, is the outdoor hot tub, where you can loll back and let the magic of the mountains work on you. The Casita, a separate little adobe house, has two guest rooms, two baths, and fireplaces. It can be used as a suite or as two separate rooms, each with a bath.

"We both are people-oriented," John says. "This is pretty much a continuation of what we were doing." Marcine adds, "Except that I'm cooking more!" A guest convinced them of the joy of a bread machine, and you can imagine how delicious the inn smells in the morning. As for which one is the chef, "If it comes out of the oven, I do it," Marcine says, "From the top, John does." Guests rave about John's "elegant" stuffed French toast or Marcine's porridge topped with vanilla ice cream—how's that to start the day? There's a social hour that often lasts much longer, giving guests a chance, as Marcine says, "to show, share, and tell," while enjoying cheese and crackers with nuts or fruit and wine and mineral water. And for you coffee hounds, know that the brew is their own special blend, Cafe del Sol.

How to get there: The inn is 1 mile north of Taos Plaza, on Highway 64/Paseo del Pueblo Norte. Turn right on unpaved road immediately alongside the Southwest Drum and Moccasin Company, and the inn is on the left, hidden behind a tall "latilla" fence that surrounds the inn's 1⅖₁₀ acres.

Innkeepers: Marcine and John Landon

Address/Telephone: 109 Mabel Dodge Lane (mailing address: P.O. Box 177); (505) 758–0287

Rooms: 7; 5 with private bath; no air conditioning (elevation 7,000 feet). No smoking inn.

Rates: \$45 to \$125, double; \$20 extra person; \$10 crib; EPB and evening refreshments.

Open: All year.

Facilities and activities: Hot tub. Nearby: Taos Plaza with restaurants, art galleries, and shops; Taos Indian Pueblo; Kit Carson Home; Millicent Rogers Museum; Martinez Hacienda.

Recommended Country Inns® Travel Club Benefit: 10% discount, Sunday–Thursday, on two-night-minimum stay, major holidays excluded; reservations must be made direct.

La Posada de Taos

TAOS, NEW MEXICO 87571

Nancy and Bill fell in love with Taos years ago when they used to come to New Mexico to visit her brother, who lived in Albuquerque. As for becoming innkeepers, Nancy says, "We've had that dream since 1981. Bill was stationed in Suffolk [England] until 1984, and ever since that day I've been collecting furniture, especially English furniture."

Bill laughs. "It all started when we were having lunch in a pub with friends. In a shop window across the street there was a cupboard . . ."

"It was an old food cupboard," Nancy says. "I told our friends, that thing is really calling to me. That was the beginning of the inn."

Bill grins. "That was the most expensive pub lunch we ever had."

Taos really spoke to him. "Wow!" he told Nancy. "We gotta find something to do in this great town." Bill was a fighter pilot in the Air Force Reserves, and acting as a consultant on the admissions process at the Air Force Academy is what brought them home from England.

"I know lots of people think they're going to do it, have an inn, but we really have!" Nancy says exultantly. "Bill went off for a walk, looked at this inn, and that was it." La Posada de Taos had been the dream of long-time innkeeper Sue Smoot, who has retired happily to Albuquerque. She could hardly have turned over her lovely inn to a more enthusiastic couple.

The result is a cozy mix of Southwestern style and English pine brought with Nancy and Bill from England. They have a photograph of the house they lived in while in England, built from 1560 to 1620—and we think *we* have homes that are historical! "It was fascinating," Nancy says. "The house consisted of two houses joined together."

Of the twenty-drawer corn chandler's chest in the entry, "Oh, it's modern," says Nancy, "It can't be over a hundred and fifty years old." Each of the merchant's drawers held a different grain—barley, rice, oats. On the shelves at the top, there's a lovely collection of Blue Willow that Nancy acquired "one piece at a time."

The Honeymoon House is a small cottage within the adobe walls, with a loft bed and a skylight overhead. Pretty romantic!

Nancy and Bill cook breakfast with zest, especially since they like to eat with their guests. We began with a cantaloupe half filled with blueberry yogurt and topped with a sprig of mint. Next came an aromatic frittata of eggs, potatoes, and leeks, which blended deliciously with tomato slices and spicy sausage. For dessert, a rich bread pudding with whipped cream kept us talking for an hour and a half, enjoying one another's company. Nancy says she likes this part almost the best.

The long dining room faces French doors onto the east garden and sunshine. Behind, in the common room, bookshelves are stacked for a good read before the tile fireplace. Several of the rooms have wood burning stoves or fireplace.

How to get there: From the traffic light at the Plaza and Kit Carson, go west on Don Fernando for 2 blocks, left on Manzanares, and take the first right onto Juanita Lane. The inn is on the right at the end of the street.

Innkeepers: Nancy and Bill Swan
Address/Telephone: 309 Juanita Lane (mailing address: P.O. Box 1118); (505) 758–8164 (fax, same) or (800) 645–4803
Rooms: 6, including 1 cottage; all with private bath, cottage with kitchen; wheelchair accessible. Pets permitted. No smoking inn.
Rates: $65 to $115, double; $15 extra person; EPB. No credit cards.
Open: All year.
Facilities and activities: Nearby: Taos Plaza with shops, art galleries, and restaurants; Taos Pueblo; Kit Carson House; Millicent Rogers Museum; Rio Grande Gorge; Taos Ski Valley; hiking; fishing; white-water rafting on Rio Grande; horseback riding; golf.

Neon Cactus Hotel

TAOS, NEW MEXICO 87571

Who among us hasn't dreamed at some time or other of the glamorous life of an old-time movie star? Sharon surrounds herself—and her guests—with all the luxurious trappings of Hollywood in the good old days when stars were stars. The Marilyn Monroe Suite, the Rita Hayworth, the James Dean—oh, what a fun getaway place this is!

Sharon has been collecting movie memorabilia from the 1930s, '40s, and '50s; her inn, with its art deco decor, is a perfect foil for the collection of rare movie photographs and posters of those times. In the Marilyn Monroe Suite, a large photograph of the star hangs above the black-satin tufted headboard, and other pictures of Marilyn are placed around the other walls. The queen-sized bed is covered with a black quilted spread; there are art deco lamps on the art deco bedside tables. It's all glamorously set off by a pink carpet and soft pink walls.

The James Dean Room is suitably masculine, with a crouched black leopard poised atop the headboard of the queen-sized bed, another on the tailored desk, and another, a little smaller, on one of the tailored bedside tables. This room has its own deck, with a wonderful view of the mountains to the east. And all the while Dean is smiling down on you from the photograph above the bed.

As for the Billie Holiday Room, "I like to

think she wouldn't be singing the blues in her room," Sharon says. This cheerful room is all pink and soft green, with a small mirror and an opened pink Japanese parasol over the bed. Billie's photos are here, and her own private deck.

The common area is tiled with warm Saltillo tile, and the clerestory windows in the living room bring in lots of bright New Mexico light. A softly quilted mauve sofa is accented by pillows of Native American weavings. Some hang on the walls, along with colorful Southwestern paintings. Sharon likes Japanese parasols and fans and has used several here. Magazines, green plants, and a fireplace help make this a most pleasant room.

Breakfast, a bountiful continental with fresh fruit, yogurt, homemade baked goodies, croissants, and bagels and cream cheese, is served in the adjoining dining room. It has a wall of windows as well as a skylight to let in even more light—I think the stars would really have shone here.

In case you want to get in shape for a screen test, the spa next door has a cardiovascular workout area, complete fitness training equipment, steam room, saunas and hot tubs, indoor and outdoor pools, aerobics classes, tennis and racquetball courts, and therapeutic massage. "Our guests get a daily discounted rate," Sharon says. Who could ask for anything more?

Feather boas, peacock feathers, pink flamingoes, snaky white lamps with black and gold shades—shades of Hollywood of the past are everywhere. The climax is the Hall of Stars photo gallery, quite a show.

How to get there: Highway 68 in town is Paseo del Pueblo Sur. The Neon Cactus is on the east side of the road, between Doña Ana Drive and Paseo del Canon (Highway 64). It's the square pink adobe with the red Spanish tile roof. The left front part of the building has a sign saying LAW OFFICES but ignore that and take the walk to the right, past the NEON CACTUS sign.

Innkeeper: Sharon Winderl
Address/Telephone: 1523 Paseo del Pueblo Sur (mailing address: Box 5702); (505) 751–1258
Rooms: 5; all with private bath. No smoking inn.
Rates: $35 to $105, double, seasonal, continental breakfast.
Open: All year.
Facilities and activities: Hot tub. Nearby: Taos Spa and Court Club; Taos Plaza with shops, galleries, and restaurants; Taos Pueblo; Kit Carson House; Millicent Rogers Museum; Rio Grande Gorge; Taos Ski Valley; hiking; fishing; white-water rafting on Rio Grande.
Recommended Country Inns® Travel Club Benefit: Stay two nights, get third night free, subject to availability.

Old Taos Guesthouse

TAOS, NEW MEXICO 87571

The moment you walk through the extra-wide front door, late of the old Taos post office, you'll be caught up in Tim's enthusiasm for anything and everything Southwestern. "We just want to accomplish what we set out to do," he says, "renovate this wonderful 150-year-old adobe hacienda, using imagination—but retaining the old Southwest flavor." He and Leslie (and daughter Malia, although she's a little young to contribute much yet) are renovating the house at the same time they're running the inn, but you'd never know everything wasn't already completed. Each guest room is different, and Tim loves to tell of the stern professor who unbent enough to say upon departure: "I have to tell you I've traveled this world, and this is one of the neatest places I've been."

Neat is right, and Tim's enthusiasm is contagious. "Look!" he says of Room 6. "Everything everybody wants in the Southwest—stained glass, vigas, *latias*, sculptured posts, adobe showers, Mexican tile, kiva fireplace, log furniture . . ." I had to holler "halt!" and he laughed. "It's so great when you complete a project and people ooh and ah," he confessed. "And we take it personally when someone's not happy." It would be difficult to be unhappy in such congenial circumstances and in such well-thought-out and complete guest rooms. It's a casual, homey, comfortable kind of place, where you can do your own thing or mingle with the other guests. A group of doctors was staying while I was there. As soon as they came back from their happy outdoor pursuits, they began to plan an evening barbecue on the patio.

The split-level traditional hacienda with Territorial windows was a guesthouse back in the 1940s. Situated on a rise over Taos, it presents a fabulous mountain scene. The Reeveses' next project is to enlarge the kitchen because, Tim says, "the kitchen is the place where people get together. So we want to build an even larger one."

While Tim is busy being the master builder, Leslie is the cook, quite a change from her previous life with the ski patrol in Santa Fe. "My fresh-baked breads and muffins are always different," she says, "but—always healthy." She also serves hot cereal, fresh fruit, yogurt, and homemade granola.

The small Shi Tzu, Sachi, greets guests with a welcoming bark, but the older, more sedate Pomeranian named Princess may not even deign to raise her head.

"Princess was deeded us with the place," Leslie says with a good-natured laugh. There is also a calico cat named Tony.

Surrounded by lovely trees so old they almost hide the inn, and on seven and a half acres of land with fabulous vistas, the Old Taos Guesthouse is already so delightful I can't imagine what future improvements Tim and Leslie have in mind. It'll be interesting to see what they come up with next.

How to get there: Take Kit Carson Road east for 1⁴⁄₁₀ miles to Witt Road. Turn south on Witt Road for ⁷⁄₁₀ mile. The inn is on the right, and there is a sign.

Innkeepers: Tim and Leslie Reeves
Address/Telephone: 1028 Witt Road (mailing address: P.O. Box 6652); (505) 758–5448
Rooms: 8; all with private bath; no air conditioning (high elevation). No smoking inn.
Rates: $60 to $105, double; $10 extra person; continental breakfast.
Open: All year.
Facilities and activities: Nearby: Taos Plaza with restaurants and shops; Indian pueblos; museums; hiking, fishing, skiing area; mountain-bike and horseback rentals.

Rancho Rio Pueblo
TAOS, NEW MEXICO 87571

Yolanda's family has been in Taos for many generations, which makes her unique among many of Taos's innkeepers. "I'm a true *Taoseña*," she says. "My father was a local doctor, and he actually made house calls here," she says of the sprawling pink adobe that she has lovingly restored. "He loved this place."

Built in the late 1800s by the Riviera family to house their twenty-two children, Yolanda was able to buy the hacienda when Mrs. Riviera died at the age of one hundred. Standing on twenty-two acres bordering Indian land and the Rio Pueblo, which gives the inn its name, the long, low adobe house is half-hidden under a stand of cottonwood and willow trees. The grounds are green and well cared for. "The land belongs to the Indians," Yolanda says, "but they're only interested in it for grazing. We get a permit from them so we can irrigate."

The walls are almost 3 feet thick, and the inn has twelve fireplaces. In keeping with the Spanish heritage of the home, the fireplaces have been built by Taos artist Carmen Velarde, whose work also is in the Smithsonian. Another well-known artist who has contributed to the inn's ambience is Taos artisan Miguel Chavez, who made much of the inn's furniture. Throughout the inn you'll find *bancos*, *nichos*, carved beams, *latillas*, vigas, Mexican-tile floors—everything the Southwest has to offer that sets it apart from the rest of the country. Enhancing this are the colors that Yolanda chose: soft peach for the walls and teal blue for the tilework. Guest rooms are large and restful, with thoughtful touches such as terry robes, and alarm clocks for those who might want to go skiing early in the day (the Taos Ski Valley is right at hand).

And the view from the large living-room windows along two sides of the large room is magnificent. The Taos and Sangre de Cristo mountains on the western horizon make for spectacular sunsets. Not to mention snow-covered peaks in the winter and an occasional rainbow after a spring shower.

In winter a breakfast buffet is spread in the sunny dining room; in summer there are three courtyards for al fresco meals. Off the back patio is an apple orchard dating from the building's construction, and it's now full of weathered, gnarled old trees. Breakfast is a feast of fruit and granola, buttermilk pancakes and waffles, salmon and cream cheese omelets, oatmeal and croissants, and cheeses with French bread.

Yolanda's background is public relations. "I've adopted just about everybody we've had as guests," she says. "We just sit around and talk over fresh coffee—and they decide to stay another day!" That's how relaxing it is at Rancho Rio Pueblo.

How to get there: From the McDonald's corner on the Santa Fe Road (Highway 68), turn west to Ranchitos Road. Go south on Ranchitos Road for 1⁴⁄₁₀ miles to Upper Ranchitos Road. Go north for ½ mile, and turn west on Karavas to the inn.

Innkeeper: Yolanda Devereaux
Address/Telephone: Karavas Road (mailing address: P.O. Box 2331); (505) 758–4900
Rooms: 9; all with private bath, phone, and TV; wheelchair accessible. No smoking inn.
Rates: $100 to $300, double; $25 extra person; continental breakfast.
Open: All year.
Facilities and activities: Pond. Nearby: Taos Plaza with restaurants and shops; Indian pueblos; museums; hiking, fishing, skiing area; mountain-bike and horse rentals.

Salsa de Salto

TAOS, NEW MEXICO 87571

El Salto is the big mountain on the horizon, and lovers of spicy food know how lively salsa is; and that, says Dadou Mayer, is how he gave this inn its name. To wallow in luxury beneath the rugged peaks of the Sangre de Cristo Mountains makes for quite a contrast: outdoors, the wild mountains, the mesas, and the high blue sky; indoors, an elegant home with finely crafted New Mexican furniture and gourmet food prepared by a Frenchman trained in a hotel school in Nice.

Dadou is also a skier, a former member of the Junior National French Ski Team. In one year's Grand Marnier ski race, he won the love of his life, a shining chrome convection-and-steam oven that he keeps polished to a fare-thee-well.

Of innkeeping, "It's my profession; I love it," he says with a most charming smile. Past owner of the Hotel Edelweiss up in the mountains, where he had a cooking school, he likes the change to a small inn.

"The inn is so much more personal than the hotel business," he says. "Our guests say, 'How nice of you to welcome me into your home.'"

Both Dadou and Mara know the answers to all the questions guests might ask—"or you can bet that if we don't, we'll find out for you!" they say. "We can direct guests to all the 'shouldn't miss' galleries, fishing holes to cast your fly for a native trout, the Pueblo dances and ceremonies, quaint shops, and the best restaurants."

The huge square lobby and dining area, with big windows open to the far vista of mountain and mesa, is furnished with soft beige leather sofas begging you to sink into them. The room is divided by a giant fireplace made of rocks from an old Taos Ski Valley copper mine. I asked Dadou about the row of sleigh bells on the rough wood mantel, and he shook them impishly. "I just found them somewhere and I like them," he said, grinning like a boy.

Guest rooms are large and uncluttered, with lounge chairs and tables on which to put things—a necessity, I think. Down comforters and nightly mints are nice features. There is a token television area, mostly used by hopeful amateurs to view ski and tennis tapes.

Breakfast you can bet will be grand—perhaps eggs Catalan and, on the buffet, yogurt, fresh fruit salad, cardamom and piñon-nut dill bread, cereals. Special is Chanterelle Omelet. "The chanterelle mushroom is abundant in the Southwest," Mara says. "We freeze them and love to serve these souvenirs of the summer in the winter." There's a refrigerator where guests can help themselves to ice, soda, or glasses of wine.

Great fun in July is the annual croquet tournament, with participants all bright in tennis whites and white lace dresses. Guests, "of course," may participate.

How to get there: Take Highway 68 north out of Taos; at the blinking light turn right on Highway 150, the Taos Ski Valley Road. One mile past the small town of Arroyo Seco, you'll see the inn on the right; there is a sign.

Innkeepers: Mara Kerkez and Dadou Mayer
Address/Telephone: P.O. Box 1468, El Prado 87529; (505) 776–2422
Rooms: 8; all with private bath; no air conditioning (elevation 7,000 feet). No smoking inn.
Rates: $85 to $160, double; $10 extra person; EPB.
Open: All year.
Facilities and activities: Swimming pool, hot tub, tennis court, croquet. Nearby: hiking trails, fishing in Rio Hondo, skiing in Taos Valley, Indian pueblos; 10 miles to historic Taos, with shops, restaurants, and mountain-bike rentals.

Stewart House Gallery and Inn

TAOS, NEW MEXICO 87571

If you're looking for a really funky, unusual, and different inn, you'll love the Stewart House. Innkeepers Mildred and Don will be the first to tell you so. "We were out in Carmel (where Don had an art gallery), and we thought, what's the funkiest house we know?" Don says. "I'd been representing Charles Stewart for twenty years, and Mildred told me, 'Why don't you just buy Chuck Stewart's house for an inn and a gallery?'"

Mildred chimes in, "We had never discussed it, and Don said 'What? An inn and a gallery?' I said I thought an inn would be fun, and he said, 'When do we move in?'" They closed the deal and moved out to Taos thirty days later. But Don hadn't seen the house in three years.

"It looked terrible," he says good-naturedly. "Weeds everywhere, so abused, took us six months to clean up." But in cleaning up they discovered all kinds of wonderful things Stewart used in the house. All sorts of old wooden doors, iron grills, glass, and shutters were used in odd ways as part of the house. A Victorian oval-windowed front door has become wall-and-window in the nook off the common room. The bathtub in the bathroom of the Artists' Room sports an old claw-footed tub that originally belonged to famous Taos artist R. C. Gorman. Stewart remade most of the inn's doors, some of them from doors 225 years old. He hauled stone from the Rio Grande, hung longhorns over his bed. "I still find new things, and I've lived here since 1989," Mildred says in wonderment.

"Evidently Stewart never threw anything away; he scavenged everywhere for interesting objects to incorporate into his house—and his work," Don says. Each room, guest or common room, is unique, individual, and full of surprises. Don and Mildred didn't want sterile motel rooms, and this is as different as you can get. In addition, the Cheeks live by the rule of good beds, good pillows, and good baths.

"We have two real strict rules here," Don says. "First, everybody's known by their first name, and second, if you want something and don't ask for it, it's your fault." Mildred adds that there's something special about having hot muffins and breads in the morning. "Where else can you get it?" she asks as she begins slicing three yummy loaves of wheat-and-honey bread.

Breakfast went on to include blueberry walnut pancakes, breakfast burritos, granola with bananas and yogurt, fresh-squeezed orange juice, tea, and coffee. Other mornings you might have green chili and corn pancakes or sausage and egg casserole. It's usually a buffet, and you'll be well insulated in case it's winter and Don invites you out for a snowball fight in ten-degree weather.

For other meals, four of Taos's most highly rated restaurants are within 2 miles of the inn.

How to get there: Take Highway 68 north to the blinking light at the intersection of Highways 64, 522, and 150. Turn right onto 150 (old Taos Ski Valley Road) for 6/10 mile. The inn is on the left, and there is a sign.

Innkeepers: Mildred and Don Cheek

Address/Telephone: 46 Ski Valley Road (mailing address: P.O. Box 2326); (505) 776–2913 or (800) 836–TAOS

Rooms: 5; all with private bath, 4 with TV, some with VCR; no air conditioning (high elevation). No smoking inn.

Rates: $75 to $120, double; $15 extra person; EPB.

Open: All year.

Facilities and activities: Hot tub, picnic grill area, art gallery. Nearby: Taos Plaza with restaurants and shops. Indian pueblos; museums; hiking, fishing, skiing area; mountain-bike and horseback rentals.

Taos Hacienda Inn

TAOS, NEW MEXICO 87571

"I grew up on a rambling ranch and farm," Jerry, a New Mexico native, says. "We grew cotton, grain, chilies, raised cattle. In fact, friends are bringing this year's crop of chilies for my birthday." And not a moment too soon for one of the inn's specialties, Southwest Green Chili Strata.

Jerry was in the communications business—as a news reporter, with a cable company, and other related businesses—but he always wanted to return to his beginnings. Peggy was in the hotel business, but "she was tired of hearing me talk," Jerry laughs. While staying at an inn, they saw this historic, two-story adobe hacienda. "Peggy said, 'Let's stop.' Well, it took about two minutes to decide!"

The L-shaped building is between Ranchitos Road and the southwest corner of La Loma Plaza, a historic residential square. Some of the thick adobe walls were built as far back as 1800, and served as part of the fortifications of the plaza. (Things were not as restful back then as they are now!)

There's a beautiful garden, with a fishpond in which several Koi, the large Japanese goldfish, swim lazily. The front lawn, shaded with towering old cottonwoods, has a fine view of the Sangre de Cristo Mountains. The front entrance opens into a bright glassed-in sunroom with a fountain, where I was greeted by C. C., the black cocker spaniel. "She's almost too friendly," Jerry says. "She has to stay out during breakfast."

Breakfast is a fulsome buffet, with the earlier-mentioned chilies present in several dishes besides the strata. Breakfast burritos, for instance, if you want something more than a little *picante* (spicy). I cooled off with my choice of four fruit juices and banana nut bread.

Snacks are served every afternoon, tasty treats like guacamole served with Peggy's special salsa, chips with *chili con queso* or bean dip, or crunchy trail mix, and beverages.

There are four rooms in the main house, with three others opening off the building's bendings and archways. The inn once contained the studios of several artists, and two outside suites are complete with kitchenettes and fireplaces. They can sleep up to four persons.

Guest rooms are luxurious, and each has individually designed tiles in the baths. In the Sunburst Room "the sun bursts through the window," Jerry explains. The Sky Room has a window seat and steps up to a small deck.

The inn furniture is handmade from New Mexican wood, and there are lots of books, pottery, and art. The art and pottery are for sale—the inn doubles as a showroom for Taos artists.

Happy Trails is happy-making indeed, with such faithfulness to Western motif as chaps and spurs on panelled walls, a mirror framed in a horse collar, furniture painted with Western scenes, and even a rocking horse, with a saddle, no less!

How to get there: From Highway 68 into town take La Placita Road (just past McDonald's on the right) left to Ranchitos Road (Highway 240). Then take a left to Valdez. Either turn left again to La Loma Plaza at the end of the block, where there's parking and an entrance off the Plaza, or go straight to another entrance to the inn on Ranchitos Road.

Innkeepers: Peggy and Jerry Davis
Address/Telephone: 102 La Loma Plaza (mailing address: Box 4159); (505) 758–1717 or (800) 530–3040
Rooms: 7; all with private bath and TV. No smoking inn.
Rates: $95 to $185, double, seasonally; $10 to $15 extra person; $10 less, single; EPB.
Open: All year.
Facilities and activities: Hot tub. Nearby: historicTaos Plaza, with shops, galleries, and restaurants; Taos Pueblo; Kit Carson House; Millicent Rogers Museum; Rio Grande Gorge; Taos Ski Valley; hiking; fishing; white-water rafting on Rio Grande.
Business travel: Phone in room; fax machines and typewriters available.

Willows Inn

TAOS, NEW MEXICO 87571

This lovely inn is on a corner, hidden behind high pink adobe walls. Once the home of artist E. Martin Hemmings (one of his paintings hangs in the White House), the inn is now a quiet retreat for George, an artist, and Estella, who makes sure that serenity reigns. "We have a lot of professionals who don't want to be bothered by ringing phones," she says. In the courtyard a fountain sparkles in the quiet, and even the cat, Bravo, is unobtrusive. "He came and sat under my car for three days, and I was going to throw him out. But he's such a love I kept him."

The inn is decorated in Southwestern style punctuated with interesting antiques. Every room has a New Mexican kiva fireplace and a Mexican-tile bath, fresh flowers, and whatever amenities guests may need—bottled water, chocolates from Italy, complimentary refreshments—everything, says Estella, done with special thought in mind. The comfortable overstuffed sofas and chairs in the living room are covered with Laura Ashley fabrics, and there are books and magazines scattered about. The dining room is long, with two tables, one of which is an original Duncan Phyfe. The hutch dates from 1690. "We tried to blend European and Southwestern together," the innkeepers say, and they have done so refreshingly.

Estella, born and schooled in Las Cruces, was teaching in California, and George, brought up in Brussels, was painting, when they decided to stop vacationing in Taos and live here instead. George found the property and was initially charmed by the two large willows in front. "They're the oldest in Taos," he claims. Next they decided to add on four rooms in a courtyard setting, engaging a local architect. The main house was built in 1926 by Taos Indians for Hemmings, with his studio a large, light room at the back of the courtyard.

"The architect we chose was a member of the historical society, so he knew everything had to be in keeping with the main house," Estella says. And it all fits right in, doing nothing to disturb the historical marker alongside the front door.

George is versatile: He was trained in Brussels in the hotel industry and came to this country because an uncle who worked for the railroad lured him to California. "But he always told me about Santa Fe [New Mexico], and his stories fascinated me," George says. Now he uses Hemmings's studio for his work, which is hung in the inn as well as in a gallery in town.

Estella is the chef, with George helping to serve, and served might be Belgian waffles (of course!) or German puffed pancakes or a Southwestern dish, such as an egg and cheese or egg and sausage casserole. Homemade breads and muffins and fresh-ground coffee, too. "You'll find no plastic, no paper, here," Estella says. "It's all linen, cotton, and china." She laughs. "Even a can of Pepsi looks foreign here!"

64

How to get there: From U.S. Highway 68 turn east onto Kit Carson Road (the traffic light just east of the Plaza) to Dolan. The inn is on the right.

Innkeepers: Estella Enrique and George van de Kerckhove
Address/Telephone: Kit Carson Road at Dolan (mailing address: Box 4558); (505) 758–2558
Rooms: 5; all with private bath; limited wheelchair access. Pets boarded down the street. No smoking inn.
Rates: $85 to $120, double, EPB.
Open: All year.
Facilities and activities: Lunch and dinner by reservation. Nearby: Taos Plaza with restaurants, shops, and art galleries; Taos Indian Pueblo; museums; hiking, horseback riding, skiing; tours.
Recommended Country Inns® Travel Club Benefit: 10% discount, subject to availability.

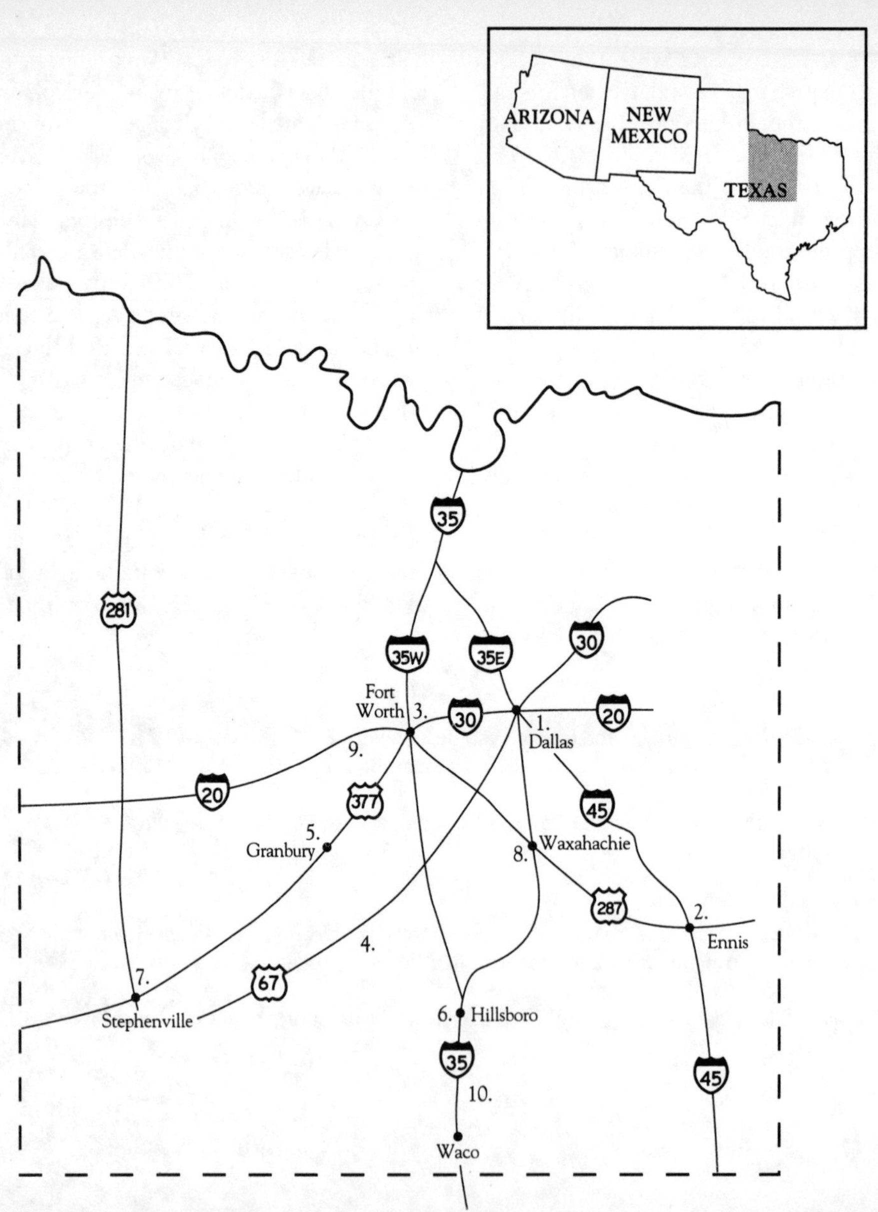

ARIZONA
NEW MEXICO
TEXAS
35
281
35W
35E
30
Fort Worth
3.
30
20
1.
Dallas
9.
20
377
45
5.
Granbury
8.
Waxahachie
287
2.
Ennis
4.
7.
67
Stephenville
6.
Hillsboro
35
45
10.
Waco

North Texas

Numbers on map refer to towns numbered below.

Hôtel St. Germain

DALLAS, TEXAS 75201

For sheer luxury, unabashed, unashamed Sybaritic living, the small and elegant Hôtel St. Germain takes the prize. Well, it's already taken several prizes, like the *Inn Business Review*'s naming the St. Germain "One of the outstanding inns of 1992."

The inn, a beautiful residence built in 1906, is architecturally imposing. The white, three-story structure has two balconies on the left and two curved porches on the right, with black wrought-iron railings, which also frame two sets of stairs to the curved driveway in front. French doors lead out, and in the stairwell, a huge twenty-four-paned window is crowned with a glass arch.

With its impressive foyer, 14-foot ceilings, sumptuous parlor, stately library, and lavish suites, it takes all the adjectives in *Roget's Thesaurus* to describe this inn adequately. The antique pieces alone are a feast for the eyes.

"My mom was an antique dealer," Claire says, pointing out the Aubusson carpets, the Mallard beds, and huge armoires. "We serve on antique Limoges—my grandmother's heavy gold china—Waterford crystal, and sterling." She alternates eight different sets of china; they're stored in the china cabinet in the small dining room.

The large dining room has bay windows of decorative glass, topped with an extravagant valence over Austrian shades. The crystal chandelier is palatial. Beyond is a romantic New Orleans–style walled courtyard. Breakfast here takes on another dimension: The chive and cheese quiche and blueberry muffins taste like nectar and ambrosia.

Soft classical music plays in the library, and there is a grand buffet piano for more personalized music. The original wallpaper is charming, and it's a treat to study the before-and-after-renovation photographs in the hall.

Suite One, a huge room decorated in rose and gray, has a rose spread and a high canopy over the bed. Suite Three has what appears to be a larger-than-life king-sized bed, which can be divided into two twins. The sitting room has a lovely antique Belgian sofa, and there's a separate dressing room. Suite Four boasts a Jacuzzi as well as a Mallard bed, a huge armoire, and a sitting area with a sofa and fireplace.

The Dangerous Liaison Suite is 600 square feet of blue, green, and gold. Beside the bed, there's a bed-lounge in the wall, a Cheval mirror, and antique Mallard furniture. In the sitting area are a fireplace and a sparkling chandelier.

The Smith Suite, on the third floor, overlooks downtown Dallas. The Napoleon sleigh bed has a crown canopy, and there is a Victorian sitting area, complete with fireplace. The padded cloth walls are another example of sheer luxury, an atmosphere that the Jacuzzi in the bath does nothing to dispel.

Hôtel St. Germain is really a taste of another world!

How to get there: From Central Expressway exit at Hall Street and turn right to Cole. At Cole turn left onto Cedar Springs, take a left onto Maple Avenue and go half a block. From North Dallas Toll Road, heading south, pass the Wycliff exit and veer to the left as you curve around to the first traffic light, which is Wolf Street. Turn left for 2½ blocks to Maple, turn right, crossing Cedar Springs to the inn, the large white mansion with a curved driveway.

Innkeeper: Claire Heymann

Address/Telephone: 2516 Maple Avenue; (214) 871–2516, fax (214) 871–0740

Rooms: 7; all with private bath, TV, and radio. Smoking permitted except in dining room.

Rates: $225 to $600, double, EPB.

Open: All year.

Facilities and activities: Dinner, lunch for 6 or more, bar service, room service, valet parking, guest privileges at The Centrum Health Club. Nearby: downtown Dallas, with Dallas Museum of Art, Kennedy Memorial, Old City Park, Reunion Tower, West End Historic District, Farmer's Market, more.

Business travel: Located in downtown Dallas. Phone in all rooms; fax.

Raphael House

ENNIS, TEXAS 75119

The Raphael House has stood in central Ennis since 1906, and since 1988 Danna has restored it to all its former glory, which was glorious indeed. Now listed on the National Register of Historic Places, Raphael House follows the precept of fine hotels "to provide the very best," Danna says. Now president of the Heritage Society, Danna also is on the board of the Ellis County Historical Society and a member of the Historic Landmark Commission. Yet she confesses to acquiring the house as sort of a lark. Visiting her family after a buying trip to New York (she was a buyer for several Austin stores), she came to look at the house "before it was torn down or burned. Once Ennis Avenue was lined with big houses like this, but this is the only one left." She returned three times and finally made an offer to buy from the last of the Raphaels, a patient in a nursing home. Before she knew it, she was the new owner of the wonderful old house and was fortunate to be able to buy much of the original furniture.

"I feel as if I adopted a family," she says as she shows off the many family photographs that she "inherited." The walls are covered with Raphaels, one of the first families in Ennis back at the turn of the century, when they built the first department store, the Big Store. Rooms are named for the Raphael family members who lived in them. Julia's Room has its original set of white French furniture from 1918, bought by sister Wilhelmina but kept by her parents. "They wouldn't let Wilhelmina take the set with her because they didn't like the man she married," Danna is delighted to explain.

Ernest's Room has a beautiful tiger oak chest, hidden under a coat of paint when Danna acquired it. "I was having it stripped—I was going to sell it. But the strippers called me and said, 'I think you ought to have a look at this.'"

The library is stocked with old books as well as new ones, magazines, a television, and a VCR. The entry is so huge that it holds a large grand piano, which Danna encourages guests to play. "Sometimes they'll sing," she says, "and it's so nice to come in at night and hear them."

Brian is a great cook ("and gardener and carpenter," adds Danna), and breakfasts are as rich as the house, with French toast stuffed with strawberries and cream cheese or what Danna calls her Tex-Czech breakfast with local Kolabasse sausage and marvelous strudel stuffed to the rim with apples, pears, pecans, and coconut. For the health conscious there are egg substitutes, turkey sausage, and lots of fruit.

How to get there: Ennis is on Highway 287, which becomes Ennis Avenue. Raphael House is at the northwest corner of Ennis and Preston Street.

Innkeepers: Danna Cody Wolf and Brian Wolf
Address/Telephone: 500 West Ennis Avenue; (214) 875–1555
Rooms: 6; all with private bath; TV available. Smoking in sun room and on porches.
Rates: $68 to $150, double; $10 less weekdays; EPB.
Open: All year.
Facilities and activities: Lunch, dinner, tea, and receptions by reservation, cooking classes spring and fall. Nearby: Colonial Tennis and Health Club, shopping area's more than 100 antiques shops, Landmark Commission driving tour, spring Bluebonnet Trail, Railroad Museum.
Business travel: Metroline to Dallas. Fax and copier; corporate rate with light breakfast, $52.
Recommended Country Inns® Travel Club Benefit: 10% discount, Monday–Thursday, subject to availability.

Miss Molly's

FORT WORTH, TEXAS 76106

Set right in the center of the authentic Old West area of Fort Worth, Miss Molly's has a partial address because the inn is upstairs, with the front door framed between two storefronts. One is the Star Cafe, a classic cowboy place to eat in Fort Worth. When you reach the top of the steps, you'll be in what was once a popular bordello, and you might even meet the ghosts of Butch Cassidy and the Sundance Kid. No kidding—Fort Worth was a favorite breathing spot for the outlaws, as well as for other gunslingers, rodeo cowboys, and drovers, who weren't too proud to mix with cattle barons and wealthy oilmen at "Miss Josie's," as Miss Molly's once was called.

Before that the historic inn was a prim and proper hotel and boardinghouse. Once again it has been returned to respectability—although there's still plenty of lively entertainment around this Wild West area with its saloons, Western gear shops, and mounted policemen.

Miss Molly's guest rooms reflect the glory days, with the Cowboy Room done up in boots and saddle and the Cattlemen's with longhorns mounted on the wall. The Gunslinger has a rogue's gallery of photos, but Miss Amelie's is all prissy, with lace curtains and hand-worked linens from her boardinghouse days. As for Miss Josie's, her room is decorated in elaborate Victorian, complete with draped ceiling and red velvet hangings.

There's a marriage certificate in Miss Amelie's room. "If she knew that her room was next to Miss Josie's, Fort Worth's most famous madam . . ." Susan rolls her eyes in mock alarm.

Bathrooms are complete with old-fashioned claw-footed tubs, pedestal basins, and pull-chain toilets. But something new has been added: "Hot baths used to cost extra," Susan says, "but since we moved the plumbing indoors, they're included in the rate."

The continental breakfast is homemade, with hearty specialty breads and muffins and lots of fresh fruit. It's served beneath the stained glass skylight in the parlor, and then it's off to one of the monthly events in busy Fort Worth, whether it's February's Last Great Gunfight, June's Chisholm Trail Roundup, or December's Texas Circuit Rodeo Finals. Fort Worth boasts, "Here is where the West begins," and Miss Molly's is just the sort of place to put you in the mood to relive those "good old days."

How to get there: Take I–35 north from downtown Fort Worth and exit at 28th Street at the FORT WORTH STOCKYARDS sign. Go to North Main and turn left to West Exchange (the third traffic light). Turn right, and the inn is on the left; there is a sign over the Star Cafe.

Innkeepers: Susan and Mark Hancock
Address/Telephone: 109½ West Exchange; (817) 626–1522
Rooms: 8; 1 with private bath. No smoking inn.
Rates: $75 to $150, single or double; $10 extra person; continental breakfast; Weekday rates available.
Open: All year.
Facilities and activities: Out the front door: Stockyards Historic Area with rodeos and cattle auctions, restaurants and shops, monthly special events. Nearby: Fort Worth museums, water garden, botanical and Japanese garden, zoo, Sundance Square, Tarantula Steam Train, Stockyards Station; children's amusement park, Cowtown Corrals, horseback riding.
Business travel: Located 2½ miles from downtown Fort Worth, 30 miles from Dallas; business rates.
Recommended Country Inns® Travel Club Benefit: 10% discount, Monday–Thursday, subject to availability.

Inn on the River

GLEN ROSE, TEXAS 76043

The inn is on the river, all right—the beautiful Paluxy River, framed along the spacious back gardens by three famous old oaks. The oaks are "The Singing Trees" of an Elvis Presley recording, and the lyrics were by a guest of the inn when it was the Snyder Sanitarium.

Located in the center of Glen Rose, this interesting building began life as a sanitarium for good health. Glen Rose was known for its salubrious mineral waters back in 1919 when the inn was built, and Amy is proud of the Texas Historical Commission's marker in front of the building. A large square structure, the inn has a wonderful spacious lobby with furnishings of comfortable overstuffed pieces and light wicker, making an inviting gathering place for guests.

Each room and suite is individually decorated with a refreshing choice of wallpaper, custom bedding, antique wardrobes, and white-tiled bathrooms, creating pleasant dreams. There is a ceiling fan in each room. A small museum on the second floor tells the history of the house; it's a repository of photographs and other memorabilia from when it was the Snyder Sanitarium, as well as details of the building's renovation in 1984.

Breakfast in the sunny, sparkling dining room "means bountiful," Amy promises, and she certainly lives up to it. You'll be served at least three courses. A feast of chef Jon Chadwick's specialties, beginning with fresh-squeezed orange juice is followed by a fruit course changing daily, depending upon what's in the local market. Next come scrambled eggs with chives or homemade sausage baked with eggs and cheese, potato pancakes, or cheese grits. Breakfast at Inn on the River is an honest-to-goodness meal, and coffee's always out for the early birds.

The rest of the day and night, beverages and cookies are always available in the dining room.

One of the best things is the river. "It's always cool down here, even on the hottest nights," says Amy. During the day there's fishing for sand bass and bluegills. At night I sat outside and watched the moon rise over the tops of those three 250-year-old trees, and I could see how the river and the trees made the old sanitarium a perfect place for an inn.

The Great Blue Heron Meeting House overlooking the river is a delightful place for a meeting or a retreat. "We're here for our guests," Amy says, "a quiet and peaceful retreat."

How to get there: The county courthouse on the square faces Barnard Street. With the courthouse on the right, go on down Barnard 2 blocks. The inn is on the left.

Innkeeper: Amy Guinn
Address/Telephone: 205 Southwest Barnard Street; (817) 897–2101
Rooms: 22, including 3 suites; all with private bath. No smoking inn.
Rates: $70 to $140, single or double, EPB.
Open: All year except the last two weeks in December.
Facilities and activities: Dinner Friday and Saturday with reservations; meeting house for conferences and retreats. Nearby: historic town square with restaurants, shops, and galleries; Dinosaur State Park, with renowned dinosaur tracks; Fossil Rim Wildlife Center; Texas Amphitheater June through October.
Recommended Country Inns® Travel Club Benefit: 10% dsicount, Monday–Thursday.

Doyle House on the Lake

GRANBURY, TEXAS 76048

Driving up the residential street to the Doyle House, you wonder how it can live up to its name of "on the lake." But although the view from the front parlor window is of the house across the street, from the back there's a sweep of shade trees and green lawn that does indeed go all the way down to Lake Granbury.

Linda and Patrick kept moving between Texas and Illinois, and in Illinois Linda had a gourmet kitchen shop. "This is a business we've always been intrigued by," Linda says. "Patrick was an army brat, and he was always saying he had no roots. We looked only for a little bit when he found them. We came to the right place at the right time, bought the house empty and in very good shape. Then we added all our own furnishings, and the house is just the right size. It's like having guests in your home."

It's definitely like visiting friends when you step into the living room with its pink walls and mauve carpet, the baby grand in front of the picture window, the wing chair pulled up to the flowered sofa. Green plants fill the corners and the hearth in front of the white fireplace.

Emily Doyle once lived here with her doctor father, who built the house sometime around 1880 on the bank of the lake. The room named after her has a pretty pink spread on the four-poster king-sized bed, and the pale green carpet makes a pleasing contrast. The Jacuzzi in the bath is sunken, and there's a separate sitting room with bookshelves and furniture of cherry and mahogany. It has a separate entrance, as do all the guest quarters.

The Carriage House is a paneled two-room suite with a queen-sized bed plus a trundle, and a refrigerator, microwave, and coffee maker. There are books here, too, and the decor is Shaker. The outside deck has a lovely old tree smack in the middle.

The Pool Cottage also offers kitchen privileges, with a "micro kitchen" in a closet. Large, it has a second door opening right onto the pool, and a covered deck for lounging. Decor here is Mission-style. Books and games are handy, and the futon sofa becomes a double bed.

During the week breakfast is continental, with fresh fruit and juice, apricot bread or sour cream coffeecake, but on weekends Linda serves specialties such as stuffed French toast with apricot sauce and ham cakes with fresh fruit garnish. Of course, there's always juice and coffee.

It's just a short stroll to Granbury's historic town square—the whole square is on the National Register of Historic Places. Plays and musicals are presented at the Granbury Opera House most weekends.

If your tastes run to the macabre, the Hood County Jail just off the square, built in 1885, still has the original cell block and hanging tower.

Nearby Acton State Park is the smallest state park in Texas. The reason it's there is because it contains the grave of Elizabeth Crockett, Davy Crockett's second wife.

How to get there: From I–20 west take either Highway 171 south to FM 51 or Highway 377 to Granbury to Historic Square. Go 1 block west to Lambert and 2 blocks south to Doyle. The inn is on the right, behind a white picket fence.

Innkeepers: Linda and Patrick Stoll
Address/Telephone: 205 West Doyle; (817) 573–6492
Rooms: 1, plus 2 two-bedroom suites; all with private bath, TV, and radio. No smoking inn.
Rates: $70 to $120, double; $15 extra person; continental on weekdays, EPB on weekends.
Open: All year.
Facilities and activities: Swimming pool, barbecue pit, fishing dock, boat tie-ups, basketball, volleyball, bocce ball, horseshoes. Nearby: historic Granbury Square with shops, restaurants, and Opera House; Railroad Depot Museum; Hood County Jail; Acton State Historical Site; Lake Granbury, with boating, fishing, water sports, and cruising on the Granbury Queen; The Gulch at Granbury; 25 miles from Fort Worth, 50 miles from Dallas.

The Nutt House

GRANBURY, TEXAS 76048

Everybody loves to say that they've stayed at the Nutt House. A visit here is always good for a laugh as well as for a good inn and dining experience.

The house was built in 1893 for two blind brothers, Jesse and Jacob Nutt. I could tell it was originally a store (a grocery) by the storefront windows, now attractively hung with drapes and plants. The building became a hotel in 1919, and it owes its present fame to Mary Lou Watkins. A great-granddaughter of one of the brothers, she opened the Nutt House Restaurant in 1970. Texans came from all over the state to dine here on such good country fare as chicken and dumplings, hot-water cornbread, fresh peach cobbler, and buttermilk or pecan pie. (There are also several good restaurants on the square.) The lobby, where old-fashioned screen doors lead to the restaurant, has wooden floors and the largest Norfolk pine that I've ever seen indoors. Elaine told me that it has been there since the 1970s.

This is a real comfortable country place. The Nutt House is just like home used to be, back in "the good old days," and as informal as life was back then. "If they're coming in late, we just leave their key in the mailbox, with their name on it, and they can let themselves in," says Elaine. Coffee's always in the pot in the lobby and in the upstairs hall of the annex. Whoever gets up first plugs them in.

"People just come out in their robes to sit and visit, or play cards and dominoes."

The rooms in the hotel, all upstairs, have screen doors and ceiling fans, reminders of an earlier time, although the hotel is now air-conditioned. They're furnished as though it's still 1919, and the upstairs parlor has old ledgers and such for browsing.

The newer rooms in the annex are on the second floor, in what used to be the law offices of the Granbury lawyer who erected the building in the early 1890s. Four connecting offices form four guest suites, and their double transom doors are left intact in case guests want connecting rooms. "The doors were just too lovely to remove," Elaine says, and I agree with her.

She gives credit to Madge Peters, the former innkeeper, for assisting with the annex decor. She designed the window treatment for the 9-foot-tall windows, a combination of shutters and lace curtains, the latter all handmade by her.

The Nutt House Inn, a log cabin on Lake Granbury just 1 block from the hotel, has a deck overlooking the lake and not-too-distant woods. The two-bedroom, two-bath cabin has antique furnishings, including wrought-iron beds. Guests share a living area, dining room, and kitchen.

How to get there: The inn is on the northeast corner of the square, directly across from the Opera House.

Innkeeper: Elaine Dooley
Address/Telephone: Town Square; (817) 573–5612
Rooms: 15, plus 1 two-bedroom, two-bath cottage with kitchen; 6 with private bath, 9 share 2 baths, 1 with wheelchair access.
Rates: $39 to $85, double, EP.
Open: All year.
Facilities and activities: Restaurant open for lunch every day except Monday; dinner Friday and Saturday when Opera House is open; wheelchair access to restaurant. Nearby: the entire town square, with the Granbury Opera House, is on the National Register of Historic Places; water sports on nearby Lake Granbury; 25 miles from Fort Worth, 50 miles from Dallas.

Tarleton House

HILLSBORO, TEXAS 76645

You may be welcomed to the Tarleton House by Rosie and Jake, although they're supposed to be confined in the kitchen behind a gate. "Unless they can sneak out," Mary Temple says. Both are what she calls pound dogs: Jake is a little blonde terrier from the pound, and Rosie they found on the corner of I–35 and Rosedale in Fort Worth.

"We called her Rosie because there are lots of ladies of the evening on that corner, and they call them the Rosedale Rosies," Mary Temple explains. (Both are her given names, but she doesn't care if you call her just Mary. "That's how I can tell how long people have known me.")

There's a lot of laughter in this pretty slate-blue-and-maroon Victorian mansion 60 miles south of Dallas and Fort Worth. Gene is a national consultant for computer literacy and Mary Temple spent many years as a social worker. Being an innkeeper was not exactly her dream. "No, actually it was my younger sister's dream for *us* to have an inn," she recalls good-naturedly. "And our daughter said to Gene, 'Daddy, if we lived in a big house, I'd get married at home.'"

They were living in Arlington (outside of Fort Worth) when Gene, who reads the classified ads, told Mary to get in the car, they were going to see something. "So we just did it! I guess it's a sort of retirement for me. We mean to stay here forever, 'If the Lord is willin' and the creek don't rise!'"

All the guest rooms are spacious and have either king-sized or twin beds, except for the Green Duck Room. "It has a double bed because it's a very small room," Gene says. "It's a little like being in a barn—but with all the luxury of air conditioning and heating, and a full bath with a shower!" he adds in a hurry. It can be part of a suite called Belle's Way, which is pretty in pink, with a fabric headboard sprinkled with pink roses, an armoire, and an antique dresser. "Belle was a Tarleton employee in charge of all the other servants," Mary explains. Mrs. Tarleton, an accomplished musician, was blind. "One of my neighbors said her grandmother used to come to musicals here when she was young."

All the rooms are light and bright with lots of windows—many rooms have bays and more than one view. Sarah's Secret has a bed built in the wall under a window, but that's not the secret. You'll have to find that out for yourself.

The Tower Honeymoon Suite doesn't have a secret, but it's got a passageway through the wall to a sitting room under the gable in the turret.

The Floral Room is a regular flower bower: wallpaper, comforter, pictures on the walls, towels—everything covered with flowers. "Then," says Mary, "a guest left a pair of boots in all those flowers. We think there should be an element of surprise in every room, so now, among all the flowers, we've added our own pair of boots, and a western hat as well."

For breakfast we had a Tarleton House specialty, a biscuit cup with egg, cream cheese, scallions, and crisp bacon, served with crisp hashed-brown potatoes. Other specialties are cheese grits and a *chile relleno* casserole. Mary's fresh cranberry muffins and apple coffeecake are delicious, too.

How to get there: From I–35 take the cut-off to Hillsboro to the courthouse. From there go east on Franklin to Pleasant and north on Pleasant. The inn is on the right.

Innkeepers: Mary Temple and Gene Smith
Address/Telephone: 211 North Pleasant Street; (817) 582–7216 or (800) 823–7216
Rooms: 8, including 1 two-room suite; all with private bath, 7 with TV. No smoking inn.
Rates: $86 to $116, double, EPB. Corporate rates available.
Open: All year.
Facilities and activities: Bicycles, croquet. Nearby: golf, Hill College Civil War Museum and Research Center, Katy Railroad Station and Museum, Cell Block Museum, historic homes, Aquilla and Whitney lakes.

The Oxford House

STEPHENVILLE, TEXAS 76401

When Judge W. J. Oxford, Sr. was paid the sum of $3,000 in silver coins for trying a case back in the 1890s, he knew just what to do with such a treasure. Between 1890 and 1898, he built the Oxford House. The judge's third wife told stories of how it took one thousand loads of fill dirt, at 75 cents a load, even to make a start on the foundation, and how the lumber was brought from Fort Worth across the Bosque River.

It was a busy time at the judge's back then, and you'll still find a busy whirl at the Oxford House, what with weddings, receptions, luncheons, and dinners, as well as breakfast for inn guests.

"We even do an English tea," Paula Oxford says. "Three courses: dainty savory sandwiches, then piping hot scones and nut breads topped with butter, jam, and lemon curd, finishing with a dessert course of moist cakes, strawberry tarts, truffles, and pastries."

Bill Oxford is a third-generation Oxford attorney with close ties to the judge and the judge's interesting home. Paula and Bill live across town, and, as Paula says, "Nobody was using the old house, so it was my idea to make it into a bed and breakfast inn." There's much family history bound up in the tall Victorian manor. Marie's Suite, named for a child who grew up in the house in its early days, contains an antique seven-piece bedroom suite from the 1890s. Aunt

Mandy's Room is decorated with photographs of an aunt who was "a real pill," Paula says. "She expected to be waited on hand and foot, so they always put her in the room that was hot with sun in the summer and cold in the winter, hoping she wouldn't stay long!"

Each guest room has a private bath with antique claw-footed tub. Bubble bath and special soaps encourage you to soak and meditate—very relaxing. The Victorian charm of the inn includes a sleigh bed built in the 1890s, beveled glass mirrors, and antique armoires. Porches, reaching three-quarters of the way around the house, are made of cypress with hand-turned gingerbread trim.

"Zandra McElmurray Coweth helps me out, and she's responsible for the good food that keeps the inn humming," Paula says about Zandra's pear in brandy with crumbles on top, sausage yeast biscuits, German cinnamon rolls, or fruit swirl coffeecake. They start the day out just fine. Other meals are by reservation; if you order dinner, possibilities are chicken breast in wine sauce or seafood crepes, perhaps served with rice/apricot pilaf, mandarin orange salad, and cheesecake with praline sauce.

If you park in the back, you'll enter under an arbor. The wide back lawn has a big old swing, and there are white chairs and tables under the trees.

How to get there: Highway 108 becomes Graham through town, and the inn is 2 blocks north of the town square, on the east side of the street. There's a sign out in front.

Innkeepers: Paula and Bill Oxford
Address/Telephone: 563 North Graham Street; (817) 965–6885 or 968–8171
Rooms: 4; all with private bath. No smoking inn.
Rates: $58 to $75, double, EPB.
Open: All year.
Facilities and activities: Lunch, dinner, and afternoon tea by reservation; gazebo. Nearby: use of the Oxfords' swimming pool five minutes across town; golf and horseback riding; tour of bronzing factory; Fossil Rim Wildlife Preserve and Glen Rose dinosaur tracks forty-five minutes away; local festivals.

The Bonnynook

WAXAHACHIE, TEXAS 75165

Driving up to the Bonnynook, you'll be amazed at the garden that takes the place of a lawn. Green plants all year, and, in season, flowers, flowers everywhere—bachelor buttons, carnations, daisies, roses, chrysanthemums—and planted in the center, a plaque that reads: HISTORIC WAXAHACHIE INCORPORATED RECOGNIZES THIS PROPERTY BUILT IN 1895 AS WORTHY OF PRESERVATION.

"Both Vaughn and I were brought up in old houses," Bonnie says. "We had old furniture that didn't work in modern houses, so we said, 'Why don't we look for an old home that needs restoration? If nothing else, we'll have a home.' Soon as we walked into this house, Vaughn and I turned to each other and said, 'I think we're home.'"

The first thing that caught my eye in the double parlor was what Bonnie says is an Austrian cozy corner, a huge piece of furniture that's a sofa built into a bookshelf and a chest of drawers, with a pull-out table/desk, alongside. All sorts of interesting collectibles surround the cozy upholstering, and the piece fits beautifully in a corner of the room, a cozy corner indeed.

Most of the inn's furnishings are in keeping, giving it a distinctive European air. Bonnie is a sociologist and Vaughn an engineer, and I think neither of them has ever disposed of anything that's a legacy from their Austrian and Welsh heritages. This makes the Bonnynook practically a museum, and a comfortable and entertaining one at that.

The antique claw-footed table in the Sterling Room was rescued from Bonnie's grandmother. "She was folding linen on it," Bonnie says in amused dismay while explaining that the room is named for her favorite nephew. The Morrow Room has her granddad's trunk, still with its labels from Wales, and with Uncle Wiggly books spilling from its bottom drawer. "I grew up on Uncle Wiggly books," Bonnie says nostalgically. "As for the trunk, it's been to college five times."

Bathrooms are like greenhouses, large and bright with green plants surrounding the bathtubs. More plants bloom on the porches, both upstairs and down.

Candy, fresh flowers, and evening snacks from cheese and crackers to cookies and brownies encourage guests to comment in the comment book, which is a lot of fun. Breakfast is a combined effort because Vaughn loves to cook as much as Bonnie does, except that he has his recipes written down whereas Bonnie's are in her head. "When we get in the kitchen, anything goes!" they confess. Anything, as in shoo-fly pie, applesauce pancakes, ginger pears, shrimp creole crepes; also increased emphasis on low-fat, low-cholesterol diets. The seven-course price fixe dinners are a wonder of "Haute Texas Nouveau Victorian Cuisine."

"It's such a nice feeling, when people who were all stressed out are ready to leave, and you get a nice hug," Bonnie says. "They seem to say, 'I'm all relaxed, ready to get back.' I like to think that when people walk away from us, they have a sense of who we are, as we have a sense of who they are. I want to know people, let them know me."

How to get there: From I–35 take Business Route 287 (West Main) east; from I–45 to Ennis, take 287 west 11 miles to Waxahachie.

Innkeepers: Bonnie and Vaughn Franks
Address/Telephone: 414 West Main; (214) 938–7207
Rooms: 4; all with private bath, 2 with Jacuzzi. No smoking inn.
Rates: $70 to $100, double; $15 extra person; EPB.
Open: All year.
Facilities and activities: Coffee nook with small refrigerator; dinner Friday and Saturday 7:00 and 9:00 P.M., other nights by request. Nearby: downtown with restaurants, shops, antiques, and craft malls; historic square with famous courthouse.
Business travel: Located 30 miles from downtown Dallas. Computer, fax, separate business phone line in guest rooms.
Recommended Country Inns® Travel Club Benefit: 25% discount, Monday–Thursday, subject to availability.

St. Botolph Inn

WEATHERFORD, TEXAS 76086

Dan and Shay have named their inn after a seventh-century saint Dan claims to have had in his family. The spelling of Dan's family name has changed over time, but only slightly, from Botolph to Buttolph. Dan researched the priest's life and was inspired by what he found.

"We lived in England for 14 years," he says, "and we visited all the sites." He says that St. Botolph founded a monastery in 654 in Boston, Lincolnshire, which was known as Botolph's Town back then. His church still stands there. So with such a saintly background, it's no wonder that the inn's motto is "As for me and my house, we will serve the Lord."

The inn brochure also points out, "Come, let us pamper you."

This large, classic Queen Anne house was built in 1897. It is distinctive for its size and its gingerbread molding decorating the two large eaves and the pointed turret. The first floor is beautifully symmetrical, with matching wrap-around porches on both sides of the front door.

But first you march up the red stone steps and pass under a rugged red-brick arch leading up the rise to the inn. There you're greeted on the day of your arrival with a Victorian high tea of scones and cucumber sandwiches, Victorian cookies, and Victorian blueberry walnut cake.

Dan was in the U.S. Army for 35 years, and Shay was a Red Cross nurse. Besides England, they have lived in Korea, the Netherlands, Hawaii, Turkey, Liberia, and Vietnam; the inn furnishings reflect the furniture, art, and artifacts they have collected from what seems like all over the world.

I loved the King David Room. It has a Philippine wicker bed with half-canopy, a white-marble-and-wood washstand from England, and, best of all, a small private stairway up to a private turret room, where a breakfast table is set in case you want your own private breakfast. So cozy, with the walls of the stairway and the room covered with the same paisley cloth as the drapes in the bedroom, and the four tall, narrow, curved windows of the turret offering a rounded view below.

The St. Mark and St. Luke rooms share a large blue bath with glass tiles set in the 1950s, when that was chic. St. Mark has an antique walnut double bed. St. Luke has twin pink-covered beds, cloth wallpaper, and a wonderful Italian mirror over a Korean chest.

Breakfast can be served in your room, on the porch, around the pool, or in the formal dining room. You get to order breakfast the evening before, and there's a choice of the full Victorian breakfast, continental, or the St. Botolph Inn special of the day, which on this day was Texas pecan buttermilk pancakes served with sausage or bacon. The full meal begins with fruit juice or honey-broiled grapefruit, offers a choice of eggs (I had a hard time deciding between the coddled and the shirred with cream, so British) served with sausage or bacon, and a basket of assorted homemade breads and muffins. The continental comes with a mixed fruit compote and orange marmalade for the contents of the bread basket.

How to get there: From I–10 take exit 407 to the third traffic light, and turn left on Russell Street. Go to the fourth stop sign and turn right onto Lamar. The inn is up the hill to the right.

Innkeepers: Shay and Dan Buttolph
Address/Telephone: 808 South Lamar Street; (817) 584–1455 or (800) 868–6520
Rooms: 4; 2 with private bath. Dogs welcome. No smoking inn.
Rates: \$45 to \$75, double; \$15 extra person; EPB and afternoon refreshments.
Open: All year.
Facilities and activities: Swimming pool, lawn games, small prayer chapel, children's playground, pet kennel. Nearby: First Monday Trades Day; Peter Pan Statue of Weatherford native Mary Martin; Weatherford Junior College; 26 miles from Fort Worth, 35 miles from Dallas.

Victorian House
WEATHERFORD, TEXAS 76086

What a wonderful home this Victorian beauty is, all 10,000 square feet of it! Three stories tall, it commands an eye-catching view of the entire city.

"We claim to have the best view in town," Gregg says, and it would be hard to gainsay him. Built in 1896 by C. D. Hartnett, a local banker, high on its own hill and surrounded by several old oak trees—and one hackberry—the inn is a sensational reminder of an extravagant age.

Gregg knows about the hackberry: he cleared the grounds, all three acres of it, himself. He made a great job of it, terracing the bright green lawn up the front walk. The gabled home, surrounded by wraparound porches and with a three-story round corner turret topped by a steep, pointed roof, is spruced up with soft taupe paint, white trim, and a dark roof that appears to be lighter on the turret.

Gregg was a cost analyst for Bell Helicopter in Fort Worth and Candice was in the food business. Candice was born and raised in the hospitality industry; her family had a motel in nearby Granbury. (*The* motel in the 1950s and '60s, says Gregg.) Then friends surprised them with a gift certificate for an inn stay, and they were quite impressed.

"Everybody was real nice," Gregg says, almost with surprise. "It was different from the motel business." They decided that they wanted to look for an inn of their own, combined with a restaurant. But after looking into the food business, they decided it was too tough for them.

But nothing dampened their ardor for an inn. It took six long years to restore the Victorian House, but they have done a fantastic job of it. The 10-foot pocket doors, the transoms over them, the original millwork, the stained glass windows in the entry, and especially the stained glass in the big bay window make this house outstanding.

The single-paneled front door hardly prepares you for the space immediately inside: a wide hallway that stretches from front to back. The staircase is to the right, leading from the turret room and an open adjoining parlor. It makes a turn up to the second floor and a second wide hall, past the second-floor game room, and on up to another game room in the turret, with a view out over the expanse of green lawn to the skyline of Weatherford.

Candice and Gregg had been collecting antiques over the years, and here they found the perfect setting for their many beautiful pieces. All the downstairs guest rooms, with their outstanding antique furniture, have a private sitting porch (for people who want to smoke) and a private entrance. The rug and rocker in the number 1 Room, which were purchased from an estate sale, supposedly once belonged to President Lyndon B. Johnson. Room number 6 is huge, made all the more so by its mirrored armoire.

Breakfast is filling, with frothy whipped orange juice, a medley of fresh fruit, a ham and cheese quiche, and homemade biscuits topped with homemade apricot jam.

How to get there: Take exit 414 (Highway 180), which in town is Palo Pinto. Go west for 6 miles and turn right into the driveway of the inn, which is on the hill immediately to your right; there's a big sign on the front lawn.

Innkeepers: Candice and Gregg Barnes
Address/Telephone: 1105 Palo Pinto Street (mailing address: P.O. Box 1571); (817) 599–9600
Rooms: 7; all with private bath. No smoking inn.
Rates: $79 to $89, double; $20 extra person; EPB.
Open: All year.
Facilities and activities: Three acres of landscaped grounds; horseshoes; badminton; two game rooms for chess, cards, etc. Nearby: First Monday Trades Day; Peter Pan Statue of Weatherford native Mary Martin; Weatherford Junior College; 26 miles from Fort Worth, 35 miles from Dallas.

The Zachary Davis House

WEST, TEXAS 76691

In her youth, Marjorie says, she was bitten by the hotel bug, going to school mornings and in the afternoons working in the largest hotel in her home town of Laredo. She went on to bigger and better things in the hotel industry, and you can be sure she knows how to take good care of her guests. Turn-down service, sweets on your pillow, complimentary wine, all combined with a lovely old home decorated with perfectly color-coordinated bed linens, towels, and comforters. "We had a lot of fun picking out the linens," Marjorie says of the family who lured her back to her home state after years in California.

"They all wanted me to move back to Texas, for one thing, but I didn't want to just sit around." Marjorie, beginning such a new career, has eight grandchildren and twelve great-grandchildren, and it was a granddaughter who said, "Grannie, there's a nine-bedroom house here in West that would make a wonderful bed and breakfast—and we really need it!" They convinced her that with all her hotel experience, having an inn should be right up her alley.

In remodeling the house, which was built in 1890 for an early settler of West (originally named Bold Springs), Marjorie at first was baffled by the problem of adding a bath to each room. But it was solved very cleverly: Each room has fixtures concealed behind an attractive screen. (All except two have showers, not bathtubs.)

There's a sense of humor here. The Quack Room has a border of wallpaper ducks around the ceiling, ducky linens, and a wooden duck: "I have several doctors who ask for this room," Marjorie says with a twinkle. The Southwest Room, the smallest (a single), has the largest bathroom in the house, and the Downstairs Room, with oriental furnishings, is called that not only because that's where it is, but, says Marjorie, "I couldn't decide whether to call it the Chinese Room or the Emperor's."

Each room is different, and it's hard to make a choice. The Poppy Room has white wicker furniture to set off the bright poppy linens, whereas the Bluebonnet Room, blue and white, celebrates the Texas state flower. Mary's Room is named after a previous owner's daughter, who said, "Oh, Mrs. Devlin, I would love to have it named after me!"

Breakfast usually features Nemecek bacon or sausage—they've been in business in West since 1896—as well as all kinds of eggs, in casserole or out. The full country breakfast also alternates with French toast, chicken or beef *fajitas* (sautéed meat wrapped in flour tortillas), and hotcakes. West, known for its Czech heritage, also is famous for *kolaches*, and Marjorie is sure to serve them, but you'll probably want more from some of the town's good bakeries!

Marjorie sponsors two Little League teams on the three back acres of her land she calls her "back forty." "I like to be part of the community," she says. In the entry just beside the door is an authentic Czech costume. "It's what everybody wears, come Westfest over the Labor Day weekend."

How to get there: From I–35 take exit 353 in West and go east on Oak Street to Roberts. Turn north 1½ blocks. The inn is on the right.

Innkeeper: Marjorie Devlin
Address/Telephone: 400 North Roberts; (817) 826–3953
Rooms: 8; all with private bath. No smoking inn.
Rates: \$40 to \$60, double, EPB.
Open: All year.
Facilities and activities: Nearby: historic town, with restaurants and bakeries, antiques and craft shops; Playdium Swimming Pool; festivals; hunting and fishing at Lake Whitney; West Station Train Depot Museum; 15 miles from Waco.
Recommended Country Inns® Travel Club Benefit: 15% discount, Monday–Thursday; 10% on weekends; subject to availability.

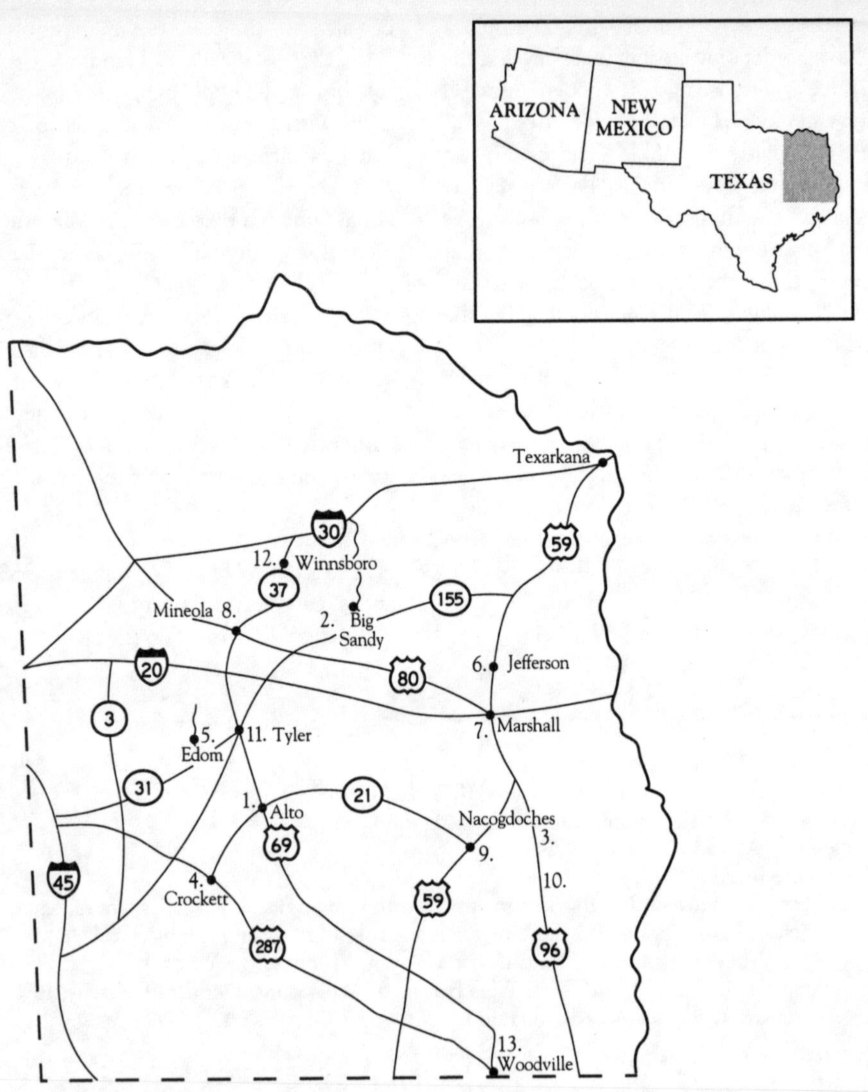
ARIZONA
NEW MEXICO
TEXAS
Texarkana
30
59
12. Winnsboro
37
155
Mineola 8.
2. Big Sandy
20
80
6. Jefferson
3
5. Edom
11. Tyler
7. Marshall
31
1. Alto
21
Nacogdoches
3.
69
9.
4. Crockett
45
59
10.
287
96
13. Woodville

East Texas

Numbers on map refer to towns numbered below.

Lincrest Lodge
ALTO, TEXAS 75925

Lincrest Lodge is just east of the small town of Alto, out in the country atop a rise with a beautiful view of the Angelina River and the green countryside.

"My mother-in-law lived here," says Chet, who was an evaluation engineer in Houston at the time. "We always came visiting. I picked up a piece of land for retirement. It was my first opportunity to build as I wanted. Each week Charlene would ask what I was doing now." He laughs, remembering. "One weekend I was putting on the third floor. She said, 'Why? Our kids don't come to visit.' I said, 'Guess we'll have to open an inn.'"

The 7,500-square-foot home, built exactly the way Chet wants it, is a split-level that looks long and low as you come up the drive. But at the rear are three stories facing the view: 35 miles over sixteen acres owned by Chet and Charlene.

"I spent six years building the house, then Charlene said, 'Get out of the way, I don't want you in the way when I decorate!'"

The results are lovely. Flowered sofas and lounge chairs are grouped around the fireplace in the living room, and the view from the wide windows seems immense. There's a door to walk out onto the porch and study the view even closer. The dining room's flowered wallpaper and formal dining set are complemented by an interesting large hutch. Guest rooms, most of which face the expansive view, are individually decorated.

A lot of partying goes on at Lincrest Lodge. The Southwest Room has a deck, and a bricked patio is below; both are party places. Special weekends include a Moonlight Weekend with a ride on the Texas State Railroad between the nearby towns of Rusk and Palestine. Or there might be a Country Western Square Dance Weekend on the patio.

The downstairs club and game room off the patio is fully equipped for all sorts of parties and meetings, with a full kitchen in addition to the kitchen upstairs. Chet and Charlene take food seriously.

"We celebrate breakfast," Chet says. "We have Sunday breakfast every morning. When people are away from home and don't have to get up and get at it, they ought to be able to enjoy a treat."

Lincrest Lodge's treats are something. A fruit bowl with melons, berries, grapefruit, strawberries and kiwi comes with crème brûlée or yogurt crème fraîche. There might be individual julienned-ham quiches with hollandaise sauce, fried tomatoes, homemade sourdough bread, scones, cereal. And don't forget the apple, blueberry, almond, or poppyseed muffins.

Dinners are special, too. Just call ahead and waiting for you will be marinated duck breast in honey mustard or ham baked in apple juice, with desserts like homemade apple pie and Black Forest cake. "Another favorite is lemon streusel cake," Charlene says.

"People are restricted by habit," Chet adds. "I urge them to try something new. For instance, most people don't know chayote squash. I do it with dill butter, and once they try it . . ."

How to get there: From Highway 69 turn east on Highway 21 for about half a mile. The lodge is up a hill to the right; there is a sign.

Innkeepers: Charlene and Chet Woj
Address/Telephone: P.O. Box 799; (409) 858–2223, fax (409) 858–2232
Rooms: 6; 1 with private bath, 1 with wheelchair access. No smoking inn.
Rates: $75, double; $30 extra person; EPB.
Open: All year.
Facilities and activities: Dinner, tea, and box lunches; game room; meeting facilities; special weekends; golf. Nearby: Caddoan Mounds State Park, Davy Crockett National Forest, Mission Tejas State Park, scenic drives.
Recommended Country Inns® Travel Club Benefit: 10% discount, subject to availability.

Annie's Country Inn
BIG SANDY, TEXAS 75755

This spanking gray-and-white dollhouse of an inn looks like one Queen Victoria might have played with in miniature. The rooms, except for the Queen Anne Room downstairs, are small, but I found them charming in every detail. Some rooms have lofts, perfect for kids.

The walls, with striped or floral wallpaper, are wainscoted; lace curtains frame the windows; fluffy, frilled, and lacy spreads and pillow shams cover the beds. Each room has a copy of an antique "safe." (It's really a refrigerator; on Saturday, when the inn and restaurant staff have their day off, your breakfast is in the safe instead of in the tearoom.)

I loved the atmosphere of camaraderie I found in the parlor when I arrived. It was early evening, and everybody was gathered around the television set, watching a vital football game. "Come join the party," they called out, waving glasses in the air.

"Looks pretty crowded to me," I answered. "There's always room for more," they said, and sure enough, space was made for me on the antique sofa and I joined them with a glass of wine.

It's always a treat to relax in a rocker on the porch or visit in the parlor with other guests, invariably interesting people. I also love the treat of the gourmet breakfast served in the tearoom across the road. There's a terrible choice: Should

I indulge in the cream-cheese-and-pecan-stuffed French toast, or should I have the strawberry crepes? Both begin with either fresh-squeezed orange juice or a delicious cold strawberry soup and a muffin.

The tearoom, with its white picket fence and circular verandas, is in one of Big Sandy's oldest homes, built in 1905. In 1982 it received the town's first official Texas Historical Marker. And yes (everyone always asks, says the innkeeper), there really is an Annie; she founded a very successful needlecraft mail-order company, Annie's Attic, which operates right out of little Big Sandy.

Both the Attic and the Tea Room have delightful displays of pretty arts and crafts: rag dolls, aprons, quilts and place mats—beware, you may be inspired to begin some needlework of your own. There even are patterns to make old-fashioned clothes for costumes and, I guess, for just plain fun.

How to get there: Big Sandy is on Highway 80 between Dallas and Longview. The inn is right in the middle of town, where Highway 155 crosses 80.

Innkeeper: William Withrow
Address/Telephone: 101 North Tyler Street; (214) 636–4355
Rooms: 13; 8 with private bath, 1 with TV. No smoking inn.
Rates: $38 to $115, double, EPB.
Open: All year.
Facilities and activities: Restaurant (closed Saturday), gift shop, needlecraft gallery. Nearby: Needlecraft Fair in July, Quilt Show in September, and Annie's Pecan Festival in November.
Business travel: Located 20 miles from Tyler. Corporate rates, phone in rooms.
Recommended Country Inns® Travel Club Benefit: 10% discount, Monday–Thursday, subject to availability.

Pine Colony Inn

CENTER, TEXAS 75935

This old hotel has been lovingly restored by daughter Regina and parents Marcille and Pershing, who pride themselves on being natives of Shelby County, one of the oldest in Texas. "Dustin is the eighth generation in the county," Regina says of her young son. "Suddenly people are into genealogy, and they come to consult with Mom; we go back more than one hundred years." Marcille writes a nostalgia column for the local paper, telling family stories like Thanksgiving in 1874 when her grandfather was a young man.

"We don't put on any front," she says, "we're all family. Guests tell us, 'We'll be back in two weeks, can we unload our car?'" There's a storeroom kept for just such a contingency. You'll find Pershing wearing his overalls, maybe sweeping the front porch. "He's just a little old country man," says his daughter fondly. As for feeling at home, "At first people want to make sure they have their room key. After a while they realize there's no need." If the front door is locked, guests can come and go at will up the side stairs to the front balcony and into the large sitting room, complete with overstuffed sofas and a television set.

The rustic hotel has dark-red Mexican tile on the first floor, what seems like acres of it, all laid by Regina and Marcille, who'll be glad to tell you how much work it was! Upstairs, they've kept the beautiful pine floors. Originally the Halley Hotel, the building was closed for seventeen years and was in bad repair. "Mom and Dad kept saying something should be done about this nice, big old building," Regina says with a laugh, "and finally we broke down and bought it."

All rooms have ceiling fans, and a fascinating touch is the network of white pipes snaking all along the ceilings. "Can you believe that's a sprinkler system?" Regina says. "It cost $20,000 even that long ago!"

Breakfast might be pancakes with homemade ribbon cane or blueberry syrup, eggs "any way," bacon, sausage, or you might be asked, "What *can* you eat?" With enough notice, Regina says, "We can run to the grocery store."

Rooms are small and simple but comfortable, with touches that make each one individual. Miss Barnhart's Room honors the woman whose bedroom suite furnishes it. The Indian Room has both pottery and paintings done by Regina. An old spinning wheel decorates the entrance hall, and a bank of old-fashioned brass mailboxes, one for each room, is set into the wall by the front door. If guests stay long enough to receive mail, they get to use one.

How to get there: Highway 87 becomes Shelbyville Street, and the inn is on the corner of Pine Street.

Innkeepers: Regina Wright; Marcille and Pershing Hughes
Address/Telephone: 500 Shelbyville Street; (409) 598–7700
Rooms: 12, including 2 suites; 10 with private bath, all with phone. No smoking inn.
Rates: $27.50, single; $45 to $55, double; EPB.
Open: All year.
Facilities and activities: Lunch and dinner, art shows, yearly quilt show. Nearby: nineteenth-century courthouse; use of swimming pool, fishing, hiking, and hunting at family's Caddo Pass Lodge; Sabine National Forest; Toledo Bend Reservoir and Pinkston Lake.
Recommended Country Inns® Travel Club Benefit: Stay two nights, get third night free.

Warfield House

CROCKETT, TEXAS 75835

Crockett is a delightful small town (about 7,000) "filled with friendly people, unique shops and restaurants, and many historic sites," Judy says in her bubbling, enthusiastic way. "Being the fifth oldest town in Texas, it has a special place for history buffs. We're certainly a visitor-friendly town and enjoy the opportunity to show off!"

Well, showing off is a Texas trait, and I for one enjoy it. The Warfield House is one of Crockett's lovely older homes, built by a Minnesotan who came to town in 1897. He took three years to complete the house, built Minnesota-style with twelve rooms, a third-floor attic, and a three-room cellar. Put together of rough-cut heart of pine, and square-head nails, it was built to last.

"I moved here from Houston when I was nine, and Jerry moved here with the General Telephone Company, and with these perfect old homes, we thought Crockett needed an inn," Judy says. "Jerry and I had this dream for four years."

The town didn't think so at first and resisted, but Judy was aided and abetted by her friend Alma Turner Sevier, who served as Judy's contractor, decorator, plumber, and designer. "She was 86 when she did the house," Judy says. "She made the drapes, made and covered the benches at the foot of the beds, did the magnolia paintings on the walls. She did so much there was no way I could completely repay her. So since the only thing she can't do is cook, I promised to give her breakfast for the rest of her life."

Alma comes often, and with good reason. We had what Judy calls a "historical" egg casserole, with bacon, biscuits, homemade "asphodel" bread, strawberry muffins, and fruit compote, and were enthralled by Alma's entertaining tales of Crockett.

Morning coffee and tea are placed on a windowseat so that guests can help themselves when they wake up. "And we have Diet Coke—a lot of people want that," it being a Texas tradition to have a Coke even before coffee in the morning.

Of course there's an Alma Room, "named in honor, too, of all the ladies who really cared about the house," says Judy. A violet-and-green color scheme and a four-poster bed make it both regal and romantic.

Ruth & Leela's Room, named for the Warfield daughters, has twin beds covered in periwinkle blue. The walls are sunny yellow, and the songbirds along the ceiling border and on the drapes are planned to invite the outdoors in. Marlene's Room, decorated so that you feel it's "your friend's home," Judy says, is in honor of another friend who helped make the inn dream come true. "My friend and her husband wanted to sell their home—this one—but didn't want to put it on the market until they consulted us. 'We want you to have it,' they said, so Jerry and I figured this was meant to be our inn."

People like to come and stay in this homey place. "I had a bank examiner who stayed a week," Judy says. Other long-term guests include two New Yorkers who stay here every year and commute the 34 miles to Centerville for business.

Judy is proud of the 19 quilts she has inherited from her mother and grandmother. The needlework in the inn is her mother's too. She found some photographs of her great-great-grandfather and his twin in an old trunk and learned that they fought barefoot in the snow at Shiloh—an interesting note for Civil War buffs.

How to get there: Entering town on Highway 287 or Highway 21 (Old Camino Real), follow the road into downtown. From downtown Courthouse Square, the inn is 3 blocks east on Houston.

Innkeepers: Judy and Jerry Teague
Address/Telephone: 712 East Houston Avenue; (409) 544–4037
Rooms: 4; all with private bath. No smoking inn.
Rates: \$68 to \$98, double, EPB. Corporate rates available.
Open: All year.
Facilities and activities: Swimming pool and hot tub. Nearby: Davy Crockett Memorial Park, Visitor Center-Museum, Fiddler's Festival, Davy Crockett National Forest, and Mission Tejas State Historic Park.

Red Rooster Square

EDOM, TEXAS 75754

Quite a surprise is this large rural-Victorian home, in a town so small it doesn't even have a post office! The original family Red Rooster was an antiques shop owned by Bob's grandfather back in Eton, Ohio; this Red Rooster is really in the country, because you're out of town as fast as you're in it. This is "real country," and I recommend lazy hours on the long front porch alternating between swing and rocking chair. But little Edom also has a lot of happy festivals, which Doris and Bob will be happy to tell you about.

The guest rooms are comfortable and bright, just about what you want your home to look like, and the downstairs bath has a luxurious Jacuzzi. The Moores have gone into the inn business because, Doris says with a laugh, "We built a too-big house!" Their children are grown, and when Doris planned the large home, Bob kept pointing out that "the kids won't be home every weekend." Nevertheless, "I built the house just like I like it," says a happy Doris, who coddles her guests instead of her children. So now they are an inn, and a very spacious, welcoming one indeed.

They're close to Canton with its famous First Mondays Trade Days. "If you go to Canton," said Doris, "you have to have show and tell. We've had a bunch of women sitting on a sheet I spread on the floor." But be sure to reserve ahead, because "that's our biggest weekend," she cautions.

The full breakfast is served family style, spread out on the bar dividing the large kitchen and den. "We always decide the night before what time to serve breakfast"; the innkeepers consult their guests, and the majority rules. Then it's your choice whether to pile your plate up and sit in the breakfast room or to relax in the den, watching television.

Either place, delicious is the sausage strata—layers of egg, cheese, sausage, and mushrooms—served with orange juice, melon and grapes, cinnamon twists, and blueberry muffins. The blueberries are grown in Edom, and big, juicy ones they are, too. They are a big crop for the area. If you don't believe it, come to the Blueberry Festival at berry harvest time.

If you're still hungry, there's also oatmeal with brown sugar and raisins, ideal for the cholesterol-conscious and "very healthy for everyone," says the chef.

And for dinner, Edom may be a *very* small town, but Doris recommends The Shed, a little restaurant serving "good home cooking." Specials on weekends are chicken-fried steak and catfish.

How to get there: The inn is 2½ miles south of Highway 64 on Highway 314. Go south off I–20 (Van exit), take Highway 314 south to Edom, and the inn is on the left.

Innkeepers: Doris and Bob Moore
Address/Telephone: Route 3, Box 3387, Ben Wheeler 75754; (903) 852–6774 or (800) 947–0393
Rooms: 3 share 2 baths; wheelchair accessible. No smoking inn.
Rates: $60, double, EPB. No credit cards.
Open: All year.
Facilities and activities: Nearby: Edom has pine-scented country lanes for hiking, crafts people, East Texas antiques stores, famous Canton First Mondays Trade Days half an hour away.

Wild Briar, The Country Inn at Edom

EDOM, TEXAS 75764

Wild Briar is a two-story manor-style brick house almost completely hidden in the trees surrounding it: oaks, sweet gum, pines, cedars, and holly. Although the inn is named for the wild berry vines on its twenty-three acres, indoors it's as British as Mary and Max can make it.

"We travel in England, and when we go, we like to visit many of the inns our rooms are named for as well as seek out new places. We want to be a true country inn, where people can stay and feel welcome." The "snug," where smoking is permitted, copies the coziness the Scotts enjoy in British pubs. There are videos of old movies, and dinner orders are taken.

Mary taught junior high school for twenty years, and she'll teach you a great deal about England and its inns. The Wild Briar presents a mix of English, Welsh, and Scottish country inns the Scotts have stayed at. Each room is named for one of their favorites. Whether you stay in Sturminster Newton, Bonthddu, Harrogate, Glebe, Thakeham, or Tresanton, you'll be glad you did.

"What do most people come and do?" I asked Mary. "Nothing!" was her mirthful answer.

The morning begins with a mug of coffee in the kitchen or on the patio, but at breakfast you'll have to exchange the mug for a cup in Mary's Spode Summer Palace pattern to match the breakfast china. Juices, fruit like grapefruit and strawberries or the huge Edom blueberries, strawberry bread, zucchini muffins, all go with "any eggs to order" and bacon or sausage. Mary often makes quiche ahead so Max won't have a problem feeding guests if it's her turn to teach Sunday school. On weekends Max makes gravy for biscuits, "his forte, not mine," Mary said.

Dinners are delicious full-course meals, perhaps starting with gumbo or broccoli-cheese soup; next comes a green or fruit salad, followed by rolled tenderloin with cornbread dressing or buttermilk-pecan breast of chicken. Family-style vegetables might be a selection of green beans, new potatoes, corn on the cob, squash, sliced fresh tomatoes, all "from our farmer friends down the road." Dessert? How about profiteroles, or mystery pie, so called because you can't tell which fruit's in it.

The Scotts are civic-minded folk; Mary serves on the city council of Edom (with a population of 300), and Max is on the water board.

How to get there: Take Highway 314 south off I–20 (Van exit) to Edom. Turn right on FM (Farm Road) 279 to FM 2339 on your left. Wild Briar is the first driveway on the left on FM 2339.

Innkeepers: Mary and Max Scott
Address/Telephone: P.O. Box 21, Ben Wheeler 75754; (903) 852–3975
Rooms: 6; all with private bath. Smoking permitted in public room ("the snug").
Rates: $100, per room, MAP. No credit cards.
Open: All year except for Tuesdays and Wednesdays when holidays fall on those days.
Facilities and activities: Dinner by reservation; gift shop of East Texas crafts. Nearby: hiking paths, craftspeople, East Texas antiques stores, Canton First Mondays Trade Days.

The Captain's Castle

JEFFERSON, TEXAS 75657

In the early 1870s Captain Thomas J. Rogers combined two houses: one of Texas Planters Architecture, which he had oxen roll on logs across town from down on the riverfront, and one already on this site. The more imposing one he attached to the front, and this is what you'll see.

"He was trying to make his house antebellum," Barbara explains. Well, I don't know how antebellum The Captain's Castle is, but it certainly is impressive, with its tall white columns and spacious grounds. It's mighty impressive on the inside, too, and it was a popular feature on the Jefferson Historic Home Tour even before the Hookers acquired it.

"I'd been on the road as a manufacturer's rep for years," Buck says. "I got tired of traveling. Some of our friends retired around here, and this is as close to Virginia as we could get without going back." Barbara and Buck are from the Tidewater section of Virginia, and they love the country around Jefferson because it reminds them of Virginia. "The rolling hills, the trees, the green—they're a lot alike." There was no sense in going back to Virginia when he retired, he says, because "I've been in Texas since 1960 and everybody's gone back there. All my friends are here."

As for Barbara, she spent those "best years of her life" raising three children, and she admits she must be one in a million because she likes to have her retired husband home. "Buck traveled three weeks out of every month, so now when he's home it's mighty nice."

The guest rooms in the main house are named for daughters and granddaughter. Katherine's Room, painted a deep, almost a hot pink, has a four-poster bed of solid mahogany, hand carved and from Indonesia. Elizabeth's Room is a light pink. It has a pretty king-sized, four-poster carved bed in a rice design as well as a copy of Thomas Jefferson's desk. Other furniture recalls Carter Braxton, and Buck was a little surprised when I said, "Carter Who?"

"Why, he signed the Declaration of Independence! If you look, you'll see his name, right at the bottom in the center!"

Teri's Room is pale blue, with a queen-sized Eastlake bed, Victorian marble-topped tables, and a flowered loveseat.

Breakfast is served on an impressive claw-footed table. It's always something good, like a Panhandle Casserole of eggs and cheese and meat, with stewed cinnamon apples, homemade biscuits, and more fruit—a compote of three to five fruits, depending on what's in season.

What's more, it's served on elegant Minton china, and Buck even knows the pattern. "It's Cockatrice."

An hour before breakfast is served, coffee arrives at your door, along with strawberry, blueberry, or apple cinnamon muffins, always homemade. "I like being at home, I like to cook and bake," Barbara says. When I say I'd prefer tea, Buck jumps right in. "Coffee, tea, orange juice, whatever you like," he says. "I've even got Coke if you want.

"I try to get people away from work, from the stuff they have to fight," he adds. "I used to do that, so when I could get away I sure did. After a while, all that traveling isn't so great!"

How to get there: Go east at the intersection of Highway 59 and Highway 49 2 blocks to Alley Street. Turn right and go 2 blocks. The Captain's Castle is on the right, on the corner of Alley and Walker.

Innkeepers: Barbara and Buck Hooker
Address/Telephone: 403 East Walker; (903) 665–2330
Rooms: 7, in 3 buildings; all with private bath and TV. No smoking inn.
Rates: $85 to $100, double; $20 extra person; EPB.
Open: All year.
Facilities and activities: Sun deck, gazebo. Nearby: Restaurants, antiques shops, historic homes, Jefferson Museum, riverboat ride, surrey ride, Mardi Gras, Springtime Pilgrimage, Christmas Candlelight Tour, Caddo Lake, Lake o' the Pines.

McKay House

JEFFERSON, TEXAS 75657

The McKay House has undergone all sorts of changes and enlargements; for starters, the roof was raised to make two lovely suites. Still imbued with the spirit of old times, Alma dresses in period costume to serve breakfast, and Joseph wields hammer and nails to continue refurbishing the historic house. The dining area has been restored, and a conservatory designed for both dining and relaxing now overlooks the lovely garden.

"McKay House is one of the oldest houses in Jefferson," Alma says, "and the oldest operating as a bed and breakfast, so we want to be as authentic as possible; we want things to be as they were back then." Television? Don't be silly, they didn't have television in the 1800s, Alma says with conviction.

The inn offers things like designer linens, Crabtree & Evelyn toiletries, fresh flowers in the rooms, and custom-made Amish quilts on the beds—wallpaper samples were sent to Indiana to have them made to match.

The Parker imagination and sense of fun are at work everywhere. The Keeping Room in the rear guest cottage is patterned after the room where Alma says pioneers did everything—cooking, eating, sleeping, bathing. The footed tub is in the dormer, the dresser is an old icebox, a chopping block is an end table; and the commode is enclosed like an outdoor privy in a little house of original wood shingles, complete with half-moon peephole. The cottage's other room is a Sunday Room, like the parlor used when farmers cleaned up and went to town for the Sabbath.

When I opened the clothes cupboard in my room and found two garments hanging there, I thought the last guests had forgotten them. But no, each guest room is complete with Victorian nightwear: a woman's nightgown and a man's sleep shirt. Alma hopes they are used.

"We want our guests to know how it was back in the 1850s," she says. They have fun wearing the vintage hats at the full sit-down breakfast in the conservatory. "When all the ladies wear their hats, you've never seen so much picture taking," Alma says with a laugh. And what a conversation starter, to get people acquainted!

Alma's "Gentleman's Breakfast" of Chicken a la McKay or honey-cured ham, cheese biscuits, and homemade strawberry bread with cream cheese and strawberry preserves is something to write home about, as are the cheese blintz soufflé and zucchini muffins. Hospitality, says Alma, is the hallmark of McKay House, and you may be called to breakfast with a tune on the old Packard pump organ. "Or better yet, just pull a few stops yourself," says Alma.

How to get there: The McKay House is located 2 blocks east of U.S. 59 and 4 blocks south of Highway 49 (Broadway).

Innkeepers: Alma Anne and Joseph Parker
Address/Telephone: 306 East Delta Street; (903) 665–7322; in Dallas (214) 348–1929
Rooms: 3, plus 2 suites in main house, 2 in rear cottage; all with private bath. No smoking inn.
Rates: \$85 to \$145, double; \$60, corporate rate; EPB. Discount on weekdays.
Open: All year.
Facilities and activities: Nearby: Jefferson restaurants and antiques shops, museums, historic homes, horse-and-carriage rides, riverboat rides, Mardi Gras, Jefferson Historic Pilgrimage in May, Candlelight Tour at Christmas.
Recommended Country Inns® Travel Club Benefit: 25% discount for stay of two nights or longer, Monday–Thursday.

Pride House
JEFFERSON, TEXAS 75657

Jefferson is the part of Texas that most seems like the Deep South, and the hospitality of the Old South is what comes naturally to innkeepers Ruthmary and daughter Sandy. Ruthmary finds innkeeping to be a life of "sharing, serving—and receiving. Wonderful people come through my life. They share with me their family, their insights, their interests—as I do in return."

They also share an inn that is one of the prides of Jefferson. Pride House was the first bed and breakfast inn in Texas, and a national magazine has called it "one of the twenty-three most romantic spots in America." Stained glass windows in every room of the house—red, blue, and amber framing the clear glass centers—together with ornate woodwork, long halls, and gingerbread trim on the porch make this house a treasure.

The parlor has an antique piano that the Historical Society asked Ruthmary to keep for them. Over it she has hung a wonderful old gilt mirror from her husband's family, "who were riverboat people, you know." Riverboating was big business on Jefferson's Big Cypress Bayou until the Civil War.

The main house has six guest rooms. The Golden Era Room next to the parlor commemorates the era of the town when more than 30,000 people lived here instead of today's 2,300. It's a lovely golden room with a romantic 9-foot half-tester bed and a large stained-glass bay window. I was equally happy in the large Blue Room with its Victorian slipper chairs and king bed. The Green Room has antique white wicker furniture; the West Room is imposing, with rich Victorian red walls and an Eastlake walnut full bed. The Bay Room, which Ruthmary and Sandy call their "lusty Victorian," is furnished with Eastlake Victorian furniture and has gold stars twinkling on the ceiling.

The other four guest rooms are at the rear in the saltbox house that Ruthmary calls Dependency—because it was the servant's quarters, and "the folks in the main house were dependent on their work."

A refreshing contrast to the Victoriana of Pride House is the common room at the rear, large and bright, with a window wall lighting up the chic black-and-white tile floor and the green plants all around. When her daughter suggested this decor, Ruthmary says she couldn't see it, until Sandy said the magic word, "green plants." Now it's the most popular gathering place in the inn.

Breakfast always includes one of Ruthmary's famous recipes from when she also had a restaurant downtown. Oh, her crème brûlée fruit parfait! Indescribably delicious! With it, perhaps bran muffins delicately redolent of almond, croissants with strawberry butter and melon preserves, and two kinds of sausage. Another morning you might be served Ruthmary's special baked pear in French cream sauce. If you catch Ruthmary or Sandy in a whimsical mood, there may be Not Eggzactly Benedict, a wonderful takeoff on you know what.

How to get there: Highway 49 becomes Broadway as it heads east into town. The Pride House is on the northwest corner of Broadway and Alley Street.

Innkeepers: Ruthmary Jordan and Sandy Spalding
Address/Telephone: 409 East Broadway; (903) 665–2675
Rooms: 10, including 1 suite (6 in main house, 4 in annex); all with private bath, 1 room for handicapped.
Rates: \$65 to \$100, double; \$10 extra person; EPB.
Open: All year.
Facilities and activities: Front porches, swings, rocking chairs, and reading material everywhere. Nearby: historic homes to tour, Jefferson Museum, railroad baron Jay Gould's railroad car.
Recommended Country Inns® Travel Club Benefit: 40% discount, Sunday–Thursday.

The Steamboat Inn

JEFFERSON, TEXAS 75657

Marian and Pete have built themselves a new-old inn, completely from scratch. "It's just like an old Greek Revival, and Pete's done it from all old materials. He went knocking on doors and old storage places to find old doors and windows." The flooring is heart of pine, and the house is so authentically antique that it's hard to believe it's new.

Marian and Pete are veteran innkeepers, but their last inn became too much for them. "We love the business," Marian says, "but our other place just grew too big."

They got started in the inn business by accident, you might say. "We were on the way to a wedding in Longview," Pete says, "and just on impulse we walked into the Chamber [of Commerce] office and asked, 'Do you know of a business for sale, we are bored to tears.' I had retired from the oil business and we were looking for something to take up the slack time." The Sorensens are from Louisiana, Cajun country, Pete looks more like a Danish sea captain, white beard, tattoo, and all, than a retired oil man. Even more surprising is that he is quite artistic; he paints—or, rather, he did before he became a busy innkeeper.

Both Pete and Marian are delighted with this "impulsive" turn in their lives. "What's nice about it," says Marian, "is that you get into the mainstream, even though you're retired." People, she says, bring the world to them. As for Pete, he roars, "We pamper the daylights out of them!"

Breakfast is delicious, and Pete is the chef. Scrambled eggs, bacon and sausage, cheese grits or hashed browns are one specialty combination. Lately, he's been making a tasty ham and Swiss cheese soufflé, crowned with hollandaise sauce. Add homemade sesame biscuits as well as fruit and orange juice, and the morning is complete. Especially since an hour before breakfast, you'll find coffee (or tea if you prefer) and muffins at your door. Pete learned to cook when he was pretty young, and he found it was something he really enjoyed. "I was next to the youngest of twelve children, and I would go to Cajun restaurants in New Orleans to learn how," he says.

Guest rooms at The Steamboat Inn are named for the steamboats that came to Jefferson when it was a wild and raucous riverboat town before the Civil War. (Today things are more sedate.)

The Golden Era Room (yes, that was a steamboat) has twin antique sleigh beds, and the old tub in the bath is something new to me. "It's skirted," Marian says as she shows it to me. "These came before the claw-foot ones." The Starlight Room has another of the interesting old tubs—and here I thought claw-footed was as old as they got!

The Runaway is pretty, with a beige lace canopy over the four-poster old rice bed, now a queen. As for the Mittie Stephens, well, it's named for a steamboat that caught fire and sank in Caddo Lake. They've recently found her, or what's left of her. "They've just been able to bring up parts of it so far," Marian says. "You can see some of the relics in the Jefferson Museum."

Each of the guest rooms has an English coal-burning fireplace. "You would not know they're really gas," Marian says, and I was almost sorry she told me.

How to get there: Follow Highway 59 into town where it becomes Jefferson Street. Go east for about 2 blocks, past Lion Street Park, and the road veers to the right and becomes Marshall. The inn is just past the stop sign, almost immediately beyond the park.

Innkeepers: Marian and Pete Sorensen
Address/Telephone: 114 North Marshall; (903) 665–8946
Rooms: 4; all with private bath and TV; wheelchair accessible. No smoking inn.
Rates: $75 to $95, double, EPB.
Open: All year.
Facilities and activities: Nearby: restaurants, antiques shops, historic homes, Jefferson Museum, riverboat ride, surrey ride, Mardi Gras, Springtime Pilgrimage, Christmas Candlelight Tour, fishing and boating on Caddo Lake and Lake o' the Pines.

Stillwater Inn

JEFFERSON, TEXAS 75657

"It's very gratifying to have guests who appreciate what we're trying to do," Sharon Stewart says earnestly, speaking both of the thoughtful yet simple decor—a complete contrast to nostalgic Victoriana—and of the restaurant, which has become an East Texas dining tradition. These innkeepers in the 1890s Eastlake Victorian home have earned a reputation for fare such as I enjoyed: grilled breast of duck served with wild rice or potatoes pureed with garlic and cream; a carrot terrine; zucchini with herbs; and for dessert, Concord cake.

Sharon and Bill pride themselves on their fancy desserts like the Concord cake, a tasty confection of chocolate meringue, chocolate mousse, whipped cream, and almonds, and on homemade ice creams like cappuccino and macadamia nut. I relaxed on a cool beige-and-white-striped sofa before the parlor fireplace and had a big delicious dish of the macadamia.

The inn's color scheme is a restful pale blue and cream. Downstairs are the bar and restaurant; upstairs are the guest quarters, constructed from light Salado pine, with dramatically pitched ceilings, skylights, and a comfortable sitting place with books and Sharon's sewing machine. The small cottage adjacent to the inn was moved onto the property and restored with the same spare lines and cool blue-and-cream color scheme, the same pencil-post pine bedstead.

In the cottage the innkeepers replaced the low ceiling with high structural beams "to give a feeling of more space," Bill says.

Breakfast is hearty and goes way beyond croissants and coffee. Added are scrambled eggs with fresh chives—"We've got an herb garden in the back," Bill says with typical enthusiasm—and Pecos melon. Everything's made from scratch by these two enthusiastic gourmets, including fresh-ground coffee.

"Not to brag," says Sharon, "but we're the only restaurant in East Texas with an espresso machine with two heads!"

They also have a light and sunny inn—clean-cut is the word that comes to mind, or maybe uncluttered. The few antiques, like the coffee table–cum–old Dutch bellows ("Hey! Where can I get one of those?" a delighted guest asked) and the furniture in the Victorian Room, all contribute to a getaway that helped unclutter my crowded mind. The white picket fence is also Sharon's pride. "It sets the house off, makes it seem so nice and 'cottagey'. . . If you knew how many times I've moved before settling here!"

A cookbook with Bill's Stillwater Inn recipes is now in print.

How to get there: Highway 49 becomes Broadway as it enters town. The inn is on the northeast corner of Broadway and Owens.

Innkeepers: Sharon and Bill Stewart
Address/Telephone: 203 East Broadway; (903) 665–8415
Rooms: 3, plus 1 cottage; all with private bath, cottage with phone and TV. No smoking inn.
Rates: $80 to $90, double, EPB.
Open: All year.
Facilities and activities: Restaurant open for dinner Tuesday–Sunday (reservation appreciated); lunch served to groups of fifteen or more; bar. Nearby: pets boarded reasonably; restaurants, antiques shops, museums, historic homes, horse-and-carriage rides, riverboat rides, Mardi Gras, Jefferson Historic Pilgrimage in May, Candlelight Tour at Christmas.
Business travel: Conference facility with wheelchair-accessible restrooms; fax and copy machines. Cottage with phone.

Cotten's Patch Inn

MARSHALL, TEXAS 75670

Cotten's Patch looks like an old farmhouse set somehow in the middle of town. The pink-painted wooden house has the sort of tall narrow windows, peaked roof, and front screened porch that can be seen in many a house on the prairie.

But inside, what a surprise! The home is filled with lovely antique furniture, decorative objets d'art, and paintings. Everywhere I looked I discovered new treasures, things like the old ironing board and iron in the dining-room alcove and the china that Jo Ann paints.

Innkeeper Jo Ann is an artist, and she has painted delightful trompe l'oeil decorations on many walls. The front hall has a painted hall tree on the wall; the kitchen has a painted rug and a latticed apple tree. I really laughed at the broom and mop painted on the pantry door. Not to be outdone by Jo Ann's artistry, Lonnie, a musician, enjoys treating guests to both organ and accordian recitals.

I had trouble picking a favorite room, a choice not made easier by Jo Ann's policy of first come first choose. "The first one here gets to see all the rooms," she says. "I always let them tour the house before others get here."

Jo Ann finds that the gentlemen often like to drink their coffee on the porch before the ladies get up, so the first one up gets to plug in the coffee. There are two pots, "one leaded, one unleaded," Jo Ann points out with a smile.

It's perfectly all right to eat in the lovely, large dining room, but like most of Jo Ann's guests, I preferred to eat in the sunny country kitchen. "Most everybody just loves to eat in the kitchen," she says. Most likely to get closer to the fresh coffee cake, say I. Jo Ann enjoys having breakfast with her guests.

If she has a group, she says she "gets carried away" into the spirit of the thing, making individual quiches or sausage balls. "When I have my homemade bread coming out of the oven, they say it drives them crazy. Homemade bread and jelly: I have a neighbor who makes mayhaw jelly just like my grandmother used to make."

Touches like ice water and magazines in the rooms, turned-down beds with candy on the pillow make Cotten's Patch a real treat. Jo Ann also provides plastic "litter bags" filled with pamphlets describing what to do in historic Marshall.

The spa on the back porch has more of Jo Ann's fun art, a painted apple tree climbing the wall and spreading on the ceiling overhead. For real is the pailful of bright red apples alongside. "I tell my guests that if they get bored in the spa, they can bob for apples," Jo Ann says with a twinkle in her eye.

How to get there: From Highway 80 go south on Alamo to Rusk. Turn right and the inn will be on the left in the middle of the 700 block.

Innkeepers: Jo Ann Cotten and Lonnie Hill
Address/Telephone: 703 East Rusk Street; (214) 938–8756
Rooms: 3 share 2½ baths; all with TV.
Rates: $75 to $85, double, EPB.
Open: All year.
Facilities and activities: Spa. Nearby: Marshall Pottery Factory, museums, Stagecoach Days in May, Fire Ant Festival in October.

Munzesheimer Manor

MINEOLA, TEXAS 75773

"We tried to create the atmosphere of when the house was built," Sherry and Bob say of the 1898 manor house that they bought, completely gutted, and put back together again. The photo album in the parlor chronicles the horrendous task they set themselves. When they began the project, Bob says, their entire family thought they were crazy. "That's nothing," Sherry chimes in. "All our friends did, too." They even got comments from strangers such as: "It is amazing that your marriage seems to be still intact!" "But," Bob says, "we've always liked to entertain and have people in the house . . . and Sherry always wanted an old house."

The large house has two parlors, a huge dining room, and guest rooms named in honor of former owners. I was in the Blasingame Room, which had both English and American antiques; the bath had a footed tub; and my armoire had a bullet embedded down low inside the door. Bob said he's darned if he knows where it came from— it came with the armoire. A Victorian nightgown and nightshirt were provided, in case I really wanted to get into the turn-of-the-century mode. Each guest room comes so equipped, which is one of the things that makes staying at this inn an adventure. I also found a tray with a bottle of St. Regis Blanc (wine without the alcohol) cooling in my room when I returned from dinner, as well as after-dinner mints.

For breakfast you'll have a full feast: perhaps fruit cup (for the Fourth of July it was red raspberries, white pear, and some of the area's huge blueberries); Bob's special scrambled eggs; pepper-cured lean bacon; and peach and blackberry jam to spread on fresh biscuits. Also on the menu are chilled blueberry soup, German pancakes, almond French toast, and a chili egg puff served with picante sour cream and hot biscuits.

It was fascinating to hear the story of how the house was reborn; Bob spoke the truth when he said, "We'll wind up sitting in the parlor and talking about it till all hours." The Cowan Room, named after Dr. Cowan, the dentist, has his black leather dental chair as an entertaining point of interest. Bob collects all sorts of memorabilia such as shoe lasts and dinner bells. Other interesting features are the stained-glass windows, the seven fireplaces, and the wraparound porch, where morning coffee and the Sunday paper made it perfect to be outdoors.

Added to the inn are three more charming rooms, which have not changed the exterior of the historic house. The Engineer's Room and the Conductor's Room foster memories of Mineola's great railroad days, and the Tack Room, built where the stable used to be, is complete with a hay loft and a "two-holer." (Indoors, for modern guests; old documents indicate that back in the good old days, the house had "a two-holer in the alley.")

How to get there: Mineola is located approximately 70 miles from Dallas and 80 miles from Shreveport at the intersection of U.S. 80 and U.S. 69 (it is also midway between Houston and Tulsa, Oklahoma).

Innkeepers: Sherry and Bob Murray
Address/Telephone: 202 North Newsom Street; (903) 569–6634
Rooms: 7, 3 in Country Cottage; all with private bath; first floor rooms wheelchair accessible. No smoking inn.
Rates: $70 to $95, per room, EPB.
Open: All year.
Facilities and activities: Dinner by reservation. Nearby: Texas Forest; Azalea and Dogwood Trails; Mineola Junction with antiques, gifts, and arts and crafts; Canton Trade Days; 25 miles from Tyler.
Recommended Country Inns® Travel Club Benefit: 10% discount, Monday–Thursday.

Mound Street Inn

NACOGDOCHES, TEXAS 75961

Nacogdoches is the blueberry capital of Texas, and Linda takes advantage of the bountiful crops to serve a delicious fruit compote topped with yogurt and blueberries. And, of course, blueberry muffins (my favorites, though, are Linda's banana/chocolate chip ones) and there's a choice of three dry cereals with bananas—or blueberries.

Linda's "glorified continental breakfast" includes her delicious homemade wheat and cheese bread and usually some of the following: zucchini grape bread, carrot apple muffins, lemon sponge jelly roll, homemade cinnamon rolls, and her own plum, peach, and blueberry jam. Breakfast is served in the dining room, on a tray out in the sun porch, or in your room.

The graceful two-story Victorian house was built in 1899, only 2 blocks from downtown. It was built for Tolbert Hardeman, a merchant whose great-uncle was a signer of the Texas Declaration of Independence. Linda has decorated with a blend of tartans and tapestries, Indian rugs and antiques, and the expansive living room and parlor are very inviting.

The house is trimmed with dentil molding, and the pair of Doric columns and preacher doors are the sort of details that earned the home inclusion in the Historic Overlay designated by the Nacogdoches Landmark and Preservation Committee. The inn is also part of the Old

Washington Square National Historic District.

Two sun porches hug the right side of the house. The downstairs one, decorated in black wicker and chintz, is a comfortable place to relax among the green plants, play a game of cards at the card table, maybe a noncompetitive game of solitaire against yourself.

The living room is somewhat Southwestern, with western rugs on the polished floor and willow chairs in front of the fireplace. The parlor has an organ that guests are welcome to play.

Linda is late of Santa Fe, New Mexico, where she managed the Preston House Inn, and she has incorporated some of the Southwestern New Mexico decor in several guest rooms as well as downstairs. Room One, the fully enclosed upstairs sun room, now a sleeping porch, is like a leafy bower amid the treetops surrounding the house. It's done in a cowboy motif. Room Four, decorated in paisleys and calicos, boasts a family-made lodgepole and a pair of Taos headboards.

Room Two has European antiques of stripped pine; Room Three has plum walls enhanced by brocades, tapestries, and floral rugs.

Nacogdoches has a lot of interesting, out-of-the-usual things to see and do; Linda says, "Come discover Nacogdoches before everyone else does!" The Old North Church is believed to be the oldest union church in Texas. An interesting piece of trivia: In Texas during the church's early days, when Texas was part of Mexico, Protestant services were unlawful.

Millard's Crossing is a group of restored nineteenth-century buildings furnished with antiques and pioneer memorabilia. If you hanker to be an archaeologist, visitors are welcome at the annual summer excavations of the Caddo Indian Mounds (June to August).

How to get there: From downtown go east on Main Street (Highway 21) 3 blocks to Mound Street. Turn left and go 2½ blocks; the inn is on the right, in the middle of the block. There is no sign; look for a light blue house at number 408.

Innkeeper: Linda Stone
Address/Telephone: 408 North Mound; (409) 569–2211
Rooms: 4; 2 with private bath. No smoking inn.
Rates: $65 to $80, double; $15 extra person; expanded continental breakfast. No credit cards.
Open: All year.
Facilities and activities: Nearby: historic downtown; Stephen F. Austin State University, Arboretum & Herb Garden; Old North Church; Millard's Crossing; Old Stone Fort; Washington Square Archaeology Site (Caddo Indian Mounds).

Capt. E. D. Downs Home

SAN AUGUSTINE, TEXAS 75972

San Augustine calls itself "the Cradle of Texas," vying with nearby Nacogdoches for the title of the oldest Anglo town in Texas. It certainly is full of Texas history, and the Capt. E. D. Downs Home is one of the reasons. This is the East Texas Pine Woods area, and lumber for the house was cut from the timberlands of the Downs family, floated down the Sabine River to a mill, barged back upstream, and transported to the site by oxen. It's still big lumber country today, and you'll see huge logs stacked alongside the road.

The Fussells bought the house in 1976. "The house, vacant, looked so sad," innkeeper Dorothy says. "The camellias outside were so pretty; I said, 'This house needs to be used.'" It was built at the turn of the century by Captain Downs, grandfather of local celebrity Ed Clark, ambassador to Australia under Lyndon B. Johnson. Clark's mother was the last of the family to live in the house.

The spacious house is bright and friendly, furnished with some antique pieces but mainly with comfortable furniture. Guest rooms are large and as cool as their names imply: The Blue Room, the Green Room, the Yellow Room. There are three fireplaces, but today they're just for show, since the house is centrally heated and cooled. Pink and red camellias surround the sun room with its white wicker furniture, books, magazines, and television.

People love to sit in the sitting room and rock and read, and there's a piano in the parlor. Dorothy says she begs her guests to play. Dorothy does not stay on the property, but her aunt, living just next door, is always available. "We all, even our guests, call her Dear Ima," Dorothy says. "It started when my children were small. We lived in Virginia, and when they wrote to her, they began their letters 'Dear Dear Ima'—they thought that was her name. She's a dear person; this whole town loves her."

So do guests, and Mary Ann, the cook, as well, by the time they leave. "She has worked for me for more than twenty years," Dorothy says. "She is such a great cook; we pride ourselves on our breakfast: sausage, bacon, eggs, our delicious biscuits and gravy." Dorothy sets her breakfast table, serves orange juice and coffee, and visits with her guests. "I've met so many lovely people. I have commercial travelers who love to sit at the kitchen table and work. I have no problem with long-distance calls; they always leave money for them—inn people are wonderful!"

Small as San Augustine is, Dorothy says she can recommend three good restaurants: Doodles, San Augustine Inn, and Faustos.

How to get there: Highway 21 becomes Main Street; the inn is 2 blocks from downtown on the corner of Congress and Main.

Innkeeper: Dorothy B. Fussell
Address/Telephone: 301 East Main Street; (409) 275–2289
Rooms: 5; 1 two-room suite with private bath, others share 2½ baths; mobile telephone available; wheelchair access to downstairs rooms and dining room. No smoking inn.
Rates: $55 to $70, double, EPB.
Open: All year.
Facilities and activities: Nearby: restaurants, historic homes and churches, El Camino Real Trail, Sabine National Forest, Toledo Bend Reservoir and Pinkston Lake.

The Mansion on Main

TEXARKANA, TEXAS 75501

If you're wondering what Scott Joplin has to do with Texarkana, the Pulitzer Prize–winning musician was from here. And the city has another reason for fame: It is two separate municipalities, one in Texas, the other in Arkansas. Squarely on the Texas–Arkansas line you'll find the nation's only Justice Building serving two states. Same with the U.S. Post Office. The Mansion on Main is near both.

The mansion was built in 1895 and has a Texas Historic Marker. The fourteen white two-story-tall columns salvaged from the St. Louis World's Fair are spectacular.

"Kay has always had a fascination with columns," Jack says. "Out of the blue, we got this flyer about the house saying 'Every old house is a great bed and breakfast inn.' We were headed to Arkansas [from Dallas] to see family and stopped by."

The inn provides guests with Victorian nightgowns for the ladies and sleepshirts for the gentlemen, following the lead of their sister inn in Jefferson, the McKay House. Both places believe in people getting into the spirit of the thing, and that includes providing fancy Victorian hats for the ladies to wear at breakfast.

The fourteen columns are a perfect foil for the pretty pink-painted mansion. If you enter by the front door, there's handsome hand-carved wood filigree work over the entrance; from the back parking lot you'll "register" at an old post-office desk. The kitchen is open and Kay says, "Come on in! Everybody comes into the kitchen."

The dining room, with a lovely small-block parquet floor, fireplace, and black oak furniture, displays Jack's collection of syrup pitchers. Kay and Jack find all sorts of interesting articles, and you never know what you'll see next (the sink in the powder room is from an old railroad car).

There's a piano in the parlor, and a paneled foyer leads upstairs to six guest rooms, from the Butler's Garret to the Governor's Suite, all furnished with period antiques.

In the upstairs hall, the telephone stand and a stereo-scopic viewer vie for interest with a section of the wall that's framed and covered with glass like a picture to reveal how the house was constructed of lathes and sisal-and-pig hair plaster.

The Lone Star Room has a cozy reading corner by the fireplace and a Family Album to enjoy. Ragland Room has a famous bed: both Lady Bird Johnson and Alex Haley slept there (at different times, of course).

The art deco Butler's Pantry, with chestnut furniture, is at the head of the back stairs, a perfect place not to disturb the rest of the house.

The inn is famous for the Gentleman's Breakfast (which ladies get to eat, too), orange pecan French toast with pure maple syrup or fresh strawberries; shirred eggs with ham, and Israeli melon; perhaps granola parfait and Chicken à la Mansion on sourdough biscuits. Chimes pleasantly call guests to table.

There's always a fireside cup of coffee or a cool lemonade on the veranda after a long day's sightseeing or attending to business.

How to get there: Take the State Line exit off I–30 to 8th and turn right to Main Street. The inn is on the left at the end of the street. Turn left into the parking lot in the rear of the inn.

Innkeepers: Kay and Jack Roberts
Address/Telephone: 802 Main Street; (903) 792–1835
Rooms: 4, plus 2 suites; all with private bath and wired for telephone and TV; wheelchair access to first floor rooms. No smoking inn.
Rates: $55 to $110, double, EPB.
Open: All year.
Facilities and activities: Guest kitchen privileges, off-street parking. Nearby: Perot Theater, Regional Arts Center, Texarkana Historical Society and Museum, Union Station, Scott Joplin Mural.
Business travel: Located in downtown Texarkana. Phone line in rooms; corporate rates.
Recommended Country Inns® Travel Club Benefit: 25% discount for stay of two nights or longer, must include the weekend.

Charnwood Hill Inn

TYLER, TEXAS 75701

If you'd like to experience the style of living enjoyed by an old-time Texas oilman, Charnwood Hill Inn is the place to be. Built around 1860 by a Professor Hand, who was headmaster of a school for girls, the mansion passed through several hands until it was purchased by H. L. Hunt in the early 1930s.

"The Hunt family extensively remodeled and redecorated," Don says. "The family moved to Dallas in 1938, but there's still a lot of interest here in the Hunt family."

I don't know what sort of furnishings the Hunts had when this gorgeous mansion was their home, but it would have to be something to equal Patsy and Don's collection. "We spent seventeen years collecting and didn't want to get rid of it," Don says. They needed to find a place worthy of such beautiful antiques, and Charnwood Hill shows them off to perfection. Patsy and Don bought the home in 1978.

This is a mansion, all right. Common areas of the inn include the formal living room, library, TV room, the Great Hall on the first floor and the Lodge on the second floor, the Garden Room, the Gathering Hall, the front and east balconies, screened swing porch, front porches, the arbor, and the beautiful east and west gardens. "Tyler's famous Azalea Trail starts right outside of this house," Don says.

Tyler also considers itself "Rose Capital of

the World," and the annual Texas Rose Festival is an important local event. Margaret Hunt was Rose Queen in 1935; and JoAnne Miller, daughter of the then-owner of the home, was Rose Queen in 1954. Both times the Queen's Tea was held in the gardens.

A pair of curved steps leads up to the white-columned entrance. The large foyer and living room are stately. The dining room is impressive, with a handmade table and ten chairs of solid pecan, a Chinoiserie breakfront displaying antique Meissen china, an oriental rug, and a delicate chandelier. It makes a contrast to the bright breakfast room, although even that, in its way, is formal, with its glass tables, chairs covered with summery floral fabric, bricked floor, and branched chandelier.

The 1,500-square-foot Art Deco Suite on the third floor was constructed for the two Hunt daughters; the gray carpet makes a perfect foil for the Chinoiserie pieces and the print fabric on a black background. The second-floor sleeping porch and one bedroom were converted into what is now called the Lodge, which has a bar, TV, and lots of room for meetings.

Breakfast is a full gourmet feast. Eggs Benedict is served with an inn specialty—a tasty breakfast potato casserole—and a mèlange of mixed fruits, and juices, coffee, and tea. If you wish, at 4:00 P.M. Patsy will serve a Lemon Tea of cheesecake with fresh fruit.

Dinners are as you like, also. "A group of Japanese guests requested Texas steak," Don says, enjoying in retrospect their enjoyment.

How to get there: From I–20 take Highway 69 south to North Broadway, which becomes South Broadway at Tyler Square. Continue south 4 blocks to Charnwood and turn left. The inn is on the right, and there's a sign.

Innkeepers: Patsy and Don Walker
Address/Telephone: 223 East Charnwood; (903) 597–3980, fax 592–3980
Rooms: 7, including 1 suite; 5 with private bath, 5 with TV. No smoking inn.
Rates: $95 to $175, double; $15 extra person, single $15 less; EPB.
Open: All year.
Facilities and activities: Tea and dinner by reservation, elevator, gift shop. Nearby: Municipal Rose Garden & Museum, Brookshire's World of Wildlife Museum and Country Store, Hudnall Planetarium, Caldwell Zoo, Azalea Trail, Texas Rose Festival, East Texas State Fair.
Business travel: Located near downtown Tyler. The Lodge for meetings.
Recommended Country Inns® Travel Club Benefit: 10% discount, subject to availability.

Rosevine Inn
TYLER, TEXAS 75702

Tyler is the "Rose Capital of the World," and Rosevine Inn is named both for the famous roses, which are shipped all over the world, and for the street it's located on. Bert is in real estate and was eager to snap up the half acre where the Pope House burned down long ago, leaving something most unusual for Tyler (and the rest of Texas): a basement. "Back in the '30s they must have built basements. I designed the house, Becca and I both decorated it, and we built it right on top of the basement of the Popes' English Tudor house, which had been vacant for a long time." Bert has turned the basement into a game room with shuffleboard, backgammon, and many a hotly contested board game.

The guest rooms are named for the flora of the area, beginning with the Rose Room, which has a high-backed antique bed, a cozy rocker, and its own small fireplace. The Bluebonnet Room, named for the Texas state flower, has a white iron bedstead and a comfy blue couch. The Azalea Room, peachy like the flowers, has a brass bed. The Sunshine Room? "Well," says Bert, "it's named for the daughter of the man who built the house that burned down, what else?" I'm not sure I follow his logic!

Becca and Bert had a great time combing the small towns of East Texas—Canton, Quitman, Tyler—to furnish the inn. Canton, 30 miles away, is famous for its First Mondays, a huge country flea-and-produce market spread out under the trees outside the small town.

Breakfast at Rosevine is hearty and delicious. There's always a hot entree like sausage quiche or French toast or omelets, served with toast and perhaps both blueberry coffeecake and applesauce muffins, along with a fruit-of-the-season cup, orange juice, and coffee and tea.

Between the welcome with wine and cheese and the delicious morning odor of fresh-brewed coffee outside in the hallway, Rosevine gives you a happy pampered feeling. "We try; what more can we say?" Bert asks with a smile.

I say that the landscaped grounds of Rosevine are so lovely that it's a difficult choice whether to laze in the hot tub under the pavilion or to play volleyball and croquet on the velvet lawn beyond the fountain in the back courtyard. Bert is the hard-working gardener. The inn is set on a slight rise of smooth green lawn; nine steps lead up to the flowerpots that mark the opening in the arched white picket fence. The path then winds across more green lawn to the front door of this charming red brick house with its backdrop of leafy trees.

How to get there: Tyler is the crossroads for many highways. Follow Highway 31 east into town to Vine Street, turn right, and the inn is the house on the right.

Innkeepers: Bert and Rebecca Powell
Address/Telephone: 415 South Vine Street; (903) 592–2221
Rooms: 5; all with private bath. No smoking inn.
Rates: $75, double; $10 extra person; EPB.
Open: All year.
Facilities and activities: Hot tub, game room. Nearby: Tyler Rose Gardens, Brick Street Shoppes, Carnegie History Center, Caldwell Zoo, Rose Festival, Azalea Trails, Historic Homes Tours.
Recommended Country Inns® Travel Club Benefit: Stay two nights, get third night free, Monday–Thursday.

Thee Hubbell House
WINNSBORO, TEXAS 75494

East Texas was more pro-Confederate than not, back in Civil War days, and quite a few mansions testify to the antebellum influence. A true East Texas Southern belle is Thee Hubbell House, its white Georgian Colonial facade catching your eye as you drive down the street. The porches and upstairs gallery sport swings and rockers, and, as Dan Hubbell says, "It's amazing how people love to sit out and rock.

"If they're my age, or older, they remember what it was like to sit out on the porch and rock. Our guests seem to enjoy staying around, and we enjoy it, too," Dan continues. Part of the pleasure stems from the fact that Dan is the mayor of Winnsboro. "We meet and greet our guests on a kind of official level," he says with a chuckle. "It seems to add a sort of prestige to our guests, to have the mayor serve them coffee."

The Hubbells chose *Thee* instead of *The* for their inn name because "it sounds cozier," they say. The inn has five charming guest rooms. There are some lovely English antiques, and Dan's grandmother's sewing chair and Laurel's grandmother's washstand testify to their native Texas roots. Two of the guest rooms are suites: the Magnolia Suite and the Master Suite, which is the inn's largest guest room, with a dining room and its own veranda.

Nostalgia reigns at Thee Hubbell House, where you can walk the 2½ blocks downtown to antiques shops and at least three churches. The front door is open so that guests can come and go as they please. The Hubbells take their peace and safety for granted and are amused when guests ask, "Is it safe to walk?"

"We tell them, of course you can walk here, even at night. Then they take off like little school kids, giggling," Dan says.

The century-old mansion has pine floors, square handmade nails, and the original wavy-glass window panes. Cabinets now surround a solid oak pie safe that was so heavy it took three men to lift it. The banister posts were made at onetime owner Colonel Stinson's sawmill; his daughter Sallie married Texas's first governor, Jim Hogg.

Breakfast is bountiful, to say the least. Begin with a baked apple stuffed with mincemeat. Next have shirred eggs, baked ham, buttermilk biscuits, grits and cream gravy, wheat raisin muffins, coffee, and juice. "We call it a Plantation Breakfast," says Laurel. "We serve in the dining room at 8:30, and sometimes our guests don't rise from the table until 11:00!" They join their guests if there are fewer than eight; if there are "more than we can handle, we don't eat at all, but we have coffee with them."

Talk about Southern hospitality: Mondays all Winnsboro restaurants are closed, so the Hubbells may say, "If you enjoy a good stew, with just crackers and a glass of milk, well, come and sit down."

How to get there: Winnsboro is on Highway 37 between I–30 and I–80. Highway 37 becomes Main Street. Turn west on Elm to number 307.

Innkeepers: Laurel and Dan Hubbell
Address/Telephone: 307 West Elm Street; (903) 342–5629
Rooms: 5, including 2 suites; all with private bath. No smoking inn.
Rates: $65 to $150, per room, EPB.
Open: All year.
Facilities and activities: Dinner by reservation. Nearby: Lake Bob Sandlin, Cypress Springs Lake, and twenty-two other lakes within a 20- to 30-mile radius; Autumn Trails Festival, Christmas Festival, spring and summer festivals.
Recommended Country Inns® Travel Club Benefit: Stay two nights, get third night free, Monday–Thursday.

The Antique Rose

WOODVILLE, TEXAS 75979

The Southern Plantation Federal–style Antique Rose was built in 1862 by S. P. McAllister, and it's pretty elegant to this day. The tidy walk bisecting the green lawn leads up to red brick steps and four square white columns on the front porch.

Denice and Jerry moved from Houston to Woodville to retire, but Denice says, "Jerry still works full time—and the inn is full time." They used to come up to East Texas to get away on weekends. "We saw this house advertised in the little *Crackerbarrel* newspaper," Denice says. "It was just like, 'This is it.' We both looked at each other, and called the Chamber [of Commerce] to see if it would be feasible."

It was not only feasible, it's been a delight. Once the hard work was finished, of course. "For the next two years we worked very hard pulling up floors, painting, all the things that come with renovating a house. Slowly it began to be not just a house, but our home."

Jerry and Denice moved to Texas from out of state more than twenty-five years ago, and it was a surprise. "Texas people are so different," they still say. "So much friendlier." Back where they came from, says Denice, you don't talk to strangers. "When I moved down here and went shopping, here was this man opening a door for me—I don't think I ever had someone open a door for me before."

As for small towns like Woodville, where you know everyone, while they were restoring the house, family and friends kept saying. "I can't believe you know so many people in just two years!"

They have planted 150 antique rose bushes in the garden, and the three guest rooms are decorated and furnished with antiques. Walls are in pale pastels; and the woodwork is white. "Do you know the *Victoria* magazine?" Denice asks. She laughs. "I don't mind giving them a plug—every time I saw something I liked, even if it was just a bowl, I tore the page out. I'd say, 'See this picture, that's how I want it done here.'" Although she chose all the wallpapers and the pretty borders, and the rugs, she also gives a "plug" to two of her sisters from Arizona.

"They came to Texas four times and spent many long hours decorating. We couldn't have done this without them."

Ashley has a high canopy bed, the kind you need steps to get into. Jessica's decor is peaches-and-cream, and there's a fireplace and a spectacular sunset view. Rebecca, blue and white, is off the upstairs porch; its wrought-iron bed is an antique.

Each guest room awaits with homemade bread, coffee, tea, and hot chocolate. "We put a little pumpkin, applesauce, or fresh apple bread in the room for a little snack." Breakfast might be individual quiches or breakfast pizza: "I make it out of crescent rolls, with browned sausage, hash browns piled on, then egg and cheddar and mild green chilies." It is yummy, and if you prefer vegetarian, Denice will leave out the sausage.

Jerry is in charge of the fresh fruit bowl, and he dresses up the kiwi and strawberries (or warmed canned apricots in winter) with whipped cream and nuts on top.

How to get there: From Highway 190 turn north onto Nellius Street. The inn is around the corner, on the left. From Highway 287 turn south onto Nellius Street, crossing West Davis and Dogwoods streets. The inn is at the end of the street, on the right.

Innkeepers: Denice and Jerry Morrison
Address/Telephone: 612 Nellius; (409) 283–8926
Rooms: 3; all with private bath. No smoking inn.
Rates: $65 to $75, double, EPB.
Open: All year.
Facilities and activities: Nearby: Antiques and gift shops, two restaurants and the Highlander Tea Room, Big Thicket National Preserve, Shivers Library and Museum, Alabama–Coushatta Indian Reservation, Heritage Village Museum.

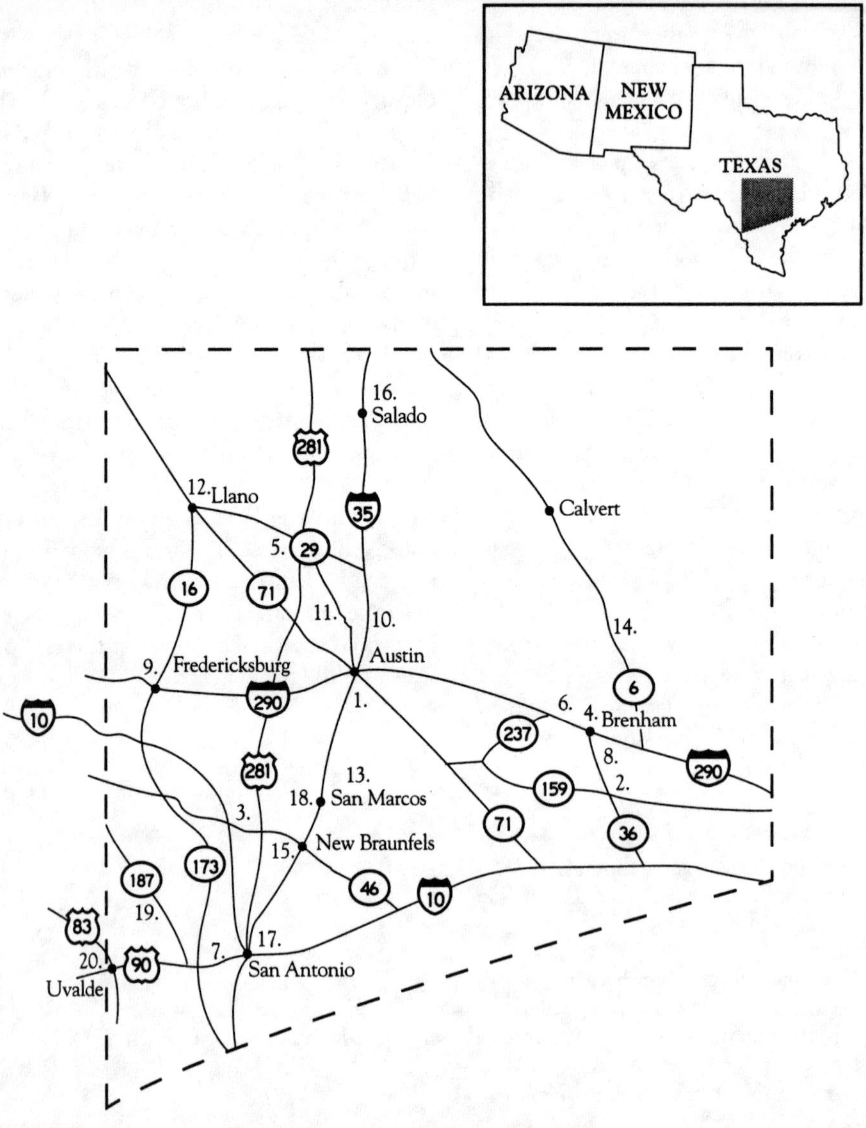

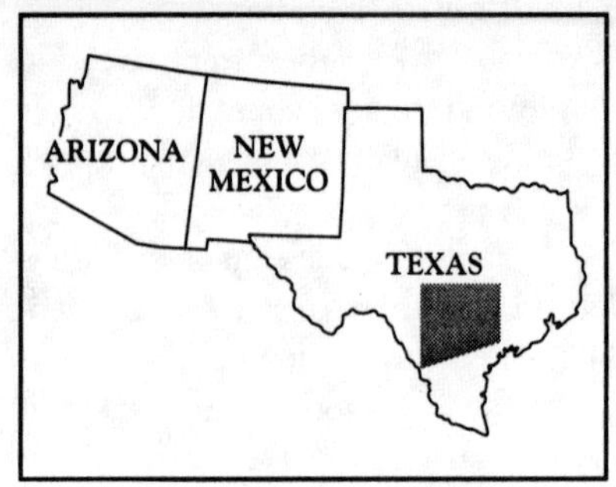
ARIZONA
NEW MEXICO
TEXAS

16. Salado
281
35
12. Llano
Calvert
5. 29
16
71
11.
10.
14.
9. Fredericksburg
Austin
290
6
10
1.
6. 4. Brenham
237
8.
290
13.
281
159
2.
18. San Marcos
3.
71
36
15. New Braunfels
173
187
46
10
19.
83
17.
7. San Antonio
20.
90
Uvalde

Central Texas

Numbers on map refer to towns numbered below.

Carrington's Bluff

AUSTIN, TEXAS 78705

Gwen and David, favorite innkeepers, are back in town after a several-year interlude in a cold climate. "I had this burning desire to go to New England," Gwen confesses. But although they loved their New England inn, Gwen got cold, homesick—and pregnant. She wanted baby Nicholas to be a Texan, too—no offense to New England!

So they are back home and happily innkeeping in this delightful house with a wonderful side garden and a view over wooded Shoal Creek Bluff. "David and I have been innkeepers for years," Gwen says, "and we hate rules; we don't have a lot of rules. We open up our home and our guests just wander around, go into the fridge for a glass of wine, or use the kitchen—just not when I'm fixing breakfast!" she adds with a laugh.

Breakfast offers Gwen's homemade granola, ham and cheese soufflé, chocolate chip banana muffins, gourmet coffee and teas, fresh fruit, and juice. After this feast all you'll want to do is lie in the hammock under the 500-year-old ivy-covered oak tree and contemplate the white clouds in the blue Texas sky.

The 1877 Texas farmhouse is situated on a one-acre tree-covered bluff. Once a twenty-two-acre original outlot of the Republic of Texas, the property was purchased by L. D. Carrington from David Burnet in 1856. L. D. owned a general store downtown, as well as the water company and the newspaper. He also served as city alderman and country commissioner. His true love was being commander of the brigade that guarded Austin from the Indians. His farmhouse, along with its 35-foot front porch, was built facing Shoal Creek Bluff. This was the perfect lookout point to watch for the Indians who lived west of Austin.

Guest rooms are named for Carringtons as well as for family members of the second owner, an Englishman who had been a vicar. In the Vicar Molesworth Room there are photos of the English vicarage on the walls. David is English, and the inn has a lovely air of an English country inn and garden. You'll know you're there when you see both Old Glory and the Union Jack flying from the side porch.

Gwen drew on her background in design to decorate in soft blues and beiges, inspired by the colors of the lovely Vermont quilt David gave her for a birthday. She has gone into quilting herself, and each guest room has an example of her art spread on the bed. The L. D. Carrington Room has a four-poster bed and a hunting horn to match the hunting-scene wallpaper; there's an antique pedal-operated sewing machine in the Martha Carrington Room. The Kathleen Molesworth Room upstairs has a view of the old oak tree and, through the boughs, Shoal Creek. (When booked with the Vicar Molesworth Room, it becomes the Molesworth Suite.) Across the street is the new Carrington's Cottage. Originally a dairy barn, the cottage displays the same decorating touches that make the inn special.

The Fullbrooks have been busy gardening, making a lovely setting for the new gazebo on the "back forty," says Gwen.

How to get there: From I–35 go west on 19th (Martin Luther King Boulevard) all the way to David Street, a small street on the right just before you reach Lamar Boulevard. Go up the short hill, and the inn is on the left just as the street curves around to the right.

Innkeepers: Gwen and David Fullbrook
Address/Telephone: 1900 David Street; (512) 479–0638
Rooms: 8; 6 with private bath, all with TV. No smoking inn.
Rates: $60 to $105, double; $15 extra person; EPB.
Open: All year.
Facilities and activities: Kitchen and laundry facilities open to guests, hammock, picnic tables. Nearby: University of Texas campus within walking distance, Town Lake, Lake Travis, museums, LBJ Library.

Fairview Inn

AUSTIN, TEXAS 78704

What a surprise this beautiful huge white-columned mansion is, barely a mile from busy downtown Austin. Surrounded by meticulous landscaping, sheltered by huge old oaks, it seems miles away in the country. "Travis Heights is a good old neighborhood," Duke says. "People are out walking their dogs, even 10:00, 10:30 at night. We sit on the porch and wave at the neighbors as they go by."

Both he and Nancy, native Texans, confess to having always harbored a burning desire to restore an old house, curbed for years—at least by Nancy—by the wonderful dollhouse in the Sun Parlor. Duke laughs. "It was supposed to take away the itch to restore." But he's bitten too, and plans to make a full-scale model of Fairview one day.

The large foyer and the spacious Great Room are perfect for guests who want to entertain. "You don't have to entertain in your bedroom," they say. The piano, a golden oldie from St. Louis in 1903, was "just in time for the 1904 World's Fair," Duke says, intimating that maybe Scott Joplin played on it. Then he laughs. "I never let facts stand in the way of a good story." The six-legged dining-room table, though, was Nancy's great-grandfather's, for a fact.

Another piece of furniture turned out to be from Nancy's family, and she had no idea of that when they bought it. The Eastlake half-tester bed in the Ambassador Room was found in Crockett (East Texas), and putting it together was rather a puzzle. A great-aunt came to visit. "Why that's great-grandmother Littlefield's bed!" she said, and told them how to put it together. "Turns out, it's been in my family more than a hundred years," Nancy says. "It had just kinda left for a while!"

The Texas Colonial Revival mansion was built in 1910. Duke points out that most of the paneling and trim is of rare heart of Longleaf Pine from Calcasieu Parish in Louisiana. The house has an Austin Historic Landmark designation and a 1993 award from the Austin Heritage Society for historic preservation. All rooms are extraordinarily spacious, but the Governor's Suite is truly Texan in scope—the Victorian Renaissance bed (now king-sized) is dwarfed in the huge room, which has a dressing room in addition to a bath. In the large enclosed sunporch there's a sofa bed and a gigantic work table. "This set up provides an excellent setting for a small business meeting," Duke says.

"We bought the house from Ima Gullett, an elderly lady who tells us stories about famous people who were entertained in the house in the past. Names I learned about in seventh-grade Texas history—it makes my hair stand on end!"

At breakfast, Belgian waffles are served with Texas pecan peach syrup; the black-bean salsa dip is served with Texas-shaped corn chips; you can slather your biscuits with "Hill Country Mud" (don't ask, just enjoy!), and the *migas* have Rio Diablo hot sauce—you'll know you're in Texas, all right. Jars of these Texas-made goodies are for sale if you want to take some home with you.

How to get there: From I–35 take the Riverside exit west to Congress Avenue. Turn left, pass the Texas State School for the Deaf on the right, and turn left on Academy. Drive 3/10 mile to Newning and turn right. The inn is the sixth house on the right. Turn into the driveway and park at the rear of the inn.

Innkeepers: Nancy and Duke Waggoner
Address/Telephone: 1304 Newning Avenue; (512) 444–4746 or (800) 310–4746
Rooms: 6, 4 in main house, 2 suites with kitchens in carriage house; all with private bath, phone, and TV. No smoking inn.
Rates: $89 to $129; $15 extra person; EPB.
Open: All year.
Facilities and activities: Nearby: University of Texas Campus and the LBJ Library, State Capitol, Zilker Park with Barton Springs and Japanese Garden, Laguna Gloria Art Museum, Elisabet Ney Museum, Umlauf Sculpture Garden; more.
Business travel: Located 1 mile from downtown Austin. Suites are good for small meetings. All rooms and suites with phone. Corporate rates.

Governor's Inn
AUSTIN, TEXAS 78705

Governor's Inn is owned by wonderful innkeepers Gwen and David Fullbrook, who have made such a success of their Carrington's Bluff Inn just a few corners away. This historical mansion was built in 1897 and for years was known as the Kenny–Lomax House—before it began another life as a fraternity house. (It's two blocks from the University of Texas campus.) Gwen and David enjoy the history of both their inns, and David was fascinated to learn that back at the turn of the century the Lomax sons played with the sons of their Carrington house. (Small world, a century removed.)

"Gwen thought up the governor theme," David says. "She visited the Governor's Mansion (which is practically around the corner, on 11th) and collected all the names." (She's Texan and she knows; David's British, so they're all strangers to him!) But each room is named for a Texas governor from way back, beginning with Sam Houston.

The mansion is impressive, with high ceilings, lots of white paneling—all original—and many porches, all surrounded by a low stone wall. Wrought-iron gates lead to the inn's many entrances, but guests use the side door off the parking lot. The happy voices of university students laughing and calling to each other as they pass by to and from class strike a warm and youthful note.

The parlor has a lovely rug over the polished wood floor, partially covering an interesting stencil whose shape is echoed by the white molding overhead. There are three dining rooms, each with a fireplace and more white-painted molding; the built-in cupboard of the center dining room is magnificent. Surrounding every doorway are moldings topped by a two-dimensional Corinthian pediment, like a miniature Grecian column—everywhere you'll see such unusual details, and all original. The Fullbrooks have done a wonderful job of restoring the home. "Rescued," David emphasizes. "After all, it was a fraternity house . . ."

Kim, resident innkeeper at the Governor's (and helped out by Gwen and David, who float back and forth between inns), likes her job, and for good reason. "It's the only work I've done that's rewarding. People really are grateful for what you do, they recognize that you're working for their pleasure."

She's particularly pleased when they ask for recipes. And no wonder, when her breakfasts include dishes like sausage and chili quiche, or Eggs Governor, and strawberry cream cheese bread.

The Governor Hamilton Room is off the parlor; all the others are on the second floor, except Ma and Pa Ferguson's Suite up on the third. As you march up the stairs, on the right wall there's an interesting lineup of prints of old shoes. At the top of the flight, hanging on the wall to the left is a huge and gorgeous handmade quilt.

David says a guest from Salem, Massachusetts, sent it to them. "I know," he says, pleased and amazed at my amazement. "She said she had no place to hang it and she wanted us to have it, we made her feel so welcome!"

How to get there: From I–35 take the MLK (19th Street) exit west to Rio Grande. Turn right and go 3 blocks to 22nd Street. Turn right and right again in the middle of the block, into the driveway of the inn, which is immediately to your right as you turn onto 22nd.

Innkeepers: Kim Harrison, Gwen and David Fullbrook
Address/Telephone: 611 West 22nd Street; (512) 477–0711
Rooms: 8; all with private bath, 4 with TV. No smoking inn.
Rates: \$60 to \$105, double; \$15 extra person; EPB.
Open: All year.
Facilities and activities: Nearby: University of Texas campus and the LBJ Library, State Capitol, Zilker Park with Barton Springs and Japanese Garden, Laguna Gloria Art Museum, Elisabet Ney Museum, Umlauf Sculpture Gardens, many fine restaurants.
Business travel: Located 5 miles from downtown Austin, 2 blocks from university. Corporate rates; phone in room.

The McCallum House

AUSTIN, TEXAS 78705

The McCallum House was built in 1907 as the home of Jane Y. McCallum, an early suffragist, her husband, Arthur, and her five children. The Danleys now have a marker from the Texas Historical Commission to authenticate the building's history. McCallum was careful to make the distinction—she was not a militant suffragette—but she had definite ideas all the same. Some of the inn furniture, such as the Blue Room set with the oval-mirrored dressing table, came with the house and reflects her taste. In the attic Nancy found the big yellow suffragette banner that now hangs in the hall: 8,000,000 WORKING WOMEN NEED TO VOTE!

The Danleys took the old house and turned it into a charming inn. Roger is a remodeling contractor, and Nancy has done some construction too. Wait until you see the dollhouse in the entry, just below the stairs.

"We did that in moments of insanity," both the Danleys say with a laugh. I would call it artistry, not insanity. It's perfectly beautiful, with downstairs ceilings decorated with molding, a hearth of real brick, and even tiny rugs needlepointed by the talented builders and decorators.

Roger's latest life-size triumph is Jane's Loft, a beautiful new attic room with 12½-foot ceilings and wonderful etched glass doors. A Victorian pattern done by hand by the Danleys decorates both the huge triangular window in the gable and the long etched panels on either side of the door leading to the big open porch.

Many guests, especially long-term ones (the Danleys often have professors visiting the University of Texas who stay for several weeks), are pleased as punch with the Garden Apartment in the back. This suite, decorated in deep rose and blue, with white wicker and a white iron daybed in the living room, has a bedroom with queen beds and a kitchen equipped for real cooking. "We've had lots of families, physicists doing research and lecturing at the university; it's a lot of fun," the Danleys say.

It's a house of porches. Adjoining the Blue Room and running along the entire side of the house is a screened porch fitted with white-wicker-and-blue-chintz furniture; I can see why folks want just to sit here and enjoy the breeze. There's a lot of sitting around the breakfast table too—that's one of the high spots of innkeeping, Nancy says. "We sit around the table and talk for *hours*."

Nancy's special dish of scrambled eggs with shaved ham, sharp cheddar, onions, and parsley is served with streusel-topped blueberry bran muffins and a fruit cup of black cherries, bananas, and peaches. Roger's specialty is a quiche with a crunchy shredded-potato crust. The filling can be ham or sausage, spinach or mushrooms, depending upon the whim of the resident chef. Also on the menu are some wonderful low-fat and no-cholesterol muffins, sweet breads, and coffeecakes.

How to get there: Exit I–35 at 38th Street and go west to Guadalupe. Turn south for 6 blocks to 32nd; turn west on 32nd. The inn is on the left.

Innkeepers: Nancy and Roger Danley
Address/Telephone: 613 West 32nd Street; (512) 451–6744
Rooms: 5, including 2 suites; all with private bath and kitchen, 4 with private porch; TDD for deaf and hearing impaired. No smoking inn.
Rates: $55 to $95, double; $15 extra person (lower rates are for three nights or more and for any night Monday through Thursday); EPB. Monthly rates available. Visa and MasterCard to secure deposit only.
Open: All year.
Facilities and activities: Nearby: many fine restaurants, University of Texas campus, LBJ Library, state capitol, Zilker Park with Barton Springs and Japanese Garden, other Austin sights.
Business travel: Located 1 mile from downtown Austin. Private phones and answering machines; fax.

Southard House

AUSTIN, TEXAS 78703

A fascinating thing about the Southard House is that the second floor was once the first floor. A photograph in the entrance hall, taken in the 1890s, shows how the house looked before the original owners hoisted it up and built a new first floor underneath around 1906. It is a very interesting Victorian Greek Revival home.

Another fascinating thing is the large world map that Regina and Kara showed me in the office; it's dotted with colored pins showing the many places in the world Southard guests come from: Europe, the length and breadth of the United States, China, New Zealand. "We've had guests from thirty-eight countries, including Russia," Regina says with delight. So you're apt to meet with pretty interesting people. The University of Texas recommends the inn to visiting architects, lawyers, and visitors to the school's Huntington Art Gallery and School of Performing Arts.

The Southards have gathered antiques from all over. The Treaty Oaks room and suite, once the parlor, has a fireplace and a bathroom sink fitted into an antique washstand. There are old-fashioned transoms over each bedroom door. I liked the antique-looking (though new) tile and the original narrow-slatted wood walls in the bathrooms. In the dining room, a nineteenth-century English oak refectory table seems 7 miles long.

While weekday breakfasts are delicious ("I call them Gourmet Continental," says Kara, who may fix home-baked peanut butter–orange bread or strawberry yogurt muffins), it's the weekend breakfasts, prepared by Regina, that are spectacular. Mexican breakfast quiche, Belgian waffles, apple pancakes, or an especially yummy egg-cheese-grits dish, served with orange juice, just-ground coffee, and hot buttered yeast bread for toast, are eaten in the shade of a green-bordered patio.

Lately Regina has been specializing in scrumptious homemade cinnamon rolls, and even Jerry has been getting into the breakfast act, fixing a fabulous fruit smoothie with a secret ingredient. Dare I tell that it's champagne?

Recommended restaurants for lunch and dinner are within walking distance—Sweetish Hill, an Austin classic, is just down the street on the corner of Blanco and 6th—and take-out food may be brought in.

The Southard House offers airport pickup, caters to special diets when requested, and takes calls for business guests. A honeymoon package includes champagne, fresh flowers, and chocolates on a silver tray. One time a guest overslept; he was awakened by Jerry, who rushed him to the airport just in time for his plane. "He says we saved his life," Regina told me with a laugh, "and he comes back to us every time he's in town."

Southard House has expanded with the three-room Peppermint Inn, located 2 blocks away.

How to get there: Take the 6th Street exit off I–35 and go west on 6th until you reach Blanco Street on your right. The inn is on the left.

Innkeepers: Regina and Jerry Southard and daughter Kara
Address/Telephone: 908 Blanco Street; (512) 474–4731
Rooms: 8, in main house and Peppermint Inn; all with private bath; downstairs rooms wheelchair accessible. Smoking permitted in public rooms.
Rates: \$49 to \$149, double, EPB weekends, continental breakfast weekdays.
Open: All year.
Facilities and activities: Nearby: four-star restaurants, shops, and galleries within 4-block walking distance; Town Lake, State Capitol, University of Texas, LBJ Library, museums.
Business travel: Located 12 blocks from downtown Austin. Phone in all rooms. Corporate rates.

The Wild Flower Inn

AUSTIN, TEXAS 78705

Bright flowers lead up to this spic-and-span square white clapboard house, flowers lining the flagstone path, flowers blooming in containers on the green lawn. Indoors, fresh flowers bloom in pots, and painted flowers bloom in the stencils Kay and her crew painted on walls and up the stairs. The effect is of light and air, of sunshine pouring in.

"I used lace curtains because I didn't want to close us in," Kay says. "I wanted to bring the outdoors in." She also likes to show her guests the outdoors; one guest from Czechoslovakia wanted to see farm and ranch land, and Kay said, "Well, get in the car," and they covered about 100 miles to see Central Texas's famous wildflowers. "Heavens, so many miles!" he exclaimed. "At home we'd be in Bohemia already!"

Kay is a rather rare thing, a native Austinite, and from an old Texas family to boot. Rooms are named for members of her family: The David G. Burnet Room is named for her great-great-grandfather, and I loved the white iron half-canopied bedstead. Dodie's Room contains the furniture of a great-aunt, and Carolyn Pearl Walker Room is furnished with pieces given to Kay's grandmother for her thirtieth anniversary. Unusual is the old daybed; there's a four-poster, too. White stenciled flowers march along the pale blue walls under the ceiling.

Kay has set some sort of record—she's gone

for five and a half weeks without repeating a breakfast menu! It became a challenge, she says, when she overheard a British guest bragging to a newcomer that Kay had not served the same thing twice in the two weeks she'd been at the Wild Flower.

"She stayed for almost six weeks, and I didn't repeat." So of course I had to ask how on earth . . . ? "I alternate sweet and savory, for one thing," she says, "and always with juice, coffee, tea, and fresh-baked bread or muffins." A favorite is Eggs Goldenrod, white sauce with hardboiled egg whites over a croissant, the yellow yolk crumbled on top—that's a savory. A sweet might be French toast stuffed with ricotta cheese, with a syrup of zest of orange, orange marmalade, and brown sugar.

The house, on a quiet, tree-lined street near the University of Texas campus, was built in 1936 for a professor. It's a dead-end street, so there's no through traffic. "Restoring it, we did the work ourselves," Kay says, making it sound easy as daughter Angela, home from college, laughs. "Easy! We moved walls," Angela says. "We discovered a covered-up inside staircase (there's an outside one up to the small porch outside the Texas Country Room), took a kitchenette out of the upstairs . . ." She helped, in between her college studies, as did son Jay.

"I stayed at an inn on a business trip," says Kay. "Claudean and I had a woodcrafts shop, and when I went back to work, I told her, 'I'm going to open a bed and breakfast.' And I have to say, it all just came together."

How to get there: From I–35 take Martin Luther King Boulevard (19th Street) west to the end at Lamar; turn right and go to the first traffic light (24th) and turn right again, staying in the right-hand lane. Turn right at the second street (Longview) to 22½ Street. The inn is on the right, on the corner of Longview and 22½.

Innkeepers: Kay Jackson and Claudean Schultz
Address/Telephone: 1200 West 22½ Street; (512) 477–9639
Rooms: 4; 2 with private bath. No smoking inn.
Rates: $59 to $75, double; $15 extra person; EPB.
Open: All year.
Facilities and activities: Nearby: restaurants, shops, Caswell Tennis Courts, Shoal Creek Hike and Bike Trail, University of Texas campus and LBJ Library.

Woodburn House

AUSTIN, TEXAS 78751

Woodburn House, built in 1909, has earned Austin City Landmark status for its architectural features. "Besides the Governor's Mansion, there's only one other home in Austin like ours," Sandra says. "The double-wrapped gallery, the woodwork of the Craftsman style, which evolved from Victorian . . ." I was convinced the moment I saw the beautiful old house, with its wide flagstone path flanked with flowering shrubs and neatly bisected at the curb by a huge, old elm tree. The name comes from Bessie Hamilton Woodburn, who lived in the house for many years. Her father, Alexander Hamilton (not the Founding Father), was Texas's provisional governor after the Civil War.

Although the Dicksons are relatively new to Austin, Herb is a Texan, and they have wasted no time becoming active in the community. "We like to belong where we belong," Sandra says. Guests have the feeling of belonging right from the start, when they're welcomed sedately by Budges the Shar-Pei, whose complete canine name is Mr. Ka Budges. Very well behaved, he minds every nuance of Sandra's voice.

The inn, as promised from the exterior, is very spacious, with 12-foot ceilings and beautiful woodwork. There are two common rooms. One, the living room, has two large maroon leather sofas and a matching chair, which you absolutely sink into—lace curtains at the windows, polished dark woodwork, oak floors, an armoire, a bookshelf as tall as the room around a corner and up to the ceiling—it's a lovely room. On the dining room's built-in corner cupboard sits an old clock that has been in Herb's family for generations. The home is filled with antiques from the Dickson family. I especially admired the dozens of handmade quilts left to the family by Grandmother Dickson.

"Guests love to bundle up in them if it gets chilly while they're enjoying the upstairs gallery," Sandra says. It was a delight to curl up on the old glider, surrounded by huge old oak and pecan trees, and watch the squirrels, the woodpeckers, the jays, and the mourning doves go about their business.

Sandra, whose family was from Guadalajara, Mexico, likes to serve a Mexican breakfast, "*Real* Mexican, not TexMex," she says. She makes her own salsa and grows her own Mexican spices. "We bake our own breakfast breads and alternate Mexican cuisine with Belgian waffles, quiches, and fluffy French toast, which are more Herb's specialties. He does all the cutting and chopping—I do all the baking," she adds. For picnic lunches she sends guests down the street to the 100-year-old Avenue B Grocery. "Owner Ross Mason is just a delight. He loves our guests and makes wonderful picnic lunches for them."

One of the nicest things about the guest rooms, aside from their spaciousness, are the tall lace-covered windows opening off the gallery in front and shaded by old trees in the back. The wide halls, the front and back stairs, the butler's pantry, the large kitchen—everything about this inn is bright and gleaming.

How to get there: From I–35 take 45th Street west to Avenue D. Turn left, and the inn is on the left at the corner of Avenue D and West 44th Street.

Innkeepers: Sandra and Herb Dickson
Address/Telephone: 4401 Avenue D; (512) 458–4335
Rooms: 4; all with private bath. Wheelchair access; devices for hearing impaired with advance notice. No smoking inn.
Rates: $70 to $85, double; $15 extra person; EPB.
Open: All year.
Facilities and activities: Exercycle. Nearby: restaurants, shops; Shipe Park with pool, tennis, basketball; Elisabet Ney Museum, many other museums; Hyde Park Walking Tour.
Business travel: Located in central Austin. Phone and work space in all rooms; corporate rates.

Ziller House
AUSTIN, TEXAS 78704

Ziller House's street, Edgecliff Terrace, is aptly named: The estate sits on the rock cliff overhanging Town Lake and facing the lights of downtown Austin; at night they seem close enough to touch.

The white, 1938 Mediterranean-style home is enclosed by greenery, both cultivated and wild, on two and a half acres. Inside, gleaming wooden floors and clean white stucco walls make an almost museumlike setting for beautiful furniture and artwork. The living room's tall, fourteenth-century Japanese screen, all black and gold lacquer, serves as a background for the deep-green leather sofa. Facing the two steps down into the room are two magnificently carved rosewood emperor chairs on each side of a large jade peach tree.

"I come from a West Texas family, but I grew up in Hong Kong," Wendy says, explaining the exquisite artifacts and furniture that make the inn so exceptional. "My father was an engineer, and my mother was French." From her mother's family come pieces like the magnificent circa 1700s buffet in the dining room.

Wendy, who's pretty down to earth amid these lovely things, just happened to be on hand when the estate was put on the market. "It was an accident," she says. "One hour after the sign went up, I saw it. It said, PERFECT FOR A BED & BREAKFAST! I'd just put Sam on a plane to

California, and I called and left an emergency message. 'What is it, what's happened?' he called back in a panic. I told him, 'I've just put a lot of money down on an inn!'" But it worked out fine.

"We like it, we live here," Sam says. "No doubts about having done the right thing."

The Wine Room is named for Sam's wine business, with wine posters on the walls and a wine-colored paisley spread on the bed, which belonged to the home's original owner. The Sun Suite has a most unusual bed, with carved-rosewood bedside tables and beautiful oriental lamps. In the adjoining sun room, the light-cherry turn-of-the-century desk and matching chair belonged to Wendy's grandmother.

Each roomy bathroom has a small built-in dressing table, original to the house. The tile is pristine, and the shower curtains are Wendy's decorative touch. Amenities include hair dryer, soaps and lotions, even an iron and ironing board in each lighted closet.

In each guest room a specially constructed cabinet contains microwave, coffee maker, refrigerator, dishes, and silverware in case you want to eat or order in. (The inn hosts lots of celebrities—business, politics, and entertainment—and Wendy says they like to hole up in their rooms after a busy day.) Breakfast is brought to your room, too, unless you prefer to eat in the dining room.

"Sam is the cook person," Wendy says. "Salmon-mousse quiche, vegetarian quiche, Black Forest ham or Canadian bacon, kippers for our British guests." But she's no mean chef, either, with her homemade breakfast tacos with homemade *chorizo*. "You make your own sausage?" I am amazed. She laughs. "You're talking to a West Texas ranch girl," she says.

How to get there: From I–35 exit at Riverside Drive and go west 1 short block to Travis Heights Avenue. Turn right, then left onto Edgecliff, which ends at the gates of the inn estate. There is parking to the left, inside the gates.

Innkeepers: Wendy Sandberg and Sam Kindred
Address/Telephone: 800 Edgecliff Terrace; (512) 462–0100 or (800) 949–5446, fax (512) 462–9166
Rooms: 4; all with private bath and TV. No smoking inn.
Rates: $95 to $110, double, EPB.
Open: All year.
Facilities and activities: Jacuzzi, gardens. Nearby: downtown Austin, Convention Center, University of Texas campus and the LBJ Library, State Capitol, Zilker Park with Barton Springs and Japanese Garden, Laguna Gloria Art Museum, Elisabet Ney Museum, Umlauf Sculpture Garden.
Business travel: Located five minutes from downtown Austin. Fax, phones in all rooms; corporate rates.

High Cotton Inn

BELLVILLE, TEXAS 77418

Anna Horton says, "We're not pretentious," but the house itself is a grande dame, a beautiful home in the best Victorian manner. It's the largest house in town and was built by a very successful cotton broker back in 1906, when cotton was king. The name High Cotton comes from a Southern expression meaning everything's rosy, which is what I can't help but feel when I visit this wonderfully relaxed inn.

Check-in time, Anna says, is "when you get here," and check-out time is "when you leave." If there's a wait, well, guests can relax by the small backyard swimming pool.

I loved the informality of choosing my own room—guests, on arrival, get a choice of the rooms that haven't been spoken for yet. This is a great way to have a tour of the inn. The rooms are named for old family friends as well as Horton antecedents. (George Horton IV is a member of the fourth generation of Hortons from Houston, 65 miles away.) I chose Uncle Buster's Room, a large corner room with lace curtains, an antique wardrobe, and two gilt-framed portraits of a stern-looking Victorian man and woman.

There's a lovely formal parlor downstairs, and by the door to the upstairs wraparound porch (there's one downstairs, too), a cheerful sitting area always has a cookie jar filled with the Hortons' famous cookies. The chocolate chip ones are something to write home about, and now you can take some home with you. Anna and George have gone into the cookie business with a small shop on the premises, and not only the chocolate chip variety are good!

The furniture is all family-antique, and I love Anna's sense of humor. "Lots of it is dead relatives," she says. "George and I got married just when all the aunts started dying, and they're all upstairs waiting to scare any guests who get out of line."

The dining-room table, however, is a back-East piece from Lancaster, Pennsylvania, a real conversation piece 66 inches wide, with twelve leaves. It vies for attention with the built-in china cabinet, whose huge plate-glass door slides up the wall—and probably, I think, overhead into the ceiling as well, it's so large. (But I haven't figured out yet how it bends.)

Breakfast might be real country, with grits, bacon, scrambled eggs, bran muffins, and biscuits. Then again, there might be a sophisticated rum-soaked cake and Anna's new whole wheat "Zen" pancakes with homemade syrup. And always Anna's special blackberry preserves, which she puts up herself.

Summer dinner was perfect—chilled cucumber soup, marinated chicken salad, fresh rolls, and snow pudding with custard sauce for dessert. Winters it's apt to be roast beef and Yorkshire pudding.

There are always animals on the inn grounds; the Hortons are soft-hearted animal lovers. Last time I was there the menagerie consisted of two dogs and two cats, and now I hear there's a pregnant pygmy goat named Lucy. She'll no doubt be a mother by the time you get there. But the animals are not allowed in the house, so if you want to see them, ask young Anna Horton.

How to get there: The inn is on Highway 36 south, on the edge of Bellville.

Innkeepers: Anna and George Horton
Address/Telephone: 214 Live Oak Street; (409) 865–9796 or (800) 321–9796
Rooms: 5 share 2½ baths. No smoking inn.
Rates: $40 to $65, double, EPB. No credit cards.
Open: All year.
Facilities and activities: Dinner for groups of ten or more; special Thanksgiving and New Year's Eve dinners for inn guests only; small swimming pool. Nearby: boarding facilities for pets, spring and fall festivals, Historic Home Tour (April), Antiques Show (October), Austin County Fair.

Ye Kendall Inn

BOERNE, TEXAS 78006

Back in the early days of Texas, there was no hotel for travelers to these parts until Erastus and Sarah Reed bought a parcel of land for $200 in 1859. They began renting out their spare rooms to horsemen and stagecoach travelers, and from being known as The Reed House, the building changed its name through the years to The King Place and the Boerne Hotel. It wasn't called Ye Kendall Inn until 1909. Today the old two-story building, of Hill Country stone, fronted by white-railed porches 200 feet along its length on both upper and lower floors, is alive again as an inn, facing the large open spaces and white gazebo of the town square.

The old place is full of mysteries. "The cellar goes into a tunnel," says Sue. "It goes to the building way down on the corner; I guess it was for stagecoach passengers to hide from the Indians." (But too bad, it's not open to the public. Never mind, there's another mystery.)

"We have a ghost who lives here," Sue confided. "I haven't seen it, but my mother says she has. She heard boots and a man's voice, and then she saw a floaty shape going up the stairs."

Perhaps it's the quiet that leads to fanciful—or real?—visions. "Guests like us mainly because it's so quiet," Sue says. "It's the Hill Country quiet—there aren't even dances here on Saturday night." But there's plenty to do all the same, with quite a few festivals held in Main

Plaza out front, like a yearly Fun Fair with arts and craft shows, dances and pig races in town, and famous Hill Country caverns nearby.

High up along the walls in the upstairs rear of the building are what Sue calls "shoot-out" windows, possibly used to defend against those same Indians the stagecoach passengers were hiding from in the tunnel.

The entire lobby and rooms opening off it contain boutiques with antiques and designer clothing, but the huge upstairs hall is for inn guests, with comfortable lounge chairs, a large dining table, and double doors opening off the long porches both front and back. The view to the front is of the green square; in the back there's a large courtyard with white tables and chairs.

Guest rooms are furnished with English and American antiques, and each has a unique personality. The Erastus Reed Room is masculine with trophy heads mounted on the wall; the Sarah Reed Room is feminine in soft yellow and white. Fascinating are the old-fashioned bathroom fixtures, right there in the rooms, although the footed tubs and the commodes are screened off; Sarah Reed's screen is of white lace.

Breakfast, supervised by Bobbie, is juice and coffee, fresh fruit, sweet rolls, and quiche, so it's more than plain continental. And the Cafe at Ye Kendall Inn has more gourmet fare, from fettucine Alfredo to chicken cordon bleu. (Or try the Boerne Special, chicken-fried steak with country gravy.)

How to get there: I–87 goes right down the middle of Boerne, and the inn is at the west end of Main Square, on Blanco, which crosses the highway.

Innkeepers: Bobbie and Don Hood and Sue Davis
Address/Telephone: 120 West Blanco; (210) 249–2138 or (800) 364–2138
Rooms: 11, including 1 suite; all with private bath and TV, 1 with wheelchair access. No smoking inn.
Rates: $80 to $125, double, continental breakfast.
Open: All year.
Facilities and activities: Cafe serving breakfast, lunch, and dinner; boutiques. Nearby: Agricultural Heritage Center; Cascade Caverns; Cave Without a Name; Guadalupe River State Park; 15 miles from San Antonio.

Heartland Country Inn

BRENHAM, TEXAS 77833

Shirley brags about her spectacular view, and it is that. The inn is high on a hill, commanding a sweeping view of 158 acres of rolling countryside.

"I always wanted a place in the country," she says, much as she enjoyed her years in nearby Houston teaching ballroom dancing. "I thought I'd have a health retreat, and with the inn I can combine both—my enjoyment of people and the serving of delicious but healthy breakfasts."

She's especially conscientious about preparing meals for people on special diets if you let her know in advance, as well as feeding folks who simply say, "Please have something healthy." She'll serve pancakes from unrefined organic flour, with pure maple syrup or honey. "But even if you're on a healthy diet, sometimes making an exception and having a treat helps you to not feel deprived."

She says guests describe her breakfast as "super colossal"—they're not hungry again until evening. Most famous is her Heartland Special: potatoes au gratin with Shirley's seasonings. "I had a guest who asked for some breakfast potatoes, 'but not just old hashed browns,' he said. So I concocted this dish and of course served everybody there at the time. Now I'm not allowed to skip it," she adds.

The good-sized inn, now composed of two buildings, originally was a small farmhouse. She was going to tear it down but her family said don't do that, add on. So add on she did, and now the main building houses a large dining room that can seat fifty, and the commercial kitchen is open for guests' use, too. There's even a huge walk-in freezer.

There are two guest rooms down and three up, all opening off a porch or a balcony (and what a view from the balconies), in the building. Rooms are very spacious and each has a trundle in addition to the main bed.

The Victorian Room and the Large Victorian downstairs share a bath and can form a two-bedroom suite. Each has a delightful velvet Victorian love seat and antique white-iron beds. Outside doors are decorated with stained-glass panels, and Large Victorian has a wonderful, large rolltop desk.

Upstairs guest rooms have cathedral ceilings and clerestory windows. The King Room is tailored, the Queen Room is more fancy, and the Princess Room is flowery. "I had a family from Paris [France]," Shirley says. "Even he liked the fancy headboard." Anyone would love the antique French love seat covered with silk brocade.

The second house has a two-story entry, with an open staircase leading up to two family suites that sleep a multitude and have their own kitchens. Downstairs there's a fine lounge area with sofa and love seat and wonderful antiques, like a 150-year-old Danish desk. On each side is a suite with two bedrooms, bath, and kitchen. The inn's lovely antiques all come from K & S Antiques in Brenham, "the best antiques shop in Texas," says Shirley.

How to get there: Heartland is about 17 miles east of Brenham. Take Highway 105 East, turn left on Highway 50, and turn right on FM 2621. Turn right onto Palestine (County Road 68) for ½ mile. Turn right at the HEARTLAND sign and go through the gate and up the hill to the inn.

Innkeeper: Shirley Sacks
Address/Telephone: Palestine Road (CR 68); Route 2, Box 446; (409) 836–1864
Rooms: 16, including 4 suites; 7 with private bath. No smoking inn.
Rates: $65 to $150, double; $20 extra person; EPB. No credit cards.
Open: All year.
Facilities and activities: Meeting house. Nearby: Tours of Bluebell Creamery, home of famous ice cream; Blinn College; historic Downtown Brenham; antiques; Hershell–Spillman antique carousel in Fireman's Park; St. Clare Monastery Miniature Horse Farm; Ellison's Greenhouses; Texas Pioneer Trail; Brenham Wildflower Trails (in spring).

Rocky Rest Inn

BURNET, TEXAS 78611

Fannie Shepperd is a most gracious and accommodating innkeeper. "Some guests like to talk," she says, "and others are tired from the trip. I see how they feel before I engage them in conversation or invite them for an evening glass of wine with me." This historic house has been Fannie's home for more than twenty-five years, and guests soon feel as much at home here as their hostess does.

Now a widow, Fannie collected many beautiful things with her husband during their years together. The parlor has both a piano and an organ, and in the dining room you'll count no fewer than four cabinets displaying a fine collection of china and glass. Fannie owes much of her interest in antiques to her late mother-in-law. "I had the patience to carry her around to antique shops," she says, "and after a while I began to like it."

The home was built in 1860 by Adam R. Johnson for his bride. Sadly, Johnson—allegedly the youngest general in the Civil War—was blinded as a result of his injuries.

You enter the spacious mansion by way of a large entry hall. Across an expanse of gleaming parquet floor there's a view past the polished wood staircase to the wide windows of the den at the back of the house. "Rocky Rest" is a misnomer; rest here is anything but rocky. All the rooms, including the guest rooms, are exceptionally large. All have antique furniture, and the master bedroom downstairs and one of the upstairs rooms sport canopied beds. On the large landing upstairs, a beautiful antique sofa and chairs upholstered in bright yellow brocade are particularly inviting.

Breakfast might be Fannie's Dutch Apple Baby, a sort of popover pastry filled with fruit, or if you prefer, scrambled eggs and sausage. Fannie can recommend several restaurants in the vicinity, but she will also cook lunch or dinner for you if you wish.

Burnet is the "Bluebonnet Capital of Texas," and in the spring the wildflowers are glorious. The inn is within walking distance of Town Square with its little shops, friendly people, and the town museum.

How to get there: Water Street is also Highway 281. The inn is on the highway, 4 blocks south of the intersection of 281 and Highway 29. The inn is on the right. A white fence and a sign are at the driveway into the inn.

Innkeeper: Fannie Shepperd
Address/Telephone: 404 South Water Street (mailing address: P.O. Box 130); (210) 756–2600
Rooms: 3; 1 with private bath, 1 with TV. Pets permitted.
Rates: $55 to $65, double; special rates for added guests; EPB. No credit cards.
Open: All year.
Facilities and activities: Lunch and dinner served by request; common room with television, piano, and books; antiques shop; thirty acres stocked with peacocks, goats, and cattle. Nearby: restaurants in town and near lake, Longhorn Caverns, Inks Lake State Park, Lake Buchanan, Vanishing Texas River Cruise, historic Fort Groghan, Hill Country Flyer steam train from Austin (50 miles away), golf course, gift and antiques shops in town square.

The Knittel Homestead

BURTON, TEXAS 77835

This old house with a rounded bulge on the outside was built in three stages. The first was in 1870, by Herman Knittel, a Confederate soldier and Texas senator who was the little town's first postmaster and merchant; today's inn kitchen and utility area were once the post office and mercantile store.

The front wing was added in 1870 as the family's residence. Herman Knittel, Jr., added the dining room, the upstairs bedrooms, and the first indoor plumbing in Burton. "But what this house is really known for," Steve says, "is the circular staircase." That accounts for the bulge, but that's not all. It was transported from Germany and took several years to get here. "It finally arrived by oxcart—and the wrong stair risers had been shipped. It had to be put in backwards!" We went to take a look, and I found it imposing all the same. "I tell people the house looks like a Mississippi steamboat," Cindy says. Would you say it's painted cream and white? "No, that's chickpea," she says with a laugh.

Two of the upstairs guest rooms open onto the wraparound porch, and the back room has its own back stairs. Bath fixtures are the original ones, and Cindy stocks all baths with Woods of Windsor soaps and bubble bath. "In these old-fashioned tubs, a bubble bath is a must," she says.

I was surprised to hear that the Blue Room in the back is "the quietest." In this village of 311 people, what could be noisy? Cindy laughs. "On Saturday nights everybody congregates out front; all the locals come down to gossip in front of the post office and the bank."

The Millers are originally from Houston. They came to Burton for the Burton Cotton Gin Festival, which was the 1993 winner of the Texas Downtown Association's award for the best festival in the state. The cotton gin itself won an award for the best restoration in the state.

"We stayed at the inn, and we loved it," Steve says. "Cindy got kinda tired of banking, and I got tired of city living." They liked what they saw, and they decided to stay. Now they are the proud owners not only of the inn but also of the cafe on the corner, which has been listed as number eight in the top ten Texas cafes.

"This is your opportunity to country dine in the historic Burton Cafe and mingle with the locals," Steve says. For breakfast, how about Bananas Foster French Toast? Or thick country–style buttermilk flannel cakes, the Knittel House egg casserole, homemade muffins filled with fruit from the Knittle orchard, Burton fresh-ground sausage or country cured bacon. Had enough? Save room for the mile-high biscuits.

Steve had years of experience in the restaurant business in Houston. The cafe was built in 1937 after the OK Saloon burned down and, he says, "When I saw the cafe, it was perfect, I loved it, all the locals—I like to say the cafe belongs to the local citizens. The folks need a place to communicate and eat."

He's so right: "It's the kind of place where I'll get a call asking, 'Is Chester there? When he comes in, have him call me.' People have packages dropped off . . ." Steve beams.

How to get there: From Highway 290 take the Burton exit 12 miles west of Brenham. Go to Main Street; the inn is on the corner of Main and Washington, opposite the post office.

Innkeepers: Cindy and Steve Miller
Address/Telephone: 502 Main; (409) 289–5102
Rooms: 3; all with private bath, TV upon request. No smoking inn.
Rates: $75 weekday, $85 weekend, double; $55 commercial rate; $15 extra person; EPB.
Open: All year.
Facilities and activities: Restaurant, bicycles. Nearby: National Archive Center for Cotton Ginning, tours of historic cotton gin, oldest operating Texaco Station in the United States, National Bike Trail; gateway to Bluebonnet Trails.

Long Point Inn

BURTON, TEXAS 77835

"We're so pleased. We never expected to be so busy and to have so many happy guests," says Jeannine. The Neinasts opened their lovely chalet-style home to guests because they wanted to share the wonderful lifestyle they have created for themselves out on the land.

"Come and feed the cows, fish the ponds, traipse the woods, listen to the quiet," they say enticingly. They especially welcome families with children. "After all," Bill says with a laugh, "we have nine grandchildren."

And when you return from the cows, the ponds, and the woods, you'll find yourself in the lap of luxury in the form of a large story-and-a-half house that is completely and wholeheartedly turned over to guests. There's a piano in the parlor—may guests play it? But of course. "In fact, we would love it if they would come and play. But so far nobody has," mourns Jeannine.

She compensates by lavishing on her guests such marvelous breakfasts as eggs Newport (with sour cream and bacon) or a casserole of cottage cheese, spiced ham, Monterey Jack cheese, mushrooms, and chili peppers, all with biscuits and homemade wild plum jam. The fruit compote is always a hit with children, "and of course we have cereal for the youngsters who want it," Bill says.

Exciting for city kids is a hike on the land and a chance to spot the deer, raccoons, possums, fox, and armadillos that live at Long Point Inn; rabbits, too, both jack and cottontail. Birds are there aplenty: bluebirds and jays, hawks and crows, robins and hummingbirds. "Kids especially like it when I take them down to feed the cattle," Bill says. "They're so gentle, they come and stick their heads in the truck for ranch cubes—that's like candy to them, and they'll take it from your hand." (They don't bite, he adds reassuringly. "They don't have the right teeth for it even if they wanted to which they don't.")

Other country doings include swimming in an old-fashioned swimming hole beneath a waterfall and fishing with a string and pole (or bring your own more sophisticated equipment) in the farm ponds. Outings include a visit to the miniature horses raised nearby. "The little folks, often that's the high point of their trip, especially if they get to see a little foal."

Pie, cookies, coffee, and always Texas's great Blue Bell Ice Cream are served in the evening. The Neinasts believe in Texas hospitality with a captial H. Long Point Inn is an ideal hideaway from the hectic pace of city living—and, for youngsters, a wonderful introduction to the joys of the countryside.

How to get there: From U.S. Highway 290 take FM 2679 to FM 390. Turn right, and Long Point Inn will be on the left on a hill not far from the intersection.

Innkeepers: Jeannine and Bill Neinast
Address/Telephone: Route 1, Box 86-A; (409) 289-3171
Rooms: 3; 2 with private bath.
Rates: $75 to $85, double; $25 extra person over age 6; EPB. Deposit required to hold reservation.
Open: All year.
Facilities and activities: Hide-a-beds, cribs, playpen, high chair, and booster chair; fishing in five ponds stocked with catfish and bass; 175 acres of cattle ranchland; swimming; hiking. Nearby: restaurants, Miniature Horse Farm at Monastery of St. Clare, Star of the Republic Museum at Washington-on-the-Brazos State Park.
Recommended Country Inns® Travel Club Benefit: 10% discount, Monday–Thursday, except March 15–May 31, subject to availability.

Landmark Inn

CASTROVILLE, TEXAS 78009

Landmark Inn is a Texas State Historical Park, and as such it's administered by the Parks and Wildlife Department. The whitewashed building has provided shelter for weary travelers for more than a century, and it may be the last bargain east of the Pecos.

The inn is on one of Texas's prettiest rivers, the Medina. The old gristmill over the underground millrace (both were built in 1854) is the place to catch lots of perch, catfish, and carp if you're an angler. The park is open all year, and the mill structures and several pieces of milling equipment can be seen along the trail that leads to the lower terraces of the river.

In keeping with the tradition of old inns, there are no telephones or televisions. Rooms are furnished with authentic period pieces, giving the nicest feeling of early Texas and pioneer days while being perfectly comfortable.

If you're lucky, you might get the room Robert E. Lee slept in, or the up- or downstairs room of the tiny bathhouse. Before the Civil War it was the only place to bathe between San Antonio and Eagle Pass. It gave up that valuable function when the lead lining the upstairs (which served as a cistern) was melted down for the Confederates.

Each room has an Alsatian motto on the wall: *"Qui tient à sa tranquillité sait respecter celles d'autres* . . . he who values his own tranquillity knows how to respect that of others." One ell of the inn lobby is a museum, with artifacts and exhibits telling the story not only of the inn but of the town as well. Castroville, which calls itself the "Little Alsace of Texas," was founded in 1844 by Henri Castro, a French Jew of Portuguese descent who brought with him 2,134 Alsatians. The ensuing mixture of French, German, Spanish, and English cultures has never obscured the ambience brought by those first homesick settlers. You'll find great bakeries, sausage houses, and restaurants in this "Little Alsace."

Inn grounds are quiet and serene. There are shady oaks and soft green lawns broken only by stepping-stones, which lead to the original kitchen (now an ice and telephone facility) and the gristmill. The park is open daily all year, and a continental breakfast is served.

A wonderfully old and oddly shaped pecan tree stands near the river. One of the Famous Trees of Texas, it marks the approximate location of Castro's encampment back in 1844. Legend has it that Geronimo was chained to the tree overnight on the way from Mexico to imprisonment in San Antonio—while his captors spent the night comfortably in the inn.

A lot goes on at Landmark Inn. To preserve the ethnic dancing of the area, Alsatian, German, Belgian, and Spanish dancers perform in authentic costume during Heritage Dance Celebration. The Living History Exhibit lauds the Texas Rangers and demonstrates the lost arts of soap making and blacksmithing.

How to get there: Just after you cross the Medina River traveling west on Highway 90, turn left on the first street, which will be Florence. The inn is on the right.

Innkeeper: Superintendent Patricia Mares
Address/Telephone: 402 Florence Street; (210) 538–2133
Rooms: 8; 4 with private bath, 6 with air conditioning, 2 with fan. No smoking inn.
Rates: \$45 to \$55, single; \$50 to \$55, double; \$7 extra person; children under 8 free; continental breakfast. No credit cards.
Open: All year.
Facilities and activities: Nearby: restaurants, fishing, historic town to explore, antiques shows twice a year, St. Louis Day Celebration (August), Old Fashioned Christmas (first weekend in December), Heritage Dance Celebration (first Saturday in April), Living History Exhibit (first Saturday in June).

The Browning Plantation

CHAPPELL HILL, TEXAS 77426

"There's no frownin' at the Brownin'" was the theme of the Browning float at a local county parade. The motto was a hit, as it very aptly describes the Browning atmosphere. This elegant antebellum mansion easily could be awed by its own splendor; but with Dick and Mildred as innkeepers, the spirit of fun rules instead.

"We have a good time," Dick says. "We feel that people are here to watch Mildred make her biscuits in the kitchen while they have their coffee. People don't want to hear how the house was put together or how old Browning died. Mildred and I tell them all *our* troubles, and we have a good laugh instead."

Still, the Ganchans have made an entertaining story of the resurrection of the old Browning plantation, which was truly a formidable undertaking. Mildred was looking for a cute little Victorian house to move to their property elsewhere when they made the mistake of stopping by to see a place that "needed a little attention." What they saw was a completely ruined mansion left over from cotton-and-slavery days.

Listed on the National Register of Historic Places, the inn once again has the fake wood graining that was the height of elegance back when the house was built in the 1850s. Daughter Meg Ganchan Rice spent ages practicing the technique as her contribution to the family restoration effort.

Upstairs guest rooms in the big house have 12-foot ceilings and massive windows and are furnished with nineteenth-century antiques, including plantation and tester beds.

Where to relax is a choice that can be difficult: the parlor, the library, or the south veranda, with its beautiful view over the vast acres of green farmland? Or for an even more breathtaking scene, climb three flights to the rooftop widow's walk that crowns the house.

And there is more. One son-in-law is such a train buff that he has built a model railroad on the property, and if he's in residence, you may be able to cajole him into a ride. "He has more rolling stock than the Santa Fe," Dick brags as he proudly shows off the new two-room "depot" he designed, a replica of a Santa Fe original. Guest rooms inside the depot have horizontal pine paneling and blue-striped-ticking curtains and bedspreads.

You'll feel like Scarlett O'Hara and Rhett at breakfast around the huge dining table, eating dishes like the inn's Eggs Sardou accompanied by a hot fruit compote. But first there's an Orange Julius eye-opener, and maybe there will also be hot biscuits. There's a social hour with snacks before dinner, too.

How to get there: From U.S. Highway 290 east of Brenham, take FM 1155 south until you come to a short jog to the left. Immediately to your right you'll see a dirt road. Turn right onto it; continue south across the cattle guard and under the arch of trees until you reach the plantation house.

Innkeepers: Mildred and Dick Ganchan
Address/Telephone: Route 1, Box 8; (409) 836–6144
Rooms: 6 in main house and Model Railroad Depot; 2 with private bath, 2 with TV. No smoking inn.
Rates: $85 to $110, double; $75 weeknights; EPB and evening snacks. No credit cards.
Open: All year.
Facilities and activities: Swimming pool, model train with 1½ miles of track, 220 acres of natural trails, fishing in lakes on property. Nearby: historic sites in Washington-on-the-Brazos and Independence, Star of the Republic Museum, miniature horses at Monastery of St. Clare; good restaurant in Brenham.

The Mulberry House
CHAPPELL HILL, TEXAS 77426

Mulberry House was the home of prosperous cotton farmer John Sterling Smith and his wife, Marie, and their descendants from 1874 to 1983. Innkeepers Katie and Myrv bought the house as a country retreat from the hustle and bustle of Houston, an hour and a half away. First they built the "barn," a suite of two bedrooms, living room, and kitchen, and lived there three years while they restored the house. Now the barn serves as both lovely guest quarters and Myrv's woodworking shop on the first floor.

Myrv is a consummate woodworking artist; examples of his fine bird carvings decorate the inn. There are hooded merganser and bobwhite families, all perched on wonderful pieces of driftwood, all detailed down to the last feather.

I wondered how Katie and Myrv had gotten into innkeeping. "Myrv was always working in the yard or in his shop, and I was always in the house," says Katie with a laugh, "and one day I was in a gift shop (on nearby Brenham's square) and a young couple was looking for a place to stay. I said, 'Come home with me,' and they did, and we had a wonderful time!"

In Miss Marie's Room, named for the lady who lived there fifty years, you'll find two wonderful Jenny Lind beds that Katie hunted down expressly for that room. The huge armoire is a find, too, and the clutch of teddy bears sitting in a corner look most pleased with their quarters.

The inn is filled with unusual antique pieces—some from the Smith family, who lived in the house 110 years.

Katie makes delicious breakfasts in the large sunny kitchen: egg and cheese soufflé, or ham, bacon and egg puff, with grits and cranberry-orange muffins. At 6:00 in the evening, before guests go out to dinner at one of Brenham's fine restaurants, there's an informal cocktail hour, with neighbors sometimes joining in. "We come and go," says Katie, "and expect our guests to make themselves at home."

"Lots of people bring their bicycles," says Myrv. "They ride from here to Washington-on-the-Brazos." A round trip of 32 miles is a good day's outing.

Chappell Hill was founded in 1847 and named for an early Texas hunter. Before the Civil War it was beginning to grow into a prominent educational and agricultural center. Today it's a charming, small village—with several annual festivals to remind Texas it's still there.

How to get there: Turn north off U.S. Highway 290 onto FM 1155 (Chappell Hill's Main Street) and drive to FM 2447 (Chestnut Street). Mulberry House is 2⁄10 mile east of the intersection.

Innkeepers: Katie and Myrv Cron
Address/Telephone: P.O. Box 5; (409) 830–1311
Rooms: 5, in main house and guest cottage; all with private bath and phone, 2 with TV. No smoking inn.
Rates: $75 to $85, double, weekends; discount during week; EPB and evening snacks. No credit cards.
Open: All year.
Facilities and activities: Large backyard, croquet. Nearby: Brenham restaurants and shops; historic Chappell Hill with restaurants, Bluebonnet Festival (April), Fourth of July parade, Scarecrow Festival (October); Washington-on-the-Brazos (capital of the Republic of Texas), Star of the Republic Museum, miniature horses at Monastery of St. Clare.

Stagecoach Inn
CHAPPELL HILL, TEXAS 77426

"We want to excel in hospitality," says Elizabeth, who is carrying on the tradition of this historic inn. The Stagecoach Inn was built in 1850 and was once a major stop for the coaches it was named for. The gorgeous grounds, like a small estate, are on a corner surrounded by a white picket fence and are ablaze with color overflowing from beds and pots of flowers. All summer long flower pots are bursting with red, white, and pink geraniums; the flower beds are bordered in scarlet begonias; and the crepe myrtle trees shower blossoms all around. There are four separate terraces from which to drink in all this beauty. "People enjoy them so much. It gets more beautiful all the time," says this proud innkeeper-gardener.

"We start the bulbs in the middle of December, especially the bearded iris," Elizabeth says of the flowers that appear at each place on the breakfast table. If it's not iris time, perhaps a sprig of rosemary will be at your place, but it will always be something from this fabulous garden.

The inn fronts on the road, and both the Coach House and Weems Cottage are on the grounds in the rear, all part of the three-acre historic site.

Breakfast can be short-order, like soft-boiled or scrambled eggs, but I vote for cook Evelyn's "secret casserole," which is still a secret from me. "She loves to let you try to work it out," says

Elizabeth, "but she's careful not to divulge it herself."

Chef Evelyn might serve eggs Elizabeth or eggs Charlotte instead, along with apple strudel, whiskey coffeecake, homemade muffins, croissants, or zucchini bread, depending upon her mood. Oh, that Evelyn surely can cook! Add grape jelly, juice of your choice, and fresh fruit in season, and you have a feast.

Sometimes Elizabeth adds her touch with a mixed fruit and yogurt combination she calls *crème fraîche*.

Whether you stay in Weems Cottage, Lottie's, or the Coach House, you have the run of the place. Weems Cottage, with two rooms and a bath, was built in 1866, and the front and back porches are full of rocking chairs, just like in the good old days. Lottie's is a 133-year-old Greek Revival house across the road from the inn, and its five rooms include two living-room areas as well as the guest rooms, all furnished with authentic Texas heirlooms and antiques. The Coach House, newly remodeled into a one-bedroom suite, is way in the back under spreading old trees. "We're flexible," says Elizabeth. "We've slept an entire bridge club, an antiques group, a football weekend—as many as fifteen to twenty guests."

Whenever you spend the night, you can have a tour of the inn, which is listed on the National Register of Historic Places.

How to get there: Turn north off U.S. Highway 290 onto FM 1155 (Chappell Hill's Main Street) and drive to FM 2447 (Chestnut Street). Stagecoach Inn is across the corner to the left, and Lottie's is on the right.

Innkeepers: Elizabeth and Harvin Moore
Address/Telephone: P.O. Box 339; (409) 836–9515
Rooms: 7; 2 in main building, 1 in Coach House with private bath, 2 in Weems Cottage, 2 in Lottie's; downstairs rooms handicapped accessible. No smoking inn.
Rates: $90 to $100, double, EPB. Business rates available. No credit cards.
Open: All year.
Facilities and activities: Beautiful grounds and garden. Nearby: good restaurants; Chappell Hill, in the heart of early Texas history; Washington-on-the-Brazos; Star of the Republic Museum; St. Clare Monastery, which raises miniature horses.
Recommended Country Inns® Travel Club Benefit: 10% discount, Monday–Thursday.

Country Cottage Inn–Nimitz Birthplace

FREDERICKSBURG, TEXAS 78624

When this cottage was built in 1850, just four years after Fredericksburg was founded, it was the only two-story house in town. Cool stone walls are more than 24 inches thick, and the hardware was forged in the owner's smithy. The walls are whitewashed; there are exposed hand-cut rafters. Most of the antique furniture was made in town in the mid-1800s.

One of the rooms is furnished with antiques from the birthplace of Admiral Chester W. Nimitz, hero of the Pacific Theater during World War II. He was born just 2 blocks away from the cottage. His grandfather's old Steamboat Hotel is now a first-class museum. Behind the museum there's a beautiful Japanese garden contributed by the people of Japan, and a block away you'll find the Walk of the Pacific War, lined with airplanes, tanks, landing craft, and other machines used in the Pacific during World War II. They're all there, out in the open, sunny hill country scenery, for kids and adults alike to touch and wonder at.

Country Cottage has other Nimitz mementos. The Pecan Room has a Nimitz night table, a chuck-wagon pie safe, an Amish quilt on the wall, and an eighteenth-century mantrap over the sofa; the coffee table is an 1825 wooden bellows from France. So many interesting details make it difficult to look at everything at once, so take your time!

The Oak Suite has its original fireplace, and guests are permitted to build a fire, but I love Jeffery Ann's admonition: "Please build only small fires!"

The inn has two new suites, the Henke Suite in the original front room of the historic house (Henke was Admiral Nimitz's maternal grandfather). The Nimitz Suite is in a part of the house that was added back in 1873, and it's full of more Nimitz family memorabilia.

The inn may be charmingly historic, but the bathrooms are beautifully modern—some of them have large whirlpool tubs. I was completely restored in one, after a wonderful day taking in all the small-town sights.

Breakfast is hot chocolate, coffee, or tea with a Southwestern egg course with home-smoked peppered tenderloin, and sometimes sweet rolls from one of Fredericksburg's famous bakeries. Two of them, Dietz's and the Fredericksburg Bakery, have been in business since the town began, and I really recommend a sweet visit. But mostly innkeeper Jeffery Ann has fresh pastries and muffins of her own for you—she loves to bake.

The old inn building is beautifully restored and scrupulously clean, and the simple structure is enhanced by Laura Ashley fabrics and bed linens. Soft terry robes and ice water in each room made me feel like a fraudulent pioneer—it wasn't like this a little over a hundred years ago, when hostile Indians were near and the living was pretty tough!

How to get there: Highway 290 goes through town, becoming Main Street, and the inn is at number 249.

Innkeeper: Jeffery Ann Webb
Address/Telephone: 249 East Main Street; (210) 997–8549
Rooms: 7 suites; all with private bath, phone, TV, refrigerator, microwave oven, coffee maker. No smoking inn.
Rates: $75 to $110, per room, EPB.
Open: All year.
Facilities and activities: Fully equipped kitchen available. Nearby: German restaurants, Admiral Nimitz Museum, Pioneer Museum, almost-monthly celebrations in historic Fredericksburg, antiques shops, small museums, LBJ National Park.
Recommended Country Inns® Travel Club Benefit: 10% discount, Monday–Thursday, except holiday periods and during local special events.

Das College Haus

FREDERICKSBURG, TEXAS 78624

Peace and serenity reign supreme in this pleasant inn, named after a quiet back street in historic Fredericksburg, a town settled in the middle of the past century by hard-working German immigrants. "Tim really gets to our guests from the city when he tells them, 'You can sit out on the porch and watch nothing come by," Myrna says.

Tim is a painter. He studied in New York, was an art professor at Colorado College, and his art work is in hotels, corporate offices, and galleries. When he was invited to be a Main Street Artist in Lufkin in East Texas, he became an adopted Texan.

As for Myrna, she was an accountant for a Lufkin firm, and her first husband was a CPA. "He died—and I ran off with an artist," she says. "Actually, we met when Tim called about a painting of his that my husband had bought before he died." The red barn at the back of the property has been restored as Tim's studio. The note out front says, "If no one answers the bell, come to the red barn in the back." Guests are invited at any time to bring their coffee and visit with the artist at work.

"We stayed at inns, and it looked like fun," Myrna says. "Tim and I both enjoy cooking, and the best thing about this is that we're doing it for the fun of it. We fell in love with the house, and we felt as if we would meet a lot of interesting people. And this makes another outlet for Tim's work," she adds, showing off the paintings on all the walls.

Myrna says that everything she has ever done has given her the experience for this. "I've raised seven children. As a mother, you have to know how to cook and take care of people. In the dining room, Tim introduces me by saying, 'This is your mother!' Well, with our guests we feel that we are a family."

The inn is filled with books on art, and Myrna is proud of an old chair, carved with lions' heads, that belonged to a sheriff of Kerr County once upon a time. The dining room of the old house is papered in a floral paper, all greens and blues and reds. The 8-foot-long table was made especially to hold a lot of people.

In the kitchen there's an old pie safe, and an ice box is tucked in the back hallway. Upstairs, off the L-shaped porch, there's the Victorian Green Suite, which can sleep six, with its sitting room containing a queen-sized sofa bed. Myrna and Tim had fun finding antique furniture—Texas sure has a lot of antiques, and not a few of them are in Fredericksburg shops.

The Country Cream Room, with a private bath across the hall, is done in pinks and blues. The bed is covered with an antique quilt, and the wash stand and library table are made of oak.

Downstairs, the Victorian Rose Room is decorated with wall covering in paisley and big cabbage roses. There's a Victrola that actually still plays; we were entertained by some old Bob Wills records.

Breakfasts, served in the dining room or upstairs porch, might be Tim's crab pancakes with jicama sauce, or peach crepes and fruit smoothies. "We're health-conscious," Myrna says.

How to get there: From East Main Street turn onto North Llano and go about 5 blocks to East College. Turn left, and the inn is on the right about a block up.

Innkeepers: Myrna and Tom Saska
Address/Telephone: 106 College Street; (512) 997–9047
Rooms: 3; all with private bath, TV, and VCR; wheelchair accessible. No smoking inn.
Rates: $70 to $85, double; $10 extra person; EPB. No credit cards.
Open: All year.
Facilities and activities: Bicycles. Nearby: public exercise track, Admiral Chester Nimitz Museum and Walk of the Pacific War, Pioneer Museum, historic Sunday Houses, Lady Bird Johnson State Park, Lyndon B. Johnson National Historical Park and LBJ State Park, Enchanted Rock State Park, antiques shops; German restaurants.
Recommended Country Inns® Travel Club Benefit: 10% discount, Monday–Thursday.

The Delforge Place

FREDERICKSBURG, TEXAS 78624

"We get some of the most interesting people," Betsy says. "That's why we settled here; this is such a vibrant, international little town, what with the Nimitz Museum and the LBJ Ranch." The Delforge Place is interesting and international itself, what with the front Map Room and the Quebec Room sporting ancient maps and other mementos from Betsy's sea-captain ancestor, head of the first merchant fleet that opened the Harbor of Yokohama to American sailing ships.

Guest room decor is ever changing, since Betsy lets her antique furniture and paintings go out on exhibit to museums on the East Coast. It follows that oriental pieces join with the American, European, and family heirlooms in furnishing the old house, once a one-room "Sunday house"—you'll have to go to Fredericksburg to find out what a Sunday house is. This one was built in 1898 by German pioneer Ferdinand Koeppen on a tract of land set aside by the German Emigration Company as a communal garden. The house was moved to its present location in 1975 and during restoration was made considerably larger.

Guests relax in one of the two *versamel*, or "gathering rooms," with coffee and tea, quiet games, or books off the shelves (or television, if they insist!). The Delforges stress that guests are welcome to come and go as they please: There's a lot to see and do in town.

And guests are sent off with a good start—one of Betsy's famous breakfasts. She has always featured her specialties of German Sour Cream Twists and San Saba French Toast (which is marinated in orange brandy and thick and crusty with orange peel and San Saba pecans. Delicious!). Now she's having fun varying them with no fewer than seven different breakfast menus. I hope you're lucky enough to catch her seven-course gourmet Fredericksburg Breakfast, a sampling of all the wonderful fruits, meats, breads, and pastries of the historical town.

"Food and fashion go together for me," Betsy says, and her past includes both food testing and fabric design. She grows her own herbs in hanging baskets over the flagstone patio. "When the apples come in the fall, we have sausage and apple crepes," which sounds to me like a great reason for an autumn visit. Betsy's avocation now is the making of gift baskets she and George call Special Day Baskets. They're loaded with all the good things produced in Fredericksburg, and people order them from all over Texas and beyond.

The Upper Deck's named for Betsy's seafaring interests. It has its own outside staircase up to the deck, bright with nautical flags flying in the breeze. Skylights and an octagon window brighten the spacious guest room, which has such original touches as weathered wooden barrels set on end as nightstands and a globe of the world on a stand, for the sailors.

How to get there: From Main Street (U.S. Highway 290) turn south on South Adams to Walnut, then left on Walnut for 3 blocks to Ettie. The inn, at 710 Ettie, is the Victorian house on the corner to your left.

Innkeepers: Betsy and George Delforge
Address/Telephone: 710 Ettie Street; (210) 997–6212
Rooms: 4 in main house, plus 2 suites in Rabke-Weber House next door; all with private bath and TV. No smoking inn.
Rates: $78 to $83, double, EPB.
Open: All year.
Facilities and activities: Lunch and dinner by reservation, picnic baskets, patio with fountain, ping-pong, pool table, sandbox. Nearby: 7 blocks away is Fredericksburg's famous Main Street, with German restaurants, and biergartens, Admiral Nimitz Museum, other historic museums, and antiques shops; LBJ Ranch approximately 15 miles east.
Business travel: Meeting and conference center, phone in all rooms; corporate rates.

Magnolia House

FREDERICKSBURG, TEXAS 78624

Geri Lilley has a lot of ambition, the right sort: She has her guests' best interests at heart. "I want to be the very best inn in Texas!" she says. "Really," she adds earnestly, "That's my ambition. I want my guests to tell me a problem or about something missing so I can fix it right now. And I try to be very flexible. We've even served breakfast to two ladies at 7:00 A.M., even though we prefer 8:30, because they were judges at a local beauty show and had to be there early."

But it's not only Geri's gung-ho attitude that makes Magnolia House special: The inn itself is warm and bright and welcoming, with large, comfortable guest rooms, the kind of parlor (and dining room) you'd like to call your own, a game room for board games, and a large patio with a fountain and a goldfish pond. The house historically is the Stein House, and although the family took the original goldfish out when they left, years ago, the only surviving member of the family called Geri recently. "Would you like some of the descendants back in the pond?" the elderly lady asked. "So now," Geri crows, "I've got goldfish out there this big!"

Hospitality shows in the sumptuous breakfast Geri and her assistant, Yolanda Martinez, take such pride in. We had fresh fruit salad with a secret "Magnolia" sauce, bran muffins, bacon and sausage, cheese quiche, and the lightest, fluffiest pecan waffles, topped with strawberries and whipped cream and/or maple syrup. I opted for the latter when Yolanda bragged that she concocts the maple syrup herself. Geri is a gourmet cook, and Yolanda is a willing disciple. The seven-course breakfast is an experience. "We've had guests for nine days and never did they have the same breakfast twice."

Although Geri has remodeled the historic house, she hasn't done away with an unusual and delightful pass-through she calls the "Mud Room." Overhanging a small washbasin is a genuine old hand pump. "All my guests have to try it," Geri says. I certainly did, and although it took some pressure, I finally got fresh spring water gurgling into the basin.

Built into the wall opposite this fun "toy" is the house's original icebox, now, of course, refrigerated. It opens on both sides of the wall, and guests can help themselves to the complimentary wine therein.

Both the Magnolia Suite and the Bluebonnet Suite have private entrances; the Magnolia has a huge living room with fireplace; the Bluebonnet has a kitchen and a very comfy rocker, which, when it was reupholstered, revealed some buried treasure: an old shilling and sixpence, "so we know it's a genuine English antique," Geri says. All rooms are large and bright and delightfully decorated by Geri, who also paints. "I retired from the oil business in Houston because I had to have back surgery. That I'm now physically fit I attribute to my guests, to all the love and caring," she says, determined to return it full measure.

How to get there: From Main Street (Highway 290 east) turn north on Adams Street to Hackberry, which runs parallel to Main. The inn is on the southeast corner of Adams and Hackberry.

Innkeeper: Geri Lilley
Address/Telephone: 101 East Hackberry; (210) 997–0306
Rooms: 6, including 2 suites; 4 with private bath, all with TV; downstairs rooms and suites wheelchair accessible.
Rates: $75 to $95, double, EPB.
Open: All year.
Facilities and activities: Porches, large patio with fountain and goldfish pond. Nearby: restaurants, antiques shops, Admiral Nimitz Museum and Walk of the Pacific War, Pioneer Museum, historic Sunday houses.

River View Inn and Farm

FREDERICKSBURG, TEXAS 78624

Breezy is the word for River View Inn and Farm. It's set on a hill in the hill country and has a breezeway that catches a round-the-clock cool wind. I could just sit there for hours, taking in the sweep of the green hills and listening to the lowing of the longhorns that Helen's neighbors raise and that sometimes graze in Helen's fields.

Helen herself raises native Texas herbs and other native Texas flora, and what a refreshing treat to have her show you her garden. "You just ought to see!"—her enthusiasm is infectious. She also has a vegetable garden close to the house, and young guests enjoy helping pick the crops, especially when they can take them home.

Helen's guests have the run of the house. The kitchen, the large and comfortably furnished living room with its big stone fireplace, the glass-enclosed sun porch, the breakfast room with its china cabinet full of heirloom china, the framed German mottoes, and the collection of framed bird pictures (mostly hummingbirds, which are Helen's favorite)—all conspire to make guests feel truly at home.

The front porch and the large upstairs area, in particular, are great for kids to read and play games in. "But we're never locked into the weather here," Helen reminds. "Not much rain, so everybody's usually out and doing, going to town or to the park."

The downstairs bedroom has a beautiful

quilt draped over a handmade cedar chest. The furnishings are 1920s Queen Anne reproductions: dressing table, dresser, bureau, bed, and chair. The bathroom tub has a Jacuzzi, a nice luxury to find out in ranch country!

Helen's breakfast is hearty enough for a rancher, too. Fresh local German sausage ("Turkey instead of German sausage for the fat-conscious"), scrambled eggs with jalapeños (but not too hot, says Helen), cheese, biscuits, fresh peach and cherry cobbler, jellies and jams.

It's all topped off by the centerpiece, fresh fruit in season, which everybody proceeds to eat. "The kids run off to play, but the grownups always linger," says Helen, "having more coffee and munching on the centerpiece." I can taste why: The county is known for blackberries, nectarines, peaches, strawberries, mangoes, and melon—watermelon, honeydew, and Persian.

The Little House That Helen Built has an old-fashioned claw-footed tub in the bathroom and a newfangled microwave oven hiding in a closet with a small refrigerator and a coffeepot. There's a queen bed and a trundle for a child and a deck in back overlooking the Pedernales River. And now there's Little House II, with an antique Jenny Lind spool bed transformed into queen size, for comfort.

You'll find that if guests aren't munching fruit or sitting on the breezeway, they'll be on the porches, rocking or swinging on the dogwood glider and waiting for the cows to come home.

How to get there: Inn is 4½ miles south of Fredericksburg on Highway 16; 1 mile south of Lady Bird Johnson Park. To the left you'll see a fence and a cattle guard. Drive over it and there you are.

Innkeeper: Helen K. Taylor
Address/Telephone: Highway 16 South; (210) 997–8555
Rooms: 5, plus 2 one-bedroom cottages; 4 with private bath, 2 with phone, 1 with TV. Pets permitted.
Rates: $75 to $85, per room, EPB. Special rates in September, January, and February.
Open: All year.
Facilities and activities: Farm acres to wander over, river to fish in, cattle to visit, vegetable garden, books and games. Nearby: Lady Bird Johnson Municipal Park, with swimming pool, tennis, and 9-hole golf course is 1³⁄₁₀ miles away; Fredericksburg has Admiral Nimitz Museum and German heritage museums.
Business travel: Corporate rates; phone in two rooms; secretarial service and fax available in Fredericksburg.

Harper Chessher Inn
GEORGETOWN, TEXAS 78626

This historic home, built in 1853, bears the name of its original owners, although the guest rooms are named for owner Leigh's daughters. Listed in the National Registry of Historic Homes, it was part of the land assigned to George Washington Glasscock, founder of Georgetown. He in turn sold to Dr. George Smithers Coleman Harper. The stone veneer of the house has been traced to Harper as the builder.

"Since this is a historic property, you have to be careful what you do," Jane says. "The city said that we could tear down some of the stone if we used it again." We go to look at the pretty little garden on the side of the house. "See that stone arch at the front? That's new, but the stone is old—it's the original."

The garden is patterned after the original one, an English garden discovered in some old photographs. Bordered walkways surround a small fountain, and the effect is very pleasant.

We cross to the garden over a long porch with black wrought-iron furniture. The door opens off Laura's Library, a book-lined room with a dining table and chairs and an interesting old sideboard. Adjoining is the big dining room, with a large table and chairs in golden wood. "The set is from Denmark," Jane says. Unusual were the long narrow tables set against two walls, with more matching chairs in front of them, making sort of a food bar facing the walls.

"Those are from a monastery in England," Jane explains as I count a total of sixteen beautiful, matching chairs.

The entire inn is decorated in a color scheme of soft pink walls, polished wood floors, and a green-patterned carpet throughout. Interesting old furniture, sofas, loveseats, and armchairs are all covered with deep rose moire. Each bed has a white crocheted spread and fluffy pillows and bolsters. Instead of art, hand-painted murals decorate the walls—flowers, vines, and objects suited to the theme of each room.

"Holly's Room is the rabbit room," Jane says, and sure enough, there are rabbits frolicking on the pink walls and a shiny white sculpted rabbit on the mantel. Melanie is the sheep or lamb room, with lambs gamboling among the flowers. Meghan's Room has a claw-footed tub in an alcove, shrouded with lace curtains. Since this is the Bird Room, pretty birds are painted among the flowers and vines. Shannon's Room has twin beds and pine furniture.

Breakfast is an assortment of homemade muffins: raspberry, strawberry, blueberry, and bran. "Blueberry seems to be the favorite," Jane says. There are also homemade biscuits with blackberry, apricot, raspberry, and strawberry jam.

High noon tea is served daily on the veranda overlooking the garden. Since it is an English garden, you'll have scones with clotted cream.

You won't find it in Mrs. Bradley's Tea Room. Instead, the room is a shop selling the crafts of Vera Bradley, a friend of Leigh's to whom she has dedicated the room, "for all the love and joy she brought to all who knew her."

How to get there: From I–35 take the Taylor–Burnet exit in Georgetown and go east (it becomes University Avenue) through three traffic lights. Go 5 blocks farther on, and turn right on College Street. The inn is on the left, 2 blocks down the street.

Innkeepers: Jane Dobrozyski and Leigh Marcus
Address/Telephone: 1309 College Street; (512) 863–4057
Rooms: 4; all with private bath; wheelchair accessible. No smoking inn.
Rates: $70 weekdays; $95 Friday to Sunday; double, continental breakfast.
Open: All year.
Facilities and activities: Nearby: Southwestern University; Old Town; Inner Space Caverns; Georgetown Lake, with swimming, boating, and fishing.

Page House Inn
GEORGETOWN, TEXAS 78628

Page House Inn sits erect like a proper 1903 Victorian lady high above the late-twentieth-century traffic roaring along Interstate 35 below. Pale yellow and gray, surrounded by a white picket fence enclosing the wraparound porches and peaked red roof, it seems aloof to the bustling business in the tearoom and inn below.

But the innkeeper is anything but aloof. Paula moved here from Iowa to be close to her family while taking care of an invalid husband. "I came with the idea that I was going to like it, and I don't have any reason not to be happy," she says happily, although she is now alone. "I enjoy meeting people, and though I work hard, when the day is done, it's done! As for the inn, my son told me he'd found a perfect location for something I might enjoy. Well, I did, restoring the three buildings—this old house, the carriage house, and the polo barn." Seems that polo was big in Georgetown back in the 1930s, and the big red barn in the back of the property now makes a wonderful meeting, conference, or party place.

Both entry hall and small lobby are filled with glass cases of gift items for sale, and the three dining rooms of the Page House Inn are pretty with lace curtains at the windows and lace cloths on the tables.

Up the long flight of stairs (these Victorian houses do have high ceilings!), a pleasant sitting area has colorful sofas, television, and game table with checkers out at the ready. Guest rooms are named for the people who once lived here. Doc and Esther Weir—why, he was a polo player. As for Joe and Olivia, "they were Mr. and Mrs. Page." And Avis? "I got permission for all the names from the family still living, and they requested that we have an Avis room; she was one of the special kids in the family."

The Carriage House Memories Room in the Carriage House sets Paula's imagination alight. "The carriage was actually stored back in here," she says, gesturing. "The horses unhooked, the tack taken next door to the tack room," and you almost can hear the jingle of the harnesses, even though it seems most improbable in the bright, modern, green-and-cream room. The old tack room next door is now Carriage Dreams, and both rooms front on a little porch.

With a tea room on the premises (and a chef), you can be sure of good food. Breakfast might be Belgian waffles and ham, or Paula's salute to the Southwest: her Piñata Bake, a delicious soufflé of eggs, crumbled sausage, peppers, onions, and mushrooms, served with miniature corn muffins. High tea is five courses: sandwiches of cucumber or jalapeño cheese ("because this is Texas"); scones and special boysenberry jam; assorted nut breads with whipped cream cheese; fruit; sweets like little Scottish shortbreads and coconut fudge tarts. No wonder dinner isn't served most evenings.

"We had our new chief of police here for a month until he got settled," Paula says. "That was real fun!" Of all her guests, she says, "I give them all the love I can while they're here."

How to get there: From I–35 take exit 260 (Leander Road) and, turning west, almost immediately turn right onto the road (more like a long driveway) just in front of the convenience store on the corner. This leads you right into the parking area in front of the inn.

Innkeeper: Paula Arand
Address/Telephone: 1000 Leander Road; (512) 863–8979
Rooms: 6 in main house and carriage house; all with private bath, 3 with TV; downstairs room wheelchair accessible. No smoking inn.
Rates: $75 to $85, double; $15 extra person; EPB.
Open: All year.
Facilities and activities: Restaurant for lunch and tea, dinner Friday and Saturday; gardens. Nearby: Southwestern University; Old Town; Inner Space Caverns; Georgetown Lake, with swimming, boating, and fishing.
Business travel: Located 26 miles from Austin. Polo Barn holds 220 for meetings, conventions, etc. Corporate rates.

Trail's End Inn

LEANDER, TEXAS 78641

Trail's End Inn is really, *really* out in the country, on six acres of land overlooking the Hill Country. From the Observation Deck (like a widow's walk) on top of the house, you can catch a glimpse of Lake Travis as well as lots of the Travis County Audubon Society Bird Sanctuary.

"At first we thought we wanted to make hiking trails," JoAnn says. "But although people can walk anywhere they want, we decided to leave the land just as is, wild." She laughs. "Tom calls it our 'Jurassic Park.' But never fear, nothing wilder than some gray fox will be lurking in the underbrush.

It all began with the Cottage, across the lawn and down about a dozen winding steps through the wilderness. It was their getaway from Austin, where Tom is a geologist-petrographer. (He tests concrete and other construction materials that have failed.) JoAnn explains: "When our children went off to college, I told Tom, 'If we don't build our dream house now, we never will,'" and she designed it herself.

The entry is large and open, two stories high. The living room walls are cranberry red with white molding, and there's a 1930s leather rocker the same color. "One of my guests said she used to rock in one like that," which pleased JoAnn no end. "I love things from the '30s and '40s," she says, and she designed the house to reflect that period. "That was such a wonderful time in American history. When you read old cookbooks and see how people managed in the Depression . . ."

The dining-room walls are a bright yellow, and in addition to the formal Country French dining set, there's a high chair waiting in the corner. "I have three children, and grandchildren; I love children," she says. There are toys and games in the living room; one corner has an old-time child's school desk. When you lift the lid, there are crayons and coloring books to amuse youngsters. Lining the stairs are soft and cuddly Raggedy Ann and Raggedy Andy, Sesame Street characters, and teddy bears.

The Blue Room upstairs has a mahogany sleigh bed and a formal sofa to lounge on. So does the Pink Room (it's walls are really pink, with flowered wallpaper on the ceiling for a change), which opens off the porch. Both rooms have unusually spacious baths.

The Cottage is a little house all to itself, with kitchen and living quarters, a bedroom with a 100-year-old bed that was handed down in JoAnn's family from Kentucky, and a bed under the low ceiling in the loft.

JoAnn's delicious banana pancakes—the batter poured over sautéed banana slices—are a breakfast specialty. For omelets she adds crisp bacon, bell pepper, onions, and cheddar cheese, asking guests, "What do you want me to leave out?" to make sure she's not serving anything someone cannot eat. With that, she serves hashed browns—"from scratch"—crisp and brown, and biscuits either plain or with bacon and cheese. She also make delicious orange-buttermilk English muffins.

How to get there: From I–35 take Highway 183 north, crossing Highway 290. From 290 go $4\frac{2}{10}$ miles, through Cedar Park, to FM 1431. Turn left and go $3\frac{7}{10}$ miles to Trail's End Road (on the left). Turn left and go $\frac{8}{10}$ mile until you come to a cluster of about eight mailboxes on the left. Turn left here onto the dirt road (there's an inn sign) and follow it around past a blue house on the right. The inn is just ahead on the left, a gray house with white trim.

Innkeepers: JoAnn and Tom Patty
Address/Telephone: 12223 Trail's End Road #7; (512) 267–2901
Rooms: 3 in main house and cottage; all with private bath and TV, kitchen in cottage. No smoking inn.
Rates: $55 to $95, double; $20 extra person; children under 10 free; EPB.
Open: All year.
Facilities and activities: Swimming pool, toys and games, gift shop. Nearby: Hill Country Flyer (steam train), Lake Travis, bird sanctuary, shops and restaurants in Cedar Park and Round Rock.
Recommended Country Inns® Travel Club Benefit: 10% discount.

The Badu House
LLANO, TEXAS 78643

The Badu House is an inn in a million, because it began life as a small-town bank. Built in 1891 for the First National of Llano, this Italian Renaissance palace housed the bank handsomely, until it failed in 1898. Then it was bought at auction by Professor N. J. Badu, a French minerologist who installed his family in the imposing red-brick-and-checkerboard-gray-granite building. It was occupied by the Badu family for more than 80 years.

Strong enough to have survived a 1900 tornado and a fire that destroyed the iron boomtown of North Llano, this building sure doesn't look like an inn, was my thought as I climbed the wide granite steps to the front door. But the stained-glass windows of the doors, one emblazoned with the letter "B," the other an "H," welcome one into another world.

The doors opened onto a wide flight of polished wood steps leading to a landing furnished with an antique desk, love seat and chairs, and a jewel-tone antique rug. I walked up a few more steps and rounded a corner to a sitting room with more Victorian settees and an antique sewing machine abandoned—a century ago?—in the midst of stitching.

Back downstairs, I found the Llanite Club on the left, which is the bar and lounge where everyone gathers when not dining or sleeping. There I was welcomed heartily and invited to inspect the bar itself, a huge slab of llanite, the rare opaline stone discovered by Professor Badu and found nowhere else in the world. Beyond the club is a lovely brick patio, facing the grounds that John has been busy landscaping.

The restaurant floors are the white marble of the bank. Solid brass hardware is decorated with an intricate flower motif. I loved the three-part shutters, which slide up and down to shade the large old-fashioned windows.

New innkeepers Karen and John serve a breakfast of coffee, juice, and homemade muffins—blueberry, apple bran—along with sweet rolls and a fresh fruit compote. "We concentrate on dinner," says John, who is the chef. Karen is the meeter and greeter, and a very pleasant and welcoming one, too.

John spent years as chef at some of Houston's and Austin's well-known eating places. But, he says, "I finally had enough of the big city. I came here to find myself; Karen and I sat on the patio of the Badu House drinking margaritas, and we both said, 'This is what we need!'"

The restaurant has a new Hill Country decor, which Karen likes to describe as Texas Chic. "We Texas-ed it up a little," she says. "More a Texas steakhouse feeling." The handmade wooden booths go well with the hearty hand-cut steaks and other specialty Texas products, like grilled quail and grilled pecan-crusted snapper. John is particularly proud of his Shiner Bock Beer Chicken, marinated in that Texas beer, along with honey, pepper, soy sauce, and garlic—mmm.

If you can get there on Wednesday night, it's Fajita Night. The half pound of chicken and beef is a delicious bargain.

How to get there: Llano is on Highway 29 where Highways 16 and 21 meet. Drive through town past the square and the courthouse, across the bridge over the Llano River, and the inn is on the left, at the corner of Highway 16 and Bessemer.

Innkeepers: Karen and John Wolsey
Address/Telephone: 601 Bessemer; (915) 247–4304
Rooms: 8, including 1 two-bedroom suite; all with private bath. Pets permitted.
Rates: $55 to $65, weekdays; $65 to $75, weekends; double, continental breakfast.
Open: All year.
Facilities and activities: Bar and lounge, dinner Wednesday through Sunday. Nearby: hunting (the "deer capital of the world"); fishing; gem and rock collecting; hiking; golf; swimming; County Museum; art, gift and antiques shops; Highland Lakes; Longhorn Caverns; Vanishing Texas River Cruises; Falls Creek Vineyard; Highland Lakes Bluebonnet Trail (spring).

Fraser House Inn

LLANO, TEXAS 78643

"Basically, I brought the house back from the dead," Belle says. "So many people in town were afraid that it was structurally unsound." But not Belle, and not Janet Hackleford, down at Acme Dry Goods: Her great-uncle William Fraser, a stone mason from Scotland, built the house—as well as the State Capitol building in Austin.

Belle restored the house imaginatively—wait until you see the fabric-covered walls in the entire house. The halls are swathed in old rose velvet, the dining room is shirred with pink roses on white, the living-room ceiling border is pleated velvet—all done by Belle herself.

"The rock for this house was quarried from the Slator Ranch outside of town; mule-drawn wagons carted it here. What fun it is to have so many people in the community tell me, 'I was married there, my parents were, too' or 'We lived in that room right there in the back corner.' Judge Morrison lived here, and he was a justice of the peace. And the house for years was a sort of boardinghouse," Belle explains.

Belle, who also works in advertising, is thrilled with innkeeping. "To tell the truth, I absolutely love the people who come here. I meet the most amazing people. One of the highlights, why, it's often 11:00, 11:30 before we get up from the breakfast table."

No wonder, when you tuck in to the meal.

After juice we had strawberries and cream and went on to French toast strata with apple-cider syrup, and link sausage with apples and a lemon brown-sugar sauce. This provides enough energy to climb Enchanted Rock, a nearby attraction of pink granite, one of the country's few exfoliated granite domes.

In the living room, Punkin the dog sits on a pale-pink velvet chair and watches the guests, while Kittycat stays outside. Prior to her work on the Fraser House Inn, Belle practiced decorating on other old houses in Llano, and her touch is unique. Not only the pleated ceiling border but also the bay window treatment, the set of Victorian overstuffed furniture, and the flowered carpet make a very pleasant parlor. Belle says she wants you to feel like you're visiting not your grandmother, but your great-grandmother!

Each guest room has a private entrance. Although Belle is installing a wonderful electronic front-door lock where you can push numbers to go in and out at will, Llano is another of these small Texas towns where it's safe to wander about any time of day or night.

Belle's policy for her guest rooms is "first come, you pick." All have queen-sized beds; downstairs it's a white-metal bedstead and pretty flowered spread and wall fabrics; upstairs, the Rose Room has an entire mirrored wall, while West Room is masculine and tailored in colors of rose and white on a black background. The two upstairs rooms are so surrounded by leafy trees that it's like sleeping in a treehouse.

Belle likes to send guests off to the Badu House Inn for dinner. "You can enjoy being wined and dined, and then walk safely home," she says. There are also four other favorite eateries about thirty minutes away, while Llano itself has no fewer than four famous barbecue restaurants.

How to get there: Llano is on Highway 29 where Highways 16 and 21 meet. Drive through town past the square and the courthouse. The inn is one and a half blocks east of the square, on the left. There is a sign.

Innkeeper: Belle Laning
Address/Telephone: 207 East Main; (915) 247–5183
Rooms: 4; all with private bath. No smoking inn.
Rates: $85, double, EPB. No credit cards except to hold reservation.
Open: All year.
Facilities and activities: Nearby: County Museum; art, gift, and antiques shops; restaurants; Highland Lakes; Longhorn Caverns; Enchanted Rock; Vanishing Texas River Cruise; Falls Creek Vineyard; Highland Lakes Bluebonnet Trail (spring); hunting (the "deer capital of the world"); fishing; gem and rock collecting; hiking; golf; swimming.

Forget-Me-Not River Inn

MARTINDALE, TEXAS 78655

Hermania joins the ranks of innkeepers who fell in love with a house and there was no turning back. "We were living in San Marcos [nearby larger town] in our 'forever' house after our years in Alaska, and I drove up to Martindale to see a friend," she says. "There was this decrepit house with a jungle around it. I didn't even get out of the car," she adds, "because I loved it so much, and I knew Ed would say *no*!" That's because she has cajoled an unwilling Edvin into buying and restoring old run-down houses before.

But you can see who won. More, wait until you see what Ed has done with this "decrepit house." At first it was one-story, with a high attic and dormers. Ed kept looking at that attic and saying, "I know there's room up there."

"He dragged in about four contractors who said it couldn't be done," Hermania says, "but he's a do-it-yourselfer." He lowered the high ceilings about 4 feet and built the most intriguing winding staircase—that was the first thing I wanted to know about. The resulting four guest rooms upstairs under the sloping roof are spacious, light, and delightfully furnished. There's a nook, as well, in the tower, called the Train Turret because youngest son Korey was into trains, and that's where he played. But when he couldn't see out of the windows—"No problem," Hermania says, "Ed just raised the floor!"

All five Rohlack offspring (grown now)

have names that begin with a K, including Kiana, which is Eskimo for "thank you"—both Hermania and Ed taught in Alaska and have many fond memories. Breakfast would have stood even a traveler in the cold north in good stead. First course was, of all things, strawberry shortcake! It was refreshing, a light, fluffy biscuit with slivered berries covered with sour cream, just slightly sweetened. Next came corn bread, split and covered with sliced hard-boiled eggs in a creamy sauce and sprinkled with fresh green scallions and garnished prettily. Coffee, tea, and fresh orange juice, of course, and Ed started it off by saying grace.

The inn is furnished in a very comfortable and eclectic fashion. Most everything has a story because Ed says Hermania is quite a bargain hunter, haunting antiques shops, garage sales, and flea markets. The rose Irish Rose Room is named in memory of the year Kiana spent in Ireland and has a big old-fashioned claw-footed tub in a corner; the Russian Ivy Room is named for son Karleton's current studying of Russian, plus there's a touch of ivy on the towels.

As for the river just outside the back door, you can catch catfish and bass "and even turtles, even if you don't want them," Hermania warns.

How to get there: From I–35 take exit 205 and go east on Highway 80 for about 5 miles until you come to the blinking light. Turn right and go to the end of the street and turn left onto Main. The inn is just down the block on the right. You can't miss it if you turn into the drive lined with huge, round metal storage tanks, left over from the days when Martindale was big in the grain business.

Innkeepers: Hermania and Edvin Rohlack
Address/Telephone: 310 Main (mailing address: Box 396); (512) 357–6835
Rooms: 7; 4 with private bath; 1 three-bedroom cottage with 1 bath. No alcoholic beverages permitted on premises; pets at discretion of innkeeper. No smoking inn.
Rates: $60 to $75, single or double; cottage, $100; EPB.
Open: All year.
Facilities and activities: On the San Marcos River with fishing, canoeing, swimming. Nearby: San Marcos with restaurants, antiques shops, historic buildings, Lyndon B. Johnson's alma mater, Southwest Texas State University; downtown Martindale with historic buildings; factory outlet mall shopping.

The Castle Inn

NAVASOTA, TEXAS 77868

This majestic Queen Anne house is well named The Castle. It is so gorgeous it's hard to describe adequately. Local craftsmen built the mansion in 1893 as a wedding present from a local businessman to his bride. Of now-extinct curly pine, decorated with ornamental brass and beveled glass, its sun porch enclosed by one hundred beveled-glass panes, the house is outstanding. You know it the minute you step into the elegant entry hall with its parquet floor, Tiffany light fixture, and the soaring 14-foot ceiling.

I love the turret on one corner, a tower that makes the house stand out among the leafy trees outside and provides circular window seats inside on the almost-room-sized stair landings. There's also a 20-foot stained-glass window in the stairwell.

The inn is furnished with antiques collected for more than thirty years by Helen and Tim. The music room has a player piano, a hand-cranked Columbia Grafanola, and a carved wooden head of Tim in an aviator's helmet (Tim is a retired airline pilot). The collection is so extensive that private tours are often arranged just to show off this magnificent property. (Tours by reservation only.)

Breakfast can be served in your room or in the upstairs sitting room next to the upstairs porch. Delicious fresh-baked muffins, English muffins, dry cereals, juice and coffee, and fresh fruit in season taste especially good in such baronial surroundings, and you can have it any time between 6:00 A.M. and the 11:00 A.M. checkout time. Evening wine and cheese, with individual loaves of hot bread, are often served on the upstairs balcony, the better to let you enjoy the evening breezes.

"A lot of times when people go out to dinner we don't know when they're coming home," says Helen, "so we leave a note telling them that their wine and cheese are waiting for them in the fridge." It's in the large upstairs hall and is also stocked with soft drinks, which are consumed "on the honor system."

Each bedroom has a fantastic antique bed, one more amazing than the next: first, a rosewood Louisiana plantation bed; then a tall half-tester; next, another half-tester, beautifully carved; and, finally, a 7½-foot-tall black bed. Antique marble-topped dressers and tables blend perfectly to scale. Another thing to marvel at is Helen's doll collection.

Helen and Tim will provide dinner if four couples want it; it might consist of Cornish hens with wild rice, broccoli hollandaise, Mediterranean salad, and a peach cobbler à la mode. Delicious!

How to get there: The inn is 4 blocks west of the Highway 6 bypass on Highway 105, which becomes Washington, Navasota's main street.

Innkeepers: Helen and Tim Urquehart
Address/Telephone: 1403 East Washington Street; (409) 825–8051
Rooms: 4; all with private bath. Smoking permitted in hallway.
Rates: $94, double; $20 extra person; continental breakfast and evening wine and cheese. Business rates available. No credit cards.
Open: All year.
Facilities and activities: Dinner if house is booked by four couples who are acquainted. Nearby: historic town with 14-foot statue of French explorer La Salle, who came to an untimely end near here in 1687, 150 years before town was formed; museum, Navasota Nostalgia Days festival in May, Main Street Project restoration.

Gruene Mansion

NEW BRAUNFELS, TEXAS 78130

"We want to become the best country inn in Texas, and we'll get there!" Sharon says confidently. A Fort Worth native with a background in real estate (Bill is from Gonzales, where he was in the oil and gas pipeline business), she and Bill not only wanted a resort, they wanted one with history. They found it in the Gruene Mansion, set on a historic cotton plantation on the banks of the Guadalupe River.

The inn is located within the Gruene (pronounced "green") Historic District on the northern edge of New Braunfels' city limits. "Bill and I really like the history of Gruene Mansion," Sharon says. "We feel as if we're caretakers of the property, and we try to carry on the tradition of *gemutlich* begun by Henry Gruene back in the mid-1800s."

Gruene Dance Hall, just down the street, is the oldest dance hall in Texas. Sharon speaks of the original owner as though she knows him. "Henry built the hall for the closeness and warmness of his friends. He also had a little house where travelers could come and stay; they just had to replace the logs for the fire. He was kind to strangers, and we wanted to live that way. It's the best way to meet people."

Wander down to Gruene Dance Hall for a beer; on weekends you can dance the Texas two-step—there's live music then. Next door, the Grist Mill Restaurant is housed in the ruins of a hundred-year-old cotton gin beneath a water tower on the banks of the Guadalupe River, with its pretty little rapids and its happy white-water rafters, many floating down from Canyon River when the water's right. You can become a river rat, too, thanks to the two outfitters on the river.

Cottages with little porches overhang the river, and they are furnished with antiques and handmade quilts; each room is different. Sharon had a great time decorating—imagine having seventeen rooms to design!

Fireside Lodge #2 has a slanted ceiling, papered with a pretty flowered wallpaper of pink and blue flowers on a black background. You can imagine the interesting contrast that makes with the rough wood paneling, made from both poplar and yellow pine. The fireplace wall is white stone; the brass bed has a colorful patchwork quilt and a crocheted afghan laid across the foot. (Feet can get chilly on cool Hill Country nights.)

Bluebonnet Lodge has huge bluebonnets painted on the walls, both bedroom and bath. The shower curtain in the bath is an old quilt (protected by a liner, of course) and dolled up with a pointed lace valance—Sharon has many original ideas. Walls in the Grand River Lodge are painted bright blue between the wood strips, and stenciled with red and yellow stylized tulips.

How to get there: From I–35 take exit 191 (Canyon Lake) and go west on Highway 306 for 1½ miles, following the Gruene Historical signs. Turn left into Gruene and go to the end of the road. The inn is on the right as you turn left onto Gruene Road.

Innkeepers: Sharon and Bill McCaskell
Address/Telephone: 1275 Gruene Road; (210) 629–2641 or –8372, fax same or (800) 299–8372
Rooms: 17, in assorted cottages on the river; all with private bath and TV. No smoking inn.
Rates: $85 to $200, double; $20 extra person; breakfast $5 extra. No credit cards.
Open: All year.
Facilities and activities: Nearby: Grist Mill Restaurant; Gruene Dance Hall; antiques; museums: Hummel, Sophienburg, Handmade Furniture, and Children's; Schlitterbahn Water Park; rafting, tubing, and swimming on Guadalupe and Comal rivers; bicycling; horseback riding; golf; tennis; Natural Bridge Caverns and Wildlife Ranch; Canyon Lake, with fishing, boating, swimming, and waterskiing; discount shopping malls.
Business travel: Located a half hour from downtown San Antonio and San Marcos. Lodge meeting facilities for 300, fax, video, computer setups available, catering.

Historic Kuebler-Waldrip Haus & Danville School Inn

NEW BRAUNFELS, TEXAS 78132

Margy (pronounced "Mar-ghee") and her son Darrell make a wonderful welcoming pair to this historic property. Set on forty-three acres of Central Texas land barely five minutes from two beautiful rivers, this is the place for total relaxation. Of the three inn cats, Double Trouble, LaVerne, and White Wings, it's LaVerne who's always lounging around. "She kind of sets the mood," Darrell says tolerantly. But it looks to me like Piggy, the big old bloodhound, ought to get the prize for slow motion. "She came with that name," Darrell explains. "I guess from her eating habits."

This region of Texas was colonized mainly by German settlers around the middle of the nineteenth century. The historic house, built in 1847, is an authentic German pioneer limestone-and-hand-hewn-timber home with fireplace and wood-burning stove. "When we got the property, it was just one room," Darrell says. "I'm thankful we were three boys, there was so much work to do." It's hard to visualize the layers of sheetrock, wallpaper, shiplap boards, and old adobe plaster they removed to show the natural beauty of stone and wood. A lot of the remodeling used old barn wood. "We tore down three barns," he explains.

The delightful surprise of an 1863 schoolhouse (with chalkboard still on the wall of the downstairs room) was moved to the property from nearby Solms. There are two sets of stairs to the two upper-level guest rooms: an outside one and one inside that leads up to a trapdoor in the upstairs hall in case the entire building is taken for meetings or family reunions—clever and cute.

Margy was a high school Spanish teacher (she goes regularly to Mexico, and wait until you see the plates and mugs you'll eat and drink from), and Darrell was in direct sales, which he didn't much like. "This is much more enjoyable, not so stressful," he says of innkeeping. "This is a very happy place." I overheard him say to some departing guests: "If nobody's coming, you're welcome to leave your things and come back if you're going into town or something."

Breakfast, which often is still going on at noon, is a full one. Peaches, bananas, and grapes, then brunch eggs with green (mild) chilies, tiny smoked sausages, potatoes with green onions, fresh rolls, jellies, butter, and hot sauce—all more than enough to feed the fourteen happy campers at the two dining room tables.

Interesting pieces of furniture are everywhere. The extra-large Rhapsody in Blue Room contains grandmother Elizabeth Fischer Kuebler's bed and piano. Guests play her piano and the one in the schoolhouse, too.

How to get there: From I–35 take exit 189 to Loop 337 west; drive 4 miles to River Road. Turn right and go 1⁸⁄₁₀ miles to the fork at Molly's Rafts & Store. Take the left fork (Hueco Springs Loop) for ¼ mile to the first mailbox on the left and the sign that says Waldrip Haus. Turn left into the inn drive.

Innkeepers: Margy and Darrell Waldrip
Address/Telephone: 1620 Hueco Springs Loop Road; (210) 625–8372, fax same or (800) 299–8372
Rooms: 7 in main house and schoolhouse; all with private bath (2 with whirlpool) and TV; wheelchair accessible. Pets at discretion of innkeepers. No smoking inn.
Rates: $85 to $125, double; $15 to $25 extra person; EPB.
Open: All year.
Facilities and activities: Volleyball, horseshoes, croquet, bird and deer watching. Nearby: museums: Hummel, Sophienburg, Handmade Furniture, and Children's; antiques in New Braunfels and Gruene; Schlitterbahn Water Park; rafting, tubing, and swimming on Guadalupe and Comal rivers; bicycling; horseback riding; golf; tennis; Natural Bridge Caverns and Wildlife Ranch; Canyon Lake, with fishing, boating, swimming and water skiing; discount shopping malls.
Business travel: Located half an hour from downtown San Antonio and San Marcos. Schoolhouse with meeting facilities and kitchen; all rooms with phone.

Prince Solms Inn

NEW BRAUNFELS, TEXAS 78130

The Prince Solms Inn is a famous Texas landmark, having been in continuous operation since immigrant German craftsmen built the handsome building in 1898. Throughout its history families of its first patrons have kept returning to this elegant yet warm and welcoming inn.

The beautifully restored building has front entry doors that are 10 feet high, with panes of exquisitely detailed etched glass. The inn shines with antique fittings gathered from all over the world. Bronzes are from Europe; solid brass doorknobs come from old Lake Shore mansions in Chicago, doors and carriage lights from old San Antonio homes. Staying here makes me feel as if I were in a mansion back in the days of the Astor, Rockefeller, and Gould railroad barons.

Guest rooms are furnished with beautiful (but sturdy) antiques, unusual light fixtures, and well-chosen, tasteful paintings and prints. Each room is named for the gloriously patterned wallpaper that decorates the walls.

New innkeeper Carmen is keeping up the tradition of hospitality of the inn. "It feels as if I have the house I've always wanted," she says.

Wolfgang's Keller, the inn restaurant, is in the cellar, but what a cellar! There are old brick walls and a fireplace—and with Wolfgang Amadeus Mozart's portrait setting the tone, the atmosphere is wonderfully Old World to match the mouth-watering continental cuisine.

I had Wolfgang's wonderful Wiener schnitzel and sampled the chef's special fettucini primavera, in a rich cream sauce, so had to forgo the sinfully rich desserts until another time. Other specials include Lobster Marquis de Lafayette, shrimp a la Wolfgang's, and Scampi Fra Diablo. Mixed drinks, wine, and champagne are readily available from the bar.

The picturesque brick-paved courtyard in the rear is a delightful place to relax.

I enjoyed the complimentary breakfast of banana fruit muffins, bagels and cream cheese, and sweetrolls from one of New Braunfels' famous bakeries, all wheeled into my room on a tea cart and beautifully served. Elegant as it is, the Prince Solms Inn provides the Hill Country friendliness that makes you feel truly at home.

How to get there: From I–35 take exit 187 to Seguin Street, then turn right around the circle to San Antonio Street. The inn is on the left.

Innkeeper: Carmen Morales
Address/Telephone: 295 East San Antonio Street; (210) 625–9169
Rooms: 10; all with private bath and phone.
Rates: $70 to $150, double; $10 extra person; continental breakfast.
Open: All year.
Facilities and activities: Dinner in Wolfgang's Keller Tuesday to Sunday. Nearby: German restaurants, antiques shops, historic museums, Wurstfest in October, tubing and rafting on Comal River, Hummel Museum.

The Inn at Salado

SALADO, TEXAS 76571

Stagecoaches used to rumble down the Old Chisholm Trail to ford Salado Creek and stop at the old Stagecoach Inn at Salado. That inn is now a restaurant and motel, but you can sample the flavor of those days by staying at the Inn at Salado, in the center of this historic Central Texas town, a very small town whose past glories include the brief hope that it would be the capital of Texas.

The town was settled predominantly by people of Scottish descent, and every November there's a "Gathering of the Clans," with Highland games and other divertisements. I loved visiting the museum to see the many colorful tartan banners hanging there, waiting for the fall event.

The Inn at Salado was built in 1872 by an early Texas statesman, Colonel James Norton, who, according to the innkeepers, donated the granite for the State Capitol building in Austin.

The Allen Hall on the grounds, circa 1901, originally was a chapel. Now it's used for meetings, gatherings, what have you. There are kitchen facilities inside as well as a stage for presentations.

The Carriage House has three guest rooms, two down and one up. The Custer Room, which has a private porch, is named for General Custer of "Custer's Last Stand" fame, simply because he camped out on the banks of Salado Creek once upon a time. The Reverend Baines Room, without a porch, is named in honor of the great-grandfather of President Lyndon Baines Johnson. The antique bed there came from the Governor Hogg estate; he was an early governor of Texas. Upstairs, the Tyler Room has a king-sized bed and a wood-burning fireplace.

Relics of Texas history are everywhere. The Baylor House, containing two guest rooms, once belonged to Mary Hardin Baylor College, an early Texas women's school originally located in Salado but now located at nearby Belton. Mary's Room and Elli's Room are the two in the house; both have porches, and Mary's Room has a queen-sized canopy bed.

Whomever they're named for, the rooms are large and comfortable. The Tyler Room is a favorite; it's bright and cheerful with lots of windows and well-stocked bookshelves.

"People like to read," Gabriele says. "We want them to make themselves at home, to use the common room, to feel free to go to the fridge with their cold drinks and wine. This is dry country, so they have to bring whatever they want to drink." Guests also make themselves very much at home with the fine assortment of games provided. And if a group of sixteen to eighteen people want to rent the entire inn, they can have complete privacy.

Pace Park down the road has a pavilion with picnic tables and grills for cookouts. A favorite pastime, when the creek is running, is to roll up your cuffs and go wading. The water is cool and clear—so refreshing!

How to get there: Take the Salado exit from I–35 and drive right into town—that's Main Street. The inn is next to Pace Park and a stone's throw from Salado Creek.

Innkeeper: Gabriele Oborski
Address/Telephone: North Main Street at Pace Park (mailing address: P.O. Box 500); (817) 947–8200
Rooms: 9, 4 in main house, 5 in cottages; all with private bath; wheelchair accessible. No smoking inn.
Rates: $90 to $105, double, EPB.
Open: All year.
Facilities and activities: Dinner by reservation, horseshoes, board games, croquet, volleyball, bicycling, walking, jogging. Nearby: golf, tennis, swimming, antiques and gift shops, restaurants, Historic Home Tour, Central Texas Area Museum, Pace Park and Salado Creek, Goodnight Amphitheater, Salado Civic Center, Dinner Theater.
Business travel: Allen Meeting Hall, catering services.

The Inn on the Creek

SALADO, TEXAS 76571

The Inn on the Creek is a collection of historic houses—Twelve Oaks, Sally's Cottage, the Holland House, and Reue House—gathered together on tree-covered land along the banks of Salado Creek. The main house, Twelve Oaks, was constructed in 1892 in nearby Cameron. After the four innkeepers moved it to the current site, they doubled the size of the building, making a total of seven guest rooms, in addition to the living and dining rooms.

Sally's one-bedroom cottage is next to Twelve Oaks; the five-bedroom annex Holland House, built in the 1880s, is just across the road; and Reue House, with four guest rooms, is down the road a piece. The buildings make a pleasant little compound under the old oak trees.

This parent–daughter–son-in-law team make a great combination. "Mom and Pop moved here from Cameron, they just loved the place," Lynn says of his in-laws. "They were intrigued by the whole idea of an inn." As for Lynn, a corporate architect, he was intrigued by the challenge of the old houses.

The inn is furnished with a collection of Victorian pieces and antiques from other periods. Family photographs, antique rugs and linens, all sorts of interesting furnishings make this a cozy getaway. Windows are hung with lace, draped with pretty valences, or covered with printed drapes to match quilted bedspreads.

"We've named the guest rooms after people who have made a significant contribution to the local community," Suzi says. In Twelve Oaks, the Rose Room, with its Victorian walnut bed covered with an antique pillowcase collection, honors Colonel Rose, who developed land in Salado. The Baines Room has warm oak furniture, the Anderson Room a gleaming brass bed and walnut accent pieces. The McKie Room, on the third floor, has its own library nook with a daybed that overlooks Salado Creek at the rear of the property.

In Holland House, the five-bedroom annex just across from Twelve Oaks, the Fletcher Room commemorates an old family name. The Alexander Room, with a four-poster bed, is named for a Salado couple. "She was an architect and he was in construction," Suzi explains.

In the Reue House, also restored from the 1880s, the Van Bibber Room has an antique walnut four-poster and a fireplace with a limestone hearth.

Not antiques but interesting all the same are the nutcrackers that Lynn and Suzi have collected. "Back in '83 we were in Rothenburg, Germany," Lynn says. "We started with the nutcrackers back then." The inn also has a nice collection of Audubon prints.

Breakfast is a treat, with a German apple puff pancake, ham/sausage loaf, sour cream coffeecake, homemade carrot muffins and cinnamon rolls, fruit, juice, and coffee.

As for weekend dinners, here's a sample menu: black-bean and corn salad; lime-seasoned salmon with salsa; brandy-glazed carrots; zesty lemon rice; mixed-berry tart. Pretty cosmopolitan for a town of 1,500!

How to get there: From I–35 heading north, take exit 283 and go north on Main Street. Turn right on Royal Street and go on to Center Circle on the left. From I–35 going south take exit 285 and go south on Main Street, past Mill Creek Drive, and over Salado Creek to Royal Street; turn left to Center Circle on the left.

Innkeepers: Suzi and Lynn Epps; Sue and Bob Whister
Address/Telephone: One Center Circle (mailing address: P.O. Box 858); (817) 947–5554
Rooms: 17; all with private bath, phone, and TV. No smoking inn.
Rates: \$75 to \$150, double; \$20 extra person; EPB.
Open: All year.
Facilities and activities: Dinner on Friday and Saturday. Nearby: Historic Salado with shops, galleries, antiques, restaurants; golf at Mill Creek Country Club; Gathering of the Clans; art festivals; corn festivals; Rolls Royce car meets; Christmas Strolls; Historic Home Tour.

The Rose Mansion

SALADO, TEXAS 76571

Lori is so happy with her work that she works closely with her fellow innkeeper at the Inn at Salado.

"We just run back and forth like crazy," she says. "Our guests get to meet both the innkeepers—but maybe not together." She enjoys visiting with her guests in the evening, those who want to sit around and talk. She's not surprised to find that most of them are looking to get away from TV, telephone, kids, and traffic. She herself is so delighted to be relaxed in Salado.

When she goes traveling she likes to be waited on and pampered, so she turns around and pampers her guests. But, on the other hand, "I let guests alone, give them their privacy, if that's what they want."

The Rose Mansion was built in 1870 by Major A. J. Rose, who made a fortune in the California Gold Rush of '49. His wife, Sallie, a cousin of Stephen F. Austin, taught elocution at Salado College (which is no more). The major's rifle and desk are in the entry, together with an interesting collection of old walking sticks.

The entire inn is done in white and shades of blue, from the blue checked wallpaper in the comfortable kitchen–sitting room, where everyone seems to gather, to the blue velvet chaise and wing chair in the Honeymoon Suite. The Quilter's Room is not the only one with a quilt—there are fine examples of this art in many of the guest rooms. Wide windows, with original glass, brighten the entire inn.

Two Texas markers and one National Register marker attest to the authenticity of Rose Mansion, in case you have doubts. On the grounds are a windmill with a cypress storage tank, a rock smoke house, and an old wagon. There are shaded seating areas and swings, too.

The Chester House on the grounds is a turn-of-the-century Greek Revival house with three bedrooms (A, B, and C, for Alice, Beatrice, and Callie). The Garrison Log Cabin is an authentically restored log cabin from the mid-1800s, with a queen-sized bed, a fireplace, and a full-sized bed up in its loft.

George's Log Cabin is of late-1800s vintage. It has two bedrooms, both with queen-sized and trundle beds, fireplace, stove, and even a private dog-trot walkway. It makes a great retreat for peace and quiet.

Breakfasts are famous for a special quiche as well as certain oat bran muffins. "They don't taste healthy, but they are," Lori confesses. She promises a gourmet dinner if you reserve in advance.

How to get there: From I–35 take Salado exit 285 going south or exit 283 going north and go down the town's Main Street to Royal Street. Turn east and go up the hill. A water tower is on the left, the inn on the right, just past the VICTORIAN OAKS sign on the right. The inn is behind a white picket fence; there is a sign.

Innkeeper: Lori Long
Address/Telephone: 1 Rose Way (mailing address: P.O. Box 500); (817) 947–8200
Rooms: 11, 4 in main house, the rest in assorted cottages around the property; some with private bath; cottages wheelchair accessible. No smoking inn.
Rates: $90 to $120, double, EPB.
Open: All year.
Facilities and activities: Dinner by reservation, horseshoes, board games, croquet, volleyball, bicycling, walking, jogging; Allen Meeting Hall, catering services. Nearby: golf, tennis, swimming, antiques and gift shops, restaurants, Historic Home Tour; Central Texas Area Museum, Pace Park and Salado Creek, Goodnight Amphitheater, Salado Civic Center, Dinner Theater.

Adams House Inn

SAN ANTONIO, TEXAS 78210

Adams House Inn is one of several beautiful old homes in San Antonio's historic King William District. Built in 1902, the inn is filled with things that have sentimental meaning to Betty. "I bought it for my home and had it restored," she says. "The original owners were in the milling and woodwork business." The finely crafted red-pine woodwork has held up beautifully. Walls in the entry, parlor, and dining room are covered with a creamy satin-striped paper, and so are the ceilings in between the beautiful wood beams.

The parlor furniture is an eclectic combination of Empire, Eastlake, and other interesting pieces. When Betty found the Empire sofa, she says she knew exactly what fabric she wanted for it. The Eastlake settee fits in beautifully, as do the platform rocker and a small carved little chair that neither Betty nor I could put a name to. "I just saw it and I liked it," she says, adding that she's been going to estate sales "for years and years."

Betty is an attorney in private practice. She is still practicing, but she changed her lifestyle to become an innkeeper as well. "I had a real serious illness and had to take off work," she says. "It makes people rethink their priorities . . ." The dining-room furniture in particular has meaning for her. "I bought it in Fannin City from a family who lived on the farm next to ours. Someone asked, 'What on earth do you want that big old monstrosity for?' For me it's just like an older sister or second mother." (It's not a monstrosity at all—it's lovely!)

The bed in Mother's Room was her mother's, the very bed she was born in. How many of us can claim that? The entire set is there. "It was the first set my parents bought after they were married." It's all intact: bed, dressing table, dresser, and a comfortable deep-red lounge. All Betty had to do was to have it refinished. What's more, the room has a secret escape to the veranda overlooking the trees shading the back yard.

Rhoda's Room also has an escape route onto the back veranda, and there's a set of private stairs outside, screened by white latticework.

Winnie and Aunt Belle have their rooms, too, with matching oak or walnut sets and other antiques. And everybody has access to the refrigerator and tea and coffee in a corner of the upstairs hall. (There are Hershey Kisses in a bowl up there, too.)

As for Sue, she lost her husband a few years back, so she gave up her florist business, although she still makes pretty floral arrangements for the inn. "I was at loose ends, so I came to San Antonio to be near my sister." She's the main cook, and a good job she does of it, too. "Blintz soufflé is my favorite, and with something you like, well, you like to serve it." Her puff pancakes are delicious, too. "It's amazing," she says. "You mix all this up and let it set overnight and then bake it in the morning. It puffs all up." It's wonderful sprinkled with powdered sugar.

"Everybody loves our bite-sized biscuits, too," she adds. "That way they can eat more and it doesn't show!"

How to get there: From I–35 take 281 south to Durango. Go west to Alamo; turn left to Adams and number 231. From I–10 take Alamo exit 155 A and go east to Adams and turn right to number 231.

Innkeepers: Betty Lancaster and Sue McKeehan
Address/Telephone: 231 Adams; (210) 224–4791 or (800) 666–4810, fax (210) 223–5125
Rooms: 5; all with private bath and TV. No smoking inn.
Rates: $75 to $85, double; $15 extra person; EPB.
Open: All year.
Facilities and activities: Parking, kitchen privileges. Nearby: The Alamo, La Villita, Convention Center, Institute of Texan Cultures, RiverCenter Mall, El Mercado, Sea World and Fiesta Texas amusement parks.
Business travel: Five blocks from downtown San Antonio. Fax and computer available, phone in rooms, corporate rates.

Beckmann Inn and Carriage House

SAN ANTONIO, TEXAS 78204

One of the many fascinating things about the Beckmann Inn is the beds with unusual tall, pointed headboards. Betty Jo and Don are from Bellville, Illinois, and they brought the beds with them. The 9-foot-tall chestnut headboard in The Suite is one they bought in St. Louis. "The original owner couldn't fit it into his house, so for twenty years it was stored in his garage." Don marvels.

The matching (as in a set, not in height!) dressing table has the maker's signature underneath the marble top, and two little pull-out glove drawers on each side of the mirror. And there is a tiny lamp shelf above each drawer.

The adjoining sunroom, in green and pink, has a wall full of wedding portraits. "That's our family," Betty Jo says. "We can't live without them."

I don't think they can live without Betty Jo's unusual collection of Anri music boxes and figurines, either. There are two shelves in The Suite and several in the Library Room, chock full. "I hadn't realized she'd collected so many until we began to do the inn," Don says with a laugh.

The pink-and-pale-green bathroom in the Library Room is the "California bath," with fixtures Betty Jo says you probably can't get in those colors nowadays.

"We researched this for three years," she says. "We were looking for a job change, and we attended a conference in Santa Fe. We wanted to learn the ups and downs." It's hard to imagine any downs for this personable pair of innkeepers.

The parquet living-room floor has an unusual decorative border, and when I admire it, Betty Jo says it came from Paris. "Paris, Texas?" is my little joke, because of course it's from the one in France.

The inn is listed as being on the National Register of Historic Places as well as within the City of San Antonio's King William Historical District—how's that for historic credentials? And the listing happens to mention a rating: Exceptional.

The house was built in 1886 by Alfred Beckmann for his bride, Marie Dorothea, daughter of the Guenther flour-mill family. Albert's father, Johan, died in 1907; his funeral was held here in the living room. Back then the address was 529 Madison, with the front door facing that street. But around 1913 the home's Victorian style was converted to Greek Revival, and the porch was circled around to the Guenther side. "It was so the front door could be moved, because there was a brothel on that street and they didn't want to have the same address!"

The Schwartzes were lucky to find the kitchen all up to date and very workable. Breakfast's first course is a glazed cranberry pear with mint and "matching" cranberry bread. "I like to make things that go together," Betty Jo says. Next comes cinnamon pecan-stuffed French toast with an apricot glaze topped with strawberries and cream, almost too pretty to eat.

"The inn, it's us," Betty Jo and Don say. "It's what we're comfortable with, our guests coming in, it's an adventure. We have people coming from coast to coast, Canadians, British . . ."

How to get there: From Loop 410 take 281 south and exit Durango. Go west to St. Marys and turn left for a short jog onto King William Street. Go 4 blocks to Guenther. Turn left. The inn is at the corner on the left, at the end of the fourth block.

Innkeepers: Betty Jo and Don Schwartz
Address/Telephone: 222 East Guenther Street; (210) 229–1449 or (800) 945–1449, fax (210) 226–5812
Rooms: 5; all with private bath. No smoking inn.
Rates: \$80 to \$130, double; \$15 extra person; EPB.
Open: All year.
Facilities and activities: Parking. Nearby: downtown with The Alamo, La Villita, Convention Center, museums, RiverCenter Mall, El Mercado.
Business travel: Located 5 blocks from downtown San Antonio, trolley stop on corner. Direct-access phone lines, fax.
Recommended Country Inns® Travel Club Benefit: 10% discount, Monday–Thursday, subject to availability.

Bed & Breakfast on the River

SAN ANTONIO, TEXAS 78204

These innkeepers make a great combination: Harry's hobby led him into innkeeping, and Dr. Zucht's hobby keeps him up in the air. Harry, who is from Ohio, is in love with the climate and the people. He was a food quality-control manager for a fast-food chain when he decided on a change. "After age fifty I figure I can do what I want to do, not what society says. This started out as a hobby . . ."

"This" turned out to be the complete renovation of the old 1916 house for Dr. Zucht. According to Harry, there was no indoor plumbing until 1923. "That's what all the lean-tos were for," he says. There are several more old homes nearby, and Harry is itching to remodel them, too. The high ceilings, original pine floors, shingled cupolas, and wraparound porch took lots of renovating, and the results are refreshing.

Dr. Zucht is a dentist who practices part-time because he'd rather be out hot-air ballooning. Between them they give their guests a darn good time. A native of San Antonio, he's around almost every morning at breakfast because "folks want things to see and do from someone who's lived here, not a concierge who might be from anywhere. After all," he says, "staying at an inn is an adventure, an unknown."

Although guest rooms are not large, they are comfortable, and best of all, each has French doors opening onto a private sunroom or a porch perched right over the famed San Antonio River and the Paseo del Rio (River Walk). Each is furnished in white wicker and some antiques, with lace curtains at the windows and cool flowered bedspreads.

Most have large armoires—the antique in Room 1 is "a knock-down," Harry says as he shows me how it could be taken apart. "They had to bring them west by wagon, and the whole thing wouldn't fit," a new and interesting piece of history for me. He modestly owns up to building the one in the Lilac Room (number 7) himself. A small part of the ceiling is sloped, because, Harry says, "I had to save that big old pecan tree outside." Leaning over the railing, I see it from the porch.

Rooms 3 and 4 can connect via the French doors and white wicker screens between their sunrooms. Rooms 5, 6, and 7 open onto a large porch over the river.

Breakfast is in the large common room separated from the kitchen by an open counter, and there are sofas and settees as well as the breakfast tables. The "Extended Continental" breakfast consists of juice and fruit, dry cereals, bagels and cream cheese, and special pastries from famed Mi Tierra Restaurant and Bakery in El Mercado (a short trolley ride away). The 10-cent Trolley wends its way through this historic area to the many downtown attractions. "People park here, and never drive again [while they're here]," Harry says. Which, in busy, bustling San Antonio, is a big plus.

And for a thrill of a lifetime, arrange for a flight with Dr. Zucht, who is a licensed hot-air balloon pilot. Weather of course permitting, a specialty is an aerial view of the sun rising over Alamo City. "We do unique things, like taking guests to be married in a balloon."

How to get there: From I–35 exit at West Durango and go east to Dwyer; from I–37 exit at East Durango and go west to Dwyer. Turn north. Woodward is the second street on the right. The inn is on the right at the end of the short street, overlooking the river.

Innkeepers: Harry Haught and A. D. Zucht

Address/Telephone: 129 Woodward Avenue; (210) 225–6333 or (800) 730–0019, fax (210) 225–6337.

Rooms: 7; all with private bath, 2 with Jacuzzi, some with TV. No smoking inn.

Rates: $99 to $119, double, extended continental breakfast.

Open: All year.

Facilities and activities: Parking, stairs down to River Walk, hot-air ballooning. Nearby: La Villita, Convention Center, RiverCenter Mall, The Alamo, El Mercado.

Business travel: Located a few blocks from downtown. Fax, copier, word processor, printer; phone in rooms.

Bonner Garden

SAN ANTONIO, TEXAS 78212

Bonner Garden is named for artist Mary Bonner, who, although she achieved some prominence locally for her etching and printmaking skills, probably was "a big fish in a small pond," says Randy. Born in 1887 in Louisiana, she moved with her family to San Antonio. In 1910 they built a house that made history: It was one of the first residences in the Southwest to use concrete. They had a pretty good reason—"Their homes in Louisiana had burned down four times," Noel says. "They wanted one that wouldn't!"

Jan and Noel are mother and father, Randy and Cindy are son and daughter-in-law, and they make a fine team, with parents concentrating on guests and offspring looking after the house. The family name is Norwegian, and Noel explains his name jokingly. "I was born on Easter," he says, "but my mother thought it was Christmas, and I was her seventh and she had run out of names."

The Palladian-style house may be a fortress of concrete reinforced with steel and cast iron, but it's softened with creamy stucco and surrounded by a lovely garden. The pretty pool, in front behind fence and foliage, looks purely decorative, but Randy says it's perfect for swimming laps.

The hot tub, atop the house on the roof garden, is wonderful for lolling while admiring the view of downtown San Antonio in the distance.

"The house was definitely a find," Jan says. The gardens alone won it a Conservation Award in 1986. She is collecting Bonner's prints, and quite a few hang on the inn walls. "In her day she was better known in the Paris of the 1920s and '30s than she was here."

The walls of the mansion are painted in varying shades of faux marble; the common rooms downstairs are a sort of terra cotta. Upstairs, some of the marbling is in soft pastels, and furniture pieces are fascinating. The Portico Room has a painted ceiling of pale blue with puffy white clouds, and a door leads out to the pool. The Ivy Room's walls are decorated with ivy on the walls; the Bridal Suite has a Jacuzzi and old tapestries; and The Studio, where Mary Bonner worked, contains an assortment of interesting Mexican pieces of furniture and an old iron four-poster bed.

The portrait over the mantel of the dining room and the tiles of the fireplace were brought from Italy. The portrait makes for a fun breakfast game: everybody gets a guess as to who—or what—it was. Conquistador? Soldier of fortune? Priest? Someone's ancestor? Whatever, it adds spice to Jan's delicious breakfasts of oven omelet with crumbled bacon, cheese, and mushrooms, or breakfast tacos of eggs and sausage, or Belgian waffles. French toast is topped with apricot sauce, and there are always fresh cinnamon rolls or a nice sticky pull-apart or sour cream coffeecake.

We sat around till noon, visiting. Jan was a high school registrar, Noel a real estate broker, Randy is a radiologist, Cindy an artist. "It's been a partnership for years," Jan says. Guests, too, are an interesting mix. "People are fun. The other night we were serenaded by a writer of women's songs. She got her guitar and sang some of her songs to us," Noel says. "None of our guests is aloof, they all mingle."

How to get there: From I–10 take the Woodlawn exit and go east to Main. Turn right (south) onto Agarita and go to number 145, which is the last house on the street. It is on the left.

Innkeepers: Jan and Noel, Randy and Cindy Stenoien
Address/Telephone: 145 East Agarita; (210) 733-4222 or (800) 396–4222, fax (210) 733–6129
Rooms: 5; all with private bath and TV. No smoking inn.
Rates: $75 to $95, double, EPB. Weekly rates available.
Open: All year.
Facilities and activities: Lap pool, hot tub, patio, Nordic Track and stationary bicycle, rooftop terrace, parking. Nearby: downtown with The Alamo, La Villita, Convention Center, museums, RiverCenter Mall, El Mercado.
Business travel: Located 1 mile from downtown San Antonio. Direct-access telephone lines, 9-foot dining-room conference table, fax and secretarial services, corporate rates.
Recommended Country Inns® Travel Club Benefit: 20% discount, Sunday–Thursday; 10%, Friday and Saturday.

Bullis House Inn

SAN ANTONIO, TEXAS 78208

Bullis House Inn and San Antonio International Hostel make for an unusual experience, because the combination offers the best of two worlds. While staying in the historic home of Civil War General John Bullis, you get to mix with travelers from all over the world: More than 90 percent of the guests staying at the hostel at the rear of the inn are international visitors, and the inn's four parlors are open to all. In interacting with hostel guests from France, England, Australia, Germany, and Japan, I felt as though I were smack in the middle of an international voyage.

The innkeepers believe that inn guests tend to be warm, open people and that the lost art of conversation revives at an inn. "Guests can read or watch television in the parlors, but since there are TVs in the rooms, mostly they come down to visit with the international hostel guests," said Nathan, one of three managers who help out when the Crosses are absent. "And the kids can keep busy with the swimming pool, or play volleyball, Ping-Pong, badminton, board games . . . there's a lot for them to do here, plus we're within five minutes of downtown with the River Walk and the Alamo."

The Bullis House, a large white Neoclassical mansion, was built by the general when he came to town from New York in 1865. But he didn't settle down. He fought hostile Indians in Texas and saw action in the Spanish-American War. The colorful general, called "Thunderbolt" by the Indians and "Friend of the Frontier" by the settlers, earned formal thanks from the Texas Legislature.

Large white columns support the front portico. Inside, parquet floors, marble fireplaces, and chandeliers attest to early Texas elegance. Guest rooms are large and high-ceilinged, and most have fireplaces—there are ten fireplaces in all! The rooms have been totally redecorated, with massive oak and cherry beds in king, queen, and full sizes. Especially fine for families is the trundle bed in each guest room; each room can accommodate four persons, and the large "family room" can sleep six.

Breakfast is fancier now, with homemade crepes or sweetheart waffles in addition to cold cereal and hot apple, cinnamon, or orange muffins, orange juice, coffee, tea, and hot chocolate. San Antonio abounds in fine restaurants, and the Crosses have many recommendations. Mexican ones in the Mercado (market) are special regional favorites. San Antonio, a warm and happy combination of Anglo and Hispanic cultures, always has some kind of parade or festival going on—I've never been in a city that parties so much. There are no strangers here!

How to get there: Take the New Braunfels–Fort Sam Houston exit off I–35 or the Grayson Street exit off Highway 281. The inn is on the corner of Grayson and Pierce, adjacent to Fort Sam Houston.

Innkeepers: Alma and Steve Cross
Address/Telephone: 621 Pierce (mailing address: P.O. Box 8059); (210) 223–9426
Rooms: 10; 1 with private bath, 9 share 2 baths, 2 with phone, all with TV; downstairs rooms wheelchair accessible. Smoking permitted except in dining room.
Rates: $49 to $79, double; extra adult $10, child $6, 3 and under no charge.
Open: All year.
Facilities and activities: continental breakfast, lunch, and high tea by reservation; hostel on premises (inn is affiliated with American Youth Hostels); parking; swimming pool, badminton, volleyball, Ping-Pong, board games. Nearby: Paseo del Rio (River Walk), with many restaurants; The Alamo, La Villita boutiques, Institute of Texas Cultures, Hertzberg Circus Museum, Brackenridge Park and Zoo, Spanish missions, Sea World and Fiesta Texas amusement parks.
Business travel: Located 2 miles from downtown San Antonio. Fax, word processor, phone.

Norton-Brackenridge House

SAN ANTONIO, TEXAS 78204

Carolyn Cole has furnished her inn with such treasured pieces of her past as her grandmother's rocking chair and her very own small one from her childhood. The room she calls the Bridal Suite, because she likes to put honeymooners in it, has a white iron bed covered with a family quilt; her grandmother's chest; and "palms, because they're a Victorian-looking plant." There's lovely white wicker furniture in the sitting area.

The downstairs bathroom has a stained-glass window, and Carolyn leaves magazines and catalogues "and razors and little bars of glycerine soap with the inn logo" for her guests' convenience. Other nice touches include roses from the rose garden in the rear.

With the help of Frances, Carolyn, who is now a seasoned innkeeper, likes to do things up right. "My idea is to do the simple, since I'm the cook, with casseroles instead of omelets-to-order for my holiday breakfasts, but to do the simple well!" she says enthusiastically. Breakfast, served either in the dining room or on the veranda, is a delicious one of honey puff pancakes, quiche, or a blintz soufflé with apricot preserves, along with fresh fruit in season. Out of season, there are delicious fruit compotes with assorted dried fruits and almonds.

Like most innkeepers, Carolyn and Frances find that the majority of their guests like to mingle, getting acquainted. "But you can take your breakfast back to your room if you prefer," Carolyn says.

The Norton-Brackenridge House was built in 1906. The handsome two-story home, with white Corinthian columns and spanking white porch railings, began life on another street. Somewhere along the way it was remodeled into four apartments. It was moved to its present location in San Antonio's historic King William district in 1985.

Carolyn and Frances have has been busy repainting, covering the old beige walls with color. The Red Room is as bright as a hot red pepper; the Peach Room is a warm terra cotta; the Blue Room is a cool Federal blue; and the Aqua Room "is now undoubtedly my favorite," Carolyn says.

How to get there: Take I–35 south to the Alamo exit and go left past Pioneer Flour Mills to Beauregard. Take a left, then a right on Madison, and the inn is the fourth house on the right.

Innkeepers: Carolyn Cole and Frances Bochat
Address/Telephone: 230 Madison; (210) 271–3442 or (800) 221–1412
Rooms: 5, including 2 suites; all with private bath and refrigerator, 4 with kitchenette, 2 with TV.
Rates: $85 to $105, per room, EPB. Corporate rates available.
Open: All year.
Facilities and activities: Nearby: The Alamo; the River Walk (Paseo del Rio) downtown, lined with restaurants, bars, and boutiques; El Mercado (market), Brackenridge Zoo, horticultural garden, Sea World and Fiesta Texas amusement parks, several fine Spanish missions.

The Ogé House

SAN ANTONIO, TEXAS 78204

If you're looking for a proper mansion, you have found it. A tall, three-story building squared off by a set of porches top and bottom, the Ogé House looms ahead at the end of the street, looking almost like a misplaced plantation house. But not too misplaced, because it's set on large, lovely grounds ending only at San Antonio's famous river.

The Ogé House (pronounced "oh-jhay"—it's French) is one of the most magnificent homes to be found in San Antonio's historic King William District of fine homes. It was built in 1857 for Louis Ogé, a pioneer cattle rancher and a Texas Ranger.

Like many old beauties, the home had become an apartment house, but it was just waiting for Sharrie and Patrick to find it. They had been looking, driving up the East Coast for six weeks, before they realized that this was where they wanted to be.

"I used to redo old houses back East," Sharrie says. "And we'd been collecting antiques for ten, twelve years." Visiting her father here, they heard that the old house might be available. "We were interviewed by a member of one of the first San Antonio families, who came originally from the Canary Islands, before they decided they would sell us the house."

The house is huge, with two guest rooms opening off the majestic lobby, which is actually the second floor, since you climb eleven steps up to the front door. Once there you'll admire the antique French set of two settees and two chairs. "They're from a private suite in the Waldorf Astoria in New York," Patrick says.

The Library, at the rear of the house, is relaxing, with soft-yellow walls, white woodwork, satin-striped sofas, and books (although "there are books all over the house," as Sharrie says). The brass bucket in The Library is filled with menus from the city's many fine eating places.

Upstairs (third floor) the Giles and Mathis suites both open onto the porch across the front of the house, while Riverview, off the landing by the back stairs, is intensely private, with its own porch and view of the river.

Down below, on the main level, the Mitchell Suite has a platform canopy bed and a daybed, perfect, Patrick says, "for three ladies traveling together." The Bluebonnet Room is done in Texas antiques, with a four-poster rolling-pin bed and the desk of an old Texas judge. But that's all you'll find of Texas.

"We're not a Texas country inn," Sharrie says. "We have more of the flavor of a small European hotel or an English country manor house."

Sharrie's "Deluxe Continental Breakfast" begins with poached pears and goes on to such delicacies as pecan log roll, apple torte, cherry cheese cake, and fruit pasties.

You can join everyone for breakfast in the dining room, take it out on the front veranda, or go out on the grounds and sit overlooking the river. "We're on one and a half acres, and when all the trees leaf out in the summer, you can't see any of the neighbors. You can't believe you're in downtown San Antonio!"

How to get there: From I–35 take 281 south and exit at Durango. Turn right and go through three traffic lights to St. Mary's. Take the first left to Pancoast, and the inn is head on at the end of the street.

Innkeepers: Sharrie and Patrick Magatagan
Address/Telephone: 209 Washington; (210) 223–2353 or (800) 242–2770, fax (210) 226–5812
Rooms: 10; all with private bath and TV. No smoking inn.
Rates: $125 to $195, double, deluxe continental breakfast.
Open: All year.
Facilities and activities: Parking. Nearby: Downtown San Antonio, with The Alamo, La Villita, Convention Center, museums, RiverCenter Mall, El Mercado.
Business travel: Located 5 blocks from downtown San Antonio. Direct-access phone lines, fax, copier, computer hookups, corporate rates.
Recommended Country Inns® Travel Club Benefit: 20% discount, Monday–Thursday, subject to availability.

San Antonio Yellow Rose

SAN ANTONIO, TEXAS 78204

Cliff is outside beautifying the garden when I arrive. "Sometimes I don't know who I am," he says, as he wipes off his hands. "Sometimes I'm the gardener, sometimes the chef, sometimes the accountant"—but always the gracious host, I finish for him, because he isn't at all impatient at being distracted from his task. "It'll keep," he says, calling for Jenny to come join us.

"Though we're from Texas, we both were working in New York," he adds. "Every day I drove through a huge cemetery on my way to work, and after a while I began to think, one day they're gonna bury me in this cold ground." He laughs as he remembers. "One day I decided, nope! I'm gonna die in Texas, where it's warm!"

Jenny too desired a different life; she was tired of the stress of the big northern city. On holidays they had stayed in inns in Great Britain, Switzerland, Italy, Canada, and both the East and West coasts, and they knew what they wanted.

The yellow-painted-brick Yellow Rose is a fine example of the many homes that were built in San Antonio's King William District more than a century ago. Built in 1879 by Charles Mueller, a German immigrant house painter, the house, like many in the neighborhood, had been a Victorian beauty. "But it slowly deteriorated," Cliff says. It has been restored from total squalor by Jenny and Cliff—you won't be able to believe it when you leaf through the photo album documenting the changes. But it was worth all the work to the Tices.

The large entry hall has Jenny's great-grandmother's settee, and there are always fresh yellow roses as you walk in. As for the piano in the living room, "we both pick at it," Cliff says. "We have recitals about once a quarter," adds Jenny. "A soprano and tenor, a piano recital, usually on Sunday afternoons. Guests are welcome."

Every room, and many of the ceilings, is covered with beautiful figured papers. "Cliff and I hung every strip," Jenny says, no mean feat with ceilings 11 and 12 feet high. "The morning after we'd done the stairwell, I got up to find it all hanging in strips down the stairs," Cliff says with great good humor. "Nothing but to put it all up again."

Also hanging on the walls are paintings by Cliff's uncle, Dick McGowan, a well-known Southwest watercolorist. Along the upstairs hall there's an interesting old meeting-house bench from Plymouth, Massachusetts, that seems a mile long. In the Victorian Rose Room, the rosewood sleigh bed dates from the 1860s. Both the Victorian Room and the Green Sage Room across the hall, with an eighteenth-century desk, have their own private baths down the hall, and the locks match the keys to each room.

As for breakfast, "Cliff's the chef," Jenny says. Cliff modestly owns up to preparing the delicious cottage-cheese soufflé, the pecan-raisin-bran muffins, the fresh biscuits and ham, the broiled Texas Ruby Red grapefruit. "I get to eat the scraps in the kitchen," Jenny pretends to complain.

"This is all about relaxing and having a good time," Cliff sums up their philosophy. "We don't want people to come and not enjoy themselves."

How to get there: From I–35 take 281 south and exit Durango. Take a right and go through three traffic lights to St. Mary's. Turn left to the second right, and that's Madison. The inn is the seventh house down the block on the right, with an American flag out front.

Innkeepers: Jenny and Cliff Tice
Address/Telephone: 229 Madison; (210) 222–9903 or (800) 950–9903
Rooms: 5; all with private bath and TV. No smoking inn.
Rates: $85 to $100, double; $10 extra person; EPB.
Open: All year.
Facilities and activities: Parking. Nearby: downtown San Antonio, with The Alamo, La Villita, Convention Center, museums, RiverCenter Mall, El Mercado.
Business travel: Located 5 blocks from downtown San Antonio. Phones in all rooms, desks in some rooms.

Terrell Castle

SAN ANTONIO, TEXAS 78208

Katherine Poulis and her daughter Nancy Haley have combined considerable talent in creating Terrell Castle. Different wings of the four-story stone mansion have been restored, from a start of three guest rooms to the present eight; the newest is the Ballroom Suite on the third floor.

The magnificent entrance hall has a red brick fireplace and built-in seats in a "coffin" niche; also restored are the parlor, library, music room, dining room, breakfast room, and enclosed porch.

The home was built in 1894 by Edwin Terrell, a San Antonio lawyer and statesman who served under President Benjamin Harrison as ambassador plenipotentiary to Belgium in the early 1890s. He fancied a castle like those he saw in Europe, and as soon as he returned home he commissioned a local architect to build one.

Well, while the Terrell Castle doesn't particularly remind me of a European castle, it certainly does impress me as a very stately mansion. The front staircase is extraordinary. Antique furniture and lace curtains set off the fine parquet floors and curved windows in the parlor. The dining room has a huge fireplace and a wood-paneled ceiling, the first like it I've seen.

Rooms used to be named for their colors, but Katherine and Nancy have now gone genealogical. There are the Giles Suite and the Terrell

Suite; also the Colonial Room; the Victorian Room; the Tower Suite; the Oval Room (with curved windows); and the Americana Room, with the best view in the house—its windows face all four directions and offer a grand fourth-floor view of San Antonio—as well as the new Ballroom Suite, in what once was the ballroom of the mansion. "We've given it an oriental flair," says Nancy, "while retaining the Victorian character of the house." Interesting . . . each room is more lovely than the next, so I leave it to you to make a choice.

All the fireplaces in the house are functional, including one with a green tiled mantel in the meeting room on the third floor.

Breakfast is "anytime guests wake up," Nancy says. It's a feast of bacon or sausage, eggs however you want them including a wonderful Mexican omelet, crisp hashed browns or creamy grits, homemade goodies like popovers and sticky buns, as well as muffins, raisin bread, biscuits, preserves, dry cereal, juice, coffee, tea, and milk. "Most of our guests don't eat lunch after that," Nancy had told me earlier, and now she reports, "and we *still* don't know of anyone who has eaten lunch the same day! We've always served everything under the sun, and we still do!"

There's a television in the large library/office, and guests can watch whenever they want. "The whole house is open to you," say Katherine and Nancy.

How to get there: Grayson Street is between Broadway and New Braunfels Street, adjacent to Fort Sam Houston.

Innkeepers: Nancy Haley and Katherine Poulis
Address/Telephone: 950 East Grayson Street; (210) 271–9145 or (800) 356–1605
Rooms: 5, plus 4 suites; all with private bath and TV. Pets permitted.
Rates: $70 to $100, double, EPB. Cribs free; assorted rates when rooms are booked as suites.
Open: All year.
Facilities and activities: Fenced dog runs in the rear. Nearby: the Paseo del Rio (River Walk) downtown, lined with restaurants, bars, and boutiques; The Alamo; several fine missions; zoo, horticultural garden, Sea World and Fiesta Texas amusement parks.

Crystal River Inn

SAN MARCOS, TEXAS 78666

Crystal River Inn rooms are named for Texas rivers because "we are river rats," Cathy says. Both she and Mike are pleased to show guests the ropes if they want to take on the nearby San Marcos River. Each guest room has its own watery personality. The Colorado Room reflects the iciness and blue color of the river, while the Pedernales Room, in blue and warm peach, is folksy and friendly. The honeymoon suite is named for the beautiful Medina. The house, designer decorated, is restfully clean and uncluttered, and the rooms carry out this feeling.

"The peace, beauty, history, and happiness of this unique chunk of Texas has been bottled up right here, just waiting to be shared," Cathy says of her inn.

The veranda upstairs is the happy-hour porch. "Usually our guests come breezing in here from Houston or Dallas, and they're all tightly wound. We prop them up on the veranda or in the atrium-sunroom, with some wine in their hands, and in an hour the change is just amazing." The Dillons also pamper guests with bedside brandy and chocolates, although many of them linger in "the library," the lovely parlor with a cozy fireplace and walls lined with bookshelves.

Crystal River Inn is also known for its knockout weekend brunch. I feasted on fruit-filled cantaloupe ring, beer biscuits that Cathy calls "beerscuits," sausage, and the pièce de résistance, bananas Foster crepes topped with *crème fraîche* and toasted slivered almonds. Cathy invented the recipe, and when she made the crepes for a Chamber of Commerce fund-raiser, people were lined up and winding out the door, waiting for them.

Other great breakfasts are sour cream–apple walnut French toast, *huevos rancheros*—and I could go on and on with a whole assortment of homemade breads like zucchini-and-apple fritter bread. You can be sure of a gourmet feast to begin the day at the Crystal River Inn!

For the adventurous, Cathy has worked up some special weekends, like the Murder Mystery one; or she can suggest an exciting river trip, gourmet cooking lessons, and a romantic interlude complete with massage—and hot-air ballooning. Just ask her for the schedule.

How to get there: Take exit 205 west off I–35. This is Highway 80, which becomes Hopkins in town. The inn is on the right just before you come to Rural Route 12 to Wimberley.

Innkeepers: Cathy and Mike Dillon
Address/Telephone: 326 West Hopkins Street; (512) 396–3739
Rooms: 11, plus 2 two-bedroom suites; 9 with private bath, 3 share common area with mini-kitchen, TV, and phone; wheelchair accessible. No smoking in rooms.
Rates: \$45 to \$85, weekdays; \$55 to \$100, weekends; EPB.
Open: All year.
Facilities and activities: Lunch and dinner by reservation only; Mystery Weekend. Nearby: San Marcos River for water sports; Southwest State University, LBJ's alma-mater; many special events in San Marcos.

Utopia on the River
UTOPIA, TEXAS 78884

Early on, Utopia had several other names, but then a town postmaster happened to read Sir Thomas More's description of Utopia. "This is it!" he cried. "Perfect climate, happy, healthy people—we live in Utopia!" and Utopia it became.

That postmaster was not far off base, and he would have felt all the more vindicated if he could have seen today's Utopia on the River, with its large, bright A-frame lobby and breakfast area. The inn is run by Polly and Aubrey Smith—well, mostly Polly, since Aubrey has been busy as sheriff of Uvalde County.

"I had managed property in San Antonio, so I knew what I was getting into," Polly says. "But weekends Aubrey has been in Utopia, and sometimes he even helps cook." The inn is on 650 acres that have been in Polly's family for more than a hundred years, and rooms are named after pioneer settlers of the area. William Ware, an ancestor of Polly's, founded the town, and of course he has a plaque on the door of one room; another is named for Polly's grandmother. Rooms are large and airy, with touches such as quilt-pattern bedspreads and colorful duck appliqués, sewn by Polly, framed over the beds. The construction of stone with wood floors is typical of this hill country area, and the view from each room is a refreshing wilderness of mesquite and pecan trees.

The inn grounds are a veritable animal preserve. To begin with, it's a working ranch; you'll drive through a flock of sheep as you wind into the property. (Just honk your horn to get them off the road.) During nature hikes you can see the likes of such exotica as axis and fallow deer, audads, black buck antelope, and even a zebra. After that, the deer, turkeys, sheep, and goats may seem pretty tame by comparison! The place is great for the children. Bird-watchers, too. Special as well is the storytelling on the river every Saturday night March through October—and in front of a cozy fire November through February.

Breakfast can be fancy, with banana bran pancakes, or hearty, with scrambled eggs and biscuits as well as juice and coffee. Then you can wander down to see the falls on the cool, clean Sabinal River, go rock and driftwood hunting, or marvel at the old cypress tree. "We think it's from 750 to 800 years old," Polly says. "Everyone wants to see it." The huge native pecan trees in front of the inn are something to see, too.

There is a collection of art and craft wares as well as T-shirts and other necessities in the loft above the dining room. Otherwise you'll feel far from the madding crowd. "We enjoy our guests," Aubrey says, "but we want to keep our tranquillity." Tranquillity and serenity are the words he uses to describe Utopia on the River.

How to get there: The inn is approximately 80 miles northwest of San Antonio. Take Highway 90 west to Sabinal, then Highway 187 north to 2 miles south of Utopia. The inn is the left; there is a sign.

Innkeepers: Polly and Aubrey Smith
Address/Telephone: Highway 187 (mailing address: P.O. Box 14); (210) 966–2444
Rooms: 12; all with private bath and TV.
Rates: $59, single; $69, double; $10 extra person; children under 6 free; EPB.
Open: All year.
Facilities and activities: Meals for large groups with planned menus; barbecue grills and picnic tables; refrigerator and microwave in some rooms, $5 extra; gift shop, pool, Jacuzzi, sauna, volleyball, horseshoes, hiking trails, fishing, hunting, tubing on river. Nearby: stables with horses for hire and one restaurant in Utopia; Lost Maples State Park.

Casa de Leona
UVALDE, TEXAS 78802

Mesquite and Spanish oak border the long drive into Casa de Leona, and catfish practically jump out of the river alongside the inn.

"A thirty-five-pound catfish was caught in our river," Carolyn Durr says, "and recently a 10.3-pound bass. Wow!" The inn has two Spanish fountains, one in the garden by the side of the house and one inside the courtyard; frisky weimaraner Chockie, short for Chocolate, will greet you there, unless you don't care for dogs. Shannon, the German shepherd, has gone to live with a Texas Ranger. "She got so protective of us she wouldn't allow guests to get out of their cars or come out of their rooms," Carolyn says. "That was obviously a little too much devotion."

While Ben administers the local hospital, Carolyn's interests are revealed by all the cookbooks in her kitchen and all the paintings hanging on the walls. One of the guest rooms, the Picasso Room, adjoins her bright studio, where china painting and jewelry making share time with painting on canvas. Business guests can use her typewriter and desk.

"I started painting in 1972, just to relax," Carolyn says. "Ben traveled, back then, and I needed to fill my time after I'd put the children to bed." She hasn't stopped; the whole inn is an art gallery, with her paintings for sale.

Each guest room is tastefully decorated, and there are some lovely antiques. "I love antiques and I would have more if they weren't so expensive," Carolyn says with a rueful laugh. Interesting decorative touches include needlepoint done by Carolyn and framed on the walls, onyx chess sets, and arrowheads found in the vicinity. In the Bethany Room, named for daughter Bethany, her tiny ruffled flower-girl dress (she was in a wedding when she was three) is framed. The Durrs are town boosters, and you'll find a packet of Uvalde "what to see" brochures, as well as a "good night Tiger" snack of Carolyn's making, in your room.

The Durrs enjoy relaxing and sipping thirst quenchers on the sun deck with guests. Some guests bring their own canoes for a float on the Leona River behind the inn, and there's fishing there, too.

"We had a guest from Houston who just threw in a line," Ben says. "He got a bass, a brim, some perch, and a carp. The carp are the biggest here, like Chinese carp." Now that Ben no longer travels, upon request the Durrs will guide inn guests across the nearby border for a shopping and dining excursion to Mexico.

Breakfast, for which there is a huge formal dining set—"we bartered two calves for it," Ben delights in telling—is what Carolyn calls Texican. Sundance eggs are scrambled and served in tortillas with refried beans, or there may be *chili rellenos*. Carolyn's homemade cinnamon rolls are a tasty ending to the meal, and there's always fresh fruit and juices.

How to get there: From Highway 90 in Uvalde take Highway 117 toward Batesville (post office on corner) for 1 mile to Highway 140, Pearsall Road. Turn left for 1 mile. Casa de Leona is on the right, and there is an inn sign at the driveway.

Innkeepers: Carolyn and Ben Durr
Address/Telephone: 1149 Pearsall Road; (210) 278–8550
Rooms: 4, plus 1 cottage; 2 with private bath, cottage with private bath and kitchenette. No smoking inn.
Rates: $55 to $79, double; $15 extra person; EPB. No credit cards.
Open: All year.
Facilities and activities: Lunch and dinner by reservation, use of washer and dryer, sun deck, balcony, gazebo, seventeen acres of wilderness on Leona River with nature trails, fishing. Nearby: many eating places, Fort Inge Historical Site, John Nance Garner Museum, First State Bank's "Petit Louvre" Briscoe collection of art.

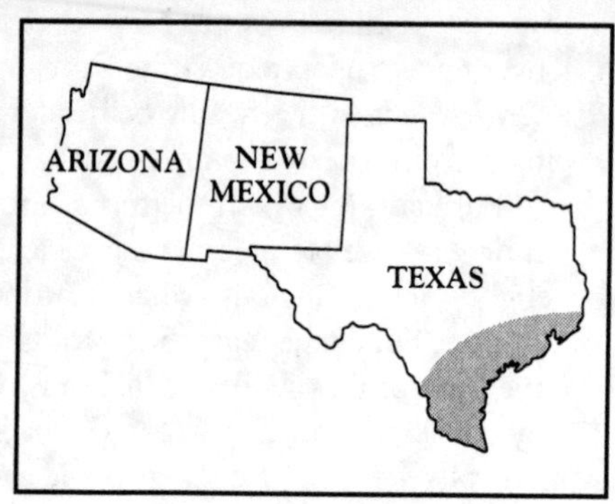
ARIZONA
NEW MEXICO
TEXAS

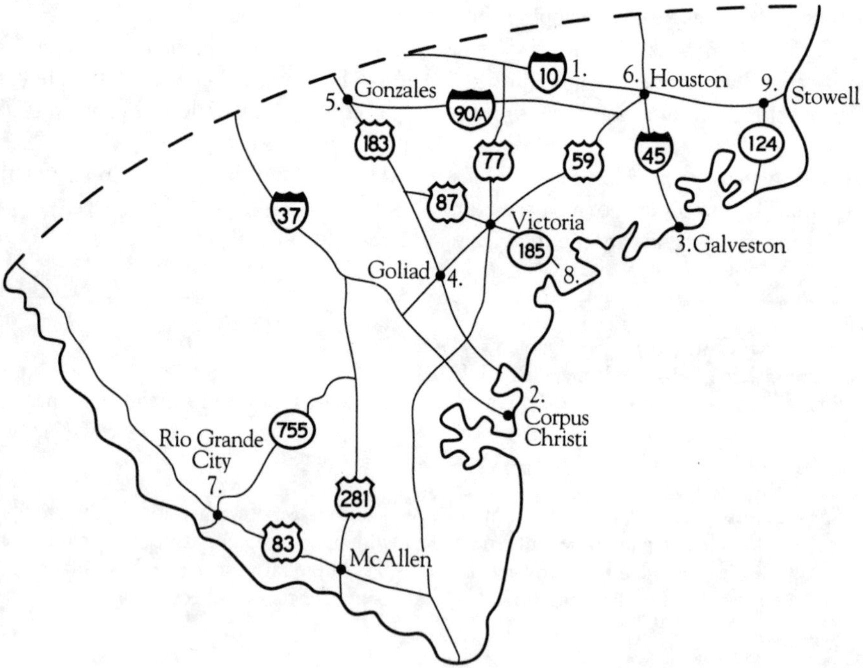

1.
10
6. Houston
9.
Stowell
5. Gonzales
90A
183
77
59
45
124
87
37
Victoria
185
3. Galveston
Goliad
4.
8.
2.
Corpus Christi
755
Rio Grande City
7.
281
83
McAllen

Gulf Coast/Border Texas

Numbers on map refer to towns numbered below.

Magnolia Oaks
COLUMBUS, TEXAS 78934

Nancy and Bob begin their guests' day with a unique offering: As Nancy serves the hearty meal, Bob accompanies himself on the guitar with an inspiring song. "I'm just a campfire singer, but I love to sing," he says as he gives us an inspiring rendition of "What a Wonderful World."

"That's what people are here for, to relax. This makes a quiet, peaceful time for people to start out their day." It works, too—we all visibly relaxed as we dug into Nancy's fresh fruit, quiche, and sausage.

Relaxing is not hard to do in this lovely Eastlake Victorian home, built in 1890 by a prominent Texan of those times—Marcus Harvey Townsend was the legislator who sponsored the bill for the purchase of the Alamo. Between the Townsends and the Stiles, the home had one other owner, the West family.

"We bought it from the West estate auction," Bob says. "Nancy's son played football with the UT Longhorns, and we kept driving through Columbus (from Houston) to Austin for the games. Nancy looked at a brochure about the sale and just about went crazy. Next Saturday, we stopped at the auction, bid for the house, and made the kick-off at one o'clock!"

The lovely color scheme is Nancy's; Bob calls her the color "schemer." She'd never stolen anything in her life, yet somehow a hotel washcloth came home from a trip with her. "I had to have those colors," she says, and the variety of terra-cotta and old rose shades is lovely.

The house was structurally excellent but cosmetically bad, and everything in the interior had to be redone "from head to toe." Did they do it themselves? "Nope," Bob says emphatically. "We're smarter than that! Nancy took forty-five minutes to do an area about yea long, so I said, okay, we're going to get help. In two days we got the whole thing stripped."

Nancy, who is a school principal in nearby Katy, also dabbles in the antiques business, so you'll find lots of interesting furniture in the inn. The Victorian Room has an old display case on the bedside table, lighted to show off the collectibles inside. On the flowered chaise a checkers game is set out and ready to play.

Another small display cabinet, in the Warren Room, is filled with a collection. The room is named for the inn's carpenter, who moved into this room and set up a cot thirty days before Nancy and Bob arrived, so eager was he to get to work. The large bathroom has a pink wicker chair, which proved to be hiding a toilet seat.

Coffee's out at 7:00 A.M. in the main Magnolia Room, with its polished wood floors, grand piano, and bevy of comfortable wing chairs, two of pale-green velvet in the bay window and two floral ones on the side. You might or might not meet Berkley, "our bed and breakfast cat," Bob explains.

The windows in the Magnolia Room are original to the house—hand-blown, looks like—and all over the outside is the most marvelous gingerbread trim, also original.

How to get there: From I–10 take the Columbus exit (mile marker 696) and go north. At the Y in the road, bear right onto Milam for about 8/10 mile. Turn left on Spring and continue for 2 blocks. The inn is on the right at number 634.

Innkeepers: Nancy and Bob Stiles
Address/Telephone: 634 Spring Street; (409) 732–2726
Rooms: 4; all with private bath, 1 with phone, 2 with TV. No smoking inn.
Rates: $80 to $120, double; $25 extra person; EPB. No credit cards.
Open: All year.
Facilities and activities: Special-occasion dinners; bicycles; croquet; chipping green; side trips to Stiles' Leanin Oaks nature ranch. Nearby: tennis, golf, horseback riding, and canoeing; restaurants; antiques shops; historic homes; Stafford Opera House Theater; Old Water Tower Museum; Walking Tours; Columbus Country Jamboree; Texas Pioneer Trail; Bluebonnet Wildflower Tours; Harris House Museum; Preston Kyle Museum; Santa Claus Museum; more.
Recommended Country Inns® Travel Club Benefit: 10% discount.

Raumonda Inn

COLUMBUS, TEXAS 78934

What a lovely mansion is the Raumonda, in a super-elegant Victorian home built in 1887. There are nine large rooms, of which three are common rooms—two large parlors and a music room with a grand piano—spacious hallways, front and back stairs, a glassed-in porch. The inn has both a formal dining room and an informal breakfast area. The Raumonda is surrounded by beautiful grounds and a cool blue swimming pool.

Buddy is the tourism director of the Columbus Area Chamber of Commerce, and he enjoys people so much that after he finished restoring the magnificent mansion, he decided to share it. "I love people," he says. "I like action all the time"—and there is always something going on at Raumonda, like live entertainment on weekends and people coming for cocktails and to view the house. "Guests are welcome to participate in all the many tourism functions we have here."

Although like most of these grand old homes, there is no access for wheelchairs, Buddy has installed an elevator for the use of his mother and anyone else who cares to ride.

"Just call me Hope," Mrs. Hope Heller Rau says with a twinkle, as she proceeds to tell a story about herself. "I told Buddy, 'Let's try it [innkeeping]. If we don't like it, we can quit.'" She adds that she told Buddy she'd move in with him only "so long as I can take my bidet and I can live in the shadow of the courthouse!" While she enjoys the privacy of her front-room suite, she's right in the middle of the action.

"I did a study," Buddy says, "and my feeling was that most people like to stay where the innkeepers live—and Mom can tell great stories of Columbus!"

Since Hope is fifth generation (and Buddy sixth), she has much to share. Families on both sides were originally Stephen F. Austin colonists, the first in Texas. The inn is furnished with beautiful family pieces. The Heller Room has the bed that belonged to Hope's father and a china cabinet brimming with family collectibles. It also can be the most private room, since it is upstairs off the back stairs.

The Hahn Room ("a family ancestor on my father's side," Buddy says) can connect with the Heller Room. It has a handsome walnut Victorian armoire almost as large as the king-sized bed. The Ilse Room is furnished with a fine suite of American Empire Revival, the wedding set of one of the Ilse daughters many years ago. The door to the front gallery is just steps away, and the door to the rear gallery is at the back of the spacious hallway. Two velvet loveseats provide a leisurely way to view the entire wall of old-time photographs in lovely frames, all of Buddy's grandparents and great-grandparents.

Breakfast, either in the dining room (with a crystal chandelier that burns candles) or in the breakfast room with its comfortable cane-back captain chairs, offers a choice of three juices, homemade banana nut muffins, and a selection of the homemade *kolaches* (Czech sweet rolls) that this area of Texas is famous for. There are also dry cereals, a dark and a light bread, and spiced figs, a specialty of the house.

How to get there: From I–10 take the Columbus exit (mile marker 696) and go north. At the Y in the road, bear right onto Milam for about 8⁄10 mile. Turn left on Spring Street, go 1 block, then take a right onto Bowie. The inn is on the left at the end of the block.

Innkeeper: R. F. "Buddy" Rau

Address/Telephone: 1100 Bowie (mailing addresss: P.O. Box 112); (409) 732–2190

Rooms: 3; 2 with private bath, all with phone and TV. Smoking permitted in designated area. Elevator to 1 room.

Rates: $80 to $120, double, EPB. Corporate rates available. No credit cards.

Open: All year.

Facilities and activities: Swimming pool. Nearby: tennis, golf, and horseback riding; restaurants; antiques shops; historic homes; Stafford Opera House Theater; Old Water Tower Museum; Walking Tours; Columbus Country Jamboree; Texas Pioneer Trail; Bluebonnet Wildflower Tours; Harris House Museum; Preston Kyle Museum; Santa Claus Museum; more.

Bay Breeze Inn

CORPUS CHRISTI, TEXAS 78404

"We're empty-nesters," Frank says, referring to the grown children who have left the family home. The home means a lot to him; he lived in it during his youth and even then didn't want to leave it. "I lived in the Tree House in back while I was in college. If I could, I would have stayed there until I was forty!" He bought the house from his mother in 1973. "I've lived all my life within walking distance of the hospital where I was born." He and Perry wanted to justify keeping it even though it was too large for the "empty-nesters," and were inspired to do that by visiting other inns.

Now, he says, thanks to Perry's culinary arts, "I've not eaten better in all our years of marriage, and I just get to eat in the kitchen." Which is hardly a hardship with dishes like fresh shrimp omelet (in season).

Frank is in real estate, and Perry has been the city's most outstanding model, according to her loyal husband. She sings at weddings, too— she's an elegant, talented lady.

The house is lovely, with a gorgeous view down to Corpus Christi Bay. "I wouldn't take anything for the view," Frank says. The living room has a bookshelf wall of bright yellow, behind the sofa, and an antique Steinway piano that belonged to Perry's grandfather. The wall behind the piano is a picture gallery of ancestors, and there's a photograph of the Ohio forebear who invented the striking match.

The Sunroom is a real treat. It runs the width of the house and is bright green and yellow, with white wicker furniture, lots of windows, and Perry's mother's childhood dollhouse. Frank says the 1930s pool table at one end of the room was probably in a bar. "I called Brunswick, the manufacturer, to find out if it was authentic; very likely it could tell many a story if it could talk."

The Tree House out back is now a large guest room with kitchen and sofa bed in addition to the queen-sized bed. There's a fireplace in the *center* of the room, and French doors open onto a deck above the treetops. The table is set with pretty blue-and-white china. "That was my mother's," Perry says.

The Nook below the deck is rustic, with wood planking on the floors and a white-painted, scrolled iron bed. "We call it our Elegant Economy Rustic Room."

Perry shines in the kitchen, turning out such tasty dishes as Pancakes Pierre and a South Texas Omelet. "It's a cheese and egg soufflé, with artichokes and salsa on the bottom." Her decision to make it depends on where people are from, she says of the spicy dish. There might be cinnamon-streusel muffins and quiche, along with seasonal fresh fruit. *Empanadas*, too, which are Mexican pastries, and you'll find a dish of *polvo* (shortbread cookies with sugar) by your bed.

Guests in the Brass Bedroom tend to sleep late, Perry says. "It's so quiet. And there's that view of the water."

The Hunt Room is masculine, great for outdoorsmen, with real trophies displaying the wildlife of South Texas. An East Indian axis deer is one such specimen, a pair of antlers is another. The twin beds have pretty paisley spreads.

Off the high-ceilinged dining room, the butler's pantry has a lovely stained-glass window.

How to get there: From I–37 turn south on Shoreline Boulevard and go 2³⁄₁₀ miles to Louisiana on the right. The inn is just down the street, on the left, and there's a sign.

Innkeepers: Perry and Frank Tomkins
Address/Telephone: 201 Louisiana; (512) 882–4123
Rooms: 4; all with private bath; wheelchair access to downstairs rooms. No smoking inn.
Rates: $57 to $85, double; $5 extra person; EPB. No credit cards.
Open: All year.
Facilities and activities: Pool table. Nearby: Spahn Hospital, downtown Corpus Christi, seawall, bicycles, fishing, windsurfing, Texas State Aquarium, Art Center, Bayfront Arts and Science Park, Botanical Gardens, Greyhound Race Track, U.S.S. Lexington Museum on the Bay, more.
Business travel: Located in downtown Corpus Christi, near Bayfront Convention Center. Phone jack in all rooms.

The Gilded Thistle

GALVESTON, TEXAS 77550

I asked innkeeper Helen Hanemann to explain The Gilded Thistle's name, because it seemed to me to be a contradiction. Helen, very much into the island's history, said that like native thistle, sturdy Texas pioneer stock sank deep and lasting roots into the sandy island soil, building a Galveston that flowered into a gilded age of culture and wealth.

Her home was part of those people and their times—in the late 1800s Galveston's Strand was known as "the Wall Street of the West"—and The Gilded Thistle is a lovely memorial to Galveston's past.

The beautiful antiques throughout the house make it an exceptionally elegant place to stay, but the atmosphere is so homey that my awe melted away to pure admiration. Helen is on duty at all times, and I joined the other guests in her kitchen, watching her arrange the fresh flowers that fill the rooms.

It wasn't hard to get used to being served on fine china, with coffee or tea from a family silver service. Breakfast, Helen says, is "whenever you want," and I took mine on the L-shaped screened porch around the dining room, especially enjoying Helen's specialty, "nut chewies," and her crispy waffles. Guests might also have Pat's fulsome scrambled eggs, country sausage, spicy baked potatoes, and homemade biscuits. "That'll take them through lunch," he says.

There's always a bowl filled with apples or other fruit on the sideboard.

Tea and coffee are available at all times, and I loved it when my morning began with orange juice and a pot of boiling water for coffee or tea at my bedroom door.

The evening snack tray could almost take the place of dinner; there are strawberries and grapes and other fruit in season, ham and cheese and roast beef sandwiches, at least four kinds of cheese, and wine. And if after that you don't feel like going out, Pat will rustle up something gourmet, like a bowl of his seafood gumbo with special rice and French bread, compliments of the house.

The Gilded Thistle has been gilded horticulturally: In recent years the inn's landscaping has won two prizes, the Springtime Broadway Beauty Contest and an award for a business in a historic building. But the climate never makes it easy and has given rise to the Texas saying that if you don't like the weather, wait a minute, it'll change. "A few years ago we had that bitter winter," Helen says. "Now we've put in lawn sprinklers and wouldn't you know—too much rain."

I overheard a visitor asking Pat what was so lively about The Gilded Thistle. Pat's answer: "Our guests."

How to get there: Stay on Highway 45 South, which becomes Broadway as soon as you cross the causeway onto Galveston Island. The inn is just beyond 18th Street, on the right.

Innkeepers: Helen and Pat Hanemann
Address/Telephone: 1805 Broadway; (409) 763–0194 or (800) 654–9380
Rooms: 3; 1 with private bath, all with TV and TTD for hearing impaired. No smoking inn.
Rates: $125 to $175, per room, EPB and snack tray in evening.
Open: All year.
Facilities and activities: Nearby: historic Ashton Villa and the Bishop's Palace; the historic Strand, with Galveston Art Center, Galveston County Historical Museum, Railroad Museum, shops and restaurants; the Seawall and Gulf Coast beaches, Moody Gardens Rainforest Pyramid, Texas Seaport Museum.
Business travel: Laptop computer, modem, fax, copier, separate trunk line; cater to small meetings for up to 20; corporate rates.

Hazelwood House
GALVESTON, TEXAS 77550

"Every inn is different," says Pat, a warm and down-to-earth person who wishes she could house everyone in an inn. "I've never had anybody here I didn't like, or who didn't like me. First they like the house—and then they like the innkeeper!" she says with a throaty chuckle.

An entrepreneurial type, Pat has remodeled ten houses in Galveston's renowned East End Historical District. She also has organized half a dozen tours to show off the charms of her beloved area, among them a Gulf Coast train ride, romantic Dinner on a Diner in a restored train dining car, and an evening at the Grand Opera House.

Hazelwood House is a Victorian charmer hidden behind a tall lattice fence, which in turn is hidden by masses of green foliage. The sign on the fence says BEWARE OF DOG, but Pat laughs: "There is no dog, just push open the gate and come on in." Steps lead up to the gingerbread porch and an interior filled with soft music, oriental rugs, and antiques. On a carved coffee table, a tray of wine, cheese, and fruit is waiting, balm for the weary traveler.

Mornings at Hazelwood House begin with a coffee or tea tray placed quietly outside your door. Pat's breakfasts, served formally in the dining room or Texas style on the porch (it's up to you) are usually Belgian waffles with whipped cream and syrup sprinkled liberally with blueberries and strawberries, a colorful feast. There may be long-link sausage, hard-boiled eggs, and yogurt, too. New are Pat's delicious cherry-pastry pizzas and other exotic pastries to start your day off sweet and lovely.

Rooms are imaginatively furnished with Pat's collection of antiques. The king-sized room has a wall of mirrors and a bed smothered in eyelet and ruffles. The tan marble bath has a Jacuzzi. "People really like that," Pat says in tones of surprise. It's no surprise to me—what a way to relax after a day of driving or sightseeing!

The double room with the carved French bed is decorated with Burmese tapestry. Its bright bath has stained-glass doors and a "throne" commode with arms. The third guest room adjoins the porch, where a hammock awaits the leisurely. The Cathedral Attic is a "wonderland of wood" with a sitting room, TV, refrigerator, and microwave.

How to get there: Go south on I–45, which becomes Broadway as soon as you cross the causeway onto Galveston Island. Turn left at 10th Street and drive to Church Street. Turn left on Church (it's one-way), and the inn is on your left at the corner of Church just before 12th Street.

Innkeeper: Pat Hazelwood

Address/Telephone: 1127 Church Street (mailing address: P.O. Box 1326); (409) 762–1668

Rooms: 4; all with private bath, 1 with TV. No smoking inn.

Rates: $75 to $125, double, EPB. Weekly and monthly discount rates; business discounts.

Open: All year.

Facilities and activities: Box lunches and beach picnics by reservation, Jacuzzi, bicycles. Nearby: swimming pool and tennis; sailboat cruises; fishing; 10 blocks to Gulf of Mexico and the Strand, historic street of shops and restaurants; Grand Opera House; Moody Gardens Rainforest Pyramid; Railroad Museum; Texas Seaport Museum.

Recommended Country Inns® Travel Club Benefit: 25% discount, subject to availability.

Michael's
GALVESTON, TEXAS 77550

Michael's is housed in an impressive red brick mansion built by Hans Guldmann, cotton exporter and vice-consul to Denmark, as a bulwark against the famous—or infamous—storms that blow in on Galveston from the Gulf of Mexico. The hurricane of 1915 destroyed much of the island but didn't touch the sturdy home, which was not yet inhabited. Even so, Guldmann was so impressed by the furor of the storm that he had the new house torn down and rebuilt atop a sloping terrace formed by storm-damaged bags of concrete. Mikey will take you down in the basement, an oddity on the sea-level island, and show you the wine cellar and the thick concrete walls.

Impressive is the Isbells' collection of Western art—Remington-inspired bronzes and paintings by Fort Worth artist Jack Bryant. Decoration was planned with an accent on light, enhancing the spaciousness of this house. The mix of family antiques and contemporary pieces together with original art is pleasing to the eye.

The rose garden, amid the broad green lawns surrounding the house, enables Mikey to fill the house with beautiful blooms and a wonderful scent. "It's great to sit out in the spring and fall, and someday we'll have a greenhouse," she says hopefully. The estate once had tennis courts, a grape arbor, and pergolas covered with roses, and Mrs. Guldmann's greenhouse (now a garden room for winter plants and a party room other times of the year) and fish pond make a charming, nostalgic picture.

All of the rooms are extraordinarily large, from the entrance hall with its sweeping center staircase to the glassed-in sunroom, bright with white wicker and green plants. Breakfast is served on Mikey's grandmother's huge dining-room table. "My mother made the chair seats," Mikey says, as I admire the rose-and-cream pattern hand worked in bargello needlepoint.

The full breakfast varies from Belgian waffles with berries to a delicious egg casserole with homemade bran muffins, and you may have it in the formal dining room or in the cheerful sunroom. Mikey's renowned for her cheesecake, and the Isbells used to serve coffee and dessert at bedtime. "But we've found that most guests come in too late or too full," she says, "so we encourage them to feel free to help themselves to whatever's in the refrigerator—or have coffee with us."

Nanny's Room, with a bright-blue iron bedstead, was once the room of the young Guldmann children's nurse and has a small antique student desk from now-defunct Terrell Military Institute. The Schoolroom, with a large green-tiled fireplace, recalls the children's classes with their tutor.

How to get there: Go south on I–45, which becomes Broadway as soon as you cross the causeway onto Galveston Island. Turn right at 35th Street, and the inn is on your right in the 1700 block.

Innkeepers: Mikey and Allen Isbell
Address/Telephone: 1715 35th Street; (409) 763–3760 or (800) 776–8302
Rooms: 4 share 1 bath. No smoking inn.
Rates: $85, double, EPB.
Open: All year.
Facilities and activities: Bicycles, rose garden with fountain. Nearby: the Strand with shops, galleries, and restaurants; historic Galveston attractions such as the Bishop's Palace, Ashton Villa, the Silk Stocking District: gambling cruise on the Gulf of Mexico; the Galveston Seawall and Gulf beaches; Moody Gardens Rainforest Pyramid; Railroad Museum; Texas Seaport Museum.
Recommended Country Inns® Travel Club Benefit: 25% discount, Monday–Thursday, subject to availability.

The Victorian Inn
GALVESTON, TEXAS 77550

Isaac Heffron, who built the first sewer systems for both Houston and Galveston and the first phase of the famous seawall now protecting the island from hurricanes, built his family a beautiful red brick residence with a wraparound veranda and a gorgeous circular porch upstairs off the master bedroom. That room is named Mauney's Room, and it was the one for me. Green and yellow, two of my favorite colors, decorate the big room, which is filled with brass, wicker, and antiques. It shares a bath with Isaac's Room, brown and turquoise with patterned cloth wallpaper. Both rooms have recently been redecorated, keeping the original color schemes.

There's not room here to describe all the beautiful things in this house. The entry hall is immense. There is a hand-carved wooden settee by the fireplace, and two more face each other at the end of the room, with a checkerboard set up for guests on the table between them. The parlor has a floor done in a hand-cut and -laid bird's-eye maple design, a hand-carved mantel, and its original crystal chandelier.

But the best part of this elegant inn is the welcome innkeeper Marcy offers to guests—I just know she loves her job. She has added personal touches and uses her own special recipes for the hearty continental breakfast that she serves.

In addition to local history lessons, guests get homemade cookies and fresh flowers in their rooms, coffee and tea any time they want in the sunny yellow butler's pantry, and perhaps a glass of sherry. Breakfast is orange juice, coffee, tea, milk, fresh fruit in season, cold cereals or hot oatmeal (depending on the temperature outdoors), quiche, French apple pie, a variety of homemade breads, croissants, and granola.

I sat on the curved upstairs porch with a refreshing glass of iced tea in my hand and rocked; a fresh breeze swept off the Gulf. Ryan's Room has a balcony and Amy's Room has an open porch, so I wasn't the only one savoring the breeze. And, of course, there's always the veranda that wraps around the house, with its view of shady green trees and other grand old houses. The third-floor suite may not have a porch, but it's a favorite hideaway for honeymooners.

The inn is a perfect setting for storybook events, and Marcy loves to plan small business meetings, weddings, and retreats. Romantic, in keeping with the ambience of the inn, is a carriage ride through the historic East End District to view many other late nineteenth-century homes, neighbors of the 1899 Victorian Inn.

Galveston is synonymous with seafood; there are many wonderful restaurants where you can get your fill of shrimp, soft-shell crab, fresh flounder, and other fruits of the sea.

How to get there: South on I–45 into Galveston; the highway becomes Broadway. Turn left at 17th; the inn is on your left when you reach the 500 block.

Innkeeper: Marcy Hanson
Address/Telephone: 511 17th Street; (409) 762–3235
Rooms: 4, plus 1 suite; suite with private bath.
Rates: $85 to $175, double, EPB.
Open: All year.
Facilities and activities: Nearby: the Strand historical district with shops, galleries, museums, and restaurants; the historic sailing ship Elissa; Railroad Museum, Seawall, and beach; restored 1894 opera house; Moody Gardens Rainforest Pyramid; Texas Seaport Museum.

The Dial House

GOLIAD, TEXAS 77963

The first thing you'll notice about the Dial House is its landscaping, which is lush and green and bountiful. Dolores is a passionate gardener, and you may have to hunt for her somewhere on her grounds.

"Everything out here, including trees, has been planted by these gnarled old hands," she says with great good humor. Dolores is also passionate about the Dial House, which is a family home furnished with pieces that were in the house "before I was born."

Dolores grew up in the Great Depression. While her parents went from one place to another, looking for work, they would send young Dolores to her Aunt Dial in Goliad.

"This was my refuge. I loved it here, and my aunt gave me the house before she died." Dolores's refuge was my delight; it is a real treat to stay here. Dolores does things like putting sheets with pink roses in the room that has pink roses all over the wallpaper. She laughs about what she calls the "vile green" wallpaper in the dining room, which she papered years ago when her aunt asked her to redo those walls.

"I don't know why I picked it—guess because I liked green. It's quite a conversation piece!"

So are the breakfast and the evening snack tray, both evidence of Dolores's supreme hospitality. The breakfasts always have two kinds of meat and several main choices, such as scrambled eggs, quiche, and sausage rolls. "In case people don't like one thing, they can have another," says Dolores. A delicious specialty is an asparagus-mushroom crepe covered with a rich cheese sauce. "Don't know whether this is better than my quiche," she says modestly, "but both get eaten all up."

There's always a big plate of fruit (I recommend particularly a bowl of Dolores's home-frozen peaches) and hot biscuits. "They're full when they leave my table," Dolores can well boast.

What Dolores calls her "evening snack tray" filled me up! There were finger sandwiches along with an old family recipe called "waxed pecan squares," old-time bread pudding with warm peach sauce, a banana cream cake with whipped cream and fresh bananas, and brownies besides. Dolores is an innkeeper who truly loves her calling and loves to see you eat.

She has two kinds of oatmeal cookies that "I keep ready to pull out at any time; German chocolate cake, cheesecake . . ." I had to cry halt—at least until the next day.

I loved relaxing in Dolores's "plant room," which she built to house her plants and collection of the dolls she played with when she was a little girl, or on the wraparound porch, lolling on the filigree chairs or swinging on either of the 5-foot-wide swings.

How to get there: From Highway 59 turn north at Mt. Auburn and go 4 blocks. The inn is on the corner of Mt. Auburn and Oak.

Innkeeper: Dolores Clarke
Address/Telephone: 306 West Oak Street (mailing address: P.O. Box 22); (512) 645–3366
Rooms: 5, including Bridal Suite; suite with private bath, all with phone and TV; wheel chair accessible. No smoking inn.
Rates: $65, double, EPB and large evening snack.
Open: All year.
Facilities and activities: Breakfast for non-inn guests; lunch and dinner by reservation (minimum four persons). Nearby: Goliad State Park, with Spanish missions and the Presidio de La Bahia, a fort infamous in Texas history; County Courthouse with "Hanging Tree"; town and antiques shops.

The Madison

GOLIAD, TEXAS 77963

The Madison is named for the Bensons' hometown in Wisconsin, and guest rooms are named for three of that state's many lakes: The Wingra, The Mendota, and The Monoma. Each reflects Joyce's elegant designing taste combined with Wallace's artistic eye. The house is the old Linburg homestead, built in 1888 in the bungalow, or craftsman, style of that time. Sitting in either one of the two parlors, with their plum-colored swags over crisp white lace curtains, it's hard to believe Wallace when he says, "This was a horror story at one time!" But you begin to when he mentions how the beautiful old oak floors were painted over—in brown—and when he describes the condition of the walls. Now the decorator floral wallpapers and coordinated borders, beautiful light fixtures, and attractive furniture make the old house picture-perfect. Many pieces are old family furniture; the comfortable sofa and matching chair were Joyce's mother's; a wonderful pre–Civil War buffet in the dining room comes from Wallace's family. "I never would have believed I'd put three buffets in a dining room," Joyce says. But all three fit in perfectly and hold the lovely linens she serves with.

Joyce was a home economist and bridal designer, Wallace a former art teacher and audio/visual consultant in the Wisconsin school system, and the inn reflects their many talents.

You'll find cheese and fruit in your room, wine and ice water, and there are tea-time and bed-time snacks. "I play it by ear," Joyce says, "depending on what I feel guests want." This guest (myself) thoroughly enjoyed tangy lemon squares and homemade *kolaches* with coffee in the evening. As for special occasions, Joyce rose to the occasion even with a pair of newlyweds who decided to arrive early. "I had to quick bake a wedding cake!" she says. You'll also get a small cake if it's your birthday or anniversary.

Joyce prides herself on her six- or seven-course breakfast, and you'll do well if you can stay the course. At any one time you might have fresh fruit and juice, homemade breads, *kolaches* and other sweet rolls, mushroom blintzes, beef tamales with enchilada sauce, roast beef hash, Swiss potatoes, a Madison specialty of eggs with cheese, and possibly tortellini with shrimp. "Mercy!" I cried, "This isn't breakfast—it's an all-you-can-eat brunch!" as Joyce added mushroom toast and spinach blintzes.

The Bensons have taken to Goliad like ducks to water, or better, like native Texans. Being active on the Goliad County Historical Commission is only one of their activities.

If you like pets, be sure to walk back to the kitchen and get acquainted with Julie, the well-behaved German shepherd, as well as a pair of beautiful cockatiels, Sugar and Spice, and E.T., the bright, black-faced lovebird.

How to get there: Go north on Jefferson Street, which is also Highway 183/77A, to the north edge of town. The inn is on the west side of the highway, just past North Street. There is a sign in the front yard and guest parking in the rear.

Innkeepers: Joyce and Wallace Benson
Address/Telephone: 707 North Jefferson; (512) 645–8693
Rooms: 3; all with private bath and TV. Smoking permitted in kitchen, on breakfast porch, and on patio.
Rates: $50 to $65, double, EPB.
Open: All year.
Facilities and activities: Lunch and dinner by prior arrangement, stationary bicycle. Nearby: restaurants; Goliad State Park has Spanish missions and the Presidio de La Bahia; County Courthouse "Hanging Tree"; antiques shops; county fair and festivals.

St. James Inn
GONZALES, TEXAS 78629

The St. James Inn occupies a home built in 1914 by a descendant of a family that was involved in Texas history right at the beginning. The first shot of the Texas Revolution was fired right here in Gonzales in October 1835.

"Walter Kokernot, who built the house, was the grandson of a merchant seaman who came over from Holland and was the captain of three ships of the Texas Navy," J. R. says. "For that, he was granted several leagues of land, which he turned into the Big Hill Ranch. His oldest son was a 'cattle gatherer.'" Cattle gatherer? J. R. laughs. "Well, he gathered what cattle he could find and made his fortune on the Chisholm Trail, which today goes right by here with the name of Highway 183."

Well, however he came by his fortune, he surely built a beautiful mansion. The house must be about 12,000 to 14,000 square feet—the Coverts aren't sure how large it is if you count the basement and the attic. Downstairs ceilings are 12 feet high, upstairs 10. The home is absolutely breathtakingly large, and the guest rooms and baths (and bathtubs!) are about the most spacious I have seen anywhere.

All the rooms are charming as well as huge: the Sunny Meadow Room, the Bluebonnet Room, the Cactus Flower Room, Josephine's Room—it's hard to make a choice. The Children's Playroom on the third floor has all sorts of nooks and crannies under the eaves. A wonderful collection of antique children's toys is in one ell, and Ann's basket collection is under the eaves outside the door. And there are other collections, all interesting, all over the inn, which also has nine fireplaces. "Guests may burn imitation logs," J. R. says, "but not real fires!"

The Coverts are fugitives from Houston; J. R. is an architect and Ann was executive director of the Republican Party of Harris County. "But I'm among Democrats here," she says with a laugh. "We just got tired of the Houston rat race—we'd been working on an escape plan for seven years."

"We found this place quite by accident," J. R. says. "I said, 'Here we are, this is what we're looking for, what can you say?' Ann said, 'Let's take it!'"

Breakfast might be pecan pancakes topped with Ann's special bananas Foster sauce. She also fixes "Treasure Basket" picnics filled with "little surprises"; "I find out something about our guests and put in little mementos. One guest crocheted, another went fishing, we're in a pecan-growing area . . . it's fun."

You can enter the inn either from the formal front porch or by the side door. Either way, you'll be floored by all the room there is to make yourself comfortable in.

How to get there: Highway 183 becomes St. Joseph in town, and St. James runs parallel to it 1 block west. The huge house is on a huge southwest corner lot at St. James and St. Andrew.

Innkeepers: Ann and J. R. Covert
Address/Telephone: 723 St. James Street; (210) 672–7066
Rooms: 4 share 4½ baths. No smoking inn.
Rates: $65 to $75, per room, EPB. Corporate rates available.
Open: All year.
Facilities and activities: Picnic baskets and dinners by reservation, tandem bicycle. Nearby: historic walking tour, Gonzales and Old Jail museums, local dinner theater, Palmetto State Park, Independence Park with nine-hole golf course and swimming pool, fishing in Guadalupe River.

Durham House

HOUSTON, TEXAS 77008

The lovely rose-carpeted living/dining area of the Durham House lends itself to comfortable chatting as well as to the many weddings and mystery evenings Marguerite delights in hosting. Each Durham House mystery is original, written for an inn setting. You don't have to spend the night in order to attend a mystery dinner—but it's certainly more fun if you can retire after the mystery has been solved to the Rose Room, with its 1860 walnut Victorian bed; or the Turret Room, with an Eastlake bedroom suite; or the Carriage House Suite, furnished entirely in American oak.

Durham House is a well-restored Queen Anne Victorian listed on the National Register of Historic Places. "I grew up in a Victorian house, in the Monte Vista section of San Antonio," Marguerite says. "And my husband did the same, only in an aunt's house in California. We're very different," she says with a laugh. "That's the only thing we have in common!" A prize possession is a photograph of J. R. Durham and his German wife taken in Galveston in 1897. Caught in the 1900 storm that all but drowned the island, the Durhams lost everything in the famous flood. They moved to Houston and built on the Heights, the highest part of town.

The Carriage House has a private entrance off the garden and its own little refrigerator, in case you want to cool a few snacks. Each bathroom in the inn has a basket with fancy French milled soap, shampoo, and the like, and each guest room has terry robes to lounge in. If you get lonesome for your pet, Clancy the basset hound is available on request.

Delicious items on the Durham House breakfast menu are apple or peach upside-down French toast or mushroom-scrambled egg casserole and homemade banana-wheat bread with strawberry butter or pumpkin-streusel muffins. "And the newest favorites," says Marguerite, "are banana–chocolate chip muffins." You also might have lemon ginger, or ginger pear, orange pecan, or fresh apple muffins. Marguerite says the best "commercial" for her muffins is that businesswomen staying at the inn want her to bake extra for them to take to their presentations. It tickles her that when they're asked, "Where did you get them?" they say, "oh, it's something I just make!"

Health conscious, Marguerite tries to stay away from fried foods. "I try not to give people eggs every day; I watch their cholesterol," although specialties are Eggs McDurham and Herbed Eggs in Ham Cups, all from Marguerite's *Durham House Cookbook*. "And I've never subscribed to the edict that bed and breakfast means breakfast at a certain time." If you must leave extra early for the airport or another commitment, Marguerite will pack you a little take-along breakfast.

The dining-room breakfront contains Marguerite's fine cut glass collection: "I especially like things Victorian." That's hardly a surprise to me!

How to get there: From I–10 (Katy Freeway) take the Studemont exit and go west along the feeder road to Heights Boulevard. Turn right and the inn is on the left about 5 blocks along.

Innkeeper: Marguerite Swanson
Address/Telephone: 921 Heights Boulevard; (713) 868–4654
Rooms: 5; 4 with private bath. No smoking inn.
Rates: $50 to $85, double, EPB.
Open: All year.
Facilities and activities: Mystery dinners, gazebo, garden, radios with cassette tapes of old-fashioned radio shows. Nearby: Houston Heights area of historical interest.
Business travel: Located five minutes from downtown Houston. Meeting space in solarium; breakfast whenever needed, no matter how early; fax; business rates.

The Highlander

HOUSTON, TEXAS 77009

When I ask Arlen if they'd named the inn The Highlander because of Scottish connections, he laughs. "Well, Georgie's Irish and I'm Scottish, but that's four generations back." So it dawned on me: Highland Avenue—The Highlander!

Remarkable is the McIrvins' garden to the right of the inn. It's a wildlife habitat, certified by the World Wildlife Federation. "The idea is to have different levels of foliage for bird and animal cover as well as fruit-bearing plants," Arlen explains. Native growth such as mandina, silver berries, and American Beauty berry provide food and cover for opossums, raccoons, and squirrels in addition to the eighteen species of birds that Georgie and Arlen have identified. It's a highlight of the Houston Garden Tour.

Georgie is into Romance with a capital R. "Every inn develops its own flavor, and our specialty has turned out to be a romantic getaway for married couples," she says. One of the romantic things she and Arlen offer is their Enchanted Evening. "It's Love and Laughter in a Box," she says, showing me a board game that couples play in the privacy of their room.

"While they're out to dinner, we set up the room with candles, lace-covered table with flowers, iced nonalcoholic wine in a silver cooler, bed turn-down with chocolates on the pillow. It takes about two hours to play the game.

One of our guests said, 'That was the most beautiful night of my life!'"

Georgie says the first time she and Arlen played, it gave them a whole new insight into their marriage. One of the questions asks what a husband would give his wife if he had all the money in the world. "Arlen looked at me and thought and thought, and I was amazed when he finally said, 'A string of real pearls.' I hadn't thought he considered me that valuable!"

I figured I'd look at the game another time when my mate was with me, but I did look at the dining-room table we were sitting at. When I admired it, Georgie had a funny story. "It was my gandmother's and I wanted to see if I could find out how old it was. There was a tag underneath a chair that said Gatesville, Georgia. I called the number and got a very puzzled man. Finally, he said, 'Lady, this is the Gatesville Prison! We make wicker, not Queen Anne!'"

Georgie and Arlen do a hearty breakfast, with homemade scones, individual fruit compotes in raspberry/rhubarb sauce, super-fluffy scrambled eggs, and breakfast ham.

I noticed the beautiful Russian blue cat noticing me. "Smokey owns the place," Georgie says. "I just live here."

Arlen was having a guitar lesson when I first arrived. As I listened to him trying out "Au Claire de la Lune," Georgie said she gave him the lessons for Christmas. "He always wanted a guitar, he bought it—but he couldn't play!"

"I'd rather give someone a memory than an object," she explains. "My parents got to the point where they could buy whatever they wanted, so I gave them memories instead. Memories you can't lose . . . or have stolen."

How to get there: From I–10 west take the Taylor exit and go north; the street becomes Watson. One block past the stop sign, turn right on Highland. Go 1½ blocks to number 607. The inn is on the left.

Innkeepers: Georgie and Arlen McIrvin

Address/Telephone: 607 Highland Avenue; (713) 861–6110 or (800) 807–6110

Rooms: 4; 2 with private bath; telephones. No alcohol, no smoking inn.

Rates: $75, double, EPB.

Open: All year.

Facilities and activities: Herb and Wildlife Habitat Garden, gazebo, Enchanted Evening, dinner by reservation. Nearby: George R. Brown Convention Center, Galleria (shopping), the Museum District (Menil and Museum of Fine Art), Astrodome, Astroworld, Houston Museum of Natural Science, Space Center, Texas Medical Center, more.

Recommended Country Inns® Travel Club Benefit: 25% discount, Monday–Thursday, subject to availability.

La Colombe d'Or

HOUSTON, TEXAS 77006

It's no surprise to find this exquisite inn so close to two art collections: The inn is patterned after one of the same name in St. Paul de Vence, France, where many famous French painters traded their work for lodging. Houston's La Colombe d'Or ("the golden dove") is hung with fine art, too, and each suite has a name I certainly recognized.

I stayed in the Van Gogh Suite, named for one of my favorite Impressionist painters. Others are named for Degas, Cézanne, Monet, and Renoir; the largest suite, up at the top, is called simply The Penthouse. The suites are decorated with fine art, although there are no original works of their namesakes.

But I didn't miss them, so swathed in beauty and luxury was I in this prince of an inn. On my coffee table I found fruit, Perrier water, and wine glasses waiting to be filled from my complimentary bottle of the inn's own imported French wine.

Owner Steve Zimmerman has succeeded in bringing to the La Colombe d'Or the casual elegance of the French Riviera. European and American antiques, as well as his own collection of prominent artists' works, are set in the luxurious house that was once the home of Exxon founder Walter Fondren and his family.

The twenty-one-room mansion, built in 1923, is divided into suites. Each consists of a huge bedroom with a sitting area and a glass-enclosed dining room where Queen Anne furniture, china plates, linen napkins, and cutlery are in readiness for breakfast. As soon as I rang in the morning, a waiter arrived with a tea cart from which he served a very French-style plate of sliced kiwi fruit, raspberries, and strawberries; orange juice; coffee; and croissants with butter and jam. I ate this artistic offering surrounded by the green leafy boughs waving outside my glass room.

You may have luncheon or dinner served in your room, too, but I feasted downstairs on meunière of shrimp and lobster, cream of potato and leek soup, the inn's Caesar salad, and capon Daniel; and as if that weren't enough, I ended with crème brûlée!

If you long to visit France, you may decide you don't have to once you've visited La Colombe d'Or. The inn is a member of *Relais et Châteaux*, a French organization that guarantees excellence, and I absolutely soaked up the hospitality, tranquillity, and luxury.

How to get there: 3410 Montrose is between Westheimer and Alabama, both Houston thoroughfares.

Innkeeper: Steve Zimmerman
Address/Telephone: 3410 Montrose Boulevard; (713) 524–7999
Rooms: 6 suites; all with private bath; wheelchair accessible.
Rates: $195 to $575, per suite, EP.
Open: All year.
Facilities and activities: Restaurant, bar. Nearby: within five minutes, Houston central business district, Houston Museum of Fine Arts, Rice University, and Menil Art Foundation; the Astrodome.
Business travel: Located 5 miles from downtown Houston. Fax, computer, typing, printer available.

The Lovett Inn

HOUSTON, TEXAS 77006

On a lovely tree-lined boulevard in Houston's Museum District, the Lovett Inn is a stately mansion on a well-landscaped corner lot. The shaded, fenced pool is hidden behind green trees and shrubs, and pretty soft-red umbrellas offer shade from the sun. The house itself is of white stucco, with reddish-brown shutters and a lovely pillared portico shading the arched front door. Huge pecan trees tower overhead.

The Lovett Inn was the home of Houston Mayor and Federal Court Judge Joseph C. Hutcheson. It was built in 1924, and Guy and Tom are waiting for the required time to elapse to claim a historical marker for the house. Guy's background is the hotel business, and Tom is a Houston developer who likes to restore old homes.

"We both constantly make upgrades for both leisure and business travelers," Guy says. There's an automated answering service for telephone calls at any time of the night as well as a message service, both boons to the business traveler. "We offer a laundry service, restaurant reservations, information on museums and shopping, cultural events."

The formal entry hall opens onto the large living room on the left (unfurnished and ready for whatever is needed for meetings and banquets); the formal dining room is to the right. Breakfast, an extended continental, offers juice and coffee, cereal, both cold and warm (oatmeal), and muffins—sometimes chocolate chip, sometimes bran, sometimes blueberry. Fruits of the season, such as fresh strawberries with banana, make a nice combination.

The dining room boasts an interesting piece of furniture: a buffet built by the judge himself. It has tin-lined drawers for iced wine, a nice touch that was new to me. I wondered how they came by it, since the judge left nothing else in the house. "A lady saw the house being fixed up," Guy says, and came in and offered it to Tom. How's that for neighborliness?

The Library is the meeting and relaxing place (except, of course, for the pool!), with its formal deep-brown wood paneling and tall windows overlooking the back deck and the garden. A stately print sofa is flanked by dark-red leather armchairs.

The guest rooms have elegant four-poster beds, lounge chairs, armoires or chests, and desks for serious work. Four are in the main house, two are in the Carriage House at the rear of the property, and the seventh, next to the Carriage House, is a regular little townhouse. It has two bedrooms, one with a king-sized bed, the other a queen and a living room, dining room, kitchen, and private patio.

There are two staircases, the formal one in the front hall and a back staircase, which squeaks a little. "We don't send guests up this way in the dead of the night," Guy laughs.

How to get there: From Highway 59 (Southwest Freeway), exit at Elgin and go west; Elgin becomes Westheimer. From Westheimer turn left on Montrose Boulevard. Go 1 block, then turn left again, onto Lovett Boulevard. The inn is on the right; there is a sign.

Innkeepers: Guy Holt and Tom Fricke
Address/Telephone: 501 Lovett Boulevard; (713) 522–5224 or (800) 779–5224
Rooms: 7 in 3 buildings; all with private bath, telephone, TV, and clock radio. Pets permitted. One smoking room.
Rates: $85 to $150, double, extended continental breakfast. No checks.
Open: All year.
Facilities and activities: Swimming pool, Jacuzzi, gazebo, garden, off-street parking. Nearby: Galleria (shopping), the Museum District (Menil and Museum of Fine Art), Astrodome, Astroworld, Houston Museum of Natural Science, Space Center, more.
Business travel: Located 5 miles from downtown Houston; George R. Brown Convention Center and Texas Medical Center nearby. Phones in rooms, fax, meeting/banquet room, answering service, business rates.

Sara's Bed & Breakfast Inn

HOUSTON, TEXAS 77008

Sara's is named for the Arledges' young daughter, who loves having an inn so much that she's become a parent's dream. "Whatever I ask, she'll do," Donna says. "She loves the idea, she loves the place, she loves to help!"

This pretty-as-a-picture Victorian is easy to love. But it wasn't always so. "To give you an idea," Donna says, "the house had no front door, no back door, and all the wood had been pulled out." It was Tillman who fell in love with the house, and every day he would say to Donna, "Just look what we could do with it."

Donna gave in. "I finally said anybody who would want something that bad ought to have it."

It's hard to believe that Sara's began life in 1910 as a small one-story Victorian cottage. The downstairs parlor is "ready to encourage guests to relax and feel right at home," Donna says, while bright bedrooms are furnished with antiques and collectibles. A circular stairway leads up to the third-floor widow's walk and a great view of the Houston skyline. Sunrise cheers early risers from the front balcony, and the large covered deck out back is a favorite lounging spot any time.

Rooms have books and luggage racks. Downstairs bedrooms have washbasins. The garden sitting area on the second floor is furnished with white wicker, and the four windows of the cupola shower the entire house with light. The Heights neighborhood has a small-town feeling, great to walk around (or jog) in, in spite of the big city only 5 miles away.

Each charming room is named after a Texas town, with decor to suit that mood. The Galveston Room has nautical beds, the Tyler Room is white wicker, the San Antonio Room is Spanish. One guest surprised his wife by telling her they were going to Austin (Texas's capital city) for the weekend, and she was certainly surprised by the Austin Room at Sara's! (She loved it.)

I was intrigued by the plate collection on the dining room walls. "That's my grandmother's collection," Donna said. "We keep adding to it."

Breakfast of hot bread or muffins, fresh fruit cup, juice, and coffee is a friendly gathering in the dining room, with the plate collection for an icebreaker if need be. But many guests are repeaters, which makes them old friends.

How to get there: From I–10 east take Shepherd Drive and turn right to 11th, then right on Heights Boulevard for 1½ blocks. The inn is on the right. From I–10 west take the Studemont exit. Make a U-turn just before Studemont and turn right at Heights Boulevard. (This is necessary because of interminable road construction.) Sara's is on the left in about 6 blocks.

Innkeepers: Donna and Tillman Arledge
Address/Telephone: 941 Heights Boulevard; (713) 868–1130 or (800) 593–1130
Rooms: 14, with 11½ baths; plus two-bedroom, two-bath suite; all with TV and VCR; wheelchair accessible. No smoking inn.
Rates: \$55 to \$150, per room; \$10 extra person; continental breakfast.
Open: All year.
Facilities and activities: Deck, sun balcony and widow's walk, television room, games. Nearby: Houston Heights area of historical interest; Farmers' Market; museums.
Business travel: Located 5 miles from downtown Houston. Enclosed garden/meeting room, fax, phones in rooms.

Webber House

HOUSTON, TEXAS 77008

If you saw the Glenn Ford movie *Final Verdict*, you've seen the Webber House. It was Ford's residence in the film, that's how imposing it is. You can see why JoAnn fell in love with it. "I decided that instead of going back to work (after having some surgery), I had to have the house; I'd open an inn."

She and Tom (who's a Jr., and son Tom is a III) were living in Conroe, north of Houston, and they were familiar with the Heights neighborhood because they'd bought a small house in the area in order to spend the night on the one day a week they came into town on business.

The Heights is Houston's most historic neighborhood, established in 1891 by a self-made millionaire from Nebraska. He patterned the lovely, tree-lined boulevard after Boston's Commonwealth Avenue, and the Heights retains a friendly, small-town atmosphere to this day. (Newscaster Dan Rather and firefighter Red Adair grew up here.)

Son Tom is the one who first saw the Webber House. "Dad," he said, "you ought to go look at that house." Built in 1907 of deep-red brick by local brickmason Samuel H. Webber, the home is listed on the National Register of Historic Places. By the time JoAnn and Tom got through restoring it, it had earned the T. C. Jester Award for Outstanding Restoration. With its intricate masonry; leaded, curved, and stained glass; 11-foot ceilings, and deep-brown cypress woodwork, the house is a masterpiece. I fell in love with the three-story staircase, its turns anchored by large, carved newel posts.

The Victorian sofa in the parlor is a treat; even if it's a reproduction, it's a beautiful hand-made one. The oval marble coffee table in front displays JoAnn's lovely collection of boxes from Syria, Delft, London's British Museum shop—there must be a dozen at least.

The large entry hall, with the parlor on the left and the polished-wood staircase to the right, leads straight to JoAnn's office and the library, "my comfy room," which is remarkable for its built-in bar–cum–ticket-booth from an English pub. (They sold beer there by the ticket.)

Breakfast in the formal dining room is a "Deluxe Continental," a fresh fruit cup of honey-dew, cantaloupe and strawberries, Dutch Bake (an apple cinnamon coffeecake), fresh bran muffins with raisins and pecans, juice, and coffee.

The spacious Victorian Room has a circular turret with curved windows overlooking the boulevard. They're covered with lace curtains, the furniture is mahogany (the bed is a four-poster), the fireplace works, and the pier glass is a nice touch. The bathroom, although private, is just opposite, and there are robes to wear while crossing the hall. The Parisian Room has pink walls with a flowery border, and the furniture is oak, with a queen-sized high-back French bed and ornate armoire.

Large and lovely is the Attic Hideaway on the third floor. There's plenty of room for a sitting area, and the view from the high windows down the boulevard is delightful. The closet door is an antique—from another English pub.

How to get there: From I–10 north take the Heights/Yale Boulevard exit and turn right on Heights Boulevard to number 1011. The inn is on the left; there is a sign in front. From I–10 south take the Studemont exit, stay in the left-hand lane, and make a U-turn under the freeway to the Heights/Yale Boulevard exit; turn right on Heights Boulevard.

Innkeepers: JoAnn and Tom Jackson
Address/Telephone: 1011 Heights Boulevard; (713) 864–9472
Rooms: 3; all with private bath, TV, and VCR. No smoking inn.
Rates: $65 to $110, double, deluxe continental breakfast.
Open: All year.
Facilities and activities: Gazebo. Nearby: Galleria (shopping), Museum District (Menil and Museum of Fine Art), Astrodome, Astroworld, Houston Museum of Natural Science, Space Center, more.
Business travel: Located 5 miles from downtown Houston; George R. Brown Convention Center and Texas Medical Center nearby. Phones in rooms; meeting/party room.
Recommended Country Inns® Travel Club Benefit: 25% discount, Monday–Thursday, subject to availability.

La Borde House

RIO GRANDE CITY, TEXAS 78582

La Borde House is still elegant, if a little worn. Even though it was built on the Texas–Mexico border in 1899, it was designed by French architects in Paris (France, not Paris, Texas!). Leather merchant François La Borde had his inn designed at Paris's Beaux Arts school as a combined home, storehouse, and inn. Its early guests were often cattle barons who sold their herds on nearby Rio Grande docks or military officers en route to California. La Borde brought to life his vision of European grandeur—and I reveled in the reconstruction of that vision. Actually, the ambience is New Orleans Creole, and I felt as Scarlett O'Hara must have felt when Rhett took her there to wallow in luxury.

Restoration in 1982 was faithful to the original as documented by old records and photographs. The inn was originally built by both European and Rio Grande artisans, and replacement brick actually was found from the same brickyard in Camargo, Mexico, that was used before.

I was entranced by opulence such as collector-quality oriental rugs and English Axminster carpets, and early ledgers also record such purchases. Each posh bedroom is named for a local history event, with antique furniture and wallpapers; and many of the papers and fabrics are duplicates of those used in the 1981 restoration of the Texas Governor's Mansion in Austin.

"It tells the whole history of the border, it's that simple," say the innkeepers. "It's dedicated to the proud past of all South Texas, and we really get a joy out of the smiles we see on people's faces as they reminisce about old times here in the valley." Old times include such mementos as Fort Ringgold, one of Texas's best-preserved old military posts, named for the first army officer killed in the battle that began the Mexican War. Interesting, too, is Lee House, once occupied by Robert E. Lee when he commanded here before the Civil War.

The restaurant is the place for great border cuisine. The Mexican plate of tacos, enchiladas, tamales, beans, and rice has a special flavor, just right for lunch.

For dinner I tried the chicken cilantro, which is sautéed in butter, seasoned with that savory south-of-the-border herb, and served on a rice bed. It was delicious. I topped it off with fried ice cream, a neat treat of frozen cream dipped in batter and deep fried in a hurry. For seafood lovers there are usually three selections, but the two favorite are the shrimp and the catfish.

How to get there: From Highway 281 take Highway 83 west, which becomes Main Street in town. The inn is on the corner of Main and Garza.

Innkeepers: Crisanto Salinas and Armandina Garza
Address/Telephone: 601 East Main Street; (210) 487–5101
Rooms: 21; all with private bath.
Rates: $59, double, historical rooms; $40, double, modern rooms; EP.
Open: All year.
Facilities and activities: Restaurant open Monday to Saturday, 11:00 A.M. to 2:00 P.M.; Friday, Saturday, and Sunday, 11:00 A.M. to 9:00 P.M. Nearby: hunting, fishing, bird watching, International Bridge to Mexico, historic Fort Ringgold.

Hotel Lafitte

SEADRIFT, TEXAS 77983

This long, white wooden building is a treasure tucked away almost where Highway 185 ends at the Gulf of Mexico. It fronts right on the water, and you may just want to sit out on the veranda and rock, lazing the day away. The Hotel Lafitte is tailor-made for a perfect getaway.

"I grew up here," says Frances, "and Weyman, he's from Victoria" (just down the road a piece). "I love old things and I wanted this building. We got married here right after we bought it, and it took us three and a half years to restore the old place. It was built in 1909 as a railroad hotel—they called this type of hotel a railroad hotel because one always sprung up at the end of a line, and the Frisco Railroad ended right out on the docks." Frances learned from an unusual guest that in an infamous storm of 1919, the seas surged right through the second-floor windows. "The gentleman came for his ninety-second birthday. He remembered the hotel from way back, and he went up to the third floor like he was a teenager!"

Hospitality begins in the parlor, where a wooden holder displays three kegs of wine for guests to help themselves. Rosé, chablis, what is your pleasure? Other pleasures of the parlor are rose-colored wing chairs flanking an organ, a soft flowered sofa, and old-fashioned lace curtains. There's a fireplace, and the walls as well as the floors are planks of wood.

The public rooms are backwards, says Frances: The parlor is the most informal, while the large lobby is formal. It boasts a player piano, a birthday gift to Frances from Weyman.

The guest rooms are airy and roomy, and those facing the front have a gorgeous ocean view. Rooms are all large and decorated becomingly, reflecting the inn's turn-of-the-century mood. Number 5 has a flapper dress of the 1920s hanging on the armoire. Room number 6 not only contains the original hotel furniture, but there's also an antique wedding dress hanging up, a gift from a friend whose grandmother wore the gown.

The two large suites are on the third floor, and the Honeymoon Suite has a rose satin bedspread, an inlaid-wood card-table set, a Jacuzzi, and not one but two chaise longues. Hedonistic luxury!

Breakfast might be a ham-and-egg casserole or a quiche along with bran muffins, fruit, and juice. For lunch and dinner the Hardings will be delighted to direct you to the family restaurant, Barkett's, where seafood specialties abound. After all, here you are on the famous Texas Gulf Coast.

How to get there: From I–10 take Highway 77 south to Victoria and Highway 185 south to Seadrift, a small town approximately 35 miles southeast of Victoria. Bay Avenue is, of course, on the bay.

Innkeepers: Frances and Weyman Harding
Address/Telephone: 302 Bay Avenue (mailing address: P.O. Box 489); (512) 785–2319
Rooms: 8, plus 2 suites; suites with private bath and TV.
Rates: $55 to $95, double; $5 less for single; EPB.
Open: All year.
Facilities and activities: Downstairs and upstairs verandas right on San Antonio Bay. Nearby: fishing, swimming, walking on the Seawall; Matagorda Island, Aransas Wildlife Refuge.

Hamilton's

STOWELL, TEXAS 77661

What a bucolic setting! "We can't get guests off the front porch," Dorothy says. "They watch the hummingbirds, the squirrels, the cattle coming up to the fence." Husband Bo is a rancher, and the Longhorns just over the fence are fascinating to city slickers.

It's birdwatching, too, that draws people. In April people from all over the world, from Britain, Australia, come to the shoreline and marshes, and to High Island, fifteen minutes from the inn. "We have Texas Cowboy Poet Bob Cahla and several other guides take people either freshwater or saltwater fishing, hunting, and on camera tours up the Trinity River looking for alligators."

We looked and sure enough, several of the critters were sunning themselves at the marsh's edge along Highway 124.

Bo's great-grandfather, James Taylor White, was the first large-scale cattle baron in Texas. He came from Louisiana in 1819, and his grandson Monroe built the home in 1899. It has remained in the family for five generations, a large, square, white plantation-type house with full porches across the front, both up and down.

"I had this big house, and we no longer needed all this room. I wanted to live in a 'real' house for a change," Dorothy explains. They built the modern ranch-style house across the road, but she hated to close the big old family place. "Rather than do that, I decided to let everybody enjoy it. And I meet the most wonderful people! We have a lot of business ladies, they feel safe, sitting on the porch, taking a walk, wandering down to the goldfish pond."

Five guest rooms are in the big house, one on the first floor and the rest on the second. The Playhouse is a delightful cottage out back under the trees, with two rooms and bath and a full porch all to yourself.

The antique furniture in the house beggars description. "Everything was here," Dorothy says of the beautiful pieces. Nothing was ever discarded; it was stored in the attic, and once Dorothy started taking it down there was no stopping her. "I thought Bo was going to kill me, the way I had him dragging stuff from the attic to be refinished. None of his friends would come by for a beer, afraid he might make them drag stuff too."

But what wonderful "stuff," every piece more special than the next. There's old Monroe's rolltop desk "that he sold lots of cows over," and a Victorian organ in the parlor. "Oh, that's my side of the family," Dorothy says. Bo's grandmother's christening dress is laid out on a quilt; an English buffet is in the dining room, a huge breakfront secretary in the parlor.

The big old kitchen is a family area also. "Some guests are more comfortable eating in the kitchen," Dorothy says. "Others want to get away from reality." Whether in the formal dining room or the kitchen, the food is delicious. Fresh fruit, peach French toast, baked-egg crepes with orange sauce, topped with kiwi and strawberries and a little sprinkle of chocolate. Pretty fancy—but that's Hamilton's. Dorothy does other fancy things, such as the "Memories Package" with a fresh flower arrangement, chilled fruit and champagne, and Godiva chocolates in your room.

How to get there: From I–10 exit at Winnie (Highway 124) and go 2 miles south to Highway 65. Turn right, and the inn is the second house on the right.

Innkeeper: Dorothy Hamilton
Address/Telephone: P.O. Box 67; (409) 296–3377, fax 296–2494
Rooms: 7 in main house and Playhouse; 2 with private bath. Smoking in kitchen/game room.
Rates: $65, double; $15 extra person; EPB.
Open: All year.
Facilities and activities: Hamilton's Antique Mall. Nearby: Larry's Old Time Trade Days, horseback riding, fishing, hunting, birdwatching, camera tours, golf.

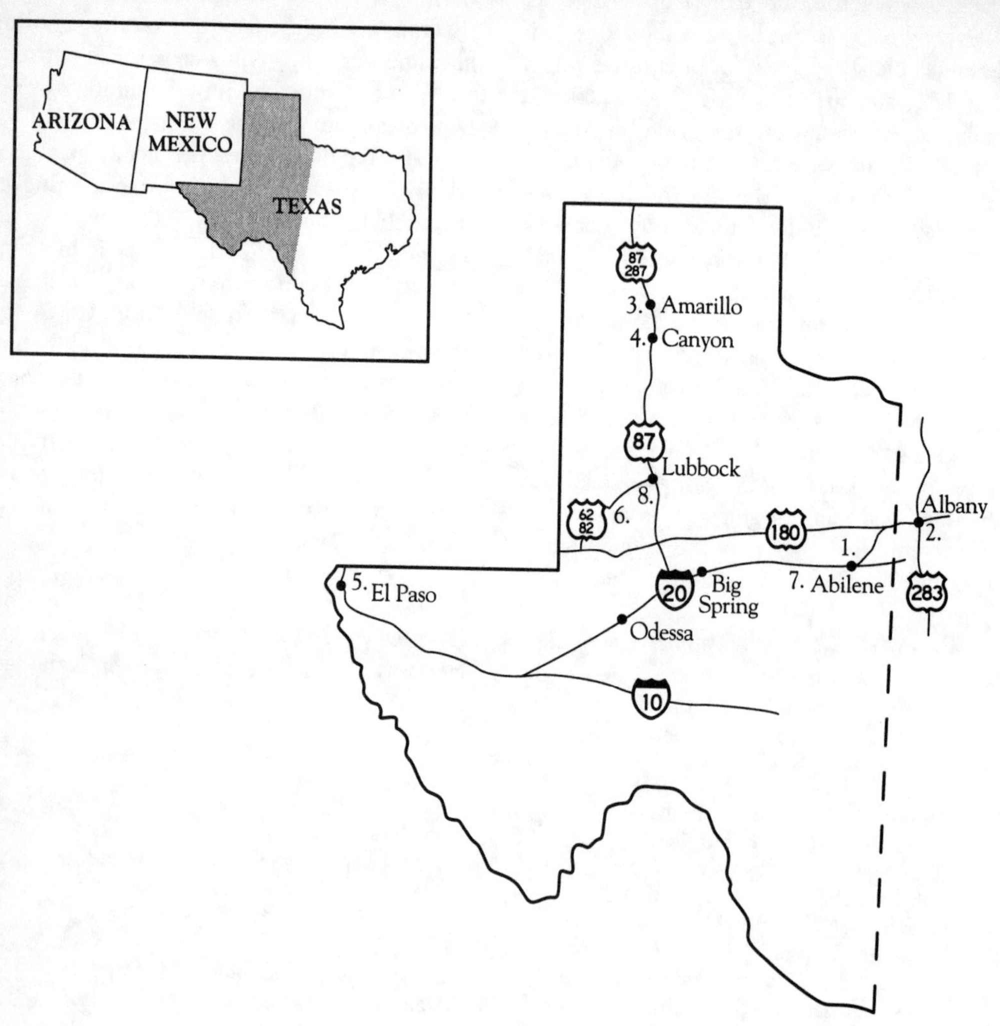
ARIZONA
NEW MEXICO
TEXAS
87 287
3. Amarillo
4. Canyon
87
Lubbock
8.
62 82
6.
180
Albany
2.
1.
5. El Paso
20
Big Spring
7. Abilene
283
Odessa
10

West Texas

Numbers on map refer to towns numbered below.

Bolin's Prairie House

ABILENE, TEXAS 79601

This large and airy prairie house was once a Victorian mansion, home of an Abilene pioneer whose name was Colonel Christmas Comfort. "He never was a colonel," Ginny says. "That was just his name." Not only names but styles change, too, and new owners in 1920 decided they preferred a simpler style. They remodeled the story-and-a-half house into a full two-story, smoothing the lines along the way.

"So it's considerably plainer than Victorian," Ginny says. "It was copied from that house across the street, whose owner back then studied with Frank Lloyd Wright in Chicago and came home and remodeled it. Guess it was just the latest thing."

Ginny, who likes to crochet, do needlework, sew, and garden, and Sam, who's a building contractor and knows how to do things right, spent months fixing up the old house, something Sam had always wanted to do. As for Ginny, she was ready to retire from bookkeeping. She finds that the house is kind of restful and peaceful. "People come here; nobody calls them and bothers them."

The inn's color scheme is mainly red, white, and blue—pale, royal, and navy blue. The living room has an old wood-burning stove, pale-blue woodwork, and shutters behind airy white lace curtains. Fabric is striped navy-and-white ticking. Large Raggedy Ann and Raggedy

Andy dolls sit contentedly in an old rocker, and I relaxed just looking at them.

Around the dining-room walls, plate racks display Ginny's assortment of Depression glass and other collectibles. "I've been collecting it for twenty years, from England, California . . . so long as it's blue, I like it," she says. The old kitchen cupboard in a corner of the dining room—you know, the old kind with a flour sifter inside the door—was Sam's grandmother's. "I can remember my grandmother making bread in one of those big old wooden bowls," Ginny says. The Bolins grew up in a small town nearby and enjoy being closer to home after living in more distant parts, although Ginny says, "We always enjoy wherever we are."

The crystal, too, that Ginny likes to use, belonged to Sam's grandmother. And upstairs in the corner of the staircase is Sam's collection of old tools in an Amish trunk. Guest rooms are spacious and light corner rooms with lots of windows and distinctive color schemes. Love is decorated in blue and beige and has comfortable wing chairs; Joy is furnished with Mamma Bolin's old bedroom set, and Ginny has used a riot of pink roses, quilted roses, striped roses (wallpaper), and rose-covered pillows in rose-colored rocking chairs. Peace, green and cream, is full of green plants, and Patience has ornate twin beds and blue wing chairs.

Breakfast is plentiful: Ginny is another innkeeper who likes to say, "They don't go away hungry." Dutch Babies (oven-baked pancakes), grits, sausage, hashed browns, baked egg dishes, homemade bread, and oatmeal with apples and cinnamon if you don't want eggs.

How to get there: From I–20 take Business Loop 20 to Grape Street; go north 6 blocks to North 5th, then east 1 block to the corner of Mulberry and North 5th streets.

Innkeepers: Ginny and Sam Bolin
Address/Telephone: 508 Mulberry; (915) 675–5855
Rooms: 4; 2 with private bath. No smoking inn.
Rates: $50 to $60, double; $10 extra person; EPB.
Open: All year.
Facilities and activities: Nearby: restaurants, fine arts museum, Grace Cultural Museum, zoo, three universities, historic Buffalo Gap Historic Village.
Business travel: Located 5 blocks from downtown Abilene. Desk with private phone line on the stair landing.

The Old Nail House Inn

ALBANY, TEXAS 76430

The Nail House was built in 1914 for Robert Nail, playwright and creator of the Fort Griffin Fandangle. All that remains of Fort Griffin, a wild Wild West settlement in the 1870s and '80s, are the ruins of several old buildings, three restored buildings, and the yearly Fort Griffin Fandangle.

The Fandangle is a show put on by the townsfolk the last two weekends in June. It's an outdoor show, a musical blend of history, hoedown, ballet, spectacles, "and a good time for everybody—those who are in the Fandangle and those who come to see it," says Joie, who sells Albany real estate when she's not innkeeping.

"I've been in real estate for years, and I was looking for an office" is how Joie got the Parsons into innkeeping. When they found the house, it took a year to renovate. Now Bill, retired, helps with the business of the inn. "Years ago we had a restaurant, I guess maybe twenty-five years." Joie laughs. "Been a day or two."

But she hasn't lost her touch with food. The Nail House's Champagne Breakfast is beautiful to behold as well as to eat: a Southwest Casserole with turkey breast and herbed tomatoes, served with oven potatoes, chips, and salsa. Mixed-fruit yogurt topped with peaches or strawberries, maybe pecan waffles—it's all delicious, whether you eat it in the formal dining room downstairs or on the sun porch. The time you want it is your choice, too.

"Sometimes I get industrious," Joie says, as if all the aforementioned food does not require industry. "Then I also make cinnamon blintzes, a cream cheese breakfast dessert."

The two-story home is right across the street from the historic Shackleford County Courthouse, the oldest courthouse in Texas "still working," she says. When you enter the inn's front door, Muffin, the official canine greeter, comes to say hello, then leaves everyone alone, so if you're a dog lover, you're out of luck. The living room boasts a pale-green Victorian love seat; the dining room has a window seat and an old grandfather's clock, a gift of Joie and Bill's three sons.

The guest rooms, on the second floor, offer a picturesque view of downtown Albany (population about 2,000). Two of them, the Oak Bedroom and the White Bedroom, open off the sun porch, which has a trundle bed to accommodate two additional guests.

The White Bedroom has white half-paneling, with a pretty, small-patterned blue wallpaper above, a white quilted spread on the antique bed, and two rust-red wing chairs in a corner.

Joie says a little lady who moved to Albany from Abilene (about 36 miles southwest) told her about the joys of innkeeping. "She actually told me how; it was fascinating." But friends and family were not so sure. "You're going to let *strangers* stay in your house?

"Luckily, my oldest son, Mike, had stayed in various inns, and he was very encouraging," Joie says.

Special touches, such as fruit baskets in your room, embroidered gowns for the ladies, plush terry robes for everyone, potted plants, and fresh flowers (in season), make the Old Nail House Inn a delightful place to stop.

How to get there: Off I–20 take Highway 6 north to Albany and follow it into town to Main Street (Highway 180). The inn is on the corner of Main and South 3rd, across the street from the Shackleford County Courthouse.

Innkeepers: Joie and Bill Parsons
Address/Telephone: 329 South 3rd (mailing address: P.O. Box 632); (915) 762–2928 or (800) 245–5163
Rooms: 3; all with private bath. No smoking inn.
Rates: $35 to $55, double; $20 extra person; EPB.
Open: All year.
Facilities and activities: Nearby: restaurants, antiques and gift shops, Shackleford County Courthouse, Old Jail Art Center, Fort Griffin State Park, Fort Griffin Fandangle Festival (June).

Galbraith House
AMARILLO, TEXAS 79102

Galbraith House was built in 1912 by a lumberman, and you should see the woodwork in this 4,000-square-foot mansion; the construction cost the princely sum, back then, of $25,000. Oh, the beautiful hand-rubbed mahogany, walnut, and oak!

"People go around with their mouths hanging open at the woodwork," Sharon says; also at the rich Bukhara oriental rugs and antiques and collectibles that fill the mansion. The home, while managed by Sharon, is owned by absentee landlords Mary Jane Johnson, an opera singer, and her husband and manager, David, who is also a consultant to a local grocery chain. With two young children, they wanted to move into a neighborhood with more young families but didn't want to part with this lovely old home. So they've turned it into an inn, one in which they'd choose to stay themselves.

Sharon is dedicated to pleasing her guests. Breakfast? "I do a really good breakfast," she says, and I doubt she could find any dissenters. Egg casseroles, omelets—"and though I try to give guests light and heathful food that remains flavorful, the men like my southern-style biscuits and gravy . . . it just depends upon who my guests are that morning." With only three or four guests, she'll cook to order, happy as a lark in the large, sunny kitchen of the big house. When guests come in there are soda and chips;

in fact, "they're welcome to what's in the refrigerator! Carrot sticks, microwave popcorn—they can do their own thing; they have free use of the kitchen, the entire house, so long as they don't swing from the chandeliers!" she adds with a laugh.

"We're not strict or rigid on check-in or -out." That, says Sharon firmly, is one of the advantages of an inn. I like her philosophy: "We're flexible; we cater to our guests. We're in the hospitality business, and the people who are the nicest get the nicest guests and the best business."

All the guest rooms are spacious and comfortable. The Christmas Room is the most popular; a king bed, a pair of lounge chairs, a large dressing table, and family photographs make it very homey. Guests have full use of the home's other rooms: living room, dining room, library, solarium, three balconies, even a butler's pantry—there's a lot of room to make yourself comfortable in.

An unusual feature of the home is the Gentlemen's Smoking Porch, a tiny outside balcony off the upstairs hall, where even back in 1912 smokers were sent. Handmade quilts by local artisans are on all the beds and many of the walls, as well as works of art by local artists.

How to get there: Take the Washington Street exit off I–40; go to 17th Street, turn east, and go 2 blocks to Polk. Turn right and the inn will be on the right at 1710.

Innkeeper: Sharon Stenstrom
Address/Telephone: 1710 South Polk Street; (806) 374–0237
Rooms: 5; all with private bath. Pets in garage. No smoking inn.
Rates: $65 to $75, double, EPB.
Open: All year.
Facilities and activities: Luncheons, teas, and dinners by reservation; television, children's playroom, patio, use of office for business. Nearby: Amarillo College, Plemons–Eakle Historic District, Amarillo Art Center, Palo Duro Canyon, *Texas* (musical drama).

Country Home

CANYON, TEXAS 79015

Just walking up the front walk, edged with flowerbeds, of this pretty little cottage makes you feel like you've come to a happy place. The white Victorian lampposts on the green lawn on each side look as if they ought to be gas-lit. The front door is Victorian to match, and the wide foyer opens onto a living room with a totally unexpected tall cathedral ceiling and picture windows opening up the rear wall.

"I never cease to be amazed at the surprised look on people's faces when they walk in the front door," Tammy says. "Guests from all those metro areas feel they've really made it. I love it when they say, 'Now this is the real Texas!'"

Well, it's true that Canyon is a rather small town, and it's true that Tammy and her mother, JoNell, live sort of on the edge of it. "It's an out-in-the-country atmosphere," she says. "We do have cattle in the fields nearby." All of which makes the Country Home feel like down-home, what with the cattle lowing softly in the peace and quiet and the pampering by the innkeepers.

The old dresser in the foyer has a pretty collection of plates. The dining room, on the right, is filled with plants and Depression chairs.

But it's the two-story living room that is such a pleasant surprise. There's an antique mantel over the fireplace, one of Tammy's handmade quilts, and Tammy's paintings on the wall. She's a teacher as well as an artist.

Her grandmother gave her an acre to build on, and she saved all her teaching money to fulfill her dream house, and a dream it is. The inn is furnished with antiques, many of which have been passed down through the family.

In the Oak Room you'll see Grandma Money's wedding dress from 1907, Grandma Jones's childhood rocker, and Great-Grandmother Fortner's treadle sewing machine.

The Honeymoon Suite downstairs has a mahogany four-poster and a whirlpool bath in its private bathroom. Upstairs, the two guest rooms share a bath with an old-fashioned claw-footed tub. They also share a loft, with a sitting area perfect for viewing clear West Texas sunsets.

Breakfast might be puffed pancakes with a hot fruit compote and sausage, or sausage quiche made with Country Home's own farm-fresh eggs, and blueberry muffins.

To cap off a perfect day, maybe touring Palo Duro Canyon and taking in the famous musical *Texas*, performed under starry skies in the canyon, snacks will be brought to your room.

When *Texas* is playing out at Palo Duro, Canyon can have up to 1,300 tourists every night (except Sunday, when it isn't performed). JoNell's home is just across the road, and Tammy and her mother have unexpectedly worked out a wonderful arrangement.

"I'm full, but we can put you up at Mom's place," Tammy has learned to say.

JoNell laughs. "We found that I can take the overflow. And it gave me a marvelous excuse to redecorate two of my rooms. I've ended up feeding people, too."

How to get there: From I–27 turn west on 4th Avenue and go to 8th Street. Turn left for 1 mile. The inn is on the right; there's a sign.

Innkeepers: Tammy and JoNell Money
Address/Telephone: Route 1, Box 447; (806) 655–7636 or 655–3635
Rooms: 3; 1 with private bath, 1 with TV. Pets permitted. No smoking inn.
Rates: $70 to $110, double; $15 extra person; EPB.
Open: All year.
Facilities and activities: Swimming pool, garden with gazebo and picnic tables, special dinners. Nearby: Palo Duro Canyon State Park and *Texas* outdoor drama in Pioneer Amphitheater, Panhandle-Plains Historical Museum, Buffalo Lake National Wildlife Refuge.

Hudspeth House

CANYON, TEXAS 79015

This huge old house has toys in the entry—you'll be greeted by antique dolls waiting for you in a cradle and a doll buggy. And each large guest room has more wonderful memorabilia to offer, thanks to the friendly citizens of this Panhandle town. Take the collection of 1912 and 1913 college yearbooks in the parlor, the ones from when West Texas State was West Texas Normal.

"An elderly lady came by the other day and brought them to us," Dave Haynie says; and it seems as if that's not unusual here. An elderly lady from Amarillo brought the Haynies the antique bridal gown that's in the Roy Room on the third floor. "She said, 'I have nobody to leave it to; no one will see it unless you display it,'" Dave reports. "We're always getting things like that. Another lady told us her daughter was in a wedding here—she was a flower girl—and she gave us this picture . . ." Which is why the Hudspeth House is so popular as the place to find out about times gone by in the territory: The Haynies offer afternoon tours of the house by reservation.

Mary Elizabeth Hudspeth came to Canyon in 1910 as a member of the faculty of the new West Texas Normal College. (A more renowned faculty member was Georgia O'Keeffe.) At first Miss Hudspeth boarded with the family that owned the house; then she acquired it for herself, taking pride in the stained glass, the fancy chandeliers, and the four fireplaces that make the house a showcase.

All the rooms are large—they just don't build the way they used to, do they? The fancy parlor with both piano and organ, the huge dining room with a table that seats fourteen under maroon velvet swags draped beneath the ceiling—it's the grandeur of the past that's fun to experience. Sally and Dave have decorated with verve and zest for the period. In the Edgar Luscombe Suite, there's an old Singer sewing machine and a dressmaker's dummy garbed in an appropriate outfit. Ready for bedtime reading on the counterpane in the Otto Stark Suite is an original edition of *Gone with the Wind*. In Henry's Room in the loft there's a teddy bear on a rockinghorse; Mollie's Rose Room has a wonderful assortment of collectibles, what my Aunt Lillian used to call "bezzagobbles."

Breakfast is set in splendor in the dining room and might be "brunch eggs Benedict." Sally has been in food service for a long time, and Dave taught school for more than seventeen years before he went into sales. Now they're busy with both their inn and local affairs. "It's just a lot of fun," they say. "You get to meet all the nice people, and you get to meet them like kinfolks."

In addition to the more usual inn stay, you can book one of four health and fitness programs the Haynies offer in their spa, where a doctor, nurse, cosmetologist, fashion consultant, masseur, and professional CPR-certified instructors are on staff. "Learn to love, laugh, and live longer" is the Haynie motto.

How to get there: From either I–27 Business or I–27 Bypass, take exit 106 (4th Avenue) west to 1904. The inn is on the right.

Innkeepers: Sally and Dave Haynie
Address/Telephone: 1905 4th Avenue; (806) 655–9800 or 655–4111
Rooms: 8; 6 with private bath. No smoking inn.
Rates: $50; $110 for entire 2-bedroom loft; EPB.
Open: All year.
Facilities and activities: Health and fitness spa, sun deck, gazebo. Nearby: Palo Duro Canyon; *Texas* (musical drama), Panhandle-Plains Historical Museum.
Recommended Country Inns® Travel Club Benefit: 10% discount, Monday–Thursday, May–August; 25% discount, Monday–Thursday, September–April.

Sunset Heights Inn

EL PASO, TEXAS 79902

Built in 1905 up in the high and mighty area of El Paso overlooking downtown, this inn on the National Register of Historic Homes is a three-story corner house of dark-yellow brick surrounded by an iron fence. Tall palm trees wave over it, and the large grounds of almost an acre are graced by roses blooming much of the year. "Twenty-nine bushes," Richard says, while he confesses that he doesn't take care of it all by himself.

Food, gourmet food, is his specialty, and you won't be able to predict what he'll feed you for breakfast because he doesn't know himself. "I don't decide what to serve until I look at my guests the evening before," he says, which brought forth a contented groan from an earlier guest, who was recovering from the morning-before feast in a corner of the beautifully decorated parlor.

The five- to seven-course meal was more like a lunch or dinner buffet to me than a breakfast. It began with prunes in cream and went on to quiche served with kiwi and purple grapes; then came Cordon Bleu chicken on rice with tomato and avocado, and eggs Benedict with papaya and star fruit, followed by angel-food cake with blueberry yogurt. This took me through the day until the champagne and late-night snacks.

Richard, late of the military, raised three

daughters by himself and learned to cook in self-defense. "We entertained a lot and couldn't afford a cook, so we all learned to cook. When the girls were small, sometimes we had sit-down dinners for thirty." But he prefers buffet because "people circulate better." Now at Sunset he has a helper in daughter Kim, responsible for many of the gourmet meals they serve.

Roni, who is a practicing physician, displays a second talent in the decorating of the inn. She did most of the pleasing color selections, while much of the furnishings are antiques from Richard's family. The parlor has a Victrola dating from 1919, and it still plays. Although the old table radio is a replica, the kerosene lamp is one Richard studied by when he was a boy on a farm in Oklahoma. "We didn't have electricity," he says. "That old lamp got me through school." But what I loved looking at was the wonderful Coromandel screen behind the old sewing machine in the parlor. Richard tells the story of how he was able to get it out of China—back when we weren't speaking to China—by shipping it through Panama.

The inn is a decorator's dream, with beautifully coordinated fabrics and wall coverings, mirrored doors, and sybaritic bathrooms. The Oriental Room has another Coromandel screen as well as a brass bed. The bathroom, with brass fixtures and a huge bathtub, is on what was once a porch. But not to worry: All the windows are now one-way mirrors.

How to get there: From I–10 West take Porfiro Diaz exit and turn right for 2 blocks to Yandell. Turn right for 6 blocks (count the ones on the right, not the left) to Randolph, and the inn is on the far corner to the left.

Innkeepers: Richard Barnett and Roni Martinez

Address/Telephone: 717 West Yandell; (919) 544–1743 or (800) 767–8513

Rooms: 10, 6 in main house, 4 in annex across the street; all with private bath, telephone, and TV; wheelchair accessible (electric chair lift from first to second floor). No smoking inn.

Rates: \$80 to \$165, double, EPB.

Open: All year.

Facilities and activities: Dinner for minimum of six people; pool and Jacuzzi. Nearby: many museums and historic fort, old Spanish missions, Tigua Indian Reservation, zoo, scenic drive, Ciudad Juárez in Mexico just across the Rio Grande.

Business travel: Located 5 blocks from downtown El Paso. Fax, all rooms have telephones.

Recommended Country Inns® Travel Club Benefit: 10% discount each night; or stay two nights, get third night free, holidays excluded; subject to availability; not good with other offers or special rates; offer good for one year from publication.

McNabb's Green Acres

ROPESVILLE, TEXAS 79358

"Come on over," Sandra says. "We'll leave the porch light on." More than that, she'll let you help with the chores. For McNabb's Green Acres is a real working cotton farm; and if you stay for two nights and three days, the inn offers a South Plains cotton tour where you'll find out how little you know about the clothes on your back. For instance, did you know that cotton grows not only in white but also in colors like brown, beige, and green?

"West Texas is the major cotton area for the United States," Sandra says. There were "modules" (bales) of cotton waiting in the fields to be picked up by the module truck from the cotton gin. The tour follows the cotton from the gin to a denim mill, and then to the Texas Tech textile department to see how it's turned into fabric.

"We like people, and what we would truly like is for the general public to see first-hand what farming is really like," says Sandra, full of enthusiastic missionary zeal.

The enthusiasm for farming is carried over to innkeeping. "The hospitality . . . could not be better!" a guest from Canada told me, fascinated by the farmers and their farming. Sandra has a sideline too; she is a florist, growing delphiniums, lilies, liatrias, and other cut flowers in her greenhouse, for sale to florists. "It's backbreaking work," she says, with a laugh that belies it.

Her other sideline is orchestrating inn weddings and honeymoon packages. She has a great sense of humor.

"My daddy's justice of the peace at Ropesville," she says. "They get married, I do the flowers, they honeymoon here—and if it doesn't work, my nephew is an attorney!"

The McNabbs are deeply entrenched in Ropesville and Texas, and Ronnie and Sandra have published a booklet on the history of the area. They moved their house from Lubbock, set it down alongside the road in the middle of 700 acres of cotton, rebricked it, and added a room. It's furnished family style, with an English tea cabinet from Waco in the living room, topped by a pewter tea service from Ronnie's mother. The hutch in the dining room belonged to Ronnie's great-grandfather, and the family clock and decorative glassware came from forebears in Marble Falls.

The wonderful old kitchen cabinet, with a flour cabinet and sifter, was going to be burned in an old shack. "I rushed over and rescued it," Sandra says.

Breakfast, as is to be expected on a real farm, is hearty. Sandy's Cotton Farm Breakfast includes quiche, sausage and salsa, sourdough biscuits and gravy, grapes from the grape arbor, and apricots from the backyard. The jam is made from wild plums. "They grow around Post and we go and pick 'em ourselves," Ronnie says—just in case they're not busy enough with the cotton.

If you stay for lunch and dinner, there are hamburgers and steaks out on the grill, a Cowboy Supper of Southwestern brisket and beans, all out by the fish pond near the grape arbor. There's a hammock in the arbor, koi goldfish in the pond, and not a sound in the air—heavenly.

How to get there: From Lubbock take Highway 82/62 to Ropesville and turn left at the blinking light at FM 41. Go east for 4 miles; McNabb's, a pink house with white columns, is on the left in the middle of the curve. There is a sign.

Innkeepers: Sandra, Ronnie, and Amy McNabb
Address/Telephone: Route 1, Box 14; (806) 562–4411
Rooms: 4; 1 with private bath, 1 with telephone. No smoking inn.
Rates: $35 to $75, double; $10 extra person; EPB. No credit cards.
Open: All year.
Facilities and activities: Lunch and dinner, Farm Tour, bicycles. Nearby: Buddy Holly Statue and Walk of Fame, Lubbock Country Museum, Lubbock Fine Arts Center, Mackenzie State Park, Lubbock Lake Landmark State Historical Park, Texas Tech Campus, National Ranching Heritage Center, Llano Estacado Winery.

Mulberry Manor

SWEETWATER, TEXAS 79556

It's a surprise to discover a mansion like Mulberry Manor in a town the size of Sweetwater (about 12,000 population). It was built in 1913 for banker, businessman, and rancher Thomas Trammell—and the architect was John Young, father of movie star Loretta Young.

Which may account for the Hollywood glamor of this show place. The focal point of the mansion is a glass-domed atrium, filled with green plants and sunshine, in the center of the house. A white, slatted fence encloses this, the heart of the house, and the inn's rooms surround it. The formal French parlor to the right of the entry is furnished in authentic Louis Quinze; the tailored parlor on the left also contains lovely pieces, garnered from all over.

"Just about everything is from estate sales and antiques shops," Beverly says. "We bought everything in this house on weekends." This gave them something to do while the house was being restored. "Auctions are really the best buy," is her advice.

"It was an old duplex, and it took thirteen months to remodel." The house had a checkered life after the Trammells were gone. To give you some idea of the scale, in 1923 it became Sweetwater and Nolan County's only hospital. Then, like many old homes, the 9,800-square-foot house was divided into apartments.

Eventually, it somehow became part of the estate of the brother of General Clair Chennault of the famous Flying Tigers.

Beverly had retired from Southwestern Bell, the Stones were living across the street, restoring that house, when this one came on the market. They sold the other and bought this.

The house has three downstairs guest rooms plus a vast suite upstairs. The separate barroom has an oversized television screen and a sitting area. The formal dining room is impressive, but so is the so-called breakfast room, with its brocaded French chairs, a beautiful mirrored sideboard, and an oriental rug on the polished wood floor.

But most exotic is the upstairs suite, which Beverly describes as "Neo-Classical." To give you an idea of the size, originally it was a ballroom. "It was an apartment, and it was horrible," Beverly shudders. Now, on the huge expanse of white carpet, the furniture is gold and black, with green plants (there's even a fern behind the king headboard). A group of statuary, busts of classical figures, occupies a corner. The adjoining bath is suitably Sybaritic.

Breakfast is as opulent as the manor. Fresh fruit compote, eggs Benedict or quiche, hashed browns, sausage or ham, biscuits and gravy, cinnamon raisin biscuits, strawberry cream cheese on croissants. And there's a big snack tray with the beverage of your choice afternoons; ours was cream puffs filled with ham salad. Who does all this? "Me. I'm the cook!" Beverly says.

Her dinners are spectacular seven-course meals, too.

And to cap it all off, Raymond takes guests for a fun ride in that shiny 1929 Model A Ford out front.

How to get there: Take exit 244 off I–20 and go north 4 blocks to Sam Houston Street and number 1400. There's a sign on the model A Ford out in front.

Innkeepers: Beverly and Raymond Stone
Address/Telephone: 1400 Sam Houston Street; (915) 235–3811 or (800) 235–3811
Rooms: 4, plus 1 two-bedroom, 1½-bath guest house; 2 rooms with private bath, 2 with TV; wheelchair accessible.
Rates: \$60 to \$200, double; \$10 extra person; EPB and afternoon snacks.
Open: All year.
Facilities and activities: Dinner by reservation, hot tub. Nearby: horseback riding; golf; Pioneer City–County Museum; lakes Sweetwater, Trammell, and Oak Creek Reservoir with fishing, boating, and water sports; World's Largest Rattlesnake Roundup (March).
Business travel: Office available with computer and fax; phones in rooms.

Country Place

WOLFFORTH, TEXAS 79382

"These are the things I like doing," Pat says: "Cooking, entertaining, meeting people—I enjoy hostessing and I really enjoy cooking. Actually, I felt raising the children was just practice, and whenever they come home to visit, I get to practice more!"

Guests feel like family, too, what with the way Pat makes you feel at home. In the wet bar next to the refrigerator, there are always snacks like cheese balls and fruit, and soft drinks. "Guests can use the fridge, make their own waffles if they want to," Pat says.

Fritz the dog came out to greet me, looking hopeful. "He's a party animal," Pat says, but he was content with a few pats before wandering off, maybe looking for that party?

The two-story ranch house is modern and new. Both living room and dining room are large and open, with light woods. The Sun Room was designed to gather heat from the West Texas sun. For entertainment there's a piano for those who can play and board games for other kinds of play.

The Country Place is really out in the country, and it's hard to remember that Lubbock is just minutes away. I wandered outside to the big yard. I could hear the horses neighing—Pat boards them—and I saw the lovely P-shaped pool and the covered patio with hot tub and barbecue grill. Big towels, robes, books, easy chairs . . . all very easy to take.

"The country roads are ideal for walking, jogging, or bicycling," Pat says. "The neighboring farms have a variety of exotic animals, which can make it pretty interesting."

Up the wide staircase, the walls are hung with family photographs. "That's my mother as a young girl," Pat points out. Windows have clean white shutters, and the color scheme of the Wicker Room is maroon and beige, complementing the wicker furniture.

In the Walnut Room, Pat likes to show off the walnut furniture, which is the set she grew up with, back in Iowa. "First my mother had it in her house, then my boys had it in college, then I got it—and had it redone." Both Wicker and Walnut share a bath.

"It's easy," Pat explains. "You have the pink towels, the others have the maroon." Everybody gets to enjoy the crewel work in the bath, done by Pat's grandmother.

The Striped Room and the Rosy Room share another bath. The Striped Room is named for the striped wallpaper and quilted spread on the queen-sized bed. The Rosy Room has soft pink walls, a rosy carpet, white French provincial furniture, and white quilts, covered with rose and pink poppies, on the twin beds.

Breakfast, says Pat, "depends on the mood of the cook." We had a Southwestern omelet with crispy hashed browns and sausage, and Pat's special bran muffins and homemade cinnamon rolls. The cook was in a good mood!

How to get there: From Lubbock take Highway 82/62 (Brownfield Highway) southwest 3–4 miles to Upland Avenue (Hayloft Restaurant sign), turn left, and go 6 miles. The inn is the last house on the right; there is a sign, and the Conover name is on the mailbox.

Innkeeper: Pat Conover
Address/Telephone: South Upland Avenue; Route 1, Box 459; (806) 863–2030
Rooms: 4; 2 with private bath, 1 with TV. No smoking inn.
Rates: $70, double, EPB and snacks.
Open: All year.
Facilities and activities: Dinner by reservation, swimming pool, hot tub, barbecue grill, bicycles, horses. Nearby: Buddy Holly Statue and Walk of Fame, Lubbock Country Museum, Lubbock Fine Arts Center, Mackenzie State Park, Lubbock Lake Landmark State Historical Park, Texas Tech Campus, National Ranching Heritage Center, Llano Estacado Winery.
Business travel: Located 12 miles from Lubbock. Small conference room.
Recommended Country Inns® Travel Club Benefit: 25% discount, subject to availability.

Indexes

Alphabetical Index to Inns

Inns with Restaurants

Inns Serving Meals by Reservation Only

Inns near Water

Inns with, or with Access to, Swimming Pools, Hot Tubs, or Spas

Inns with, or with Access to, Golf or Tennis Facilities

Inns with Downhill or Cross-Country Skiing Nearby

Inns Where Pets Are Accepted with or without Restrictions

Inns That Especially Welcome Children

Inns That Permit Smoking with or without Restrictions

Inns with Wheelchair Access

Inns for Business Travelers